One time, after submitting a storyboard to Toriyama Sensei, he gave me this advice. He said, "What makes *Dragon Ball* so distinct and quirky is how it takes an ordinary concept or design and tweaks it ever so slightly."

Sensei... Isn't that the fundamental difference between a genius and a normal person...? Anyhow, I'm working hard to cross that divide!

—**Toyotarou, 2018**

Toyotarou

Toyotarou created the manga adaptation for the *Dragon Ball Z* anime's 2015 film, *Dragon Ball Z: Resurrection F*. He is also the author of the spin-off series *Dragon Ball Heroes: Victory Mission*, which debuted in *V-Jump* in Japan in November 2012.

Akira Toriyama

Renowned worldwide for his playful, innovative storytelling and humorous, distinctive art style, Akira Toriyama burst onto the manga scene in 1980 with the wildly popular *Dr. Slump*. His hit series *Dragon Ball* (published in the U.S. as *Dragon Ball* and *Dragon Ball Z*) ran from 1984 to 1995 in Shueisha's *Weekly Shonen Jump* magazine. He is also known for his design work on video games such as *Dragon Quest*, *Chrono Trigger*, *Tobal No. 1* and *Blue Dragon*. His recent manga works include *COWA!*, *Kajika*, *Sand Land*, *Neko Majin*, *Jaco the Galactic Patrolman* and a children's book, *Toccio the Angel*. He lives with his family in Japan.

DRAGON BALL SUPER 5

SHONEN JUMP Manga Edition

STORY BY **Akira Toriyama**
ART BY **Toyotarou**

TRANSLATION **Toshikazu Aizawa, Christine Dashiell, and Caleb Cook**
LETTERING **Paolo Gattone and Chiara Antonelli**
TOUCH-UP ART **James Gaubatz**
DESIGN **Shawn Carrico**
EDITOR **Rae First**

Printed in Italy

Published by VIZ Media, LLC
P.O. Box 77010
San Francisco, CA 94107

10 9 8
First printing, May 2019
Eighth printing, May 2024

VIZ MEDIA
viz.com

SHONEN JUMP

ratings.viz.com RATED T TEEN

PARENTAL ADVISORY
DRAGON BALL SUPER is rated T for Teen and is recommended for ages 13 and up. This volume contains fantasy violence.

SHONEN JUMP MANGA

DRAGON BALL SUPER

THE DECISIVE BATTLE! FAREWELL, TRUNKS!

5

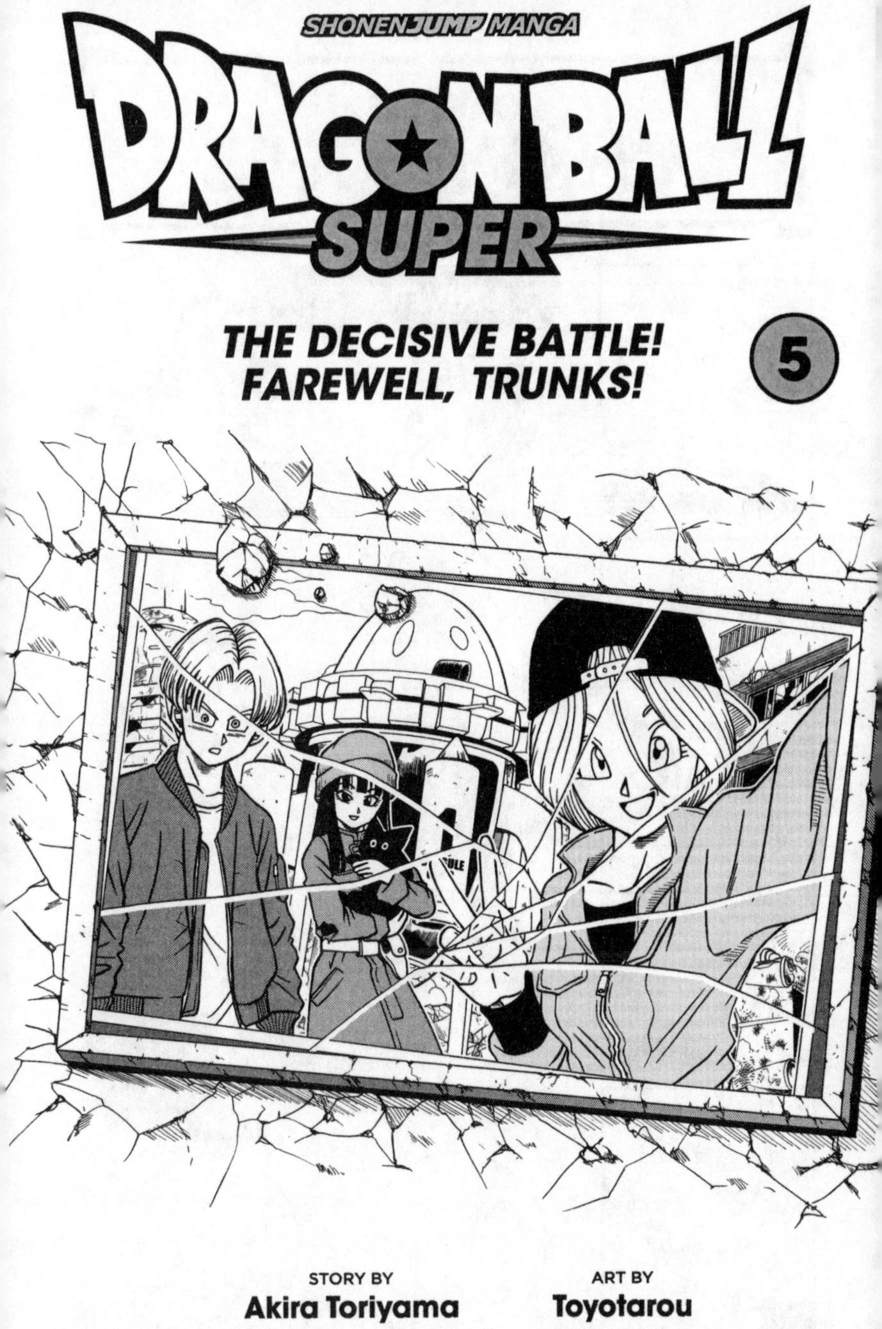

STORY BY
Akira Toriyama

ART BY
Toyotarou

CAST OF CHARACTERS

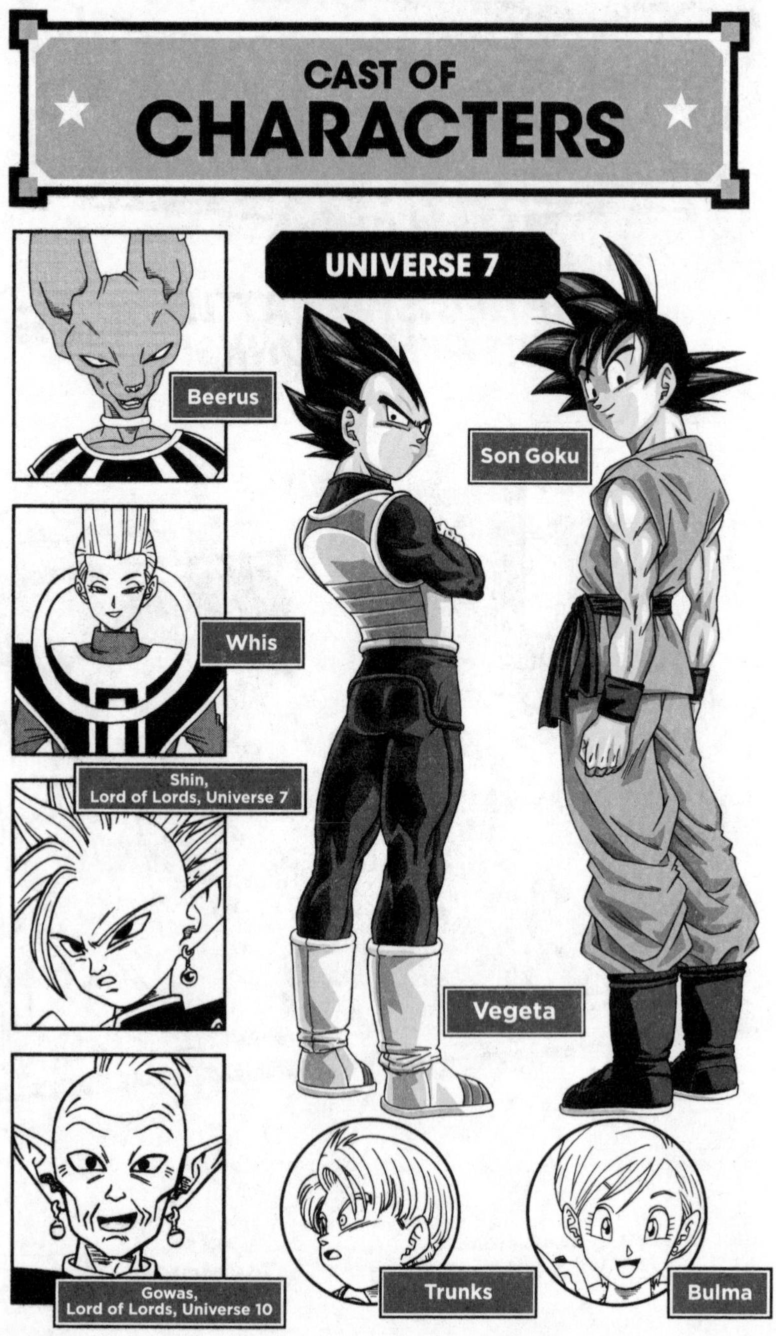
UNIVERSE 7
Beerus
Whis
Shin,
Lord of Lords, Universe 7
Gowas,
Lord of Lords, Universe 10
Son Goku
Vegeta
Trunks
Bulma

UNIVERSE 7:
Future Parallel World

Goku Black

Trunks (Future)

Zamas

God Zamas

Mai (Future)

STORY THUS FAR

A long, long time ago, Son Goku left on a journey in search of the legendary Dragon Balls—a set of seven balls that, when gathered, would summon the dragon Shenlong to grant any wish. After a great adventure, he collects them all. Later, he becomes the apprentice of Kame-Sen'nin, fights a number of vicious enemies, defeats the great Majin Boo and restores peace on Earth. Some time passes, and then Lord Beerus, the God of Destruction, suddenly awakens and sets out in search of the Super Saiyan God. Goku, by becoming the Super Saiyan God, manages to stop Beerus from destroying the Earth and starts training under him with Vegeta. One day, future Trunks appears, hoping to save the future. Goku and Vegeta travel to the future with Trunks, but they soon find themselves struggling against Goku Black and the immortal Zamas of the parallel world. Goku's attempt to seal away Zamas with the Mafū-ba fails, and when he attempts to hit back, Goku Black and Zamas use the Potara Earrings to become the all-powerful God Zamas! Thrown from one brutal battle into the next, can Goku perfect Super Saiyan Blue in time?!

5

DRAG★N BALL SUPER

TABLE! OF! CONTENTZZZ...

EPISODE 25 **Will It be Goku?! Or Zamas?!** 07

EPISODE 26 **The Decisive Battle! Farewell, Trunks!** .. 53

EPISODE 27 **Life, Training and More** 99

EPISODE 28 **The Gods of Destruction
from All 12 Universes** 145

DRAGON BALL SUPER

CHAPTER 25: WILL IT BE GOKU?! OR ZAMAS?!

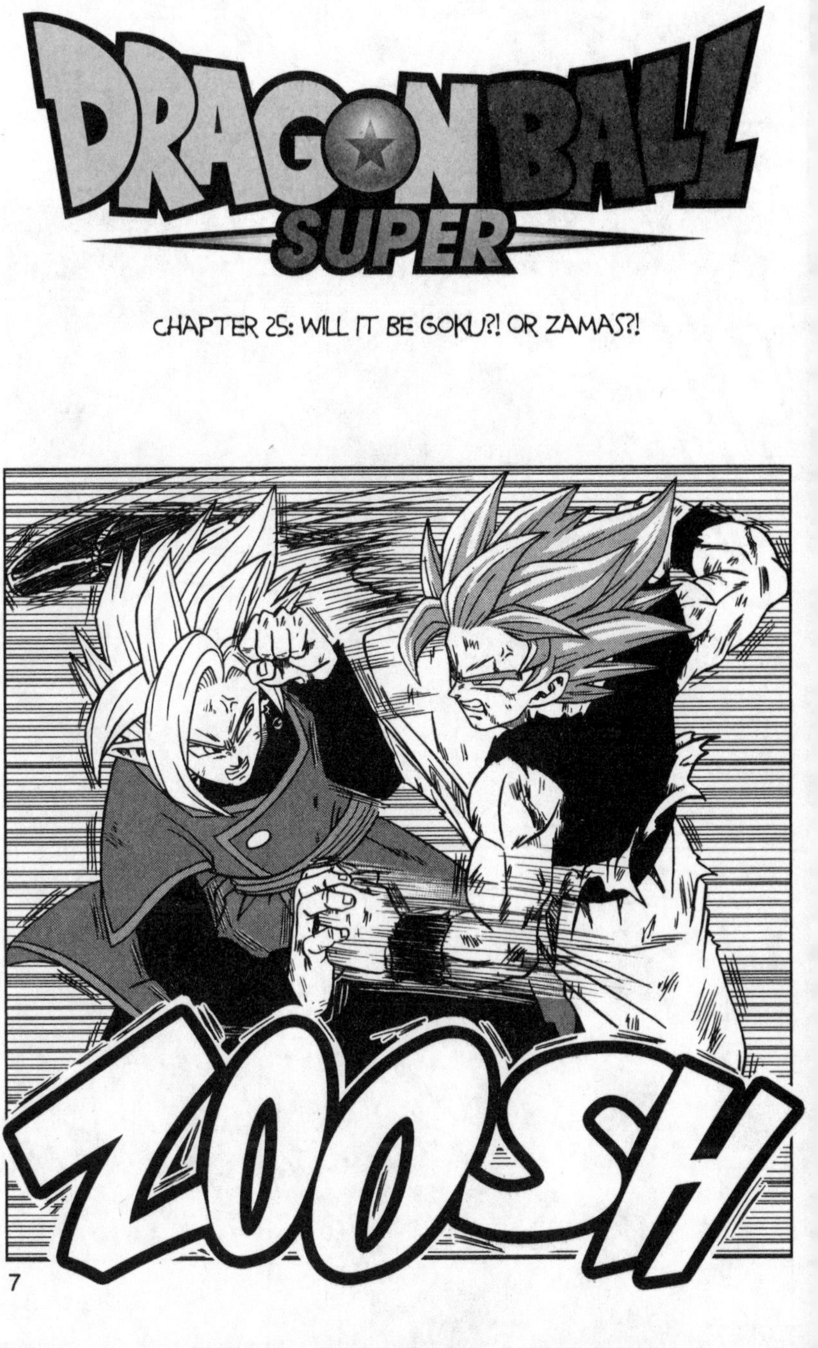
ZOOSH

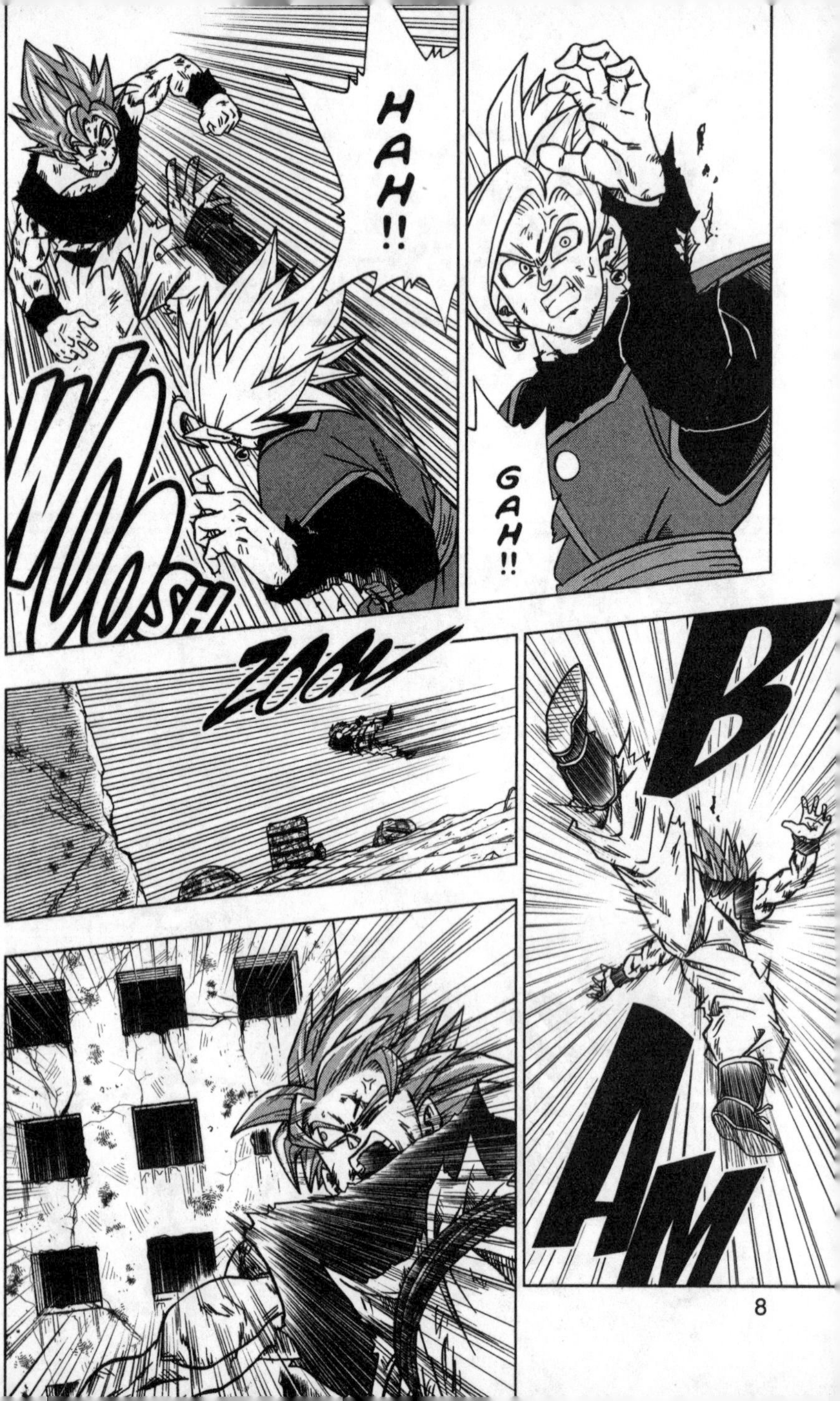
GAH!!
HAH!!
WOOSH
BAM
ZOOM

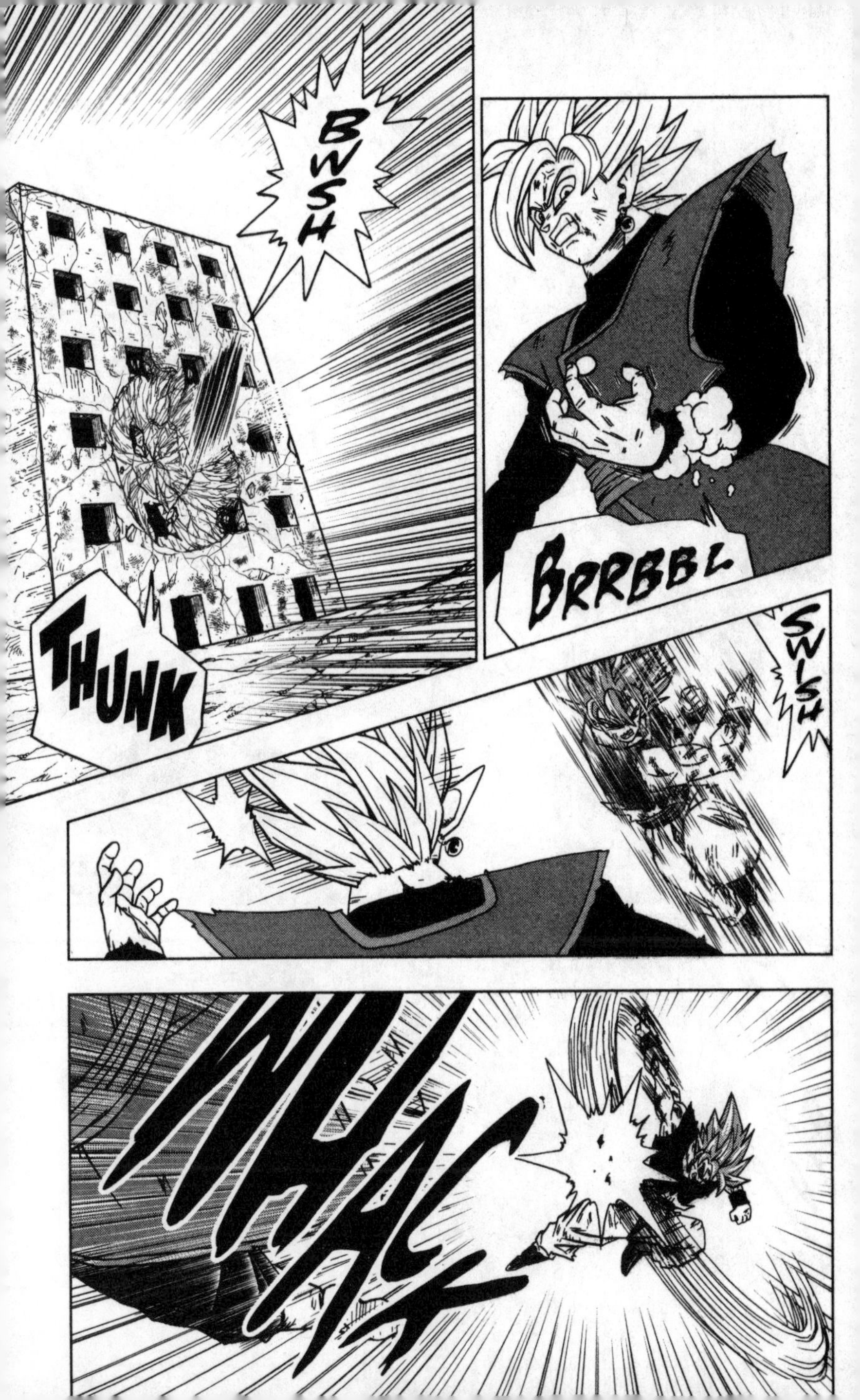
BRRBBL
BWSH
THUNK
SWISH
WHACK

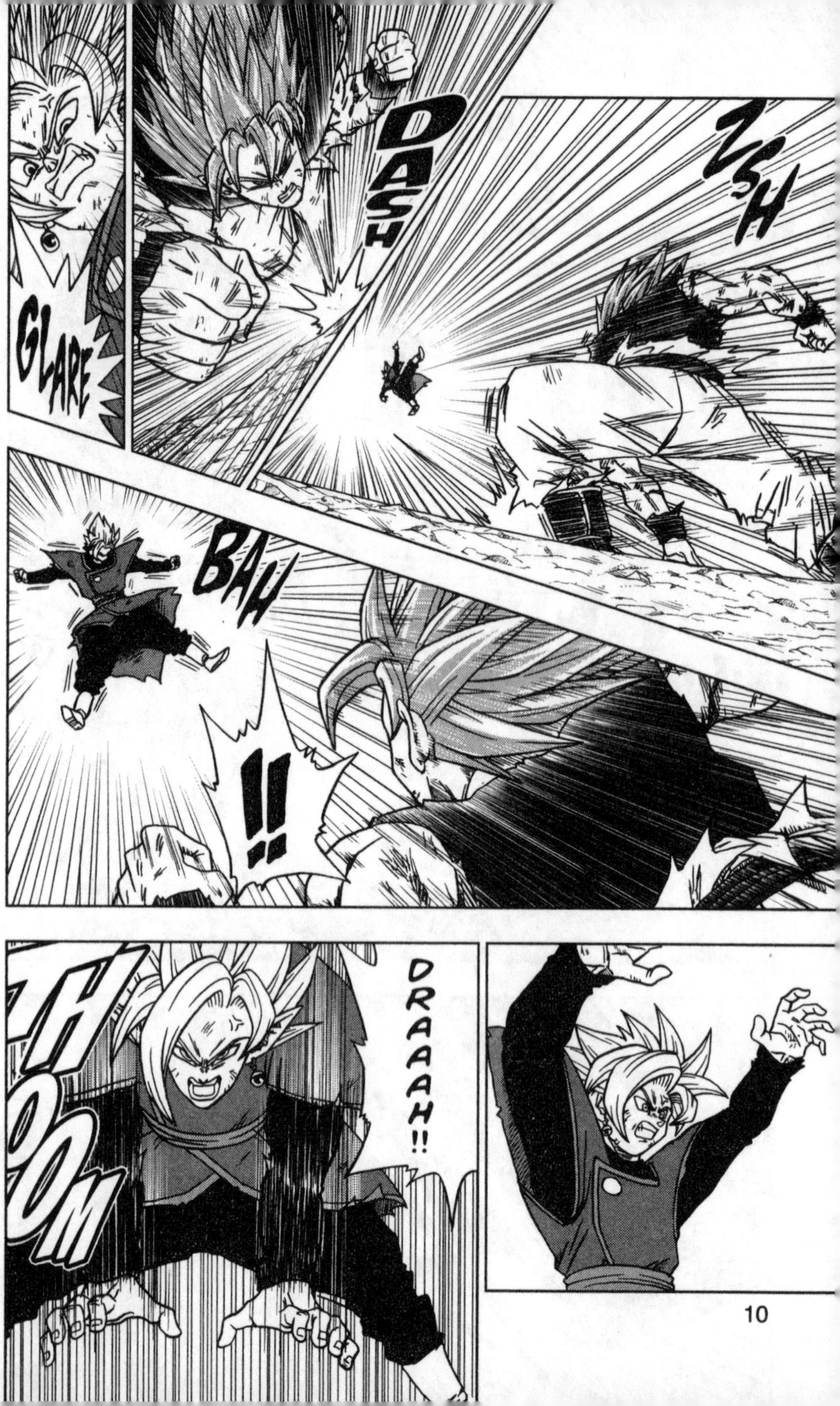
ZSH
DASH
GLARE
BAH
!!
DRAAAAH!!

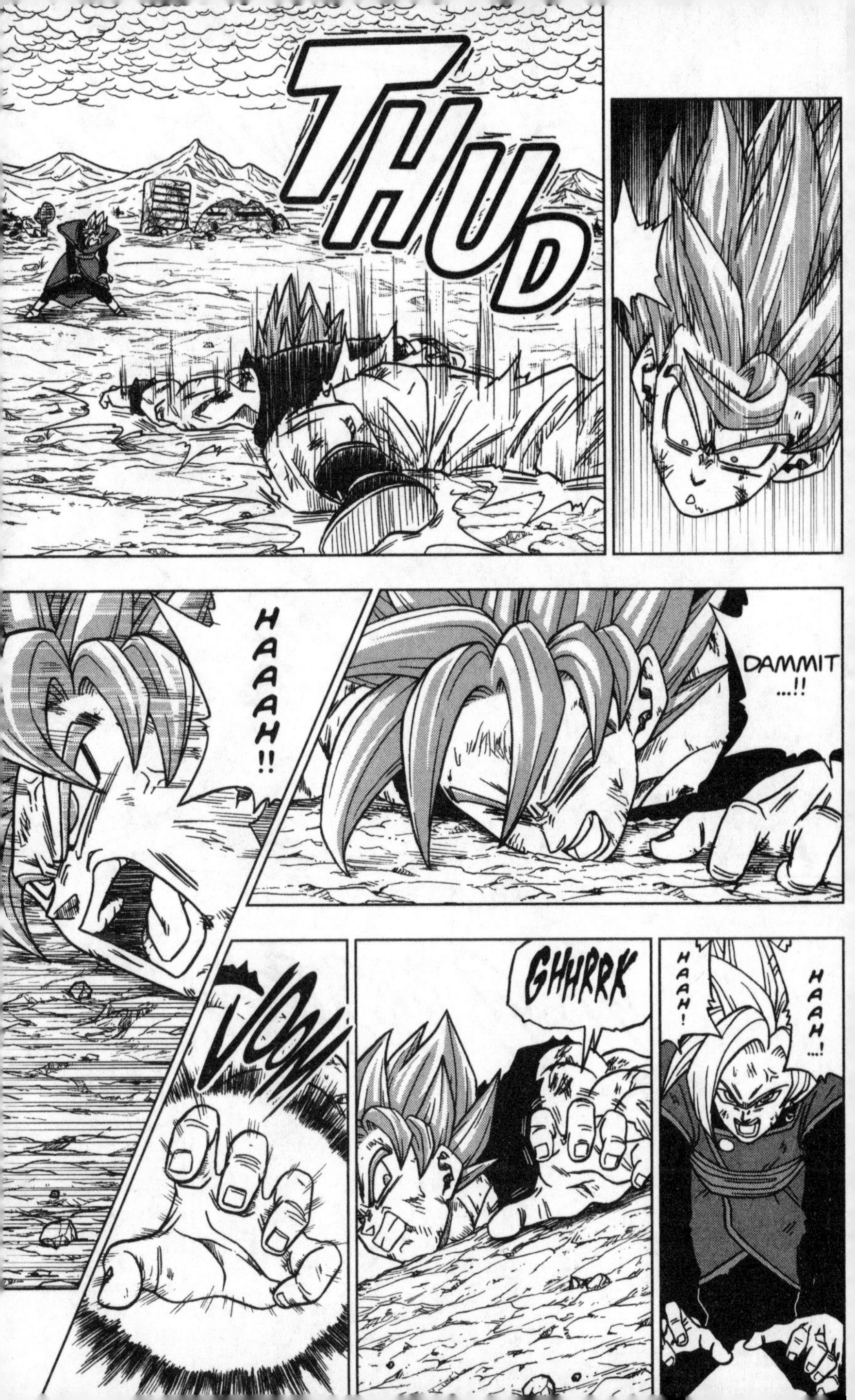
THUD
DAMMIT ...!!
HAAAAH!!
HAAAH...!
HAAAH!
GHHRRK
VOOM

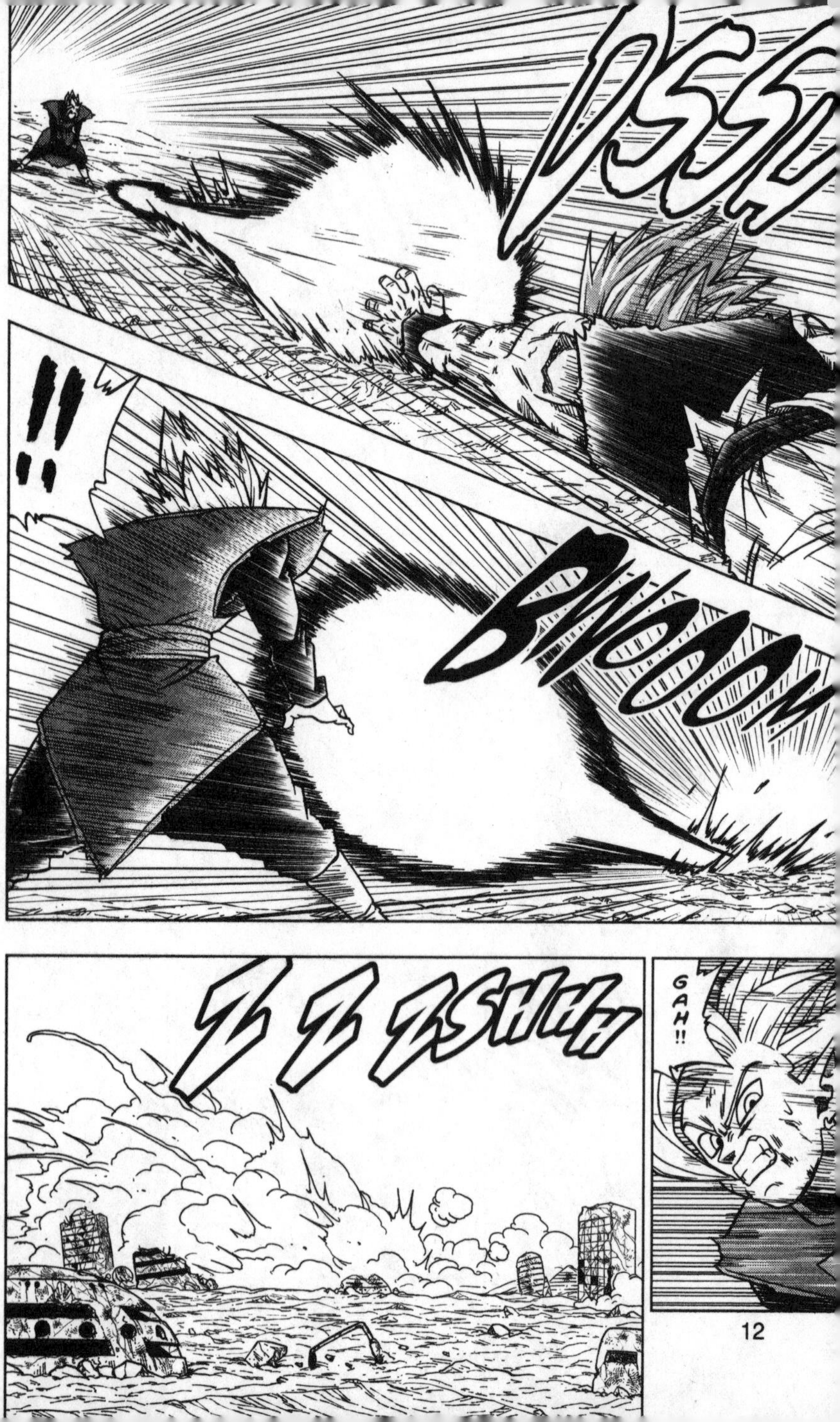
DSSH
!!
BWOOOM
GAH!!
Z Z ZSHHH

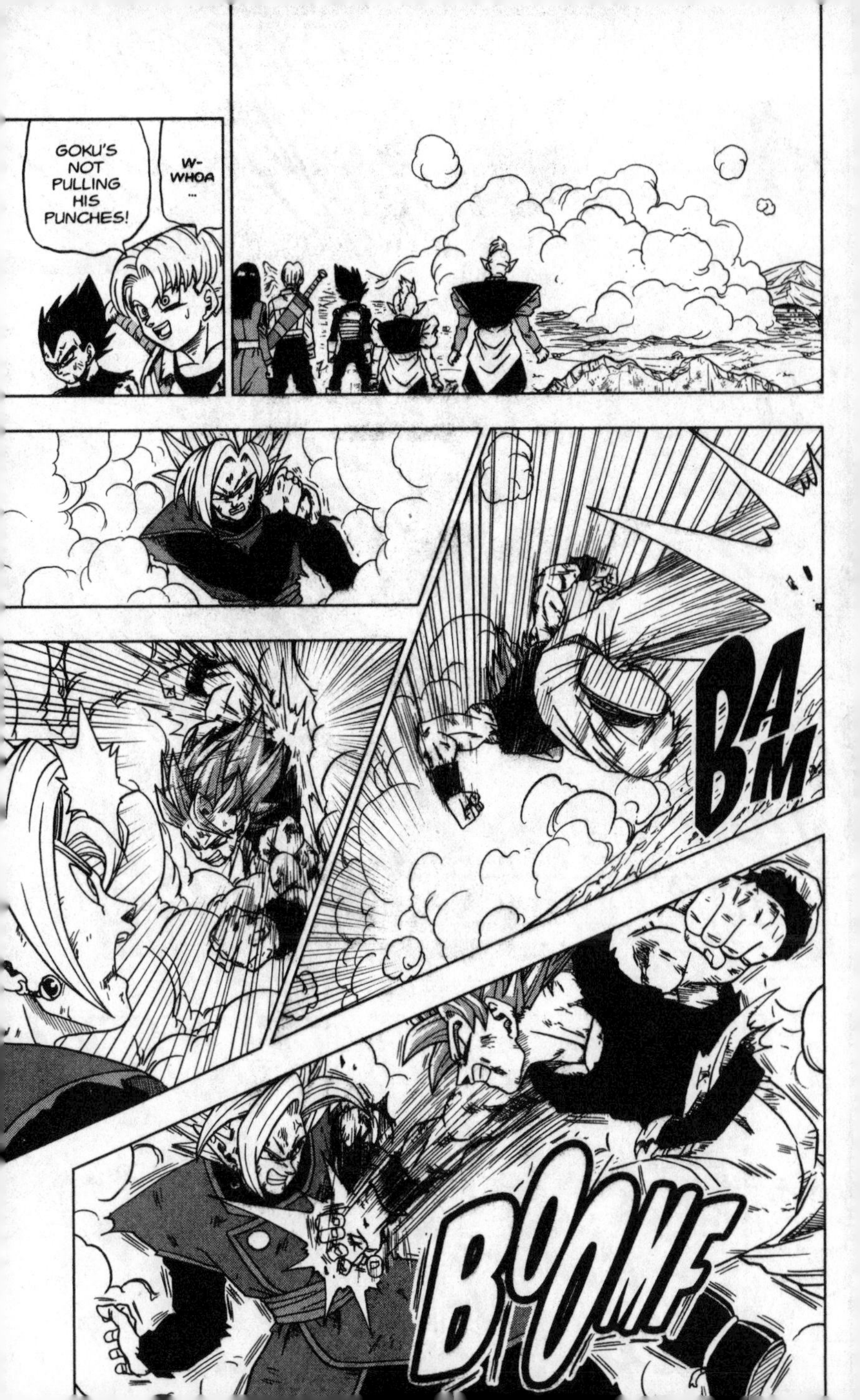
W-WHOA ...
GOKU'S NOT PULLING HIS PUNCHES!
BAM
BOOMF

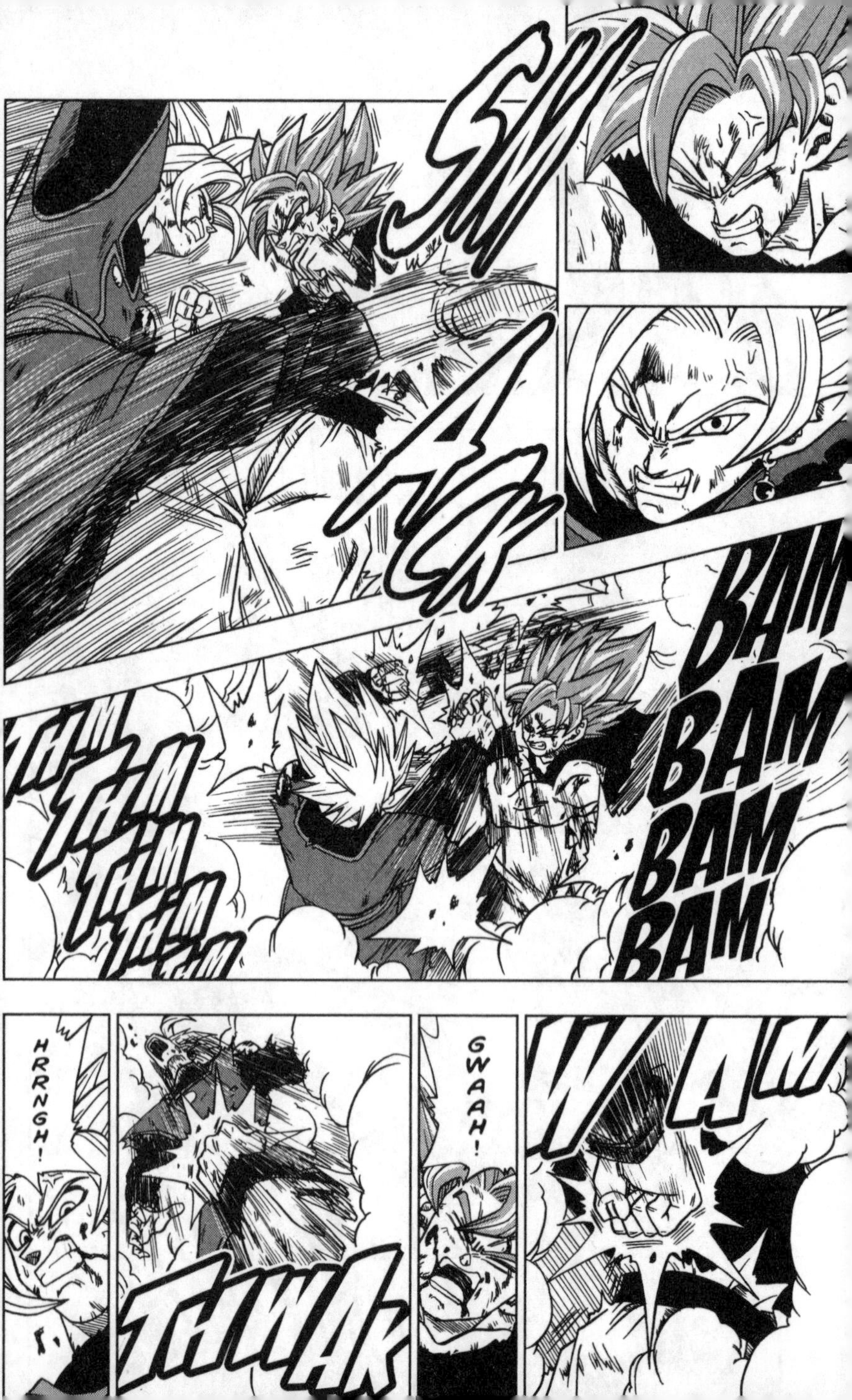
BAM
BAM
BAM
BAM
WAM
GWAAH!
THWAK
HRRNGH!

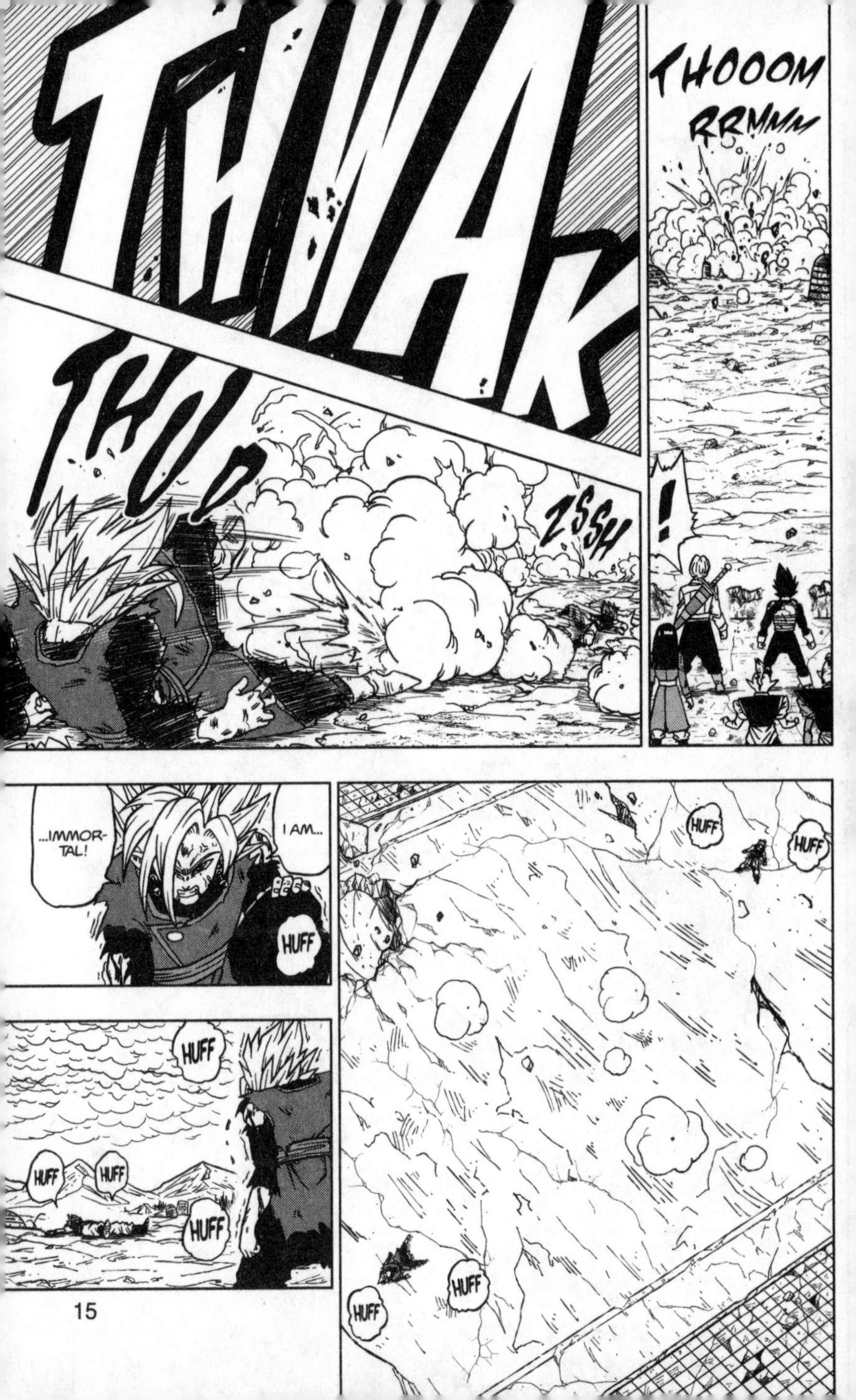
THOOOM
RRMMM
!
THWAK
THOOD
ZSSH
HUFF
HUFF
HUFF
HUFF
HUFF
I AM...
...IMMORTAL!
HUFF
HUFF
HUFF
HUFF
HUFF

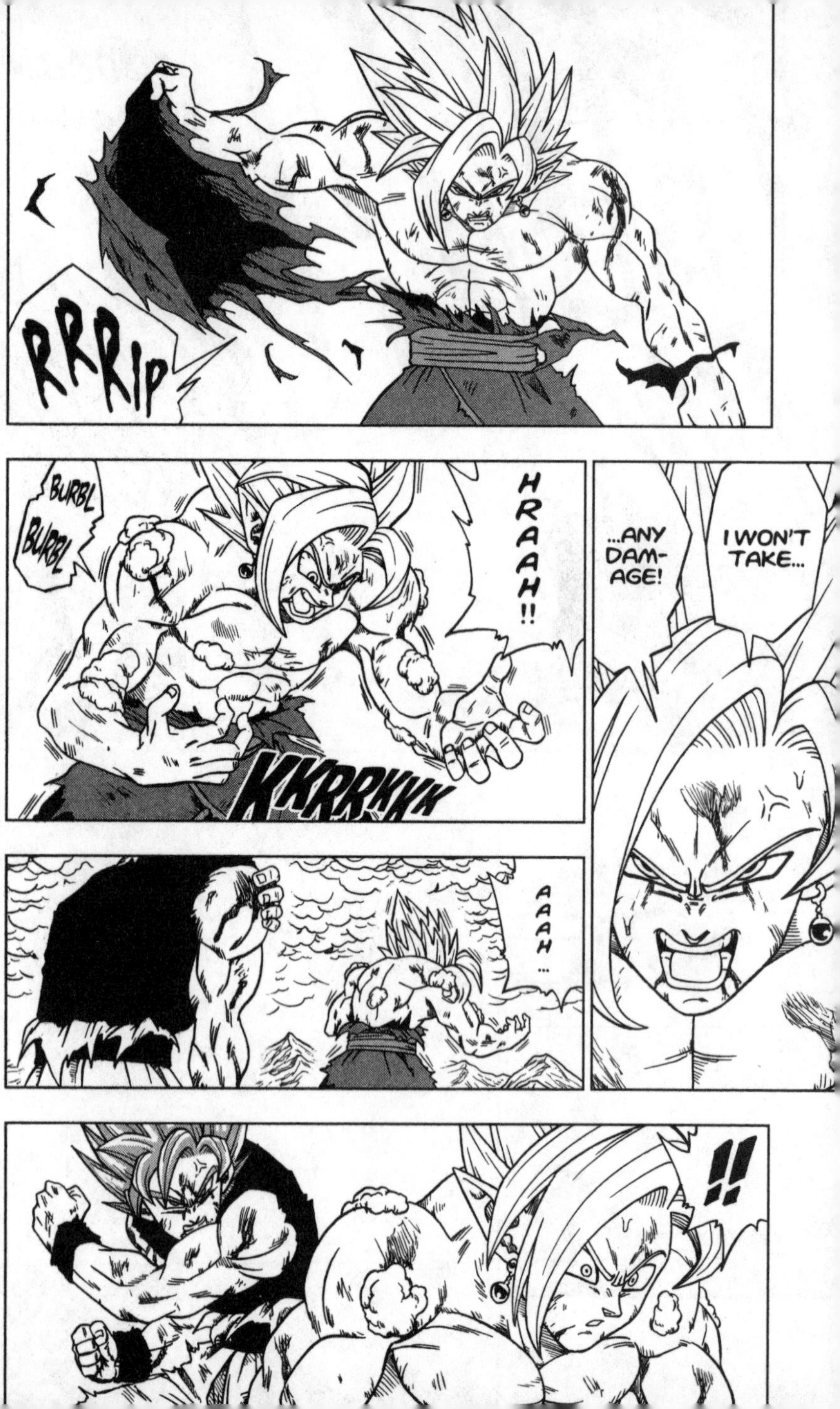
RRRIP
I WON'T TAKE...
...ANY DAM-AGE!
HRAAAH!!
BURBL BURBL
KKRRKKK
AAAAH...
!!

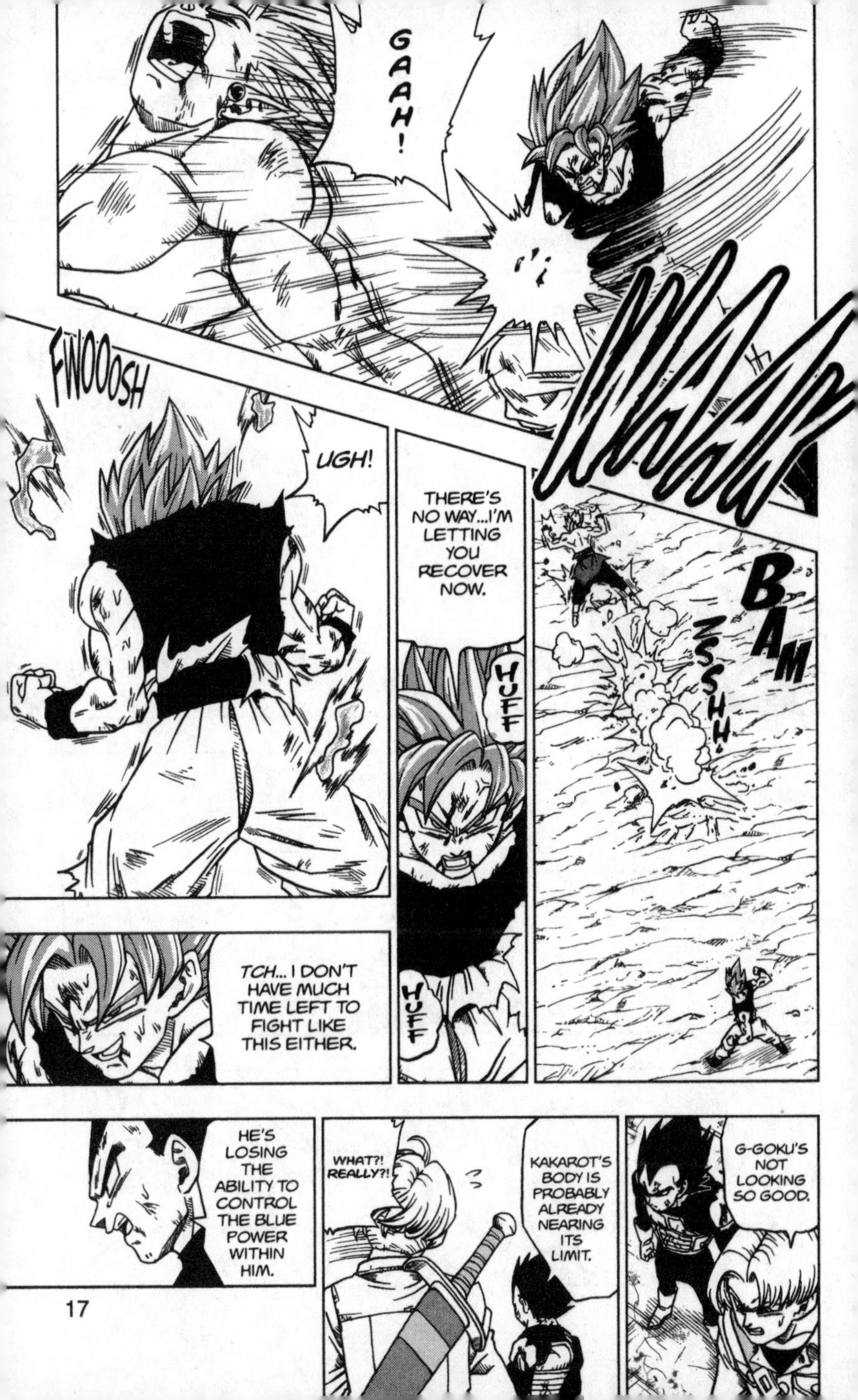
GAAH!
WHAK
BAM
ZSSHH
THERE'S NO WAY...I'M LETTING YOU RECOVER NOW.
HUFF
HUFF
FWOOOSH
UGH!
TCH... I DON'T HAVE MUCH TIME LEFT TO FIGHT LIKE THIS EITHER.
G-GOKU'S NOT LOOKING SO GOOD.
KAKAROT'S BODY IS PROBABLY ALREADY NEARING ITS LIMIT.
WHAT?! REALLY?!
HE'S LOSING THE ABILITY TO CONTROL THE BLUE POWER WITHIN HIM.

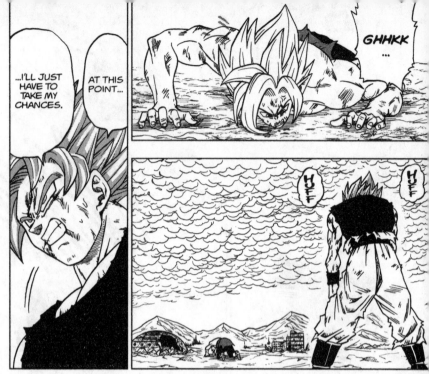

...I'LL JUST HAVE TO TAKE MY CHANCES.

AT THIS POINT...

GHHKK...

HUFF

HUFF

HUFF

HUFF

HUFF

HUFF

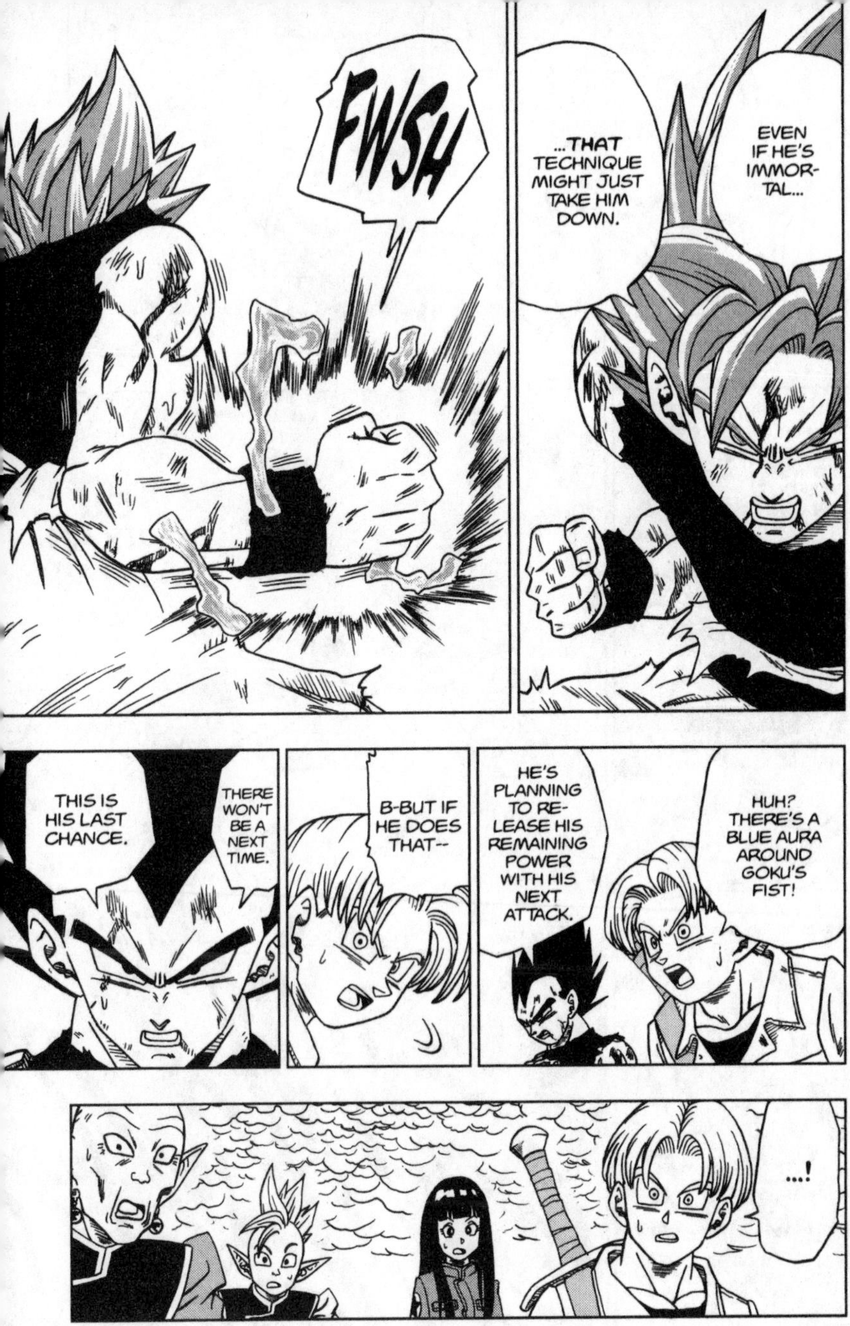
EVEN IF HE'S IMMORTAL...
...THAT TECHNIQUE MIGHT JUST TAKE HIM DOWN.
FWSH
HUH? THERE'S A BLUE AURA AROUND GOKU'S FIST!
HE'S PLANNING TO RELEASE HIS REMAINING POWER WITH HIS NEXT ATTACK.
B-BUT IF HE DOES THAT--
THERE WON'T BE A NEXT TIME.
THIS IS HIS LAST CHANCE.
...!

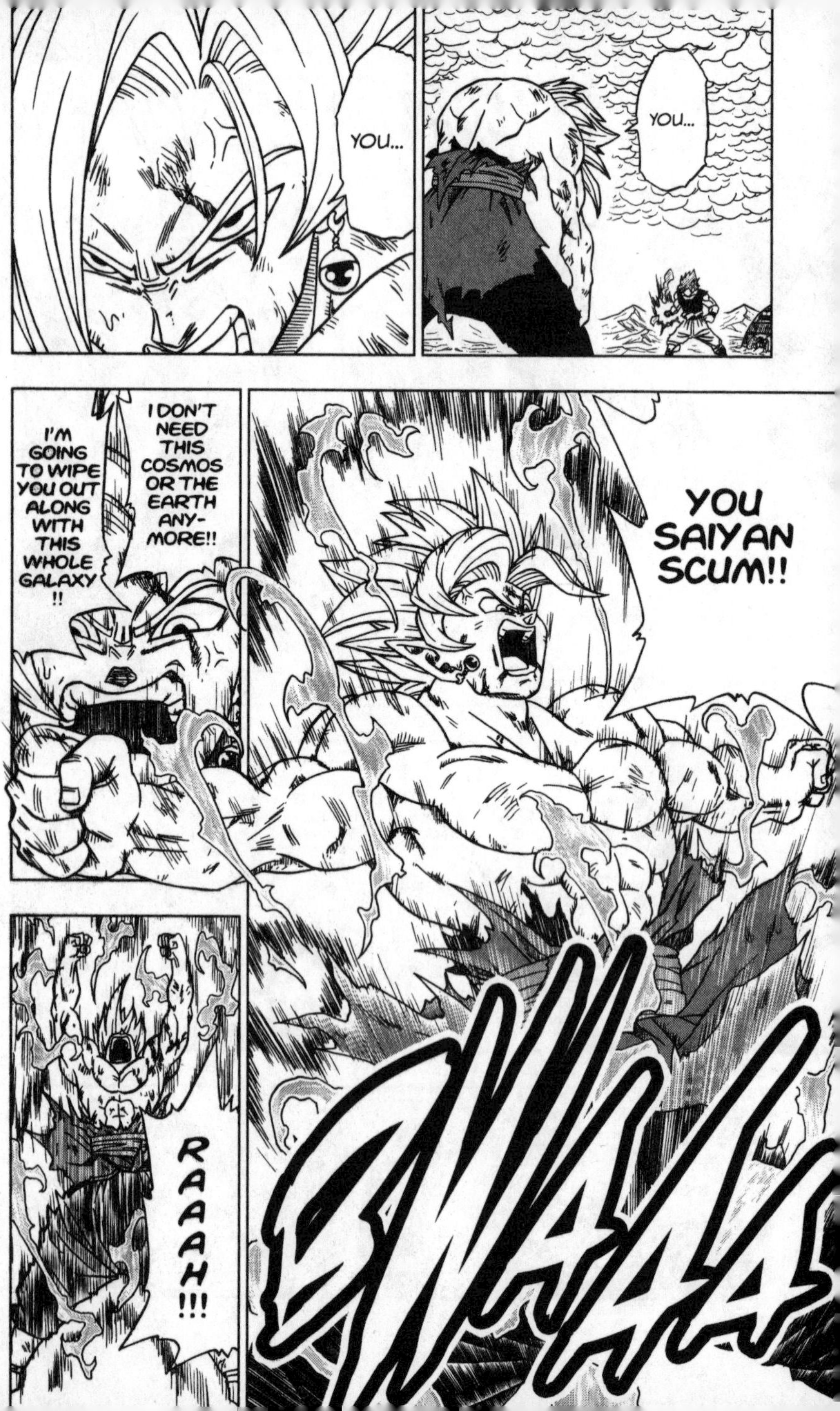
YOU...
YOU...
YOU SAIYAN SCUM!!
I DON'T NEED THIS COSMOS OR THE EARTH ANY-MORE!!
I'M GOING TO WIPE YOU OUT ALONG WITH THIS WHOLE GALAXY!!
RAAAAH!!!

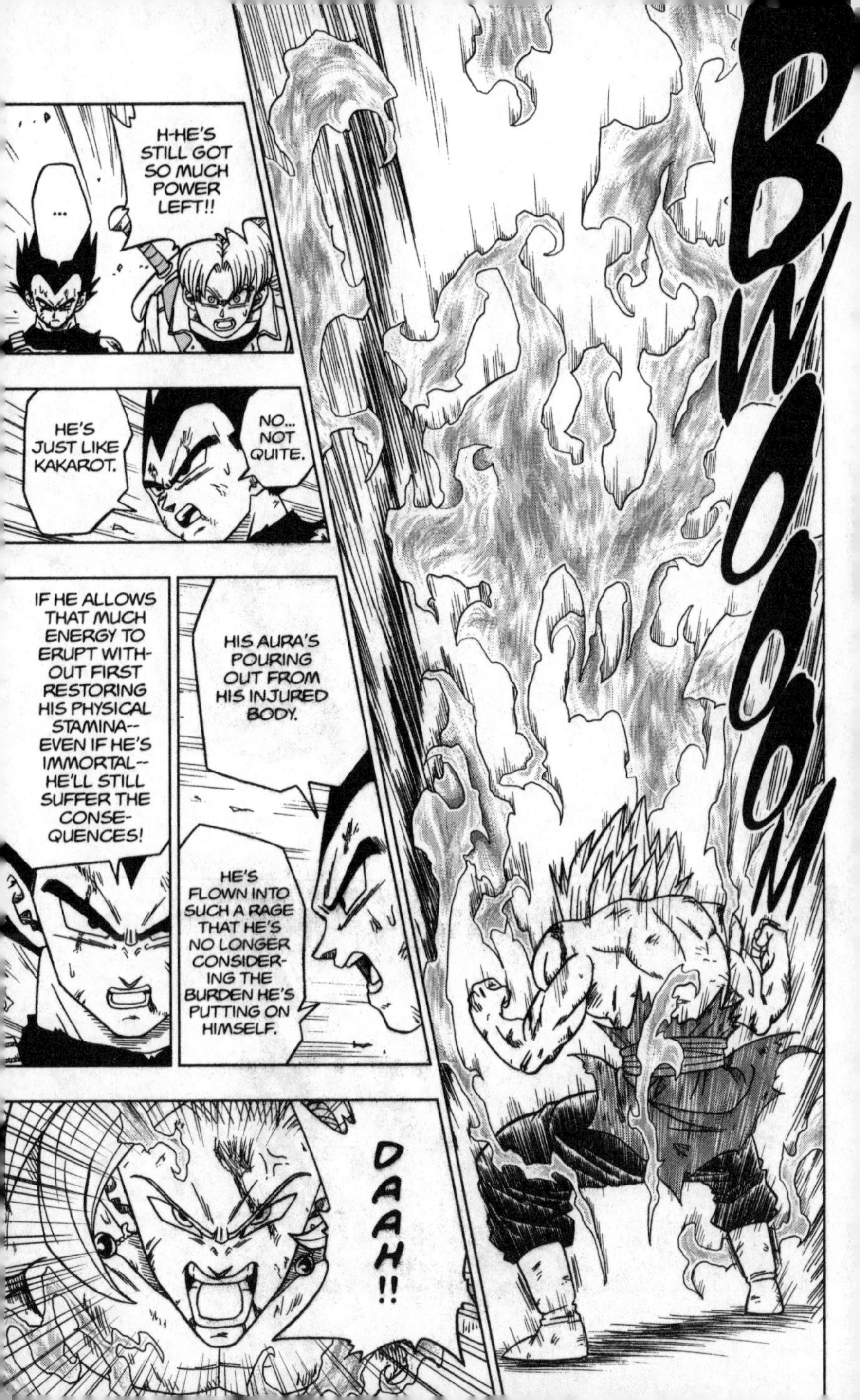
BWOOOM
H-HE'S STILL GOT SO MUCH POWER LEFT!!
...
HE'S JUST LIKE KAKAROT.
NO... NOT QUITE.
HIS AURA'S POURING OUT FROM HIS INJURED BODY.
HE'S FLOWN INTO SUCH A RAGE THAT HE'S NO LONGER CONSIDER-ING THE BURDEN HE'S PUTTING ON HIMSELF.
IF HE ALLOWS THAT MUCH ENERGY TO ERUPT WITH-OUT FIRST RESTORING HIS PHYSICAL STAMINA-- EVEN IF HE'S IMMORTAL-- HE'LL STILL SUFFER THE CONSE-QUENCES!
DAAAH!!

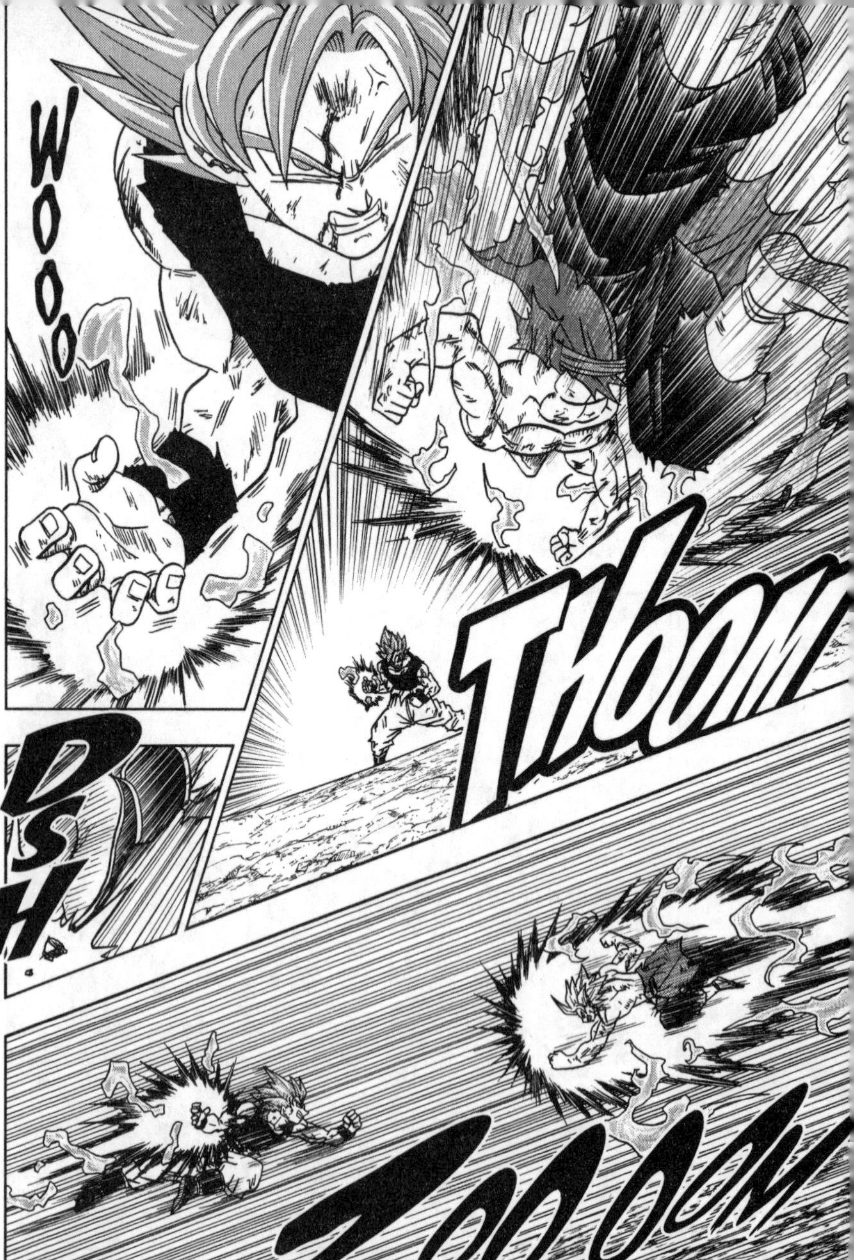
THOOM
WOOO
DSH
ZOOOM

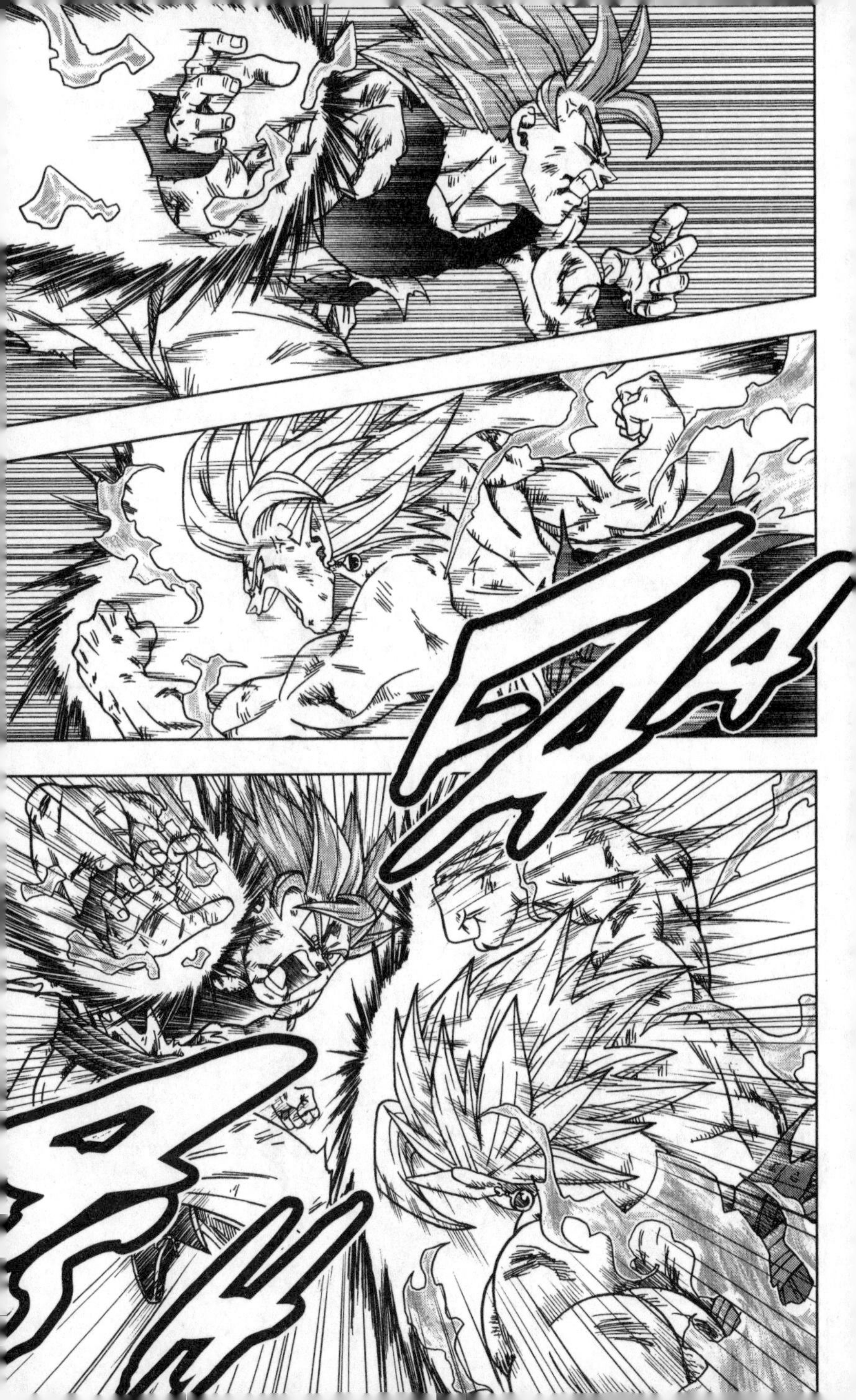

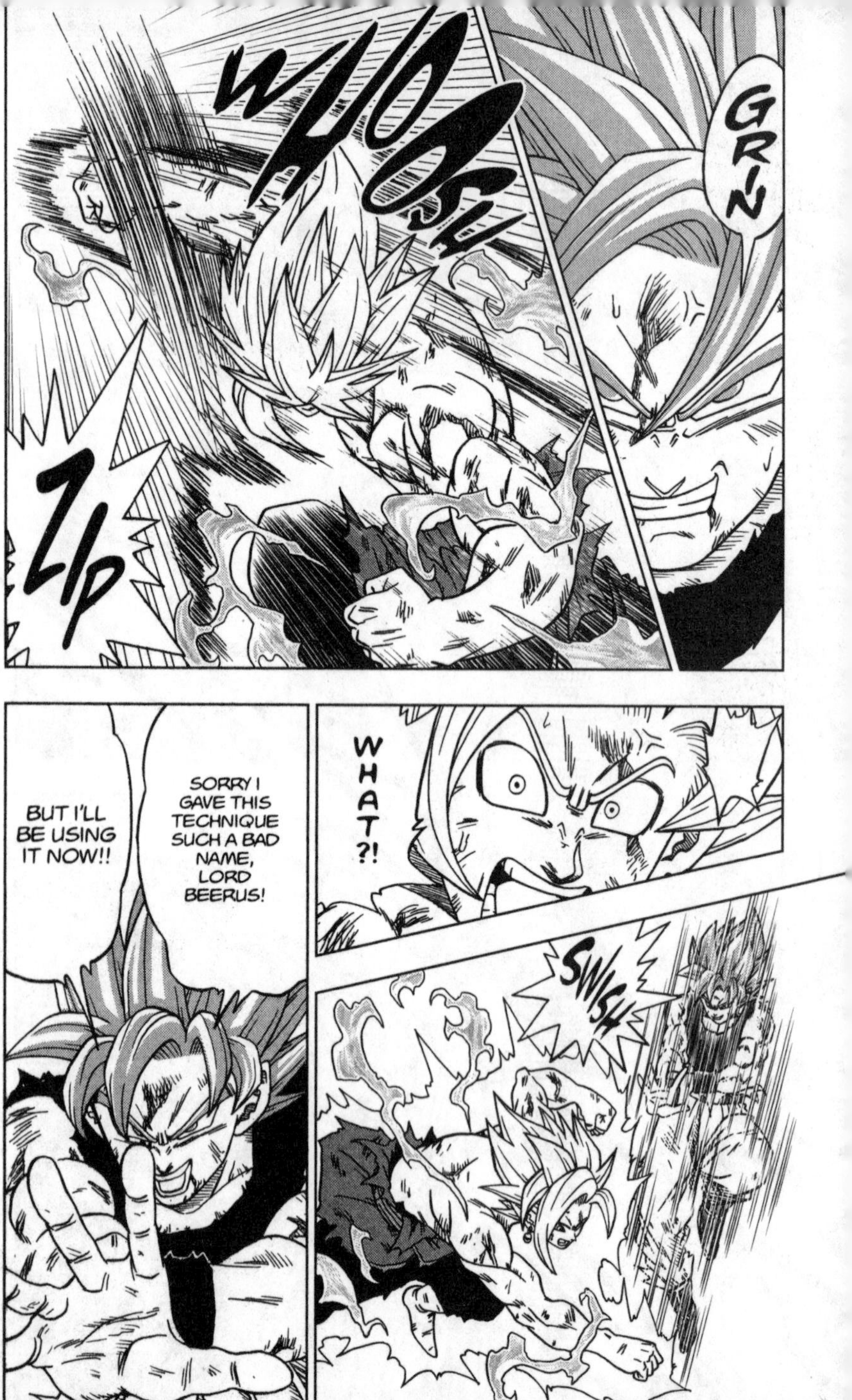
GRIN
WHOOSH
ZIP
WHAT?!
SWISH
SORRY I GAVE THIS TECHNIQUE SUCH A BAD NAME, LORD BEERUS!
BUT I'LL BE USING IT NOW!!

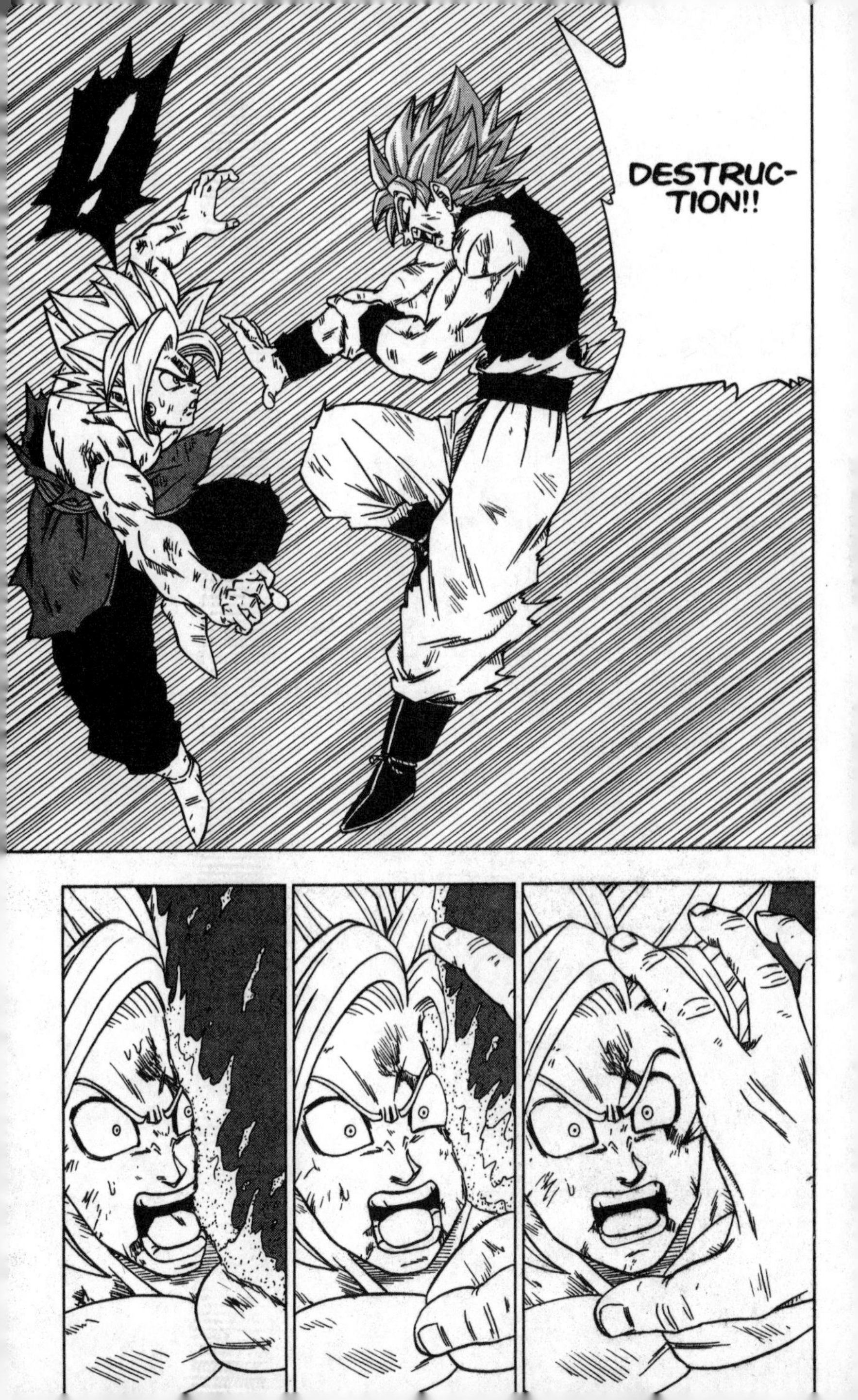
DESTRUCTION!!
!!

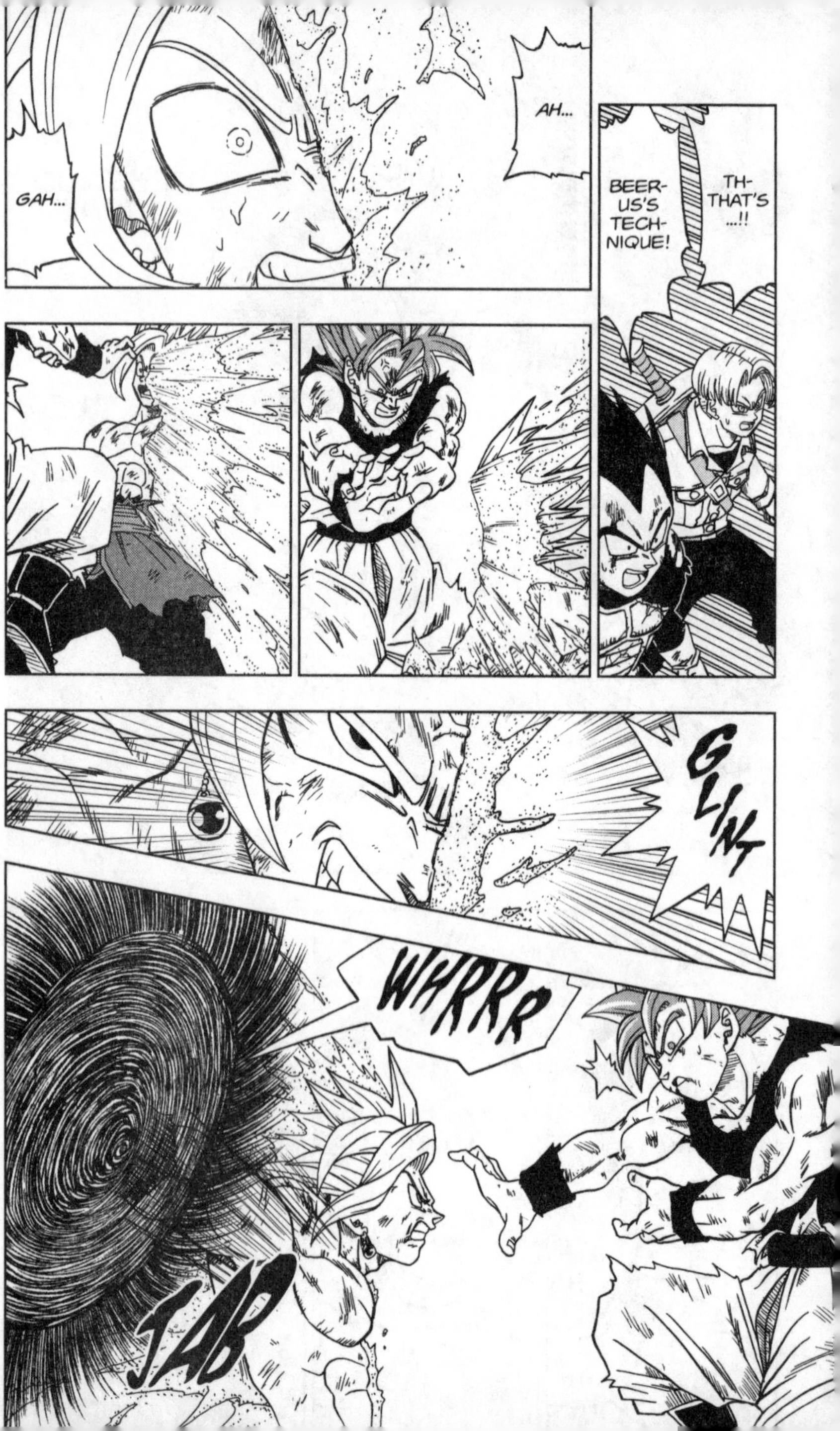
TH-THAT'S ...!!
BEER-US'S TECH-NIQUE!
AH...
GAH...
GLINT
WHRRR
JAB

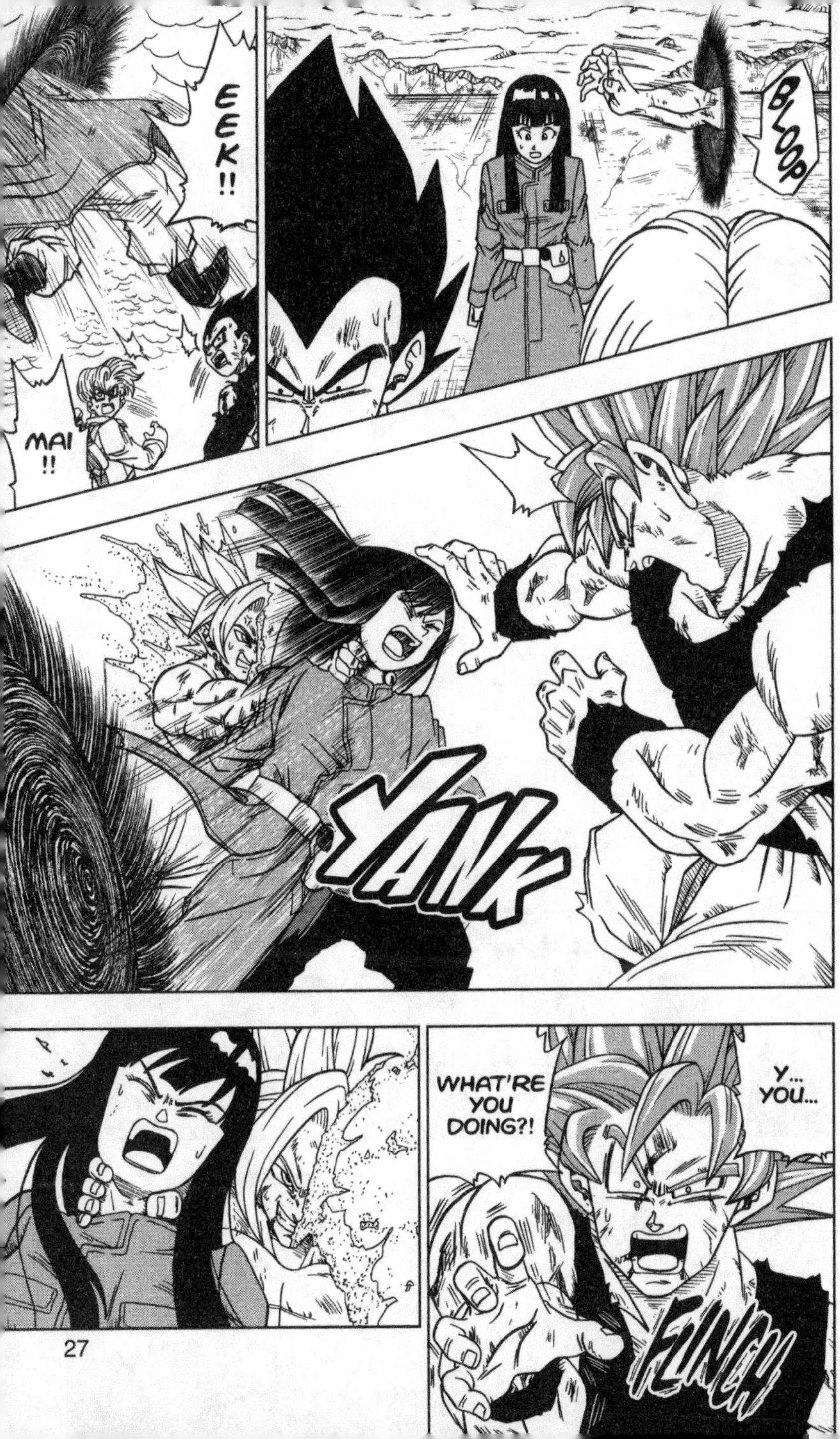
BLOOP
EEK!!
MAI!!
YANK
Y... YOU...
WHAT'RE YOU DOING?!
FLINCH

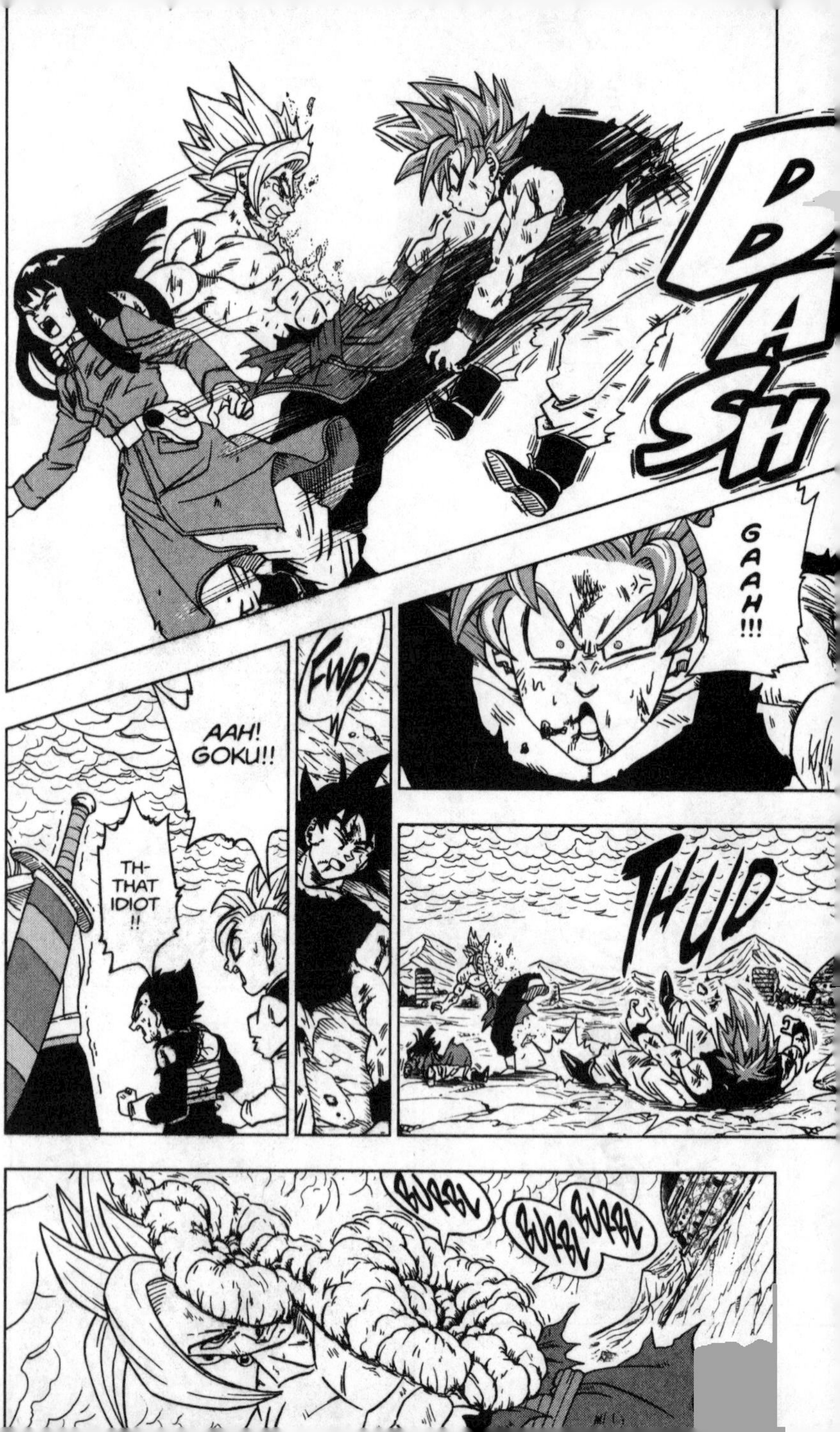
DASH
GAAH!!!
FWP
AAH! GOKU!!
TH- THAT IDIOT !!
THUD
BUBBL
BUBBL BUBBL

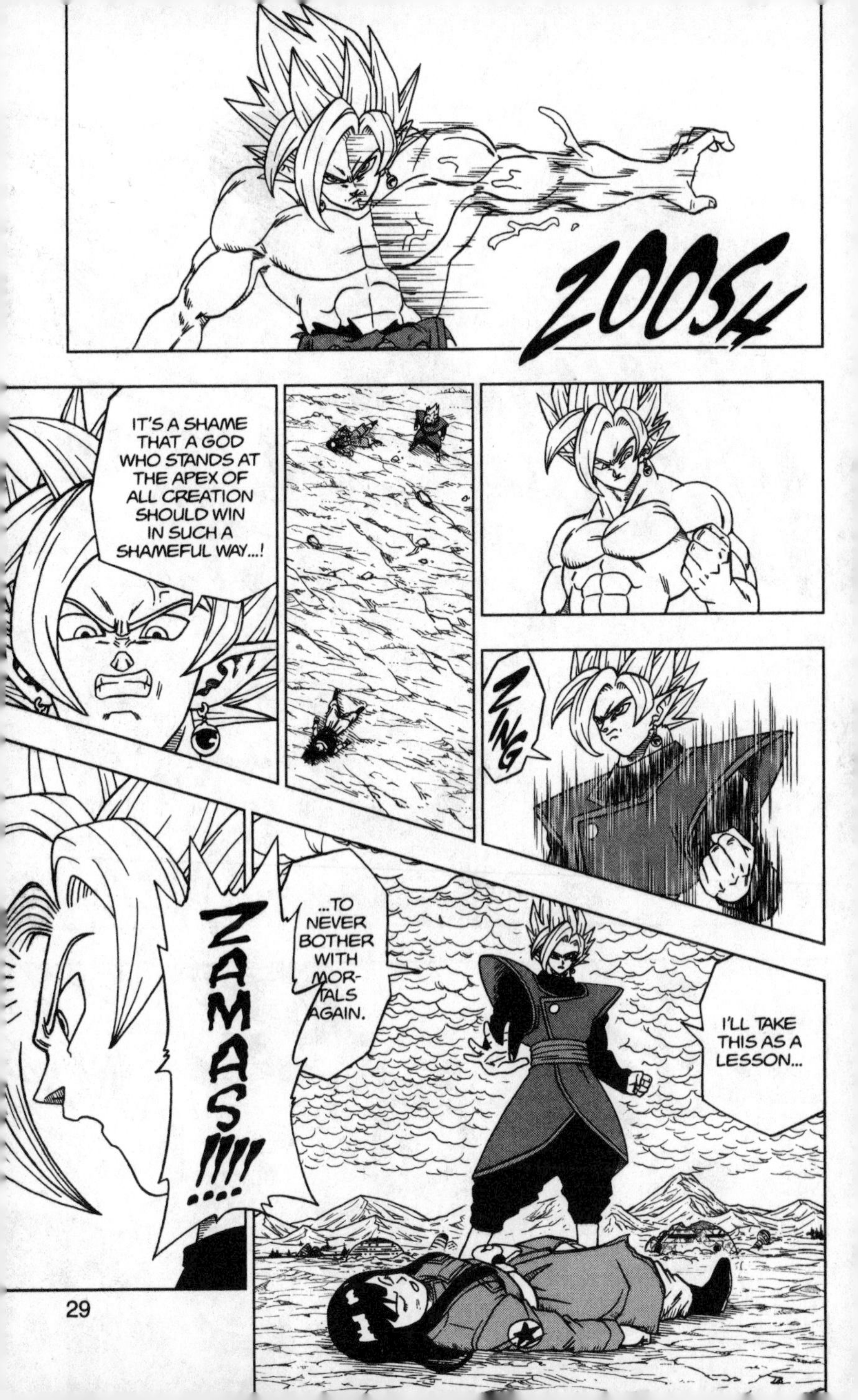
ZOOSH
ZING
IT'S A SHAME THAT A GOD WHO STANDS AT THE APEX OF ALL CREATION SHOULD WIN IN SUCH A SHAMEFUL WAY...!
I'LL TAKE THIS AS A LESSON...
...TO NEVER BOTHER WITH MOR-TALS AGAIN.
ZAMAS!!!!...

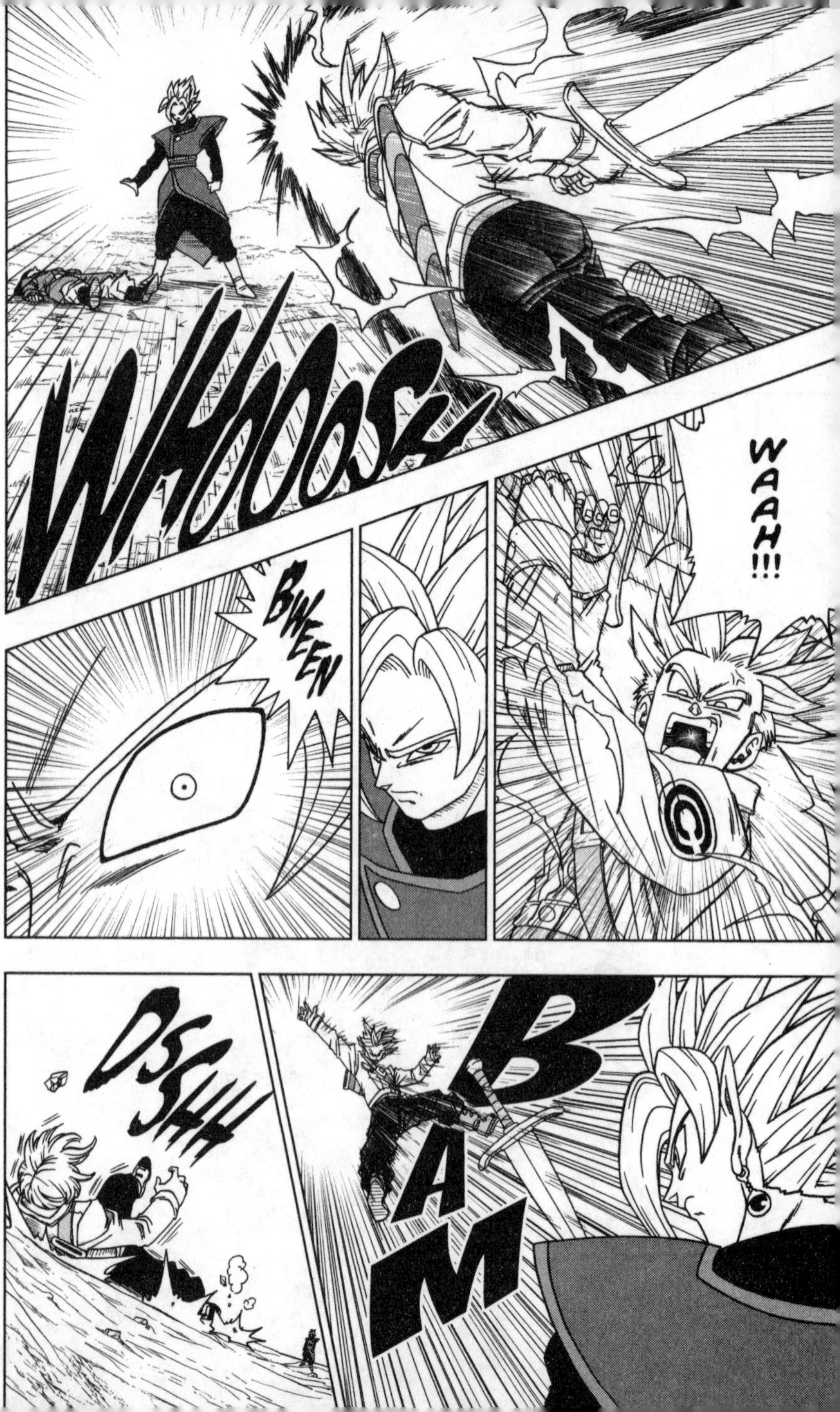
WHOOSH
WAAAH!!!
BWEEN
BAM
DSHH

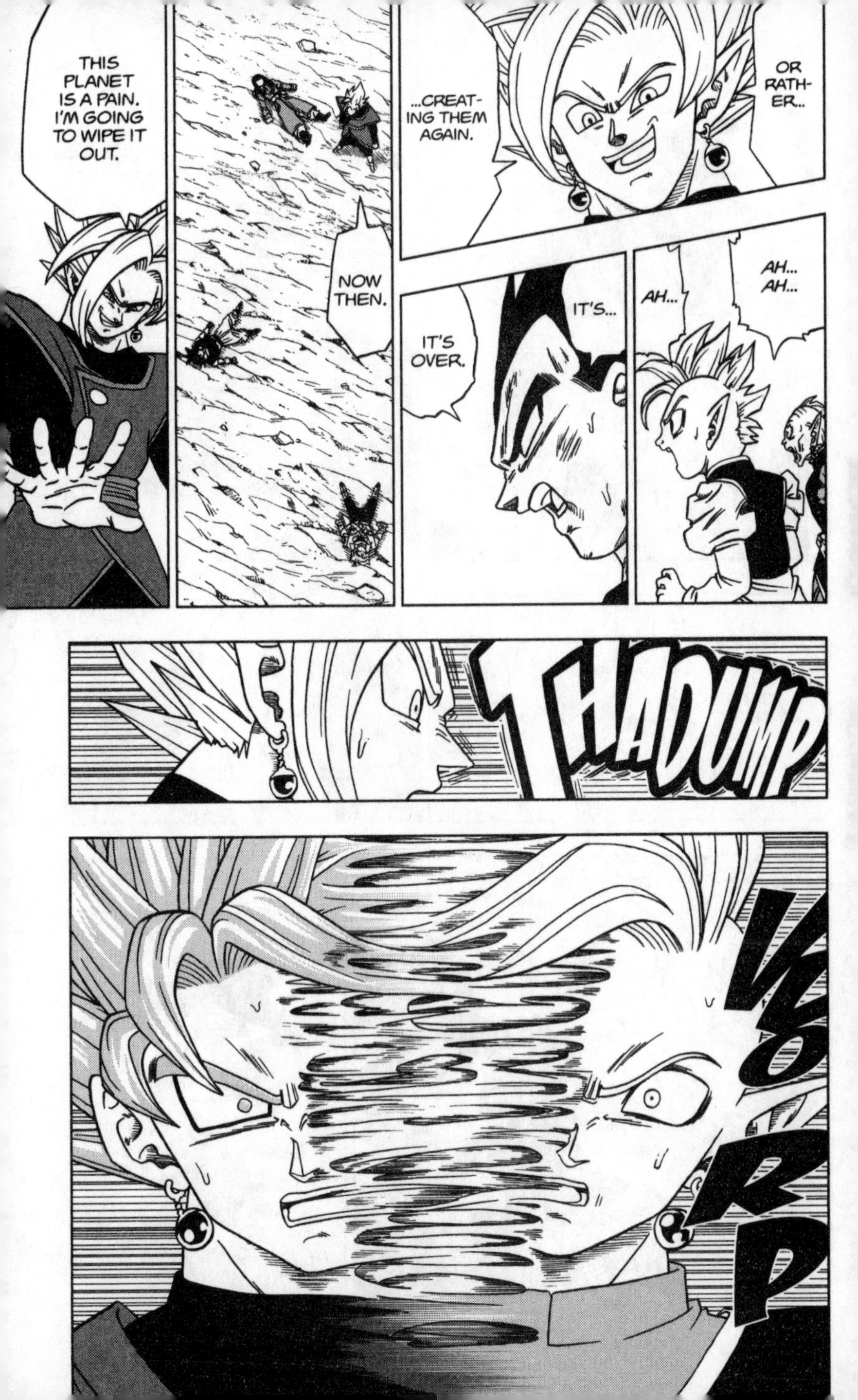
OR RATH-ER...
...CREAT-ING THEM AGAIN.
AH... AH...
AH...
IT'S...
IT'S OVER.
NOW THEN.
THIS PLANET IS A PAIN. I'M GOING TO WIPE IT OUT.
THADUMP
WOORP

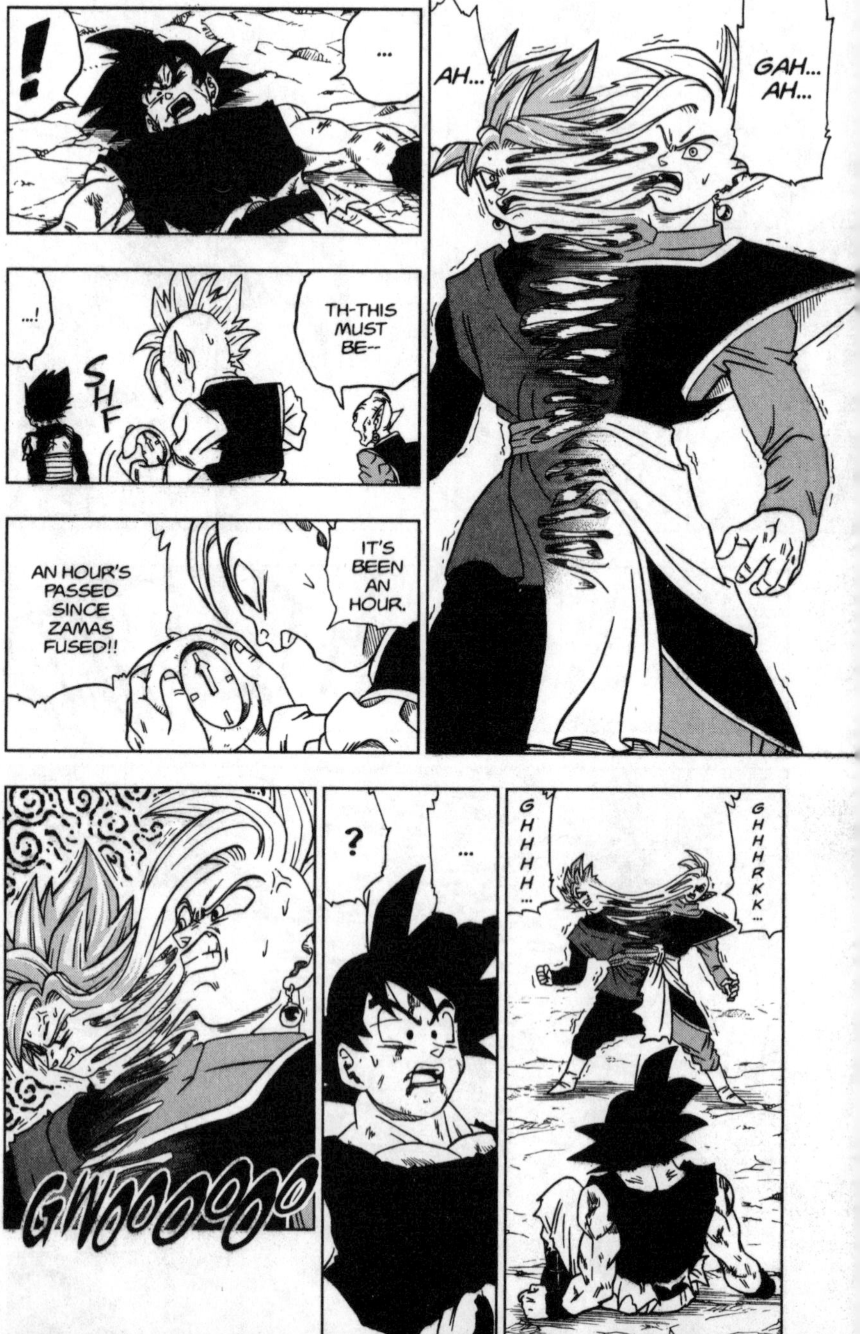
GAH... AH...
AH...
...
!
TH-THIS MUST BE--
...!
SHF
IT'S BEEN AN HOUR.
AN HOUR'S PASSED SINCE ZAMAS FUSED!!
GHHHRKK...
GHHHH...
...
?
GWOOOOOO

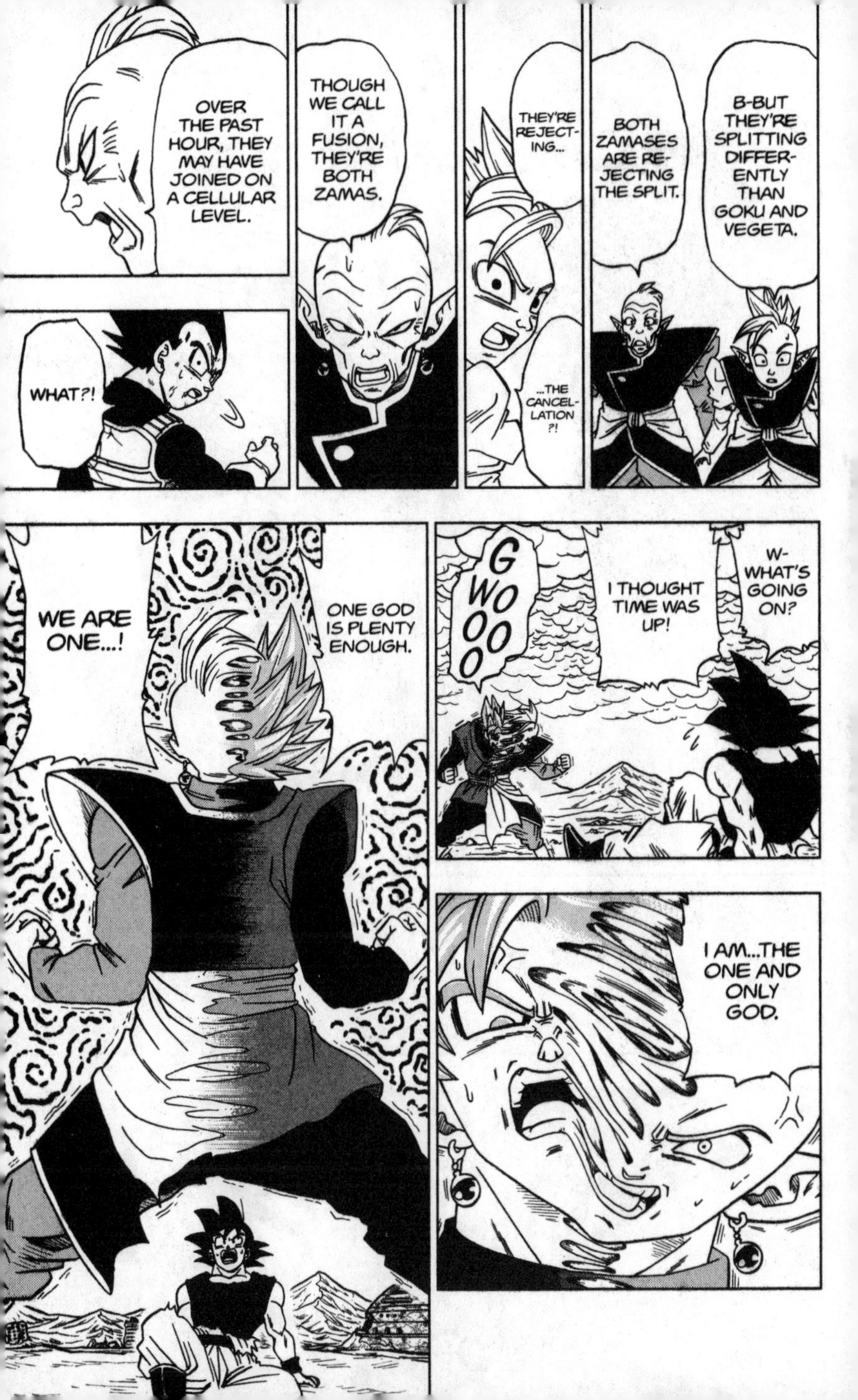
B-BUT THEY'RE SPLITTING DIFFERENTLY THAN GOKU AND VEGETA.
BOTH ZAMASES ARE REJECTING THE SPLIT.
THEY'RE REJECTING...
...THE CANCELLATION?!
THOUGH WE CALL IT A FUSION, THEY'RE BOTH ZAMAS.
OVER THE PAST HOUR, THEY MAY HAVE JOINED ON A CELLULAR LEVEL.
WHAT?!
W-WHAT'S GOING ON?
I THOUGHT TIME WAS UP!
GWOOOO
I AM...THE ONE AND ONLY GOD.
ONE GOD IS PLENTY ENOUGH.
WE ARE ONE...!

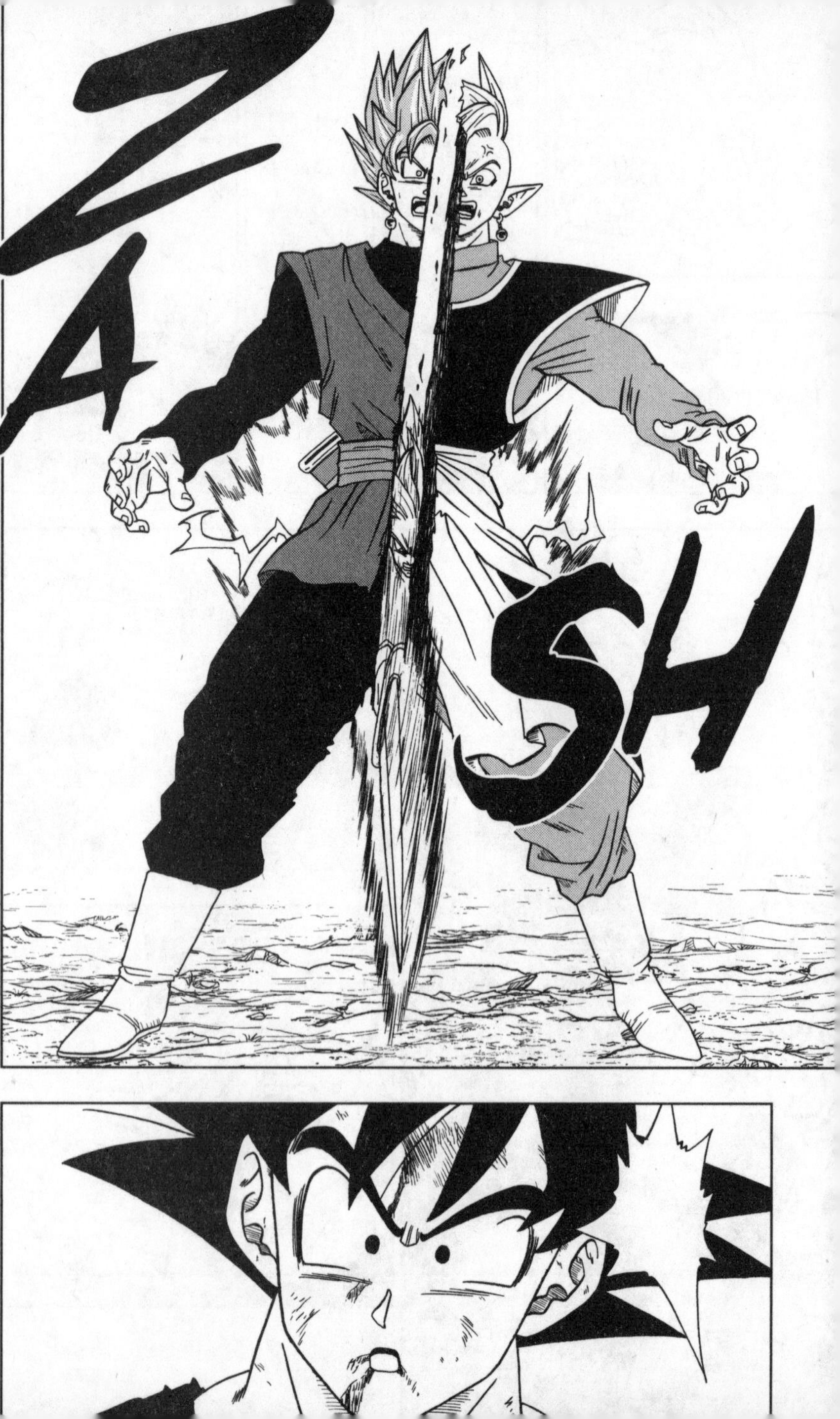
ZASH

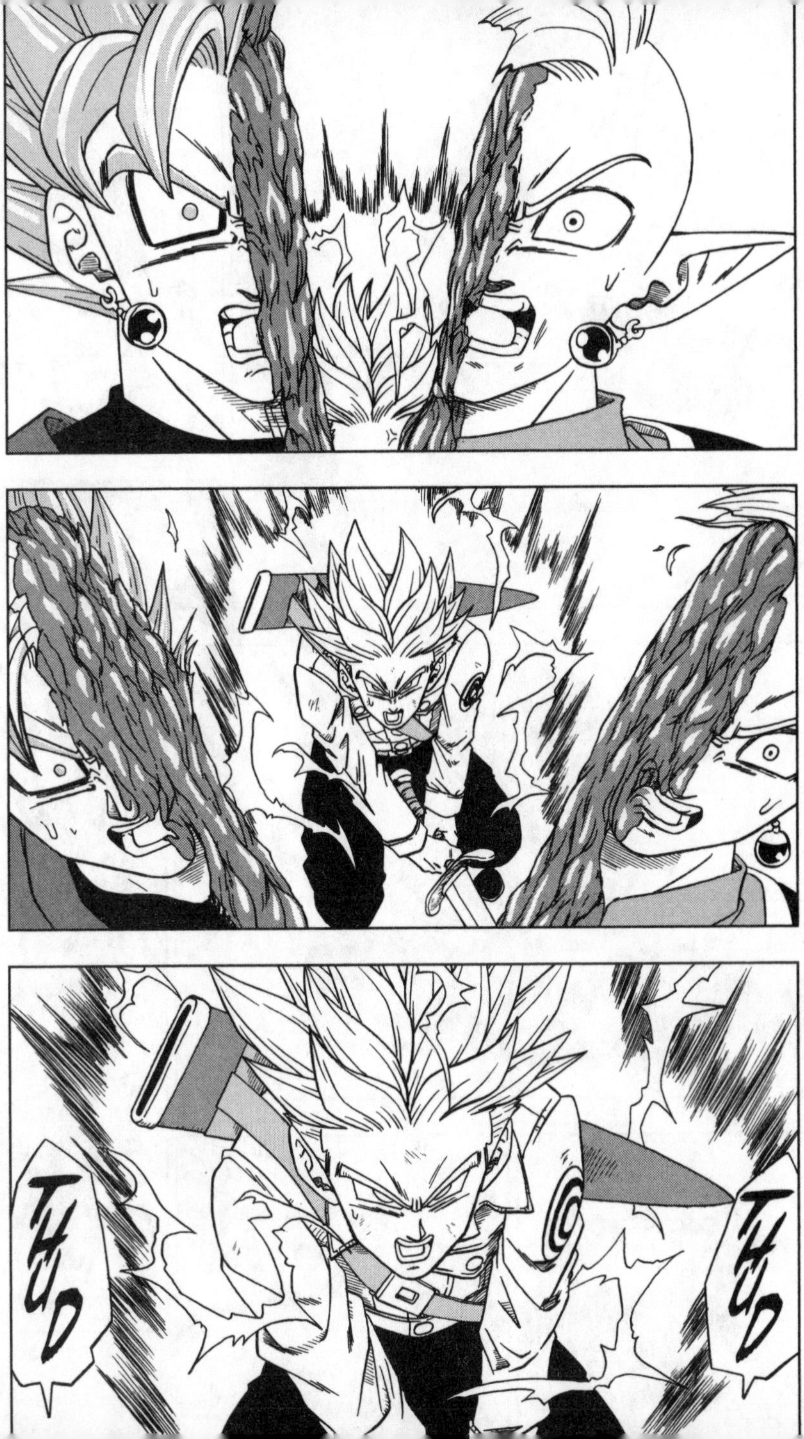
THUD
THUD

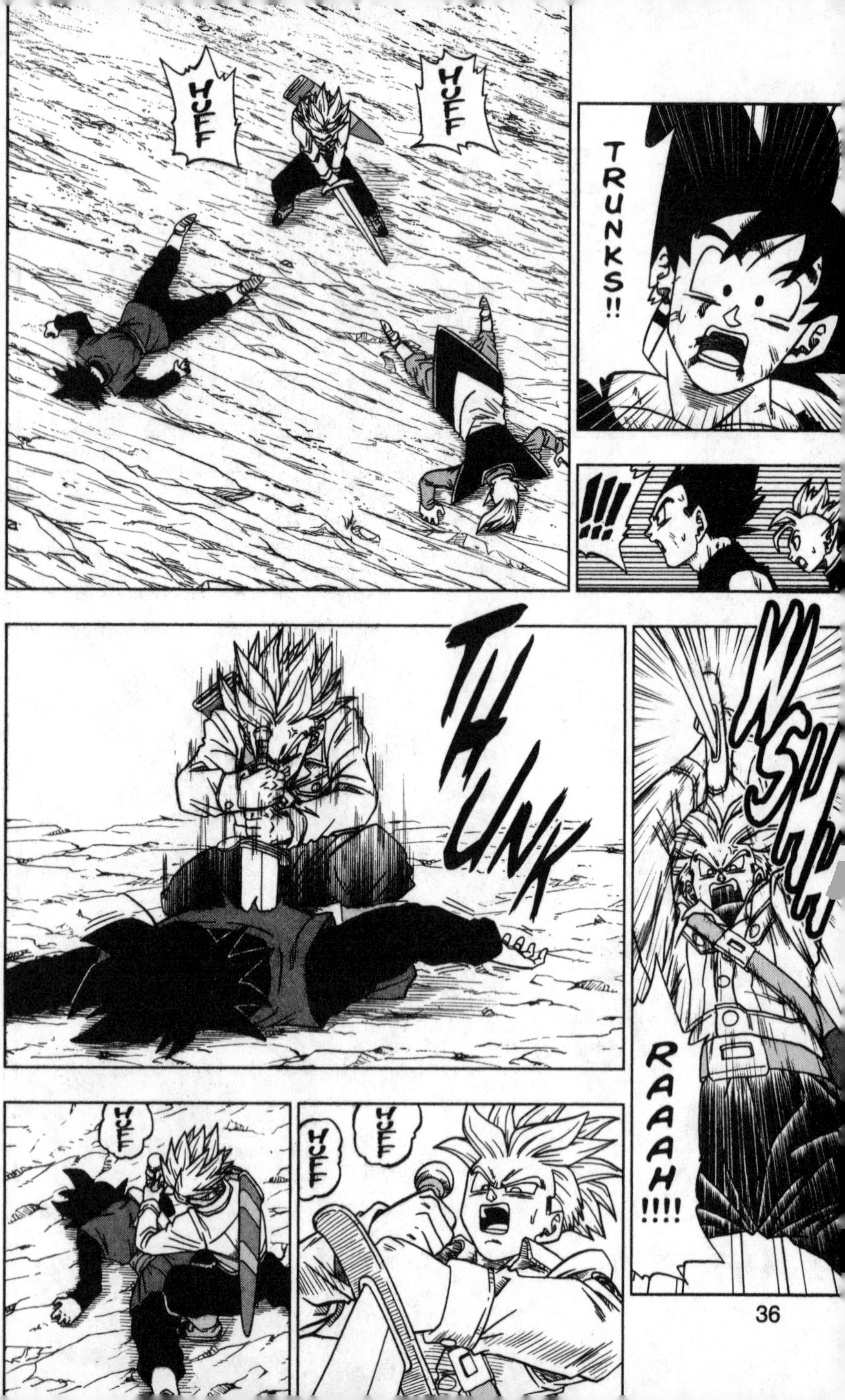
TRUNKS!!
!!!
HUFF
HUFF
RAAAAH!!!!
THUNK
HUFF
HUFF
HUFF

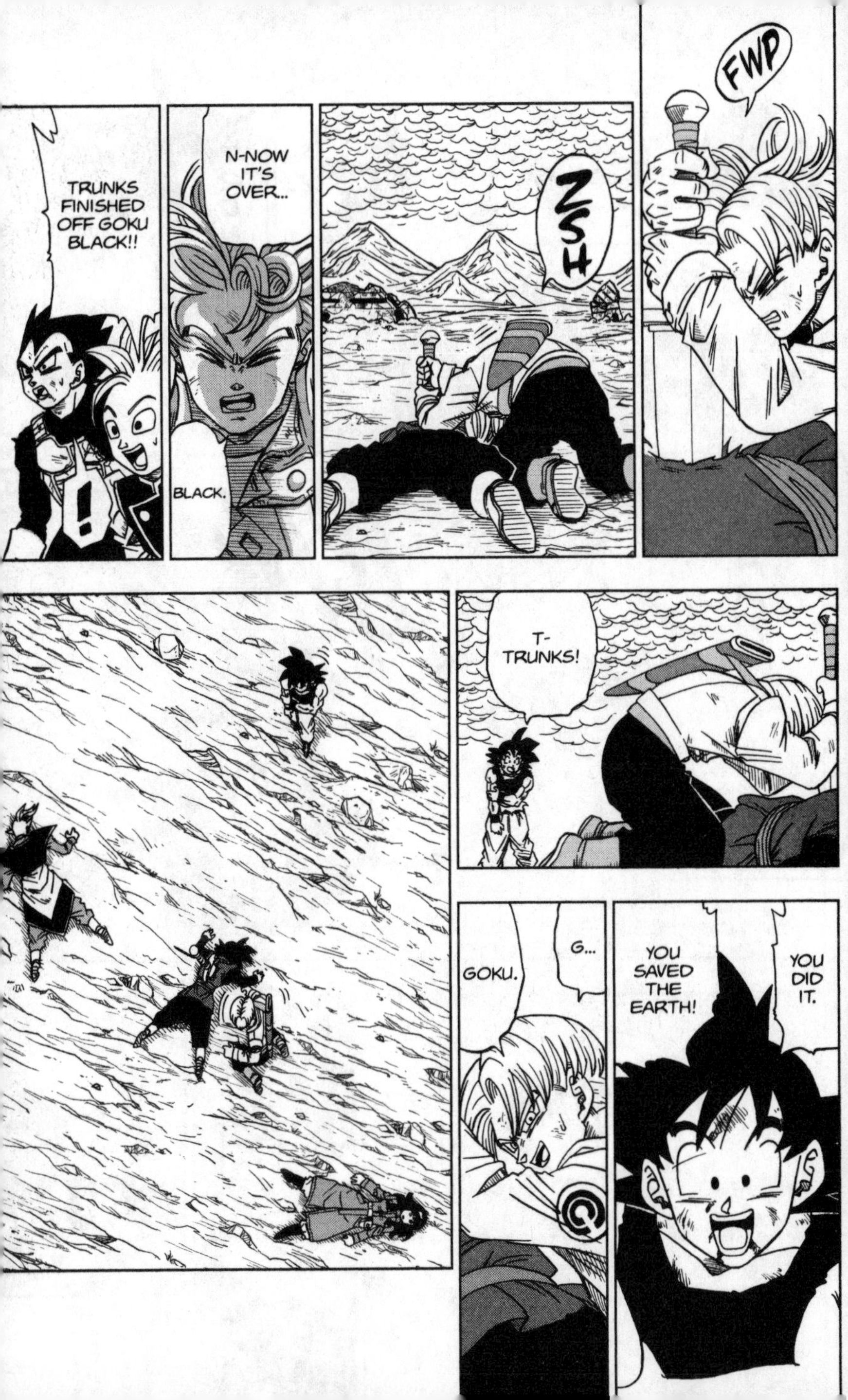
FWP
ZSH
N-NOW IT'S OVER...
BLACK.
TRUNKS FINISHED OFF GOKU BLACK!!
T-TRUNKS!
YOU DID IT.
YOU SAVED THE EARTH!
G...
GOKU.

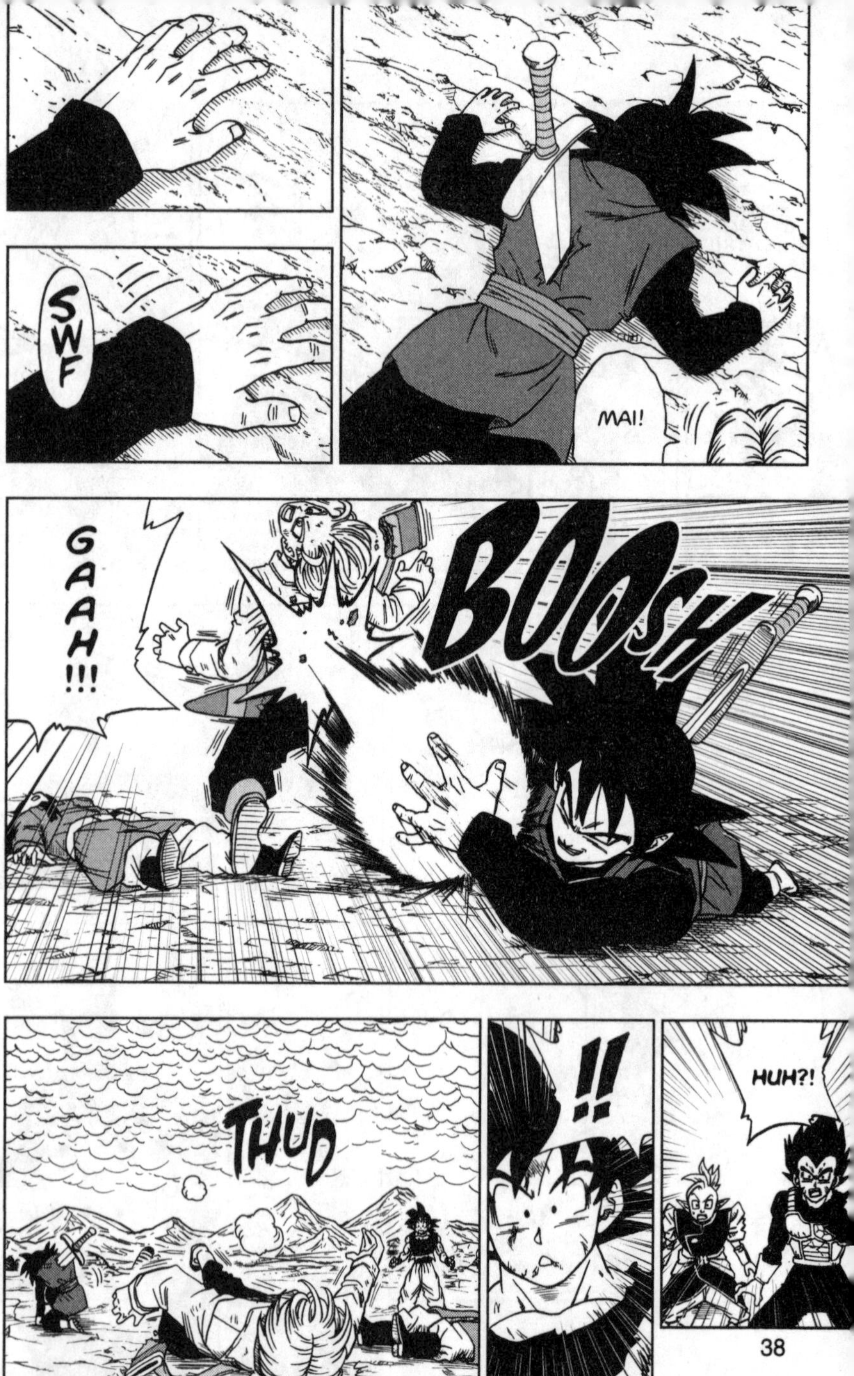
MAI!
SWF
BOOSH
GAAAH!!!
HUH?!
!!
THUD

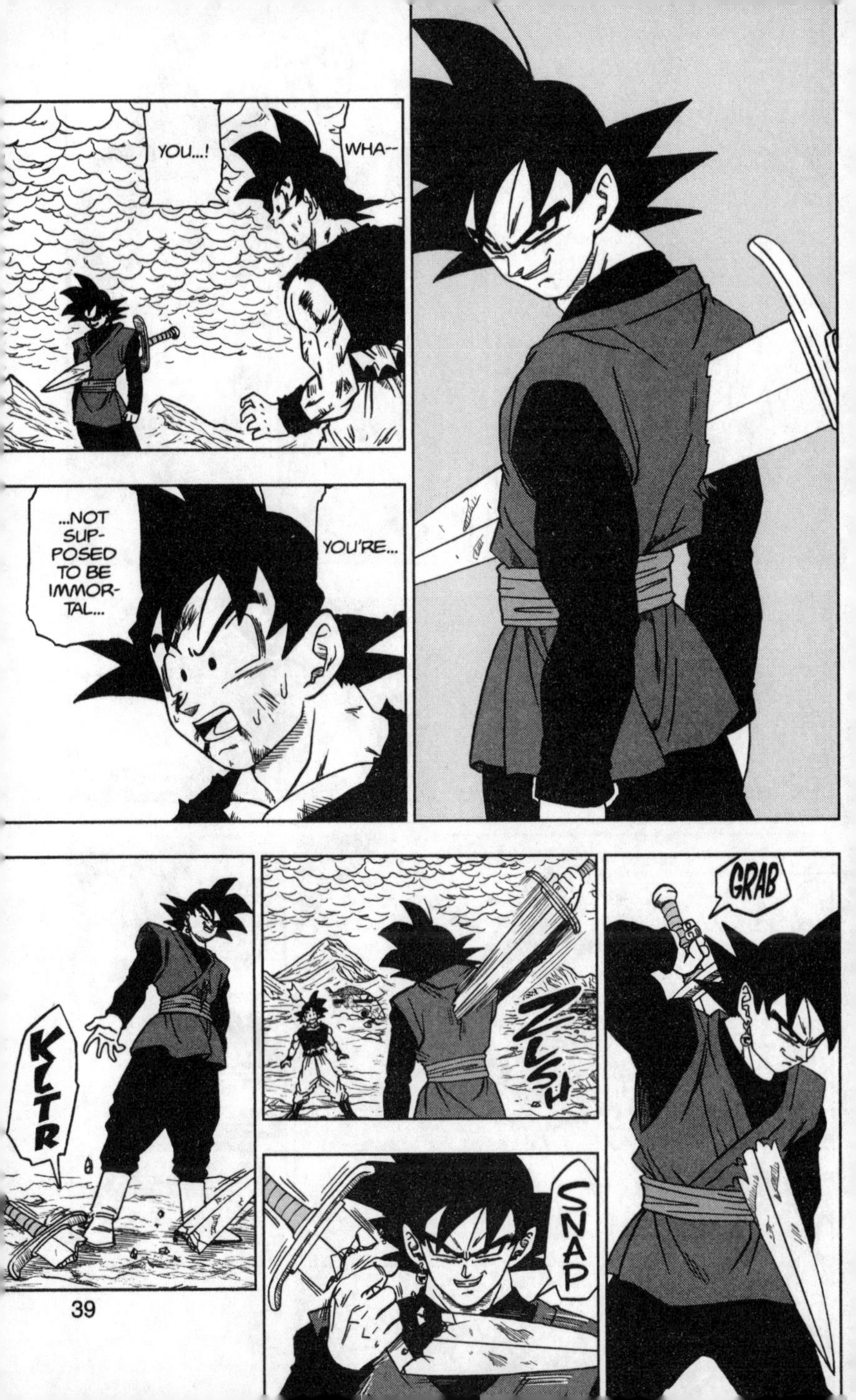
WHA--
YOU...!
YOU'RE...
...NOT SUP-POSED TO BE IMMOR-TAL...
GRAB
ZLSH
SNAP
KLTR

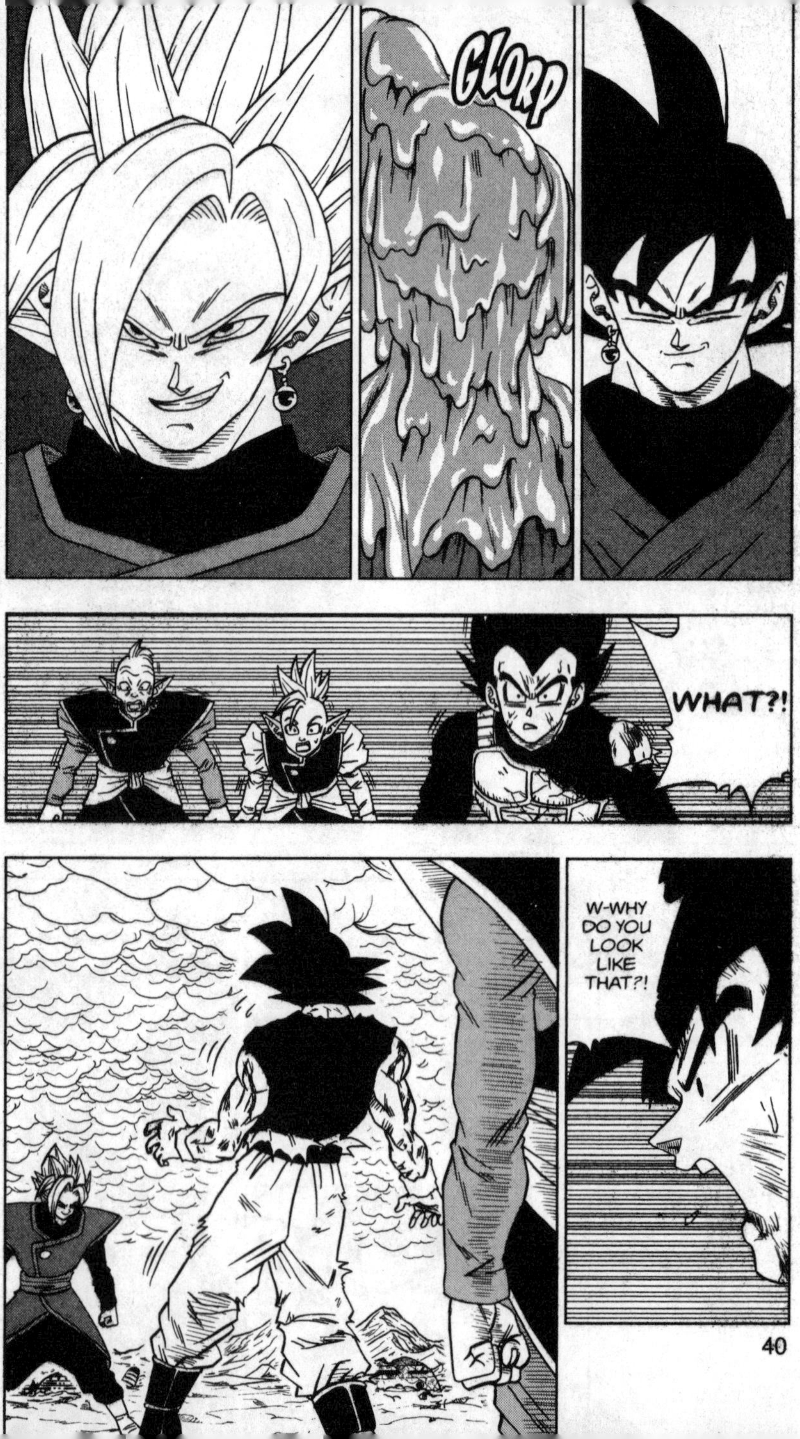

GLORP
WHAT?!
W-WHY DO YOU LOOK LIKE THAT?!

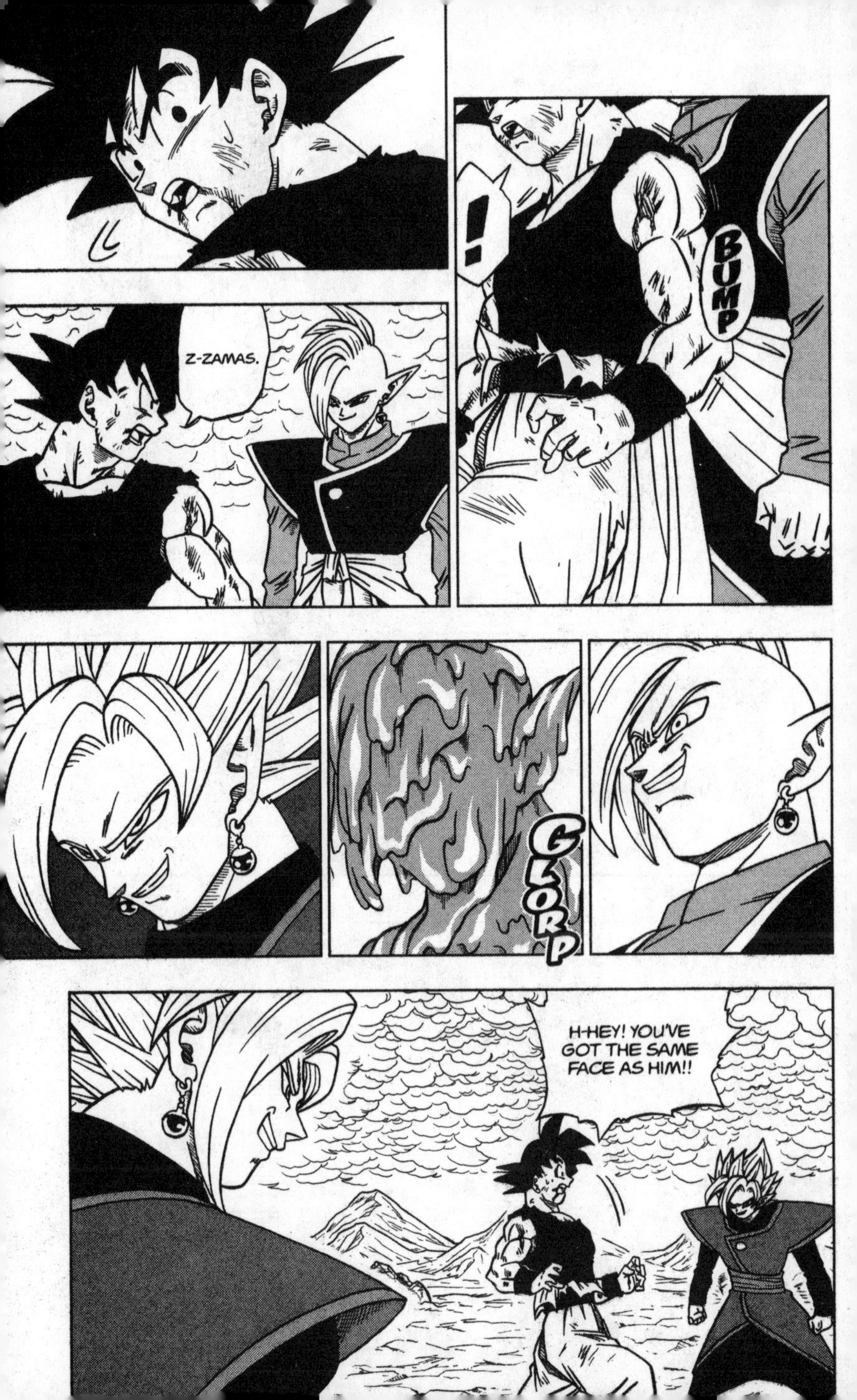
!
BUMP
Z-ZAMAS.
GLORP
H-HEY! YOU'VE GOT THE SAME FACE AS HIM!!

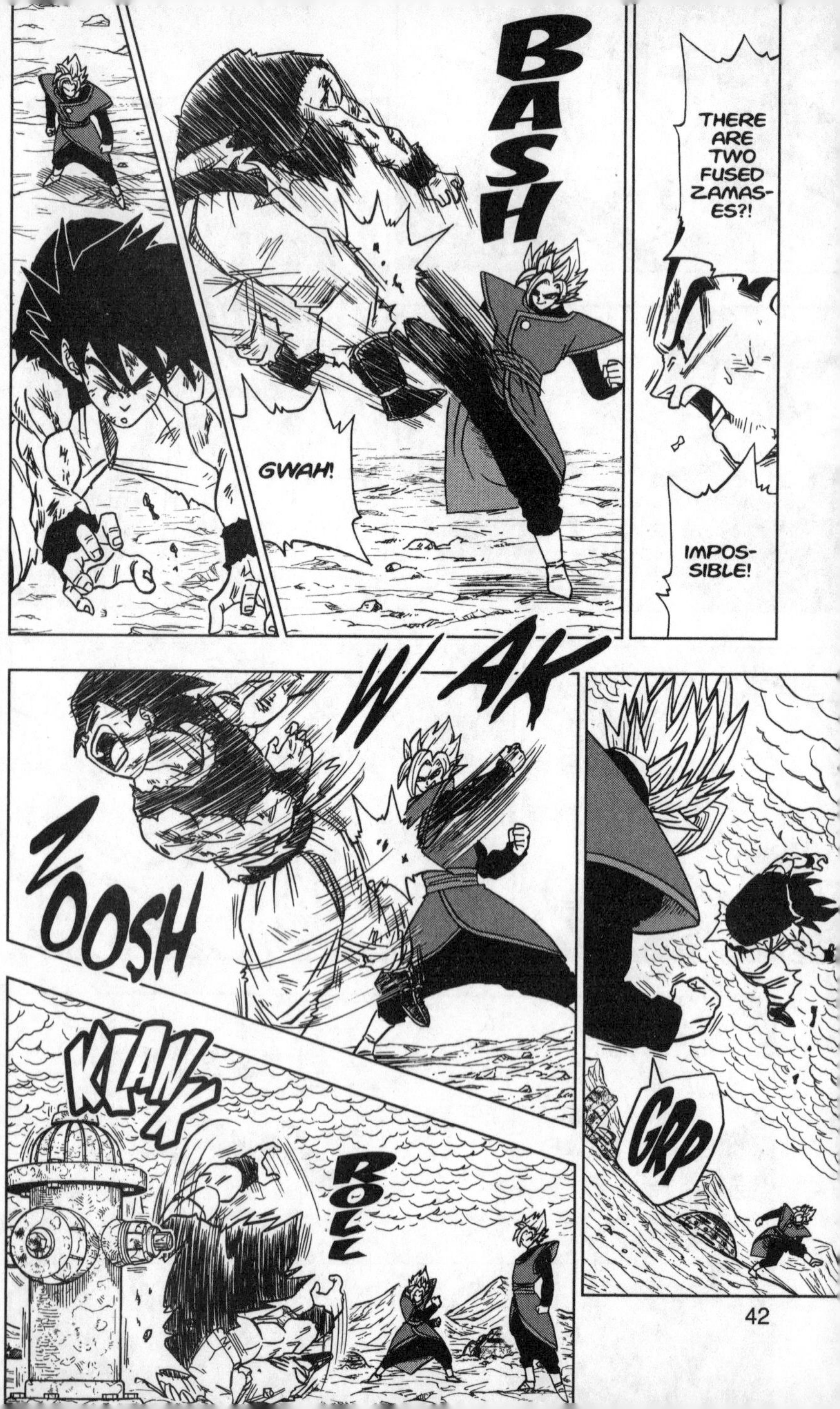
THERE ARE TWO FUSED ZAMAS-ES?!
IMPOS-SIBLE!
BASH
GWAH!
GRP
WAK
ZOOSH
KLANK
ROLL

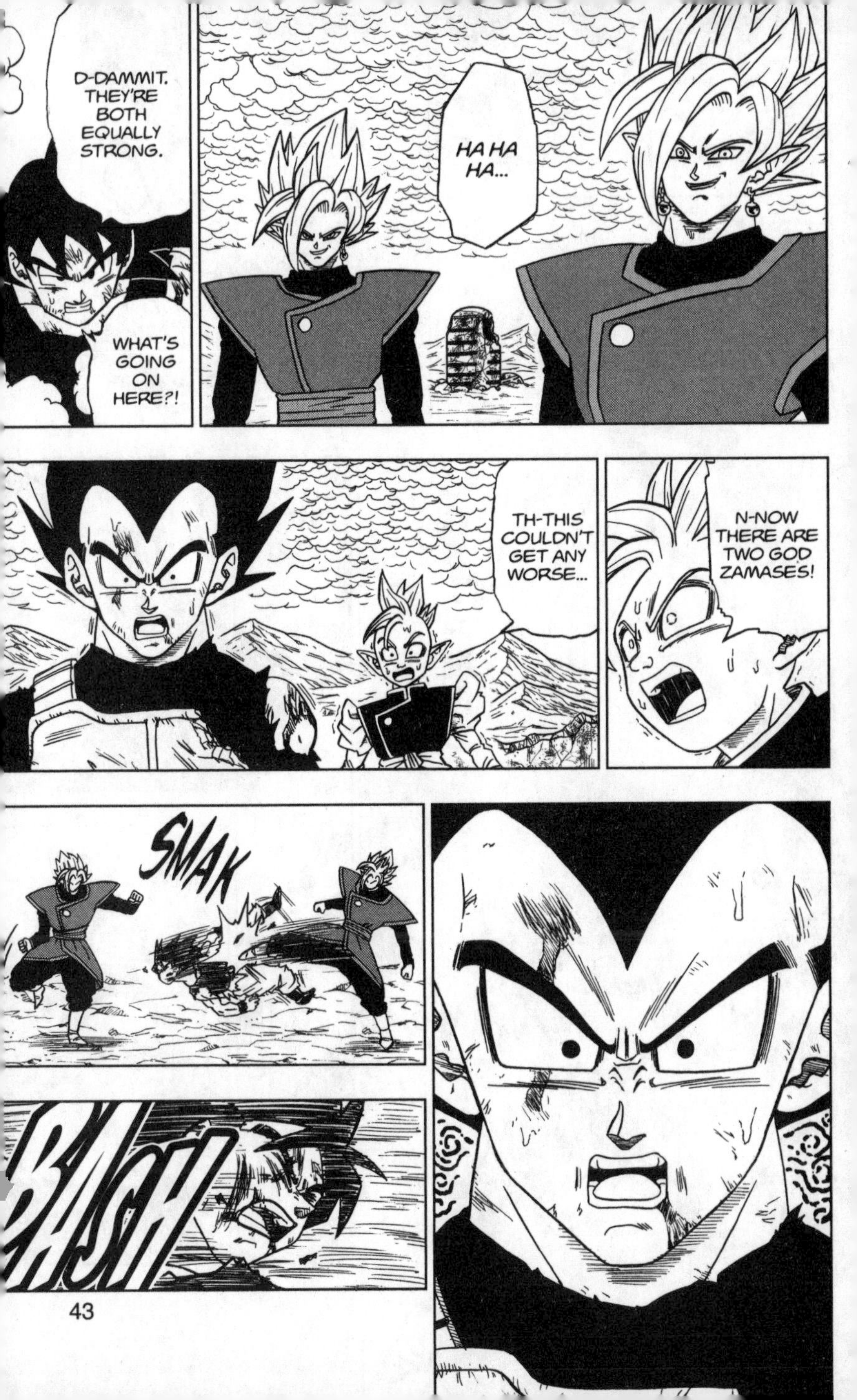
HA HA HA...
D-DAMMIT. THEY'RE BOTH EQUALLY STRONG.
WHAT'S GOING ON HERE?!
N-NOW THERE ARE TWO GOD ZAMASES!
TH-THIS COULDN'T GET ANY WORSE...
SMAK
BASH

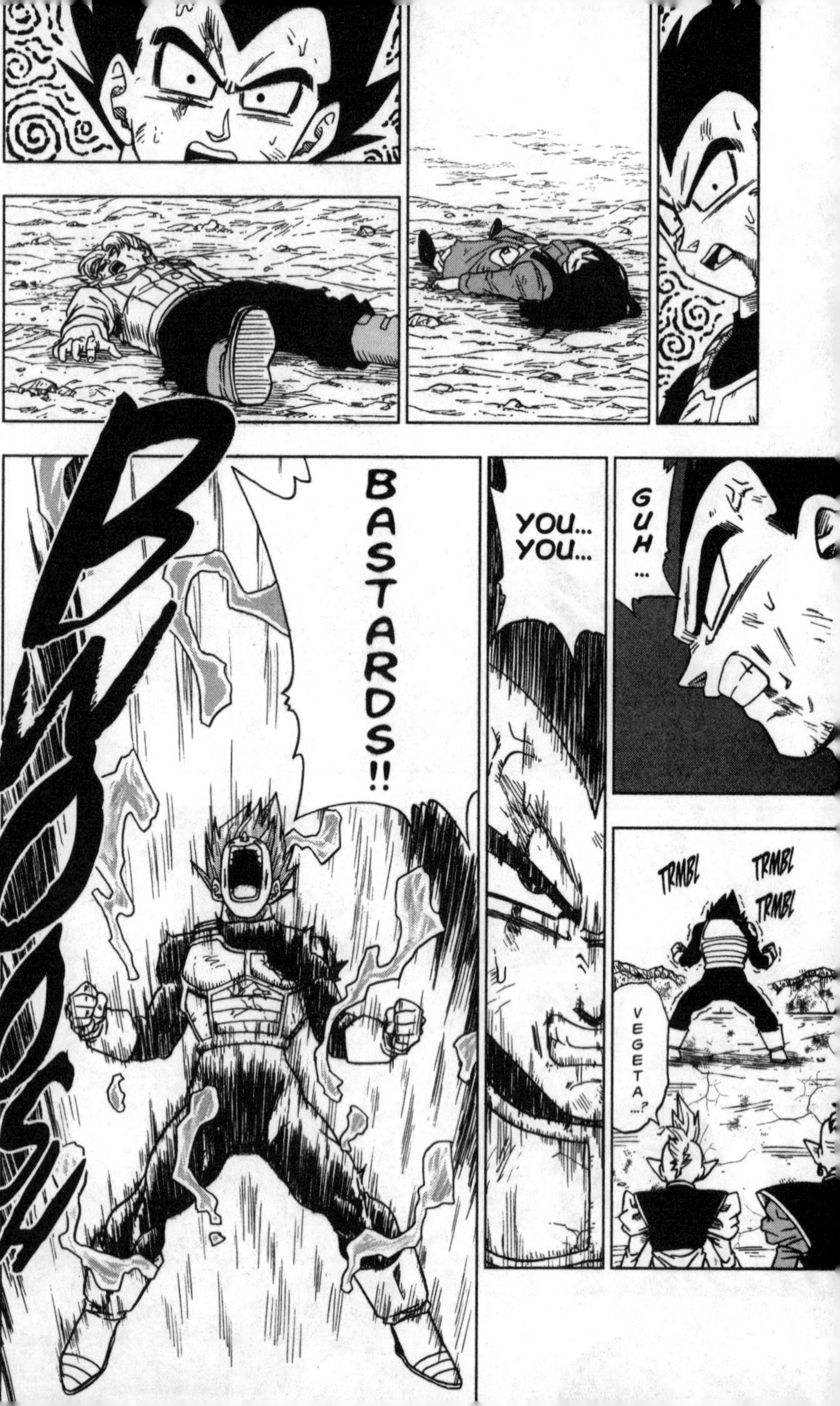
GUH...
TRMBL
TRMBL
TRMBL
VEGETA...?
YOU... YOU...
BASTARDS!!
BWOOSH

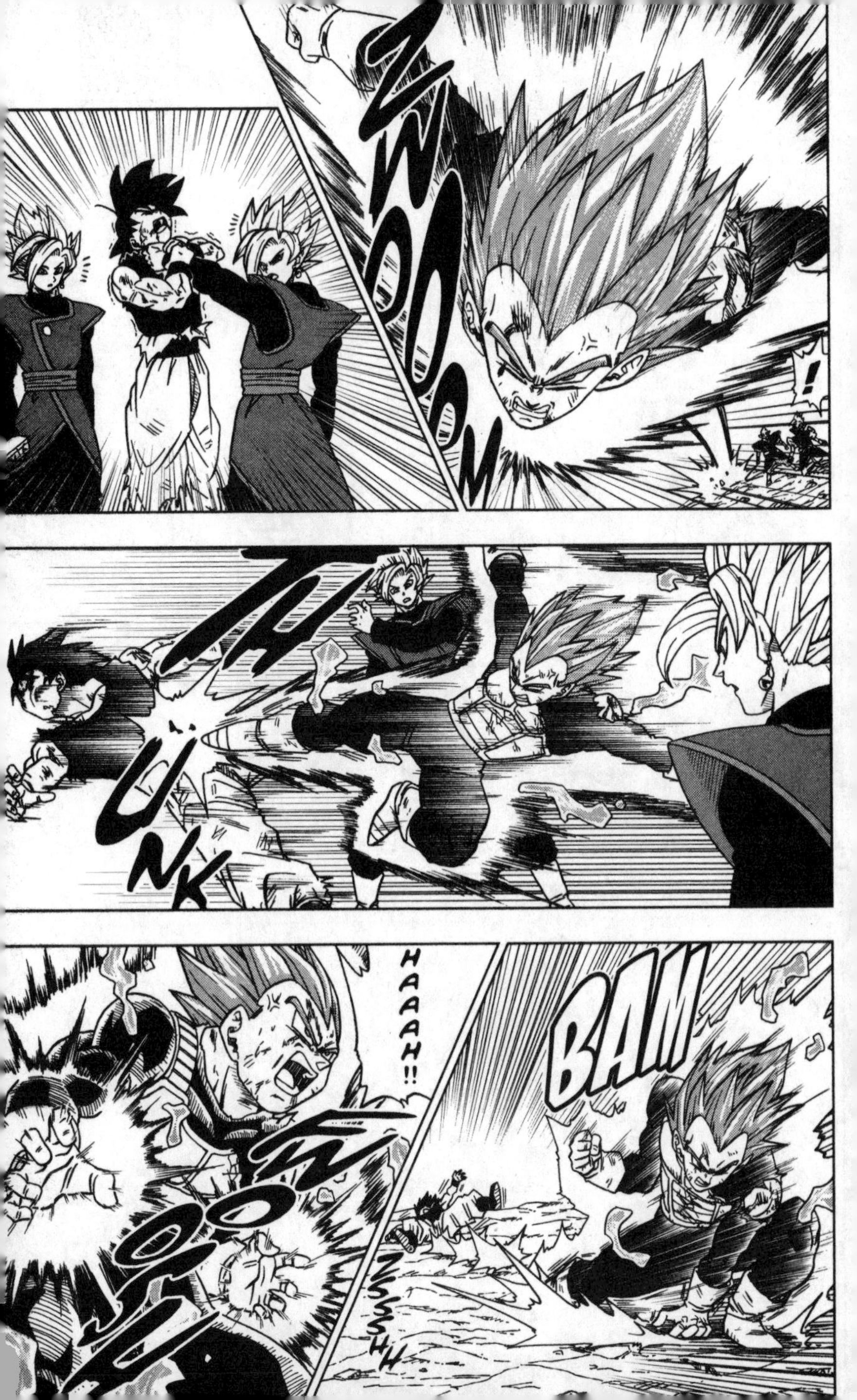
ZWOOOM
!
THUNK
BAM
ZSSSHH
HAAAAH!!
WOOSH

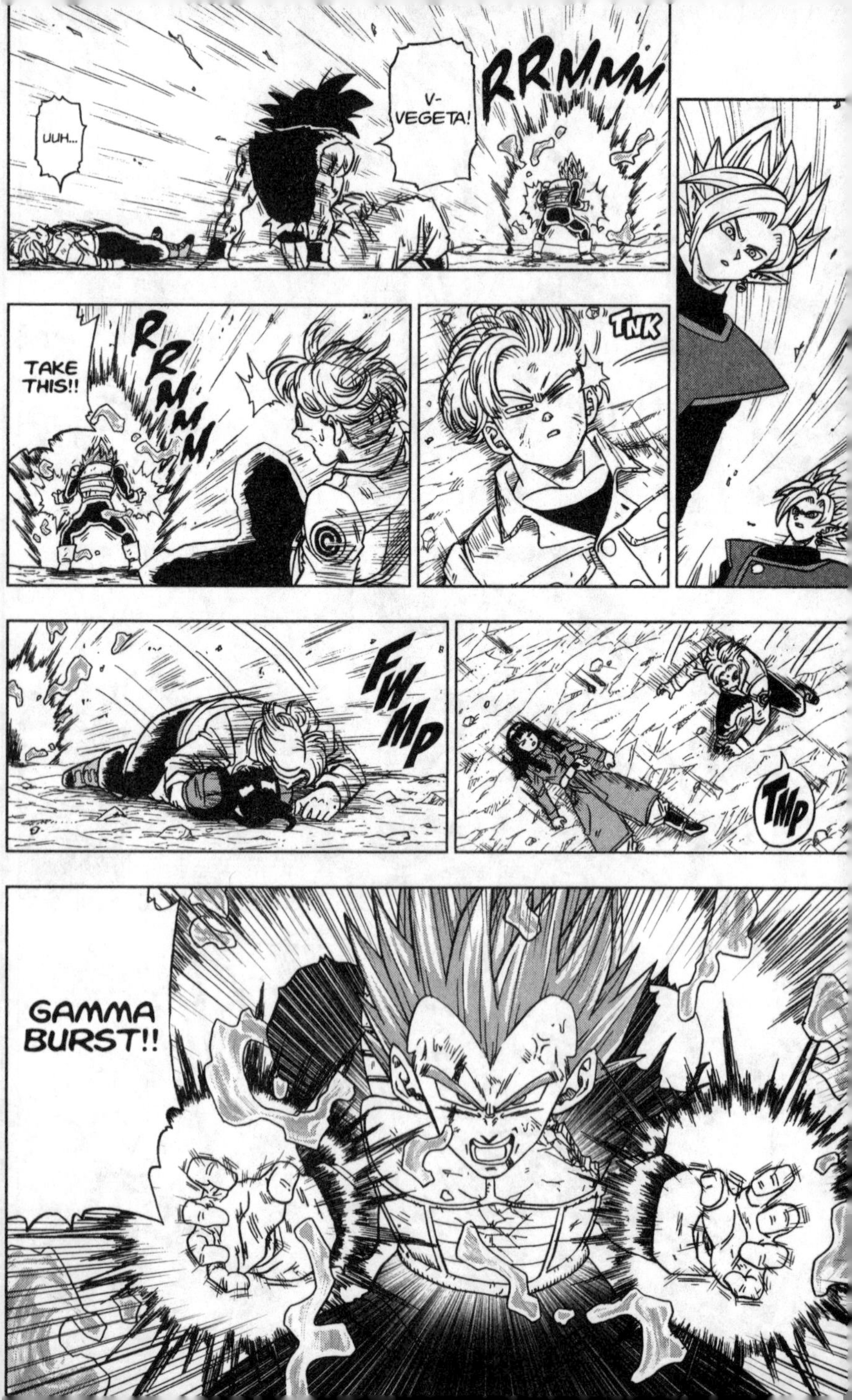
RRMMM
V-VEGETA!
UUH...
TNK
RRMMM
TAKE THIS!!
TMP
FWMP
GAMMA BURST!!

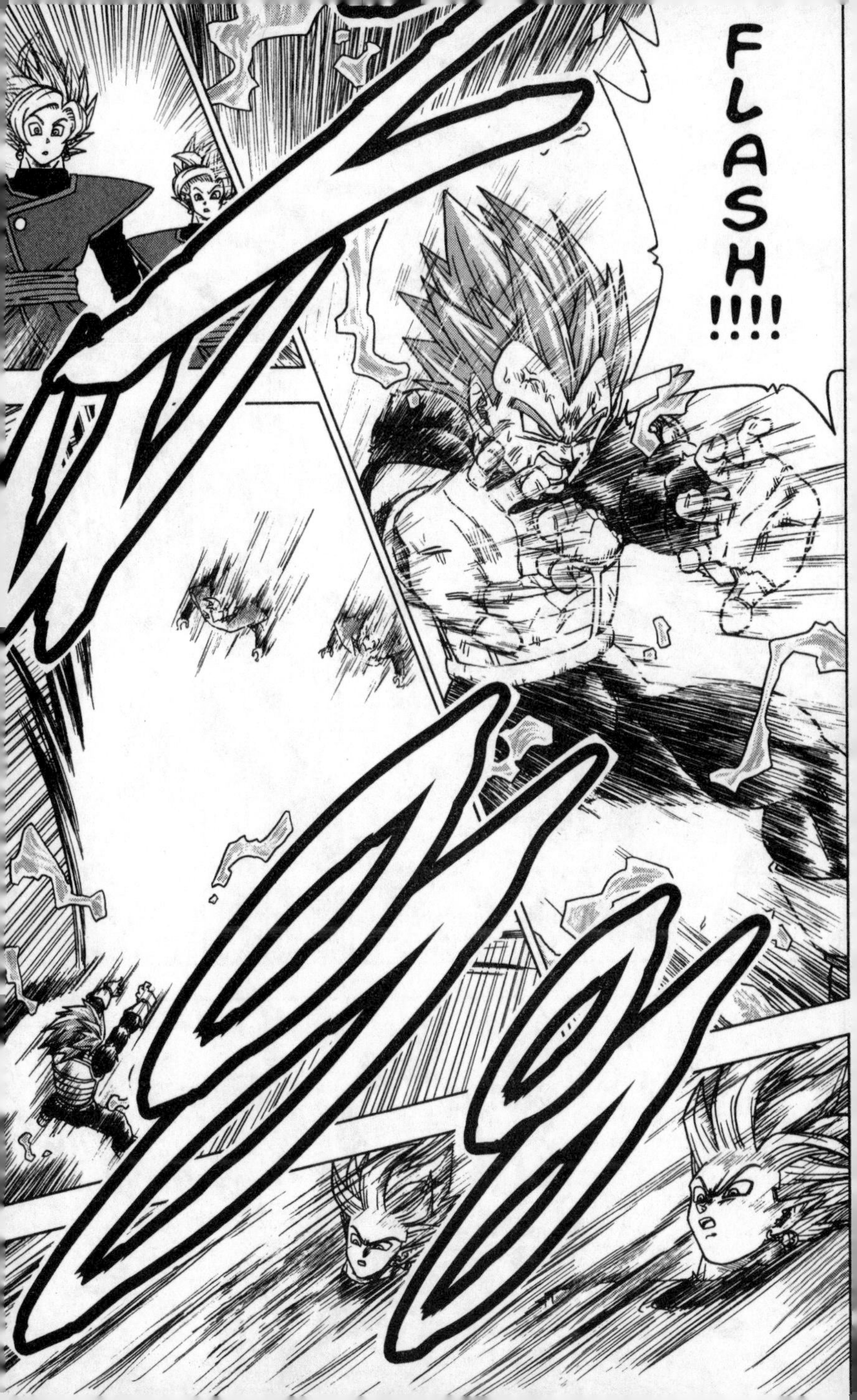
FLASH!!!!

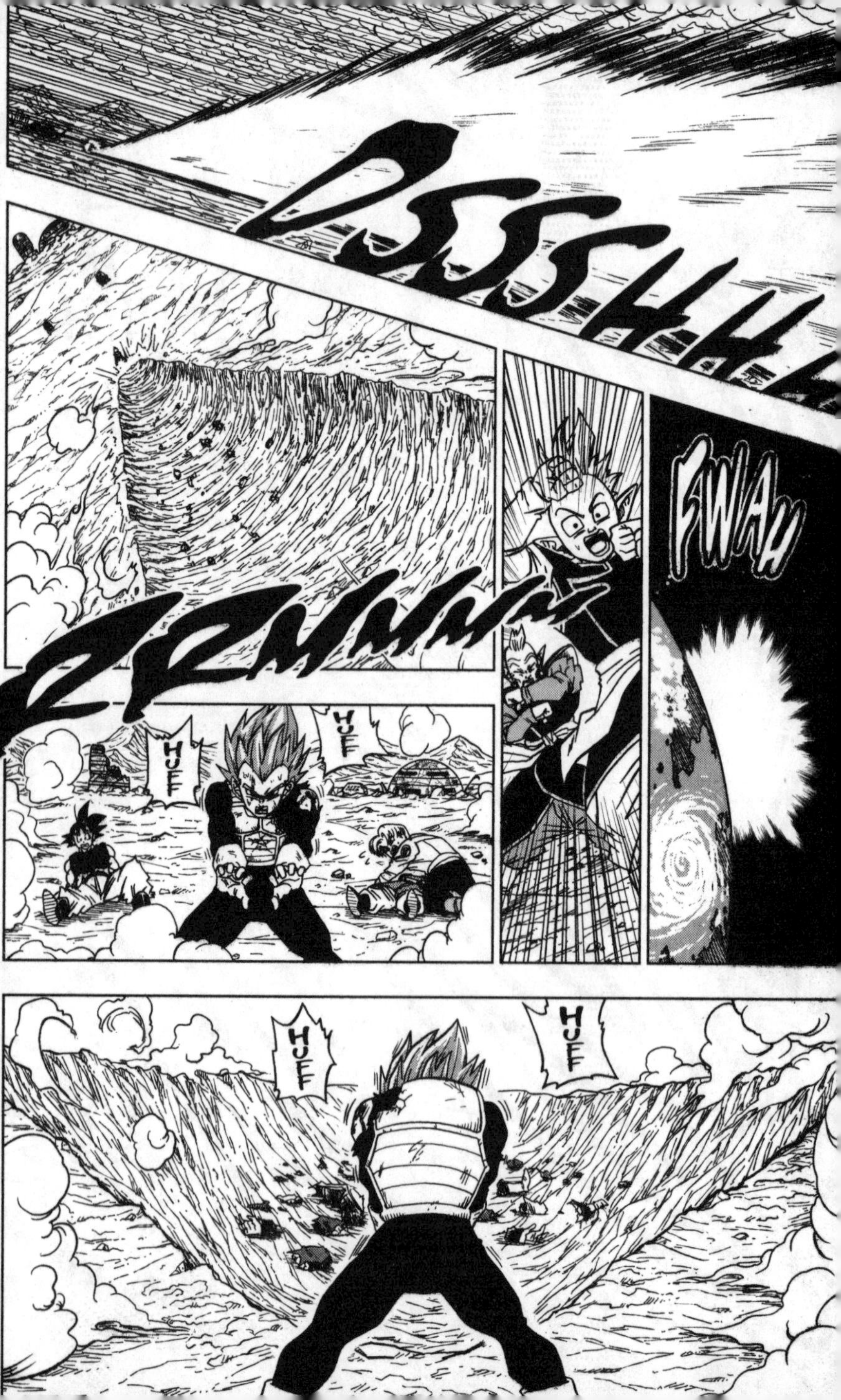
DSSHHH
FWAH
ZRMMMM
HUFF
HUFF
HUFF
HUFF

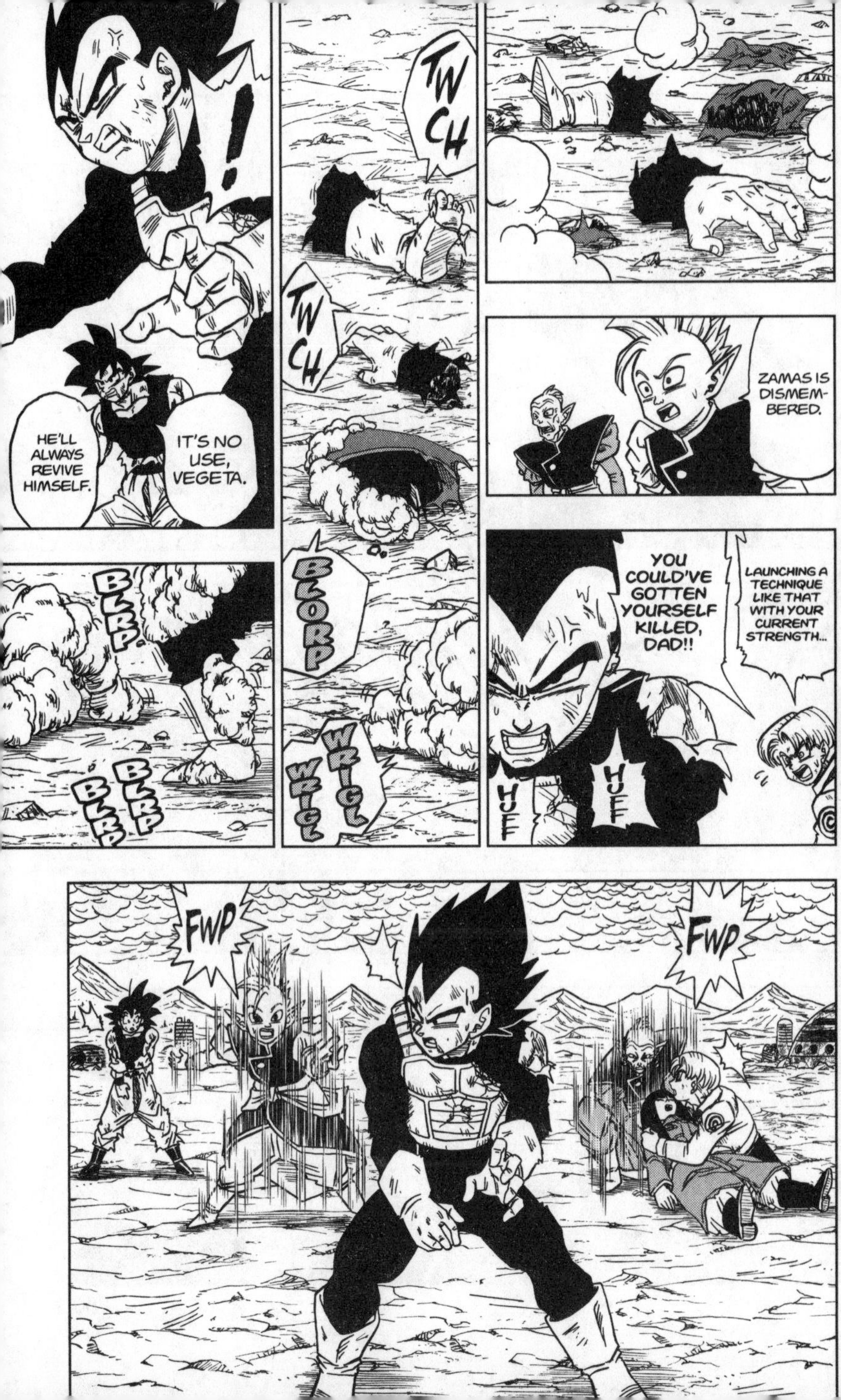
ZAMAS IS DISMEMBERED.
LAUNCHING A TECHNIQUE LIKE THAT WITH YOUR CURRENT STRENGTH...
YOU COULD'VE GOTTEN YOURSELF KILLED, DAD!!
HUF
HUF
TWCH
TWCH
BLORP
WRIGL
WRIGL
!
IT'S NO USE, VEGETA.
HE'LL ALWAYS REVIVE HIMSELF.
BLRP
BLRP
BLRP
FWP
FWP

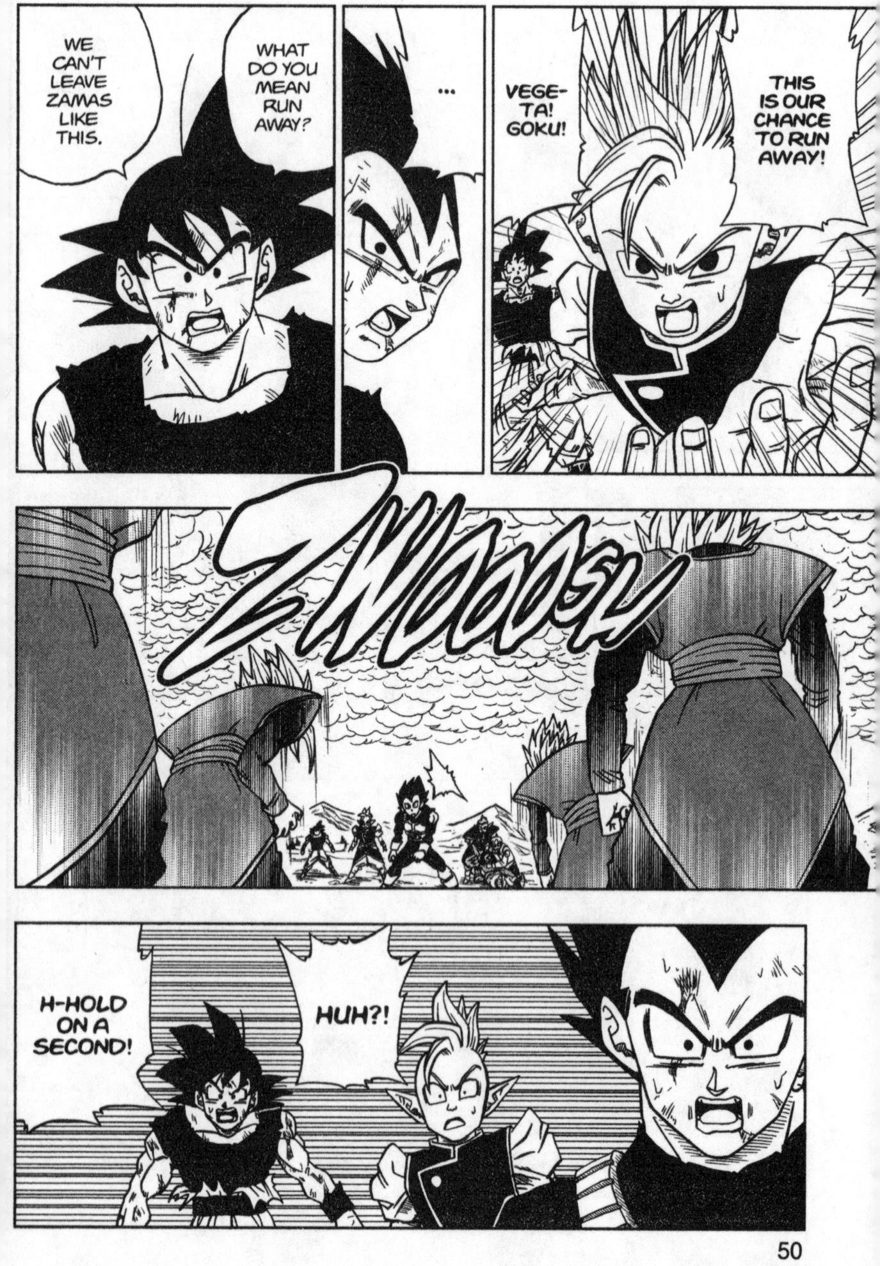
THIS IS OUR CHANCE TO RUN AWAY!
VEGE-TA! GOKU!
...
WHAT DO YOU MEAN RUN AWAY?
WE CAN'T LEAVE ZAMAS LIKE THIS.
ZWOOSH
HUH?!
H-HOLD ON A SECOND!

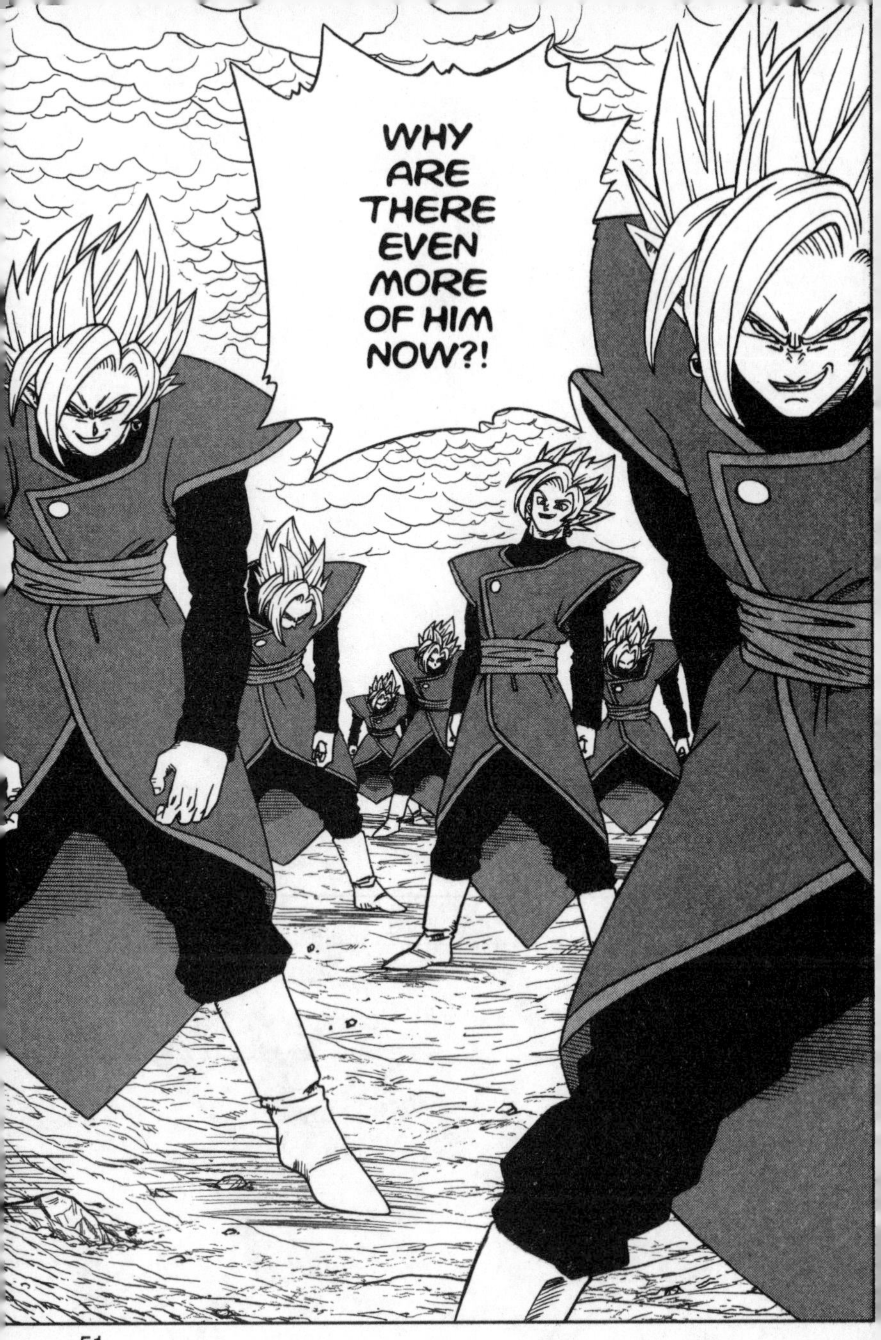
WHY ARE THERE EVEN MORE OF HIM NOW?!

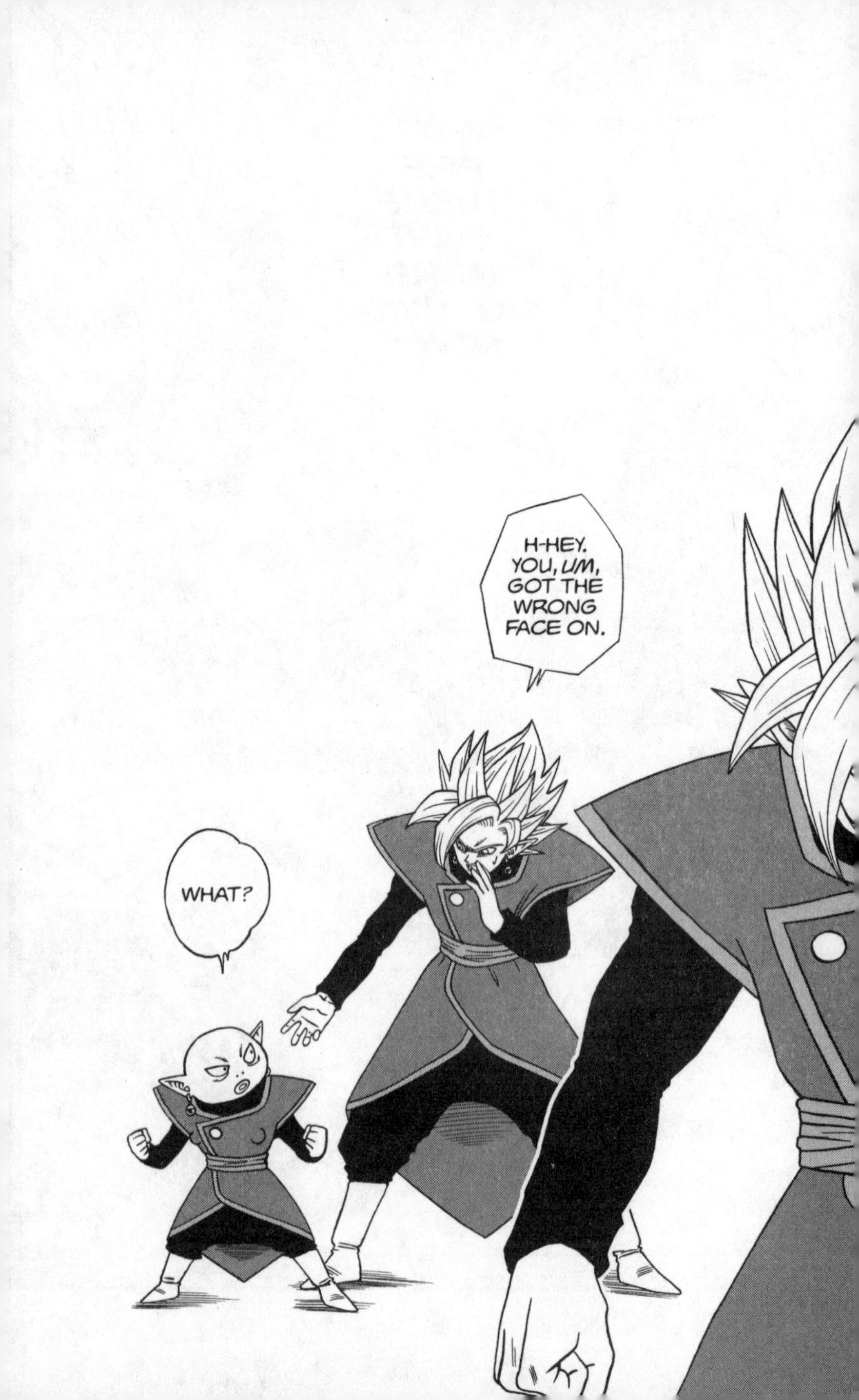
H-HEY. YOU, UM, GOT THE WRONG FACE ON.
WHAT?

DRAGON BALL SUPER

CHAPTER 26: THE DECISIVE BATTLE! FAREWELL, TRUNKS!

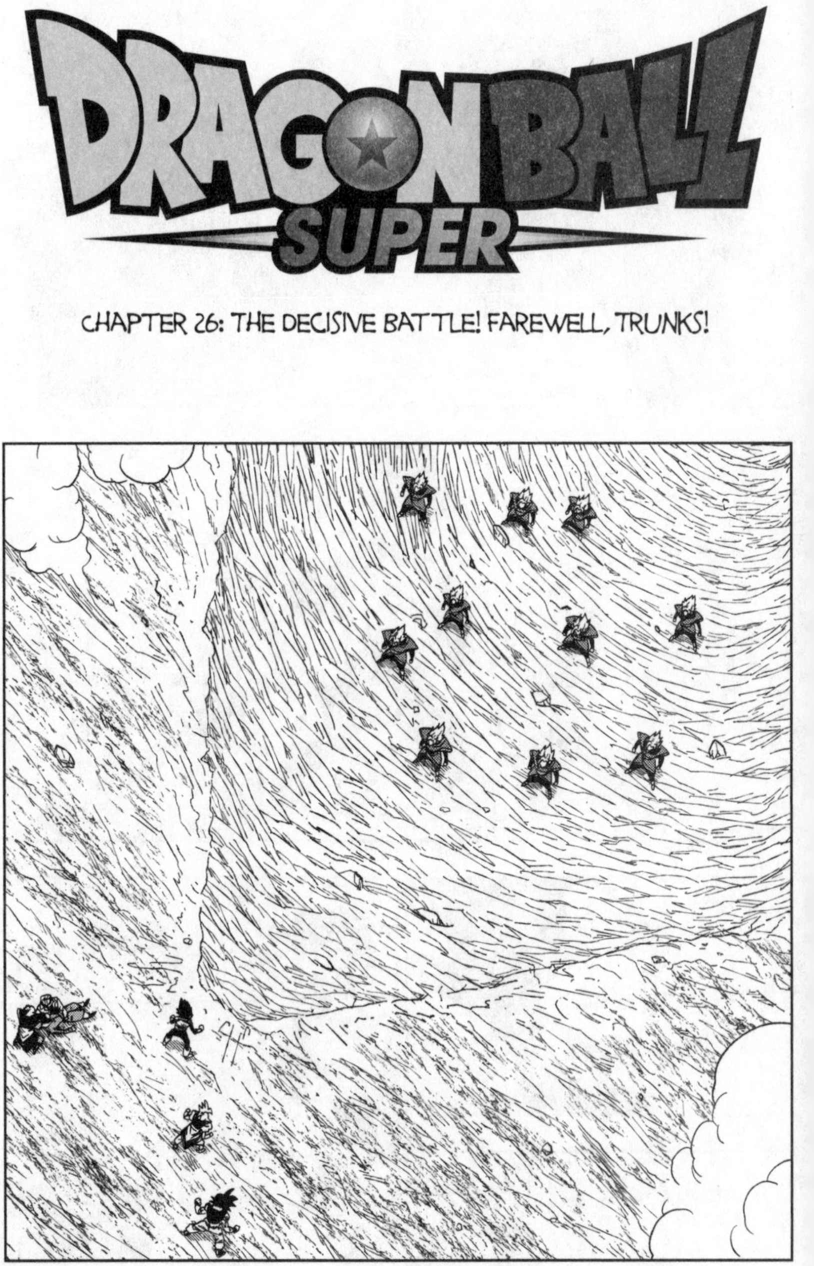

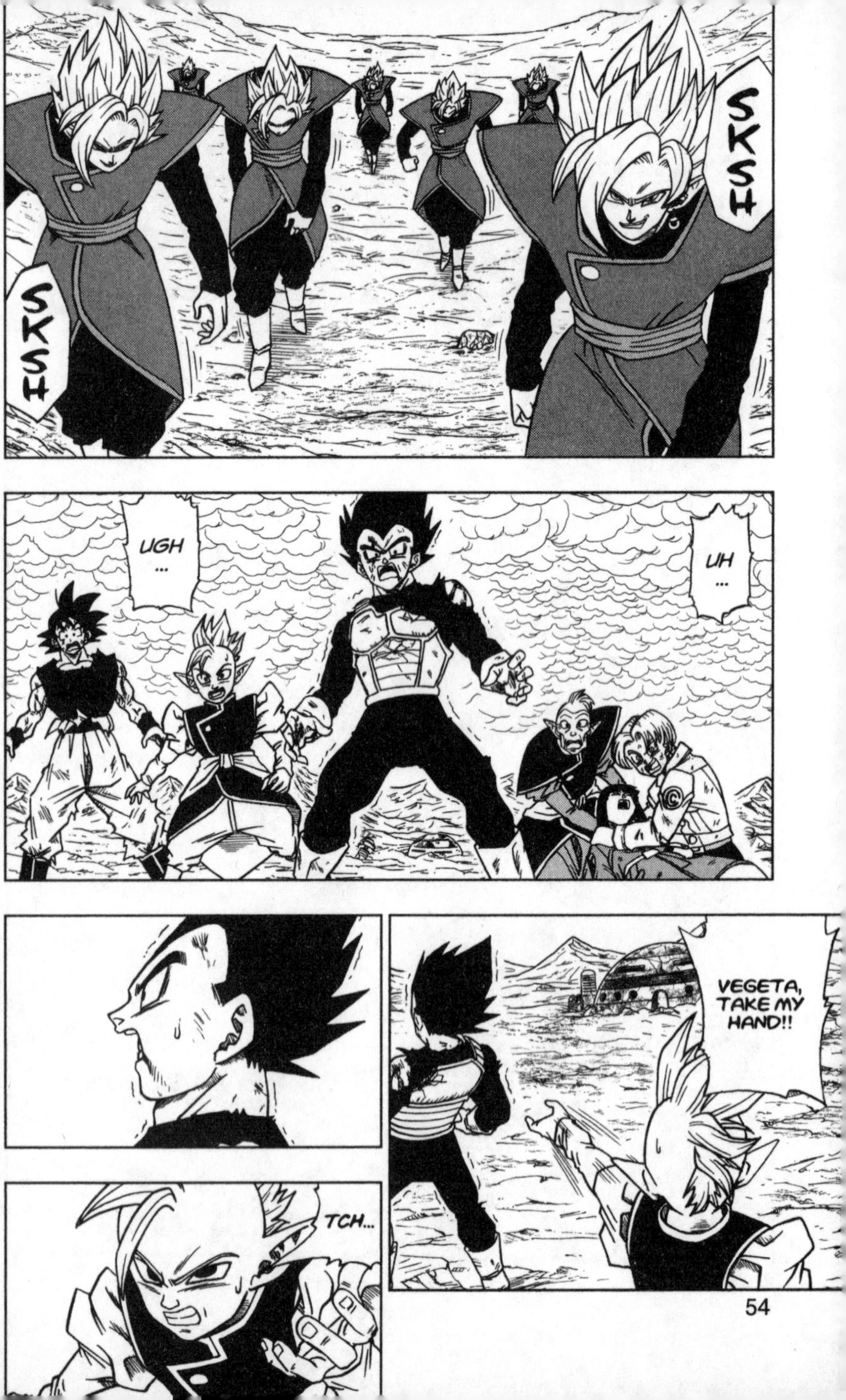
SKSH
SKSH
UH ...
UGH ...
VEGETA, TAKE MY HAND!!
TCH...

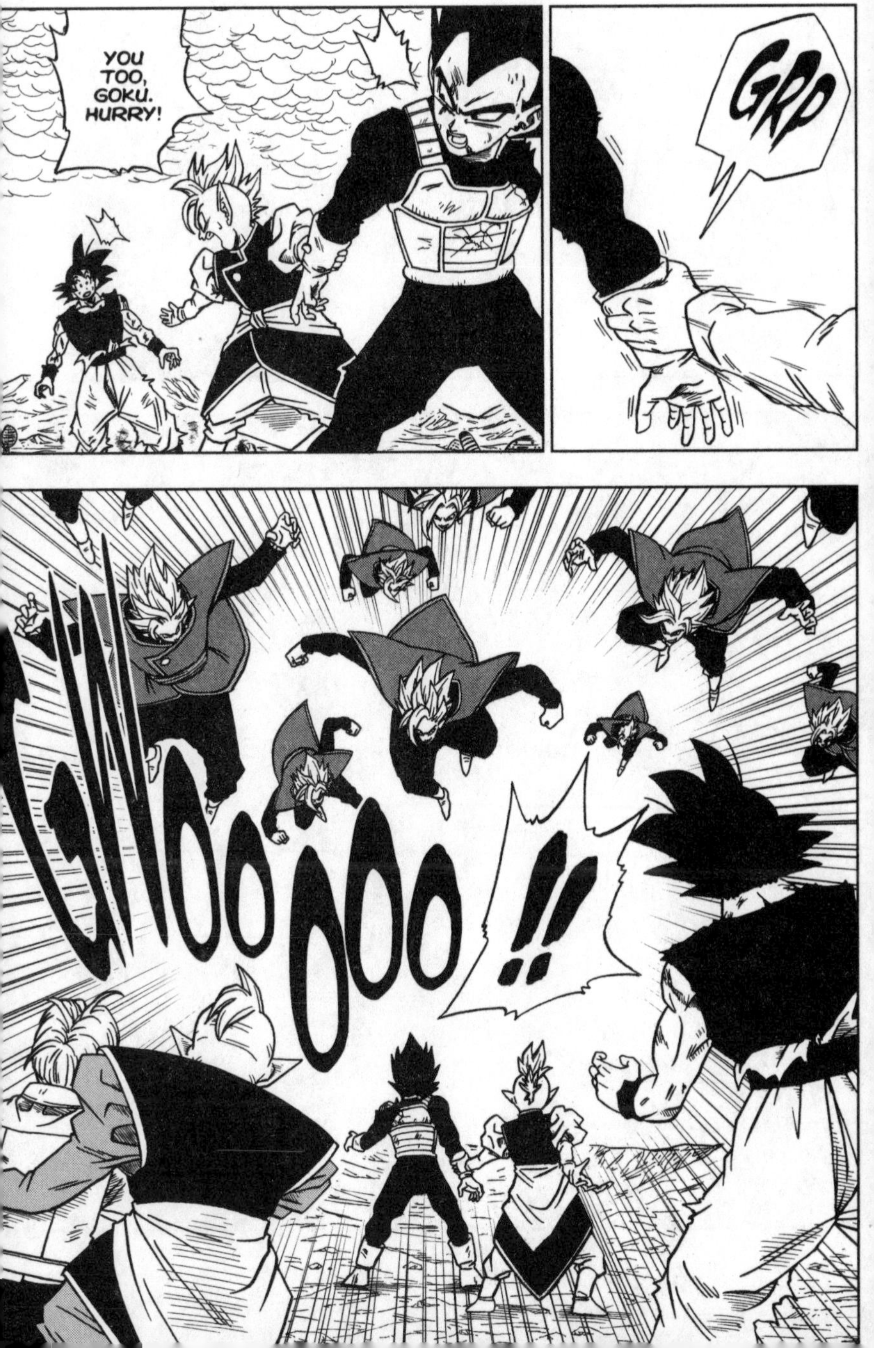
GRP
YOU TOO, GOKU. HURRY!
GWOOOOO!!

GRP

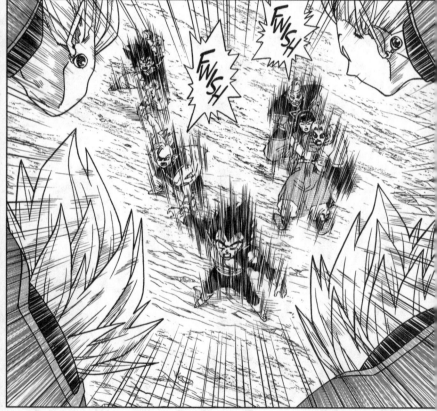

FINISH

FINISH

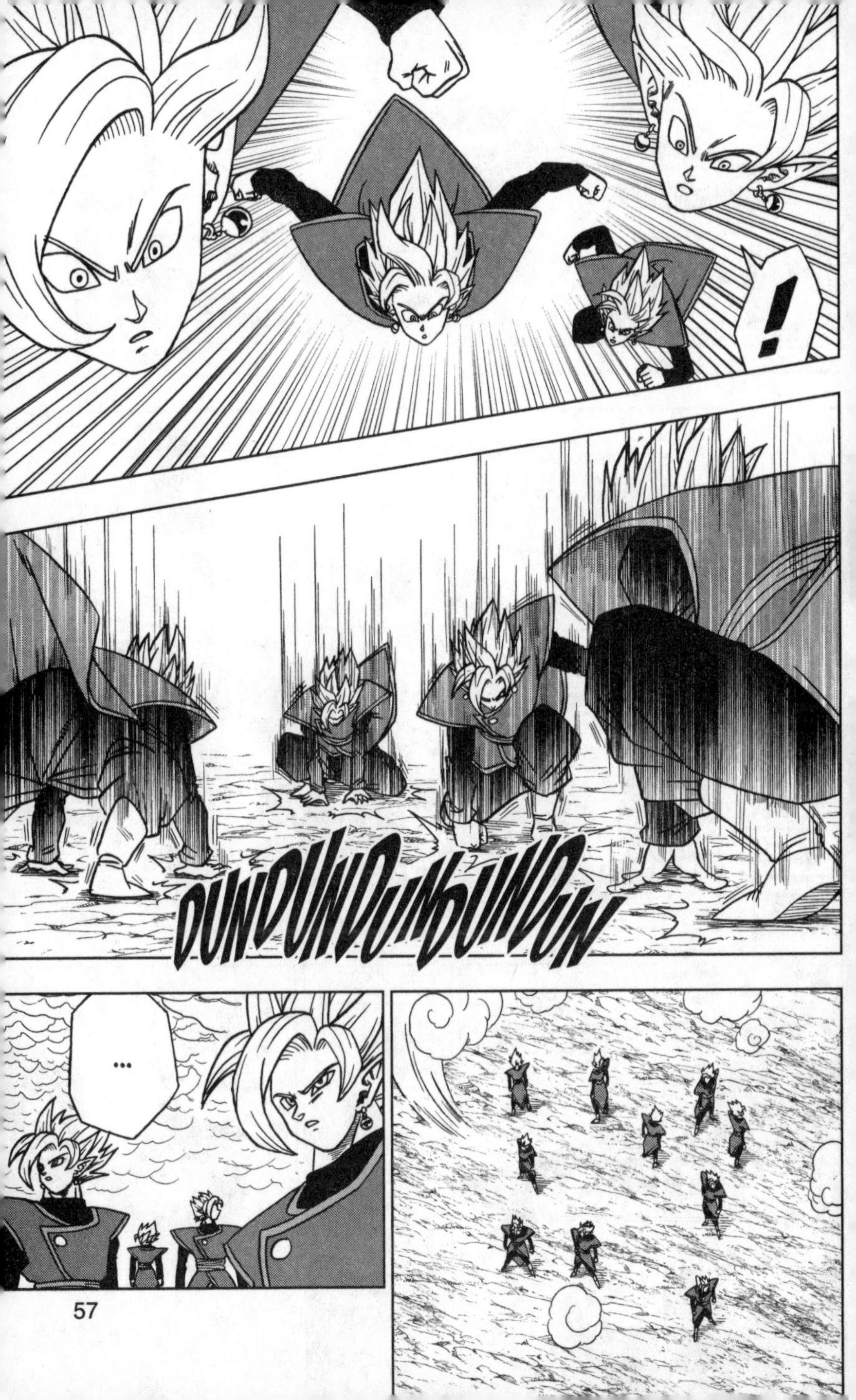
!
DUNDUNDUNDUNDUNDUN
...

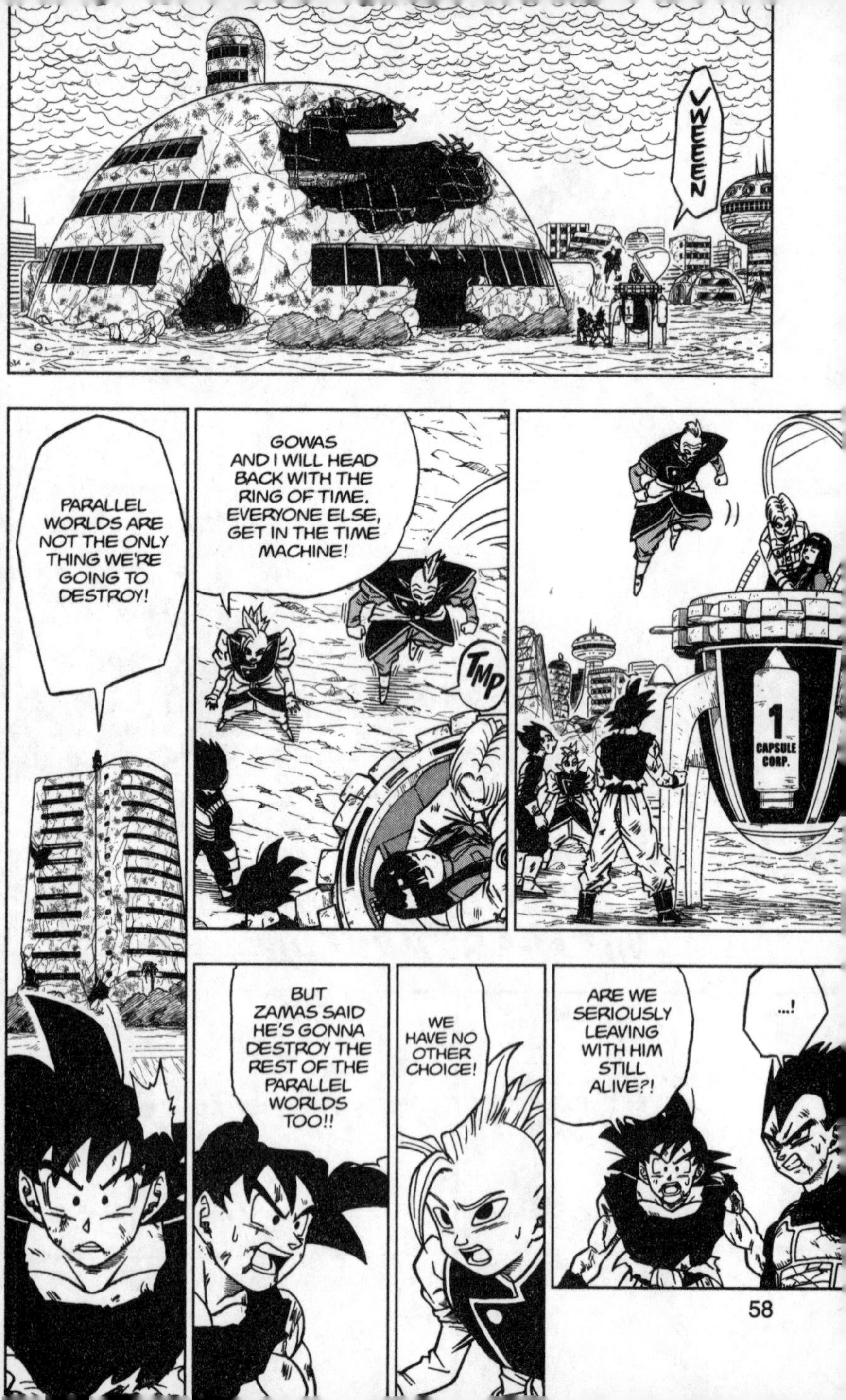
VWEEEN
GOWAS AND I WILL HEAD BACK WITH THE RING OF TIME. EVERYONE ELSE, GET IN THE TIME MACHINE!
TMP
1 CAPSULE CORP.
...!
ARE WE SERIOUSLY LEAVING WITH HIM STILL ALIVE?!
WE HAVE NO OTHER CHOICE!
BUT ZAMAS SAID HE'S GONNA DESTROY THE REST OF THE PARALLEL WORLDS TOO!!
PARALLEL WORLDS ARE NOT THE ONLY THING WE'RE GOING TO DESTROY!

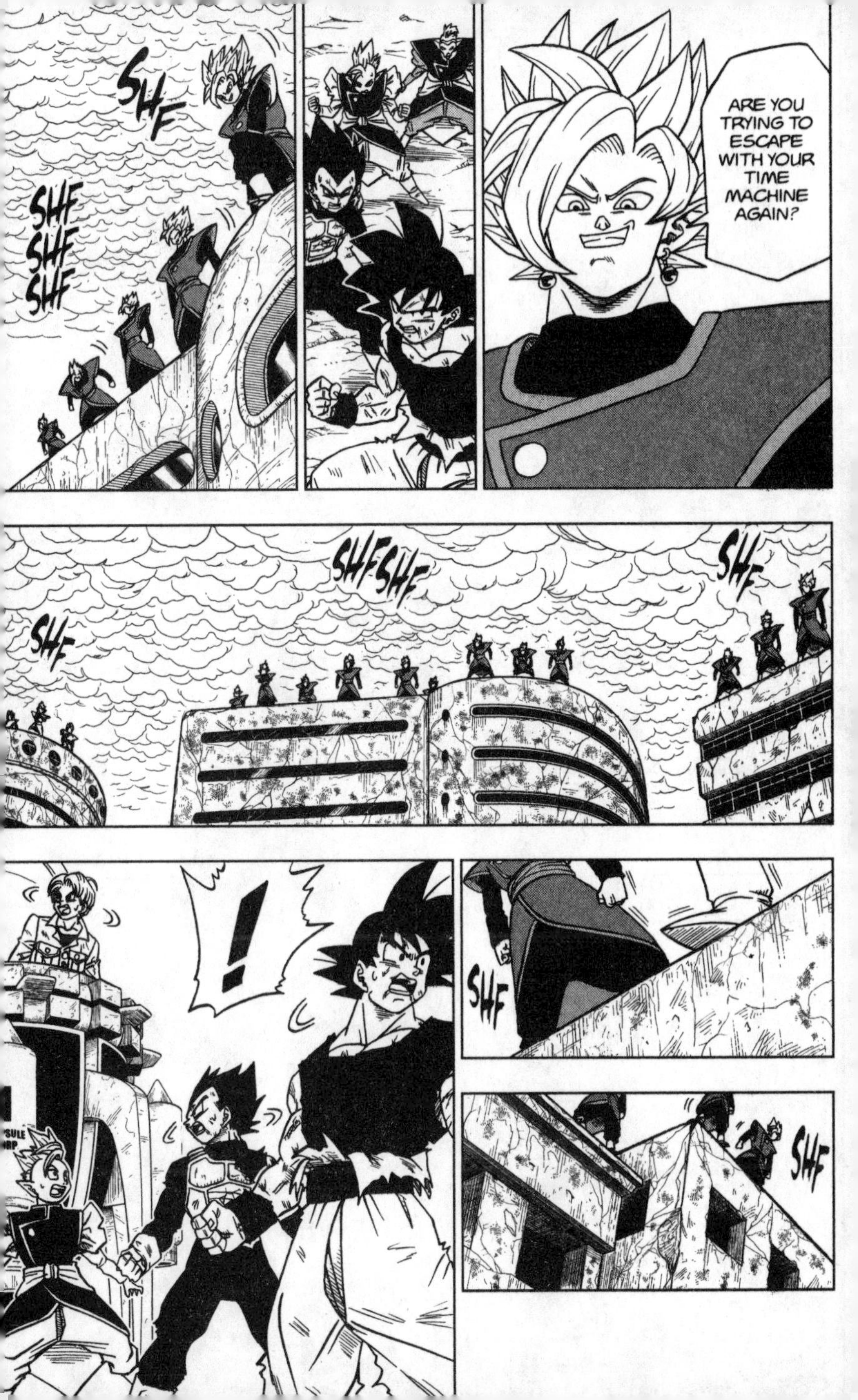
ARE YOU TRYING TO ESCAPE WITH YOUR TIME MACHINE AGAIN?
SHF
SHF SHF SHF
SHF
SHFSHF
SHF
SHF
SHF
!

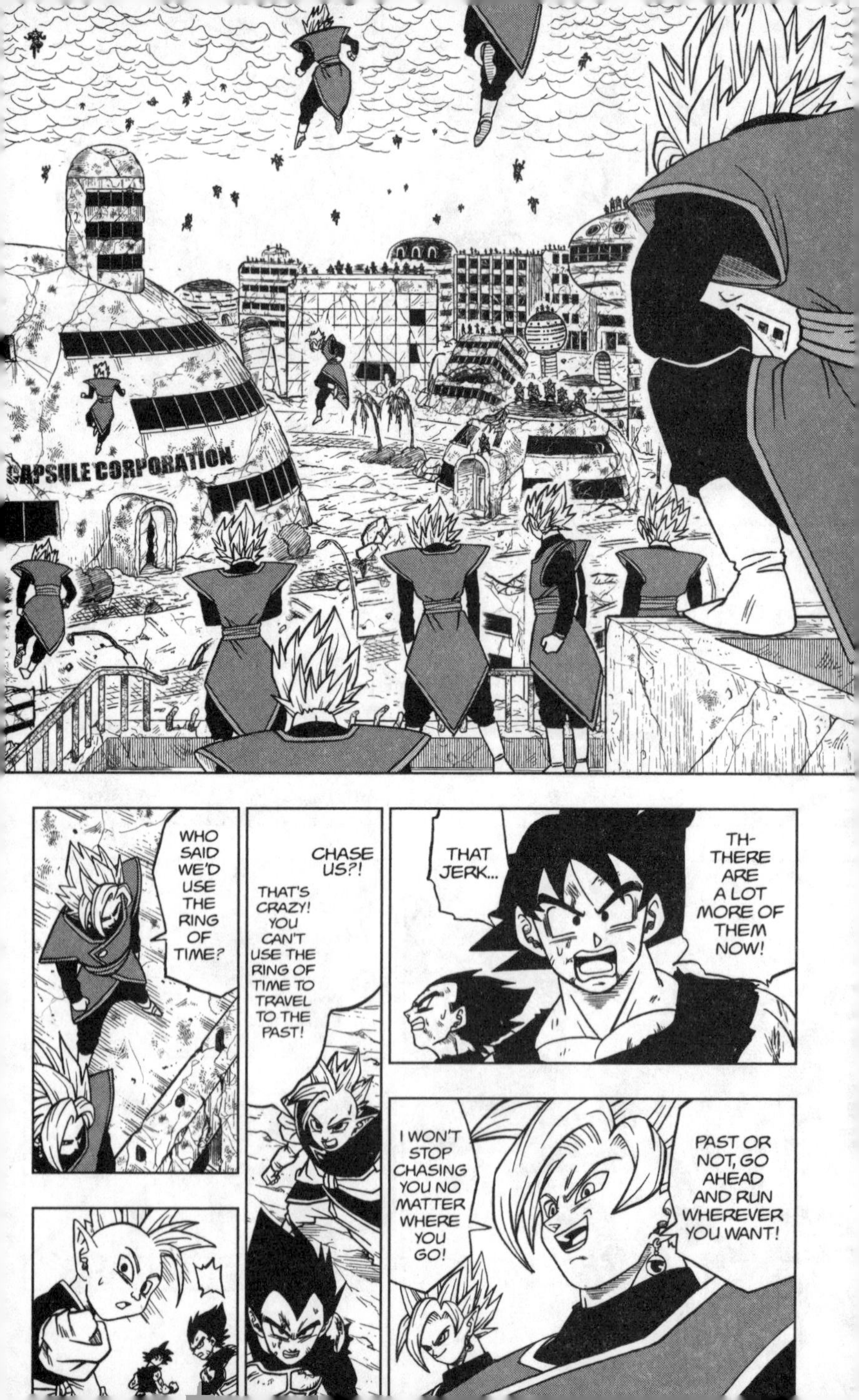
CAPSULE CORPORATION
TH- THERE ARE A LOT MORE OF THEM NOW!
THAT JERK...
PAST OR NOT, GO AHEAD AND RUN WHEREVER YOU WANT!
I WON'T STOP CHASING YOU NO MATTER WHERE YOU GO!
CHASE US?!
THAT'S CRAZY! YOU CAN'T USE THE RING OF TIME TO TRAVEL TO THE PAST!
WHO SAID WE'D USE THE RING OF TIME?

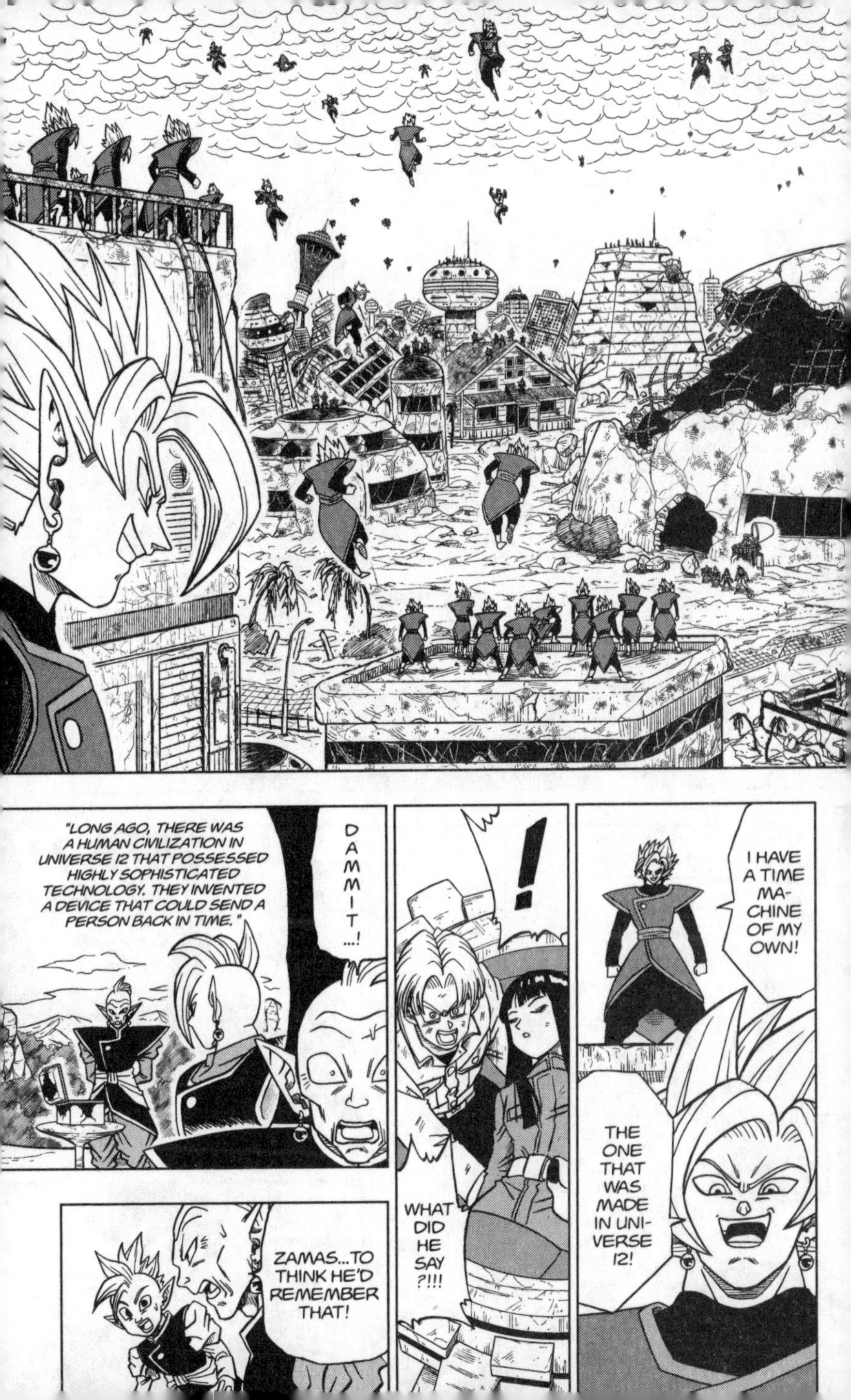
I HAVE A TIME MACHINE OF MY OWN!
THE ONE THAT WAS MADE IN UNIVERSE 12!
!
WHAT DID HE SAY?!!!
DAMMIT...!
"LONG AGO, THERE WAS A HUMAN CIVILIZATION IN UNIVERSE 12 THAT POSSESSED HIGHLY SOPHISTICATED TECHNOLOGY. THEY INVENTED A DEVICE THAT COULD SEND A PERSON BACK IN TIME."
ZAMAS...TO THINK HE'D REMEMBER THAT!

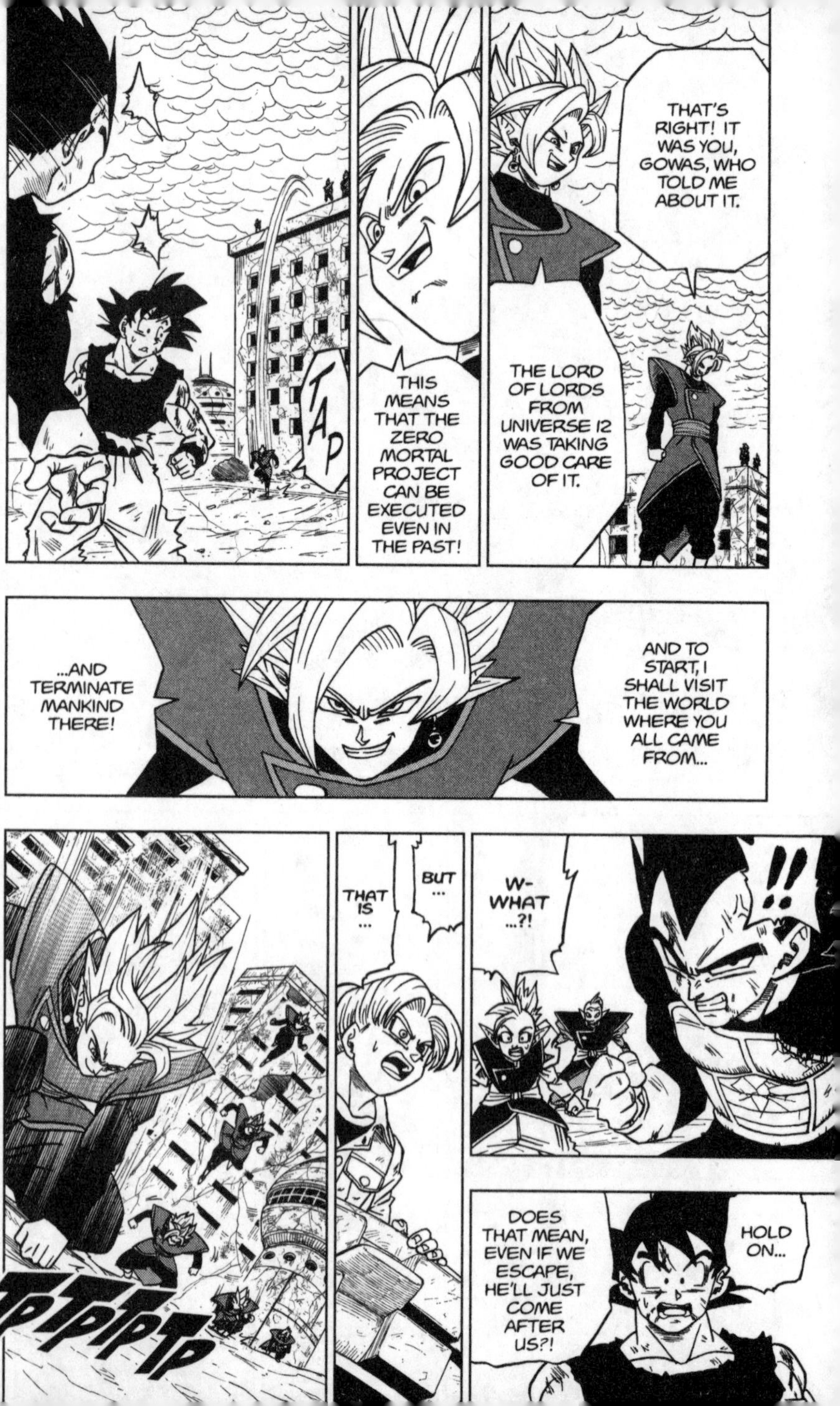
THAT'S RIGHT! IT WAS YOU, GOWAS, WHO TOLD ME ABOUT IT.
THE LORD OF LORDS FROM UNIVERSE 12 WAS TAKING GOOD CARE OF IT.
THIS MEANS THAT THE ZERO MORTAL PROJECT CAN BE EXECUTED EVEN IN THE PAST!
TAP
AND TO START, I SHALL VISIT THE WORLD WHERE YOU ALL CAME FROM...
...AND TERMINATE MANKIND THERE!
!!
W-WHAT...?!
HOLD ON...
DOES THAT MEAN, EVEN IF WE ESCAPE, HE'LL JUST COME AFTER US?!
BUT...
THAT IS...
TPTPTPTP

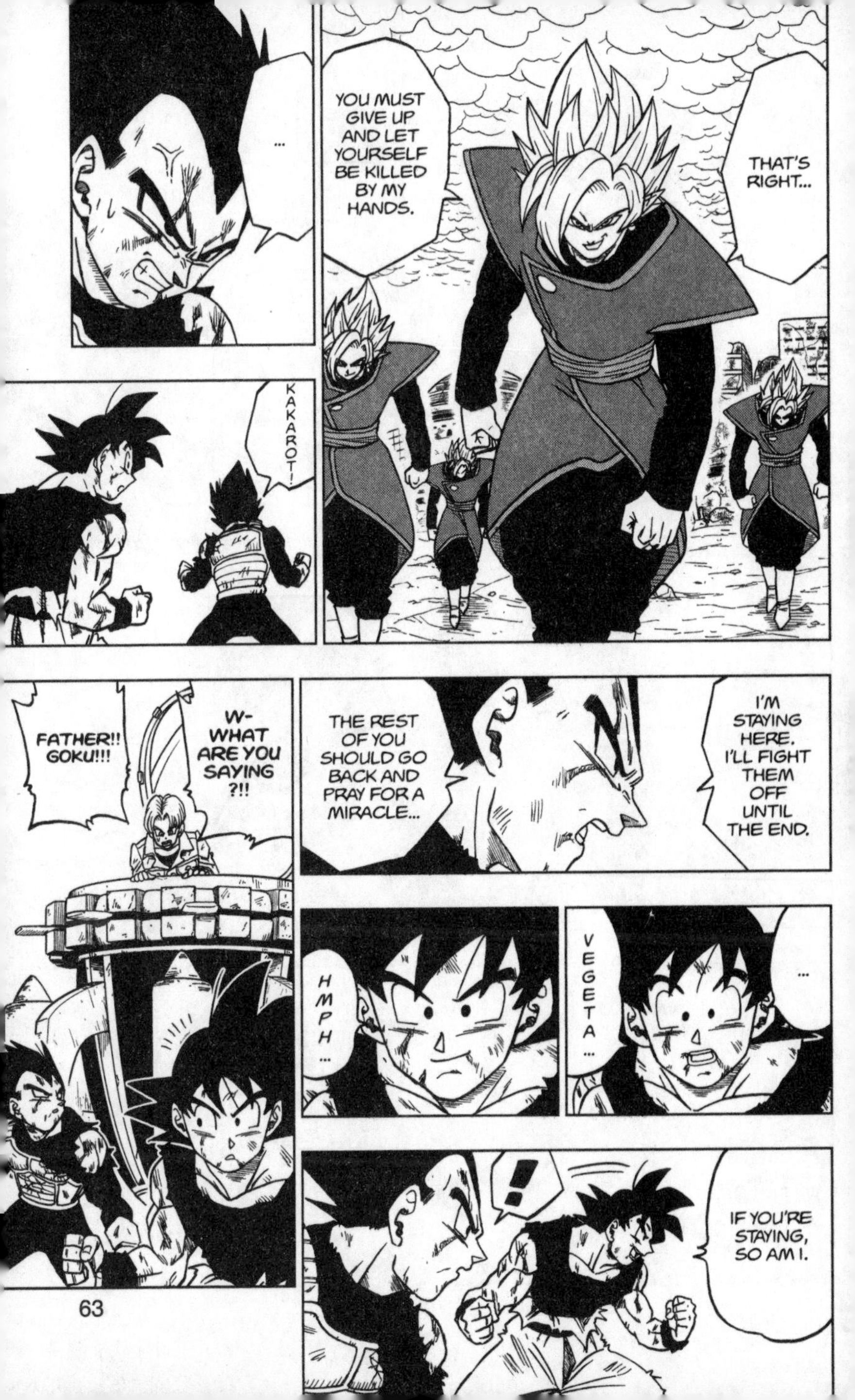
THAT'S RIGHT...
YOU MUST GIVE UP AND LET YOURSELF BE KILLED BY MY HANDS.
...
KAKAROT!
I'M STAYING HERE. I'LL FIGHT THEM OFF UNTIL THE END.
THE REST OF YOU SHOULD GO BACK AND PRAY FOR A MIRACLE...
...
VEGETA...
HMPH...
IF YOU'RE STAYING, SO AM I.
!
W-WHAT ARE YOU SAYING?!!
FATHER!! GOKU!!!

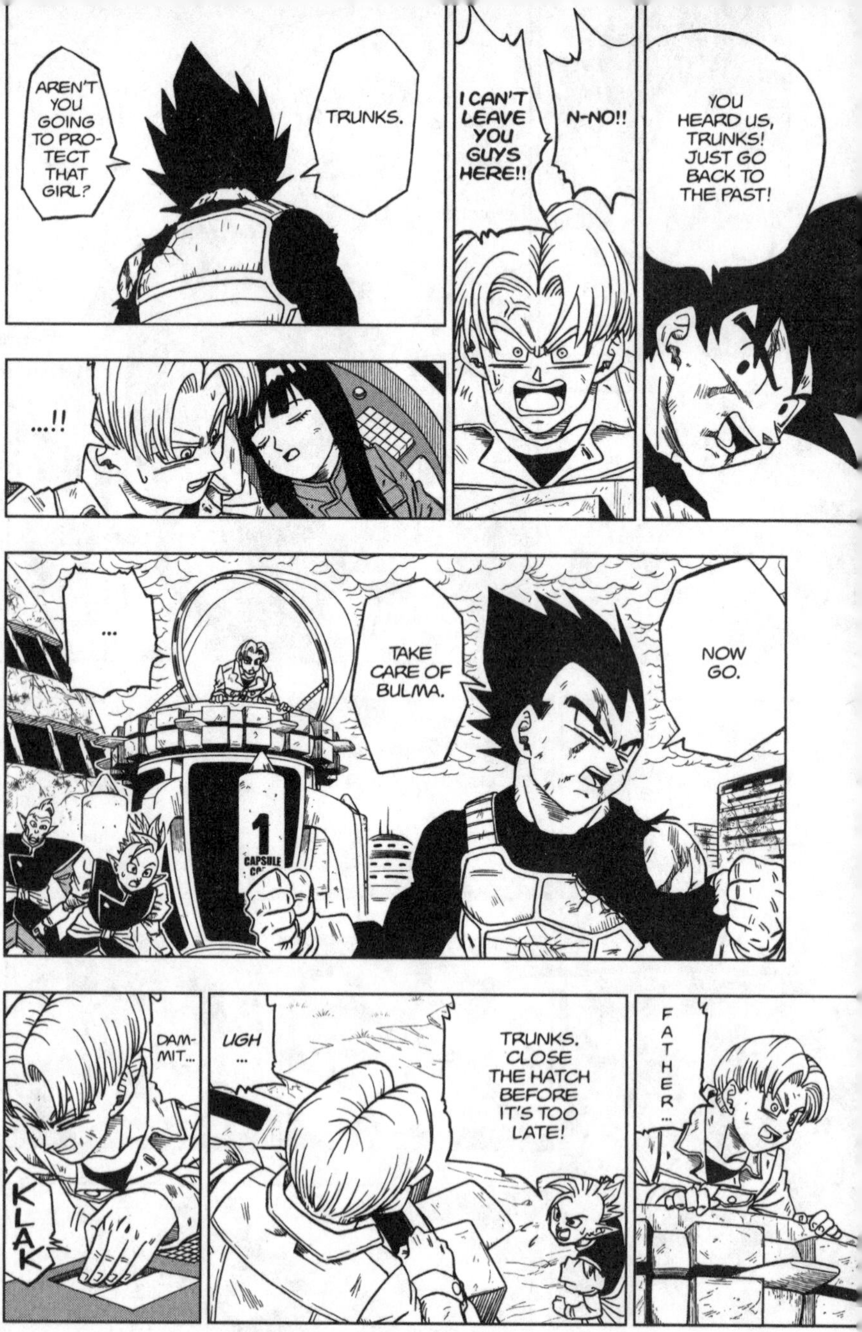
YOU HEARD US, TRUNKS! JUST GO BACK TO THE PAST!
N-NO!!
I CAN'T LEAVE YOU GUYS HERE!!
TRUNKS.
AREN'T YOU GOING TO PROTECT THAT GIRL?
...!!
NOW GO.
TAKE CARE OF BULMA.
1
CAPSULE
...
FATHER...
TRUNKS. CLOSE THE HATCH BEFORE IT'S TOO LATE!
UGH ...
DAM-MIT...
KLAK

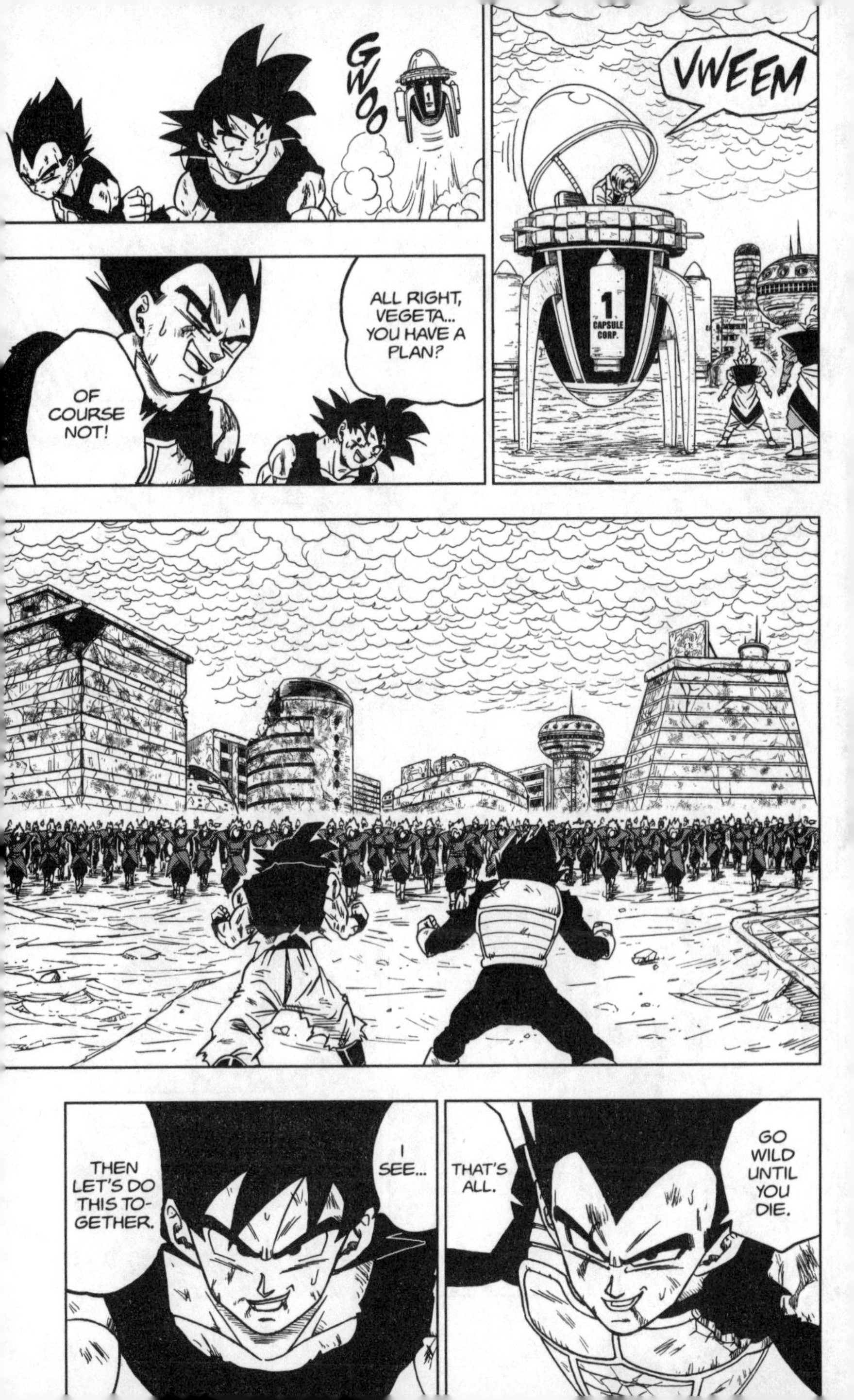
VWEEM
1
CAPSULE CORP.
GWOO
ALL RIGHT, VEGETA... YOU HAVE A PLAN?
OF COURSE NOT!
GO WILD UNTIL YOU DIE.
THAT'S ALL.
I SEE...
THEN LET'S DO THIS TOGETHER.

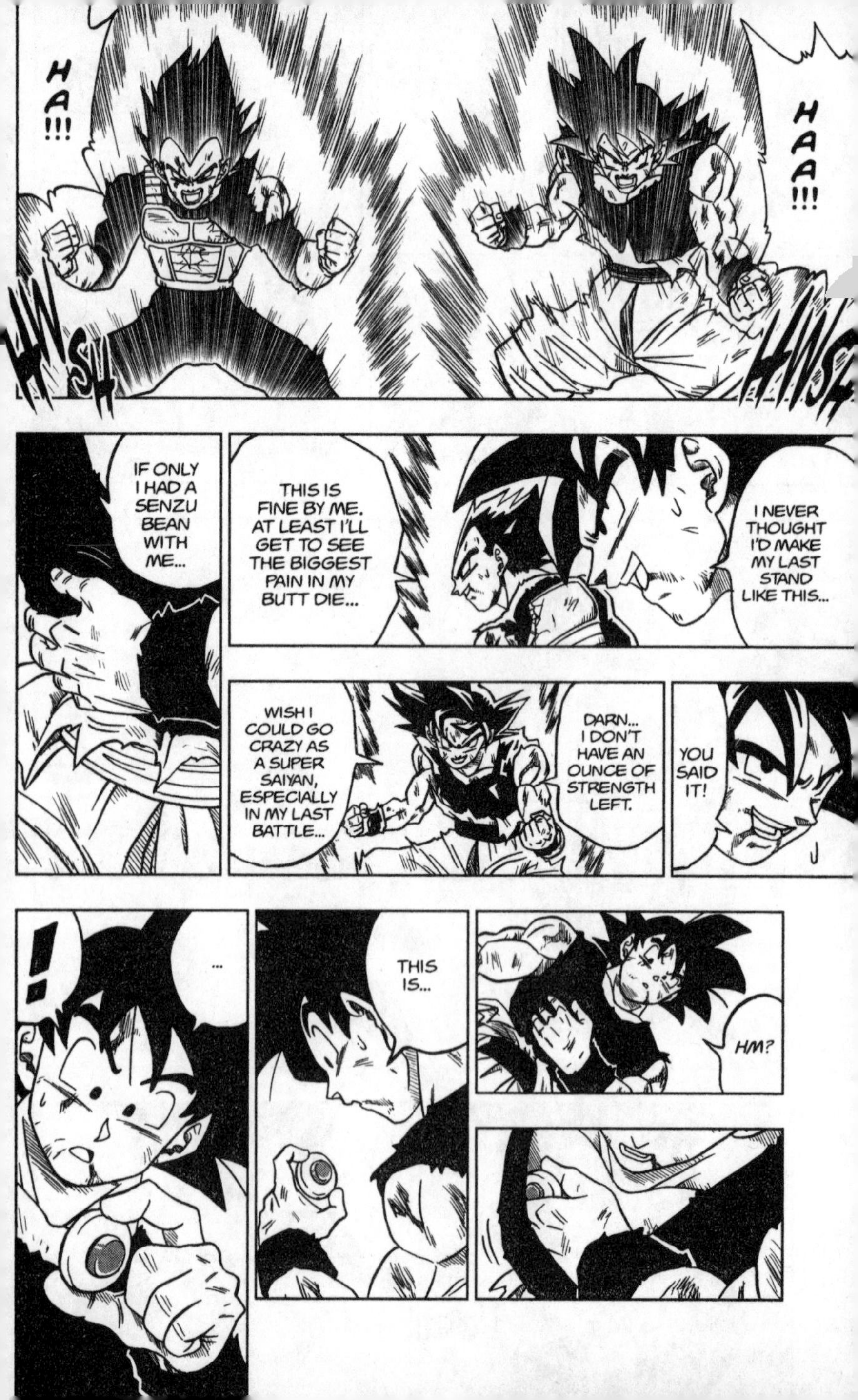
HAA!!!
HWSH
HA!!!
HWSH
I NEVER THOUGHT I'D MAKE MY LAST STAND LIKE THIS...
THIS IS FINE BY ME. AT LEAST I'LL GET TO SEE THE BIGGEST PAIN IN MY BUTT DIE...
YOU SAID IT!
DARN... I DON'T HAVE AN OUNCE OF STRENGTH LEFT.
WISH I COULD GO CRAZY AS A SUPER SAIYAN, ESPECIALLY IN MY LAST BATTLE...
IF ONLY I HAD A SENZU BEAN WITH ME...
HM?
THIS IS...
...
!

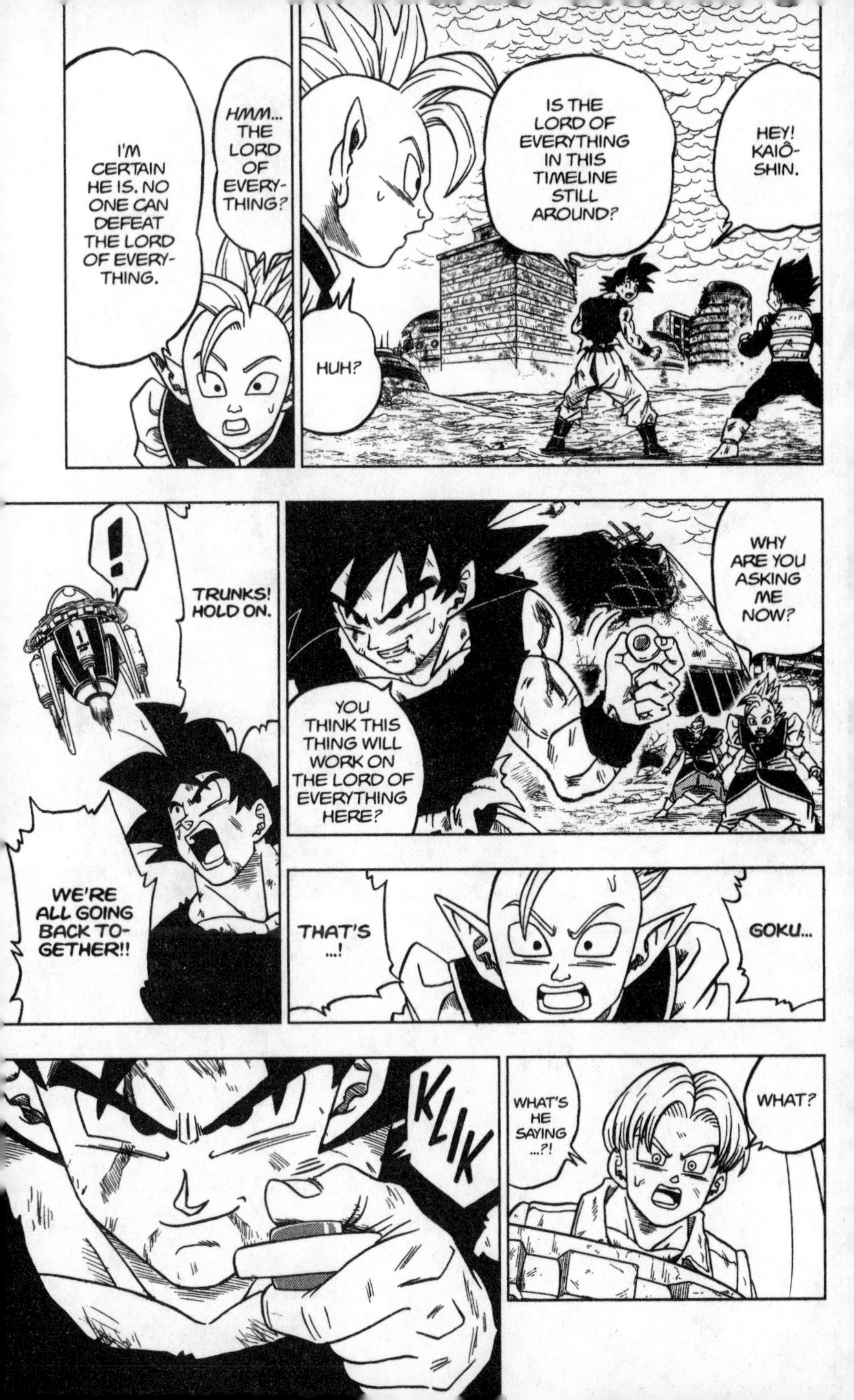
HEY! KAIÔ-SHIN.
IS THE LORD OF EVERYTHING IN THIS TIMELINE STILL AROUND?
HUH?
HMM... THE LORD OF EVERY-THING?
I'M CERTAIN HE IS. NO ONE CAN DEFEAT THE LORD OF EVERY-THING.
WHY ARE YOU ASKING ME NOW?
YOU THINK THIS THING WILL WORK ON THE LORD OF EVERYTHING HERE?
GOKU...
THAT'S ...!
!
TRUNKS! HOLD ON.
WE'RE ALL GOING BACK TO-GETHER!!
WHAT?
WHAT'S HE SAYING ...?!
KLIK

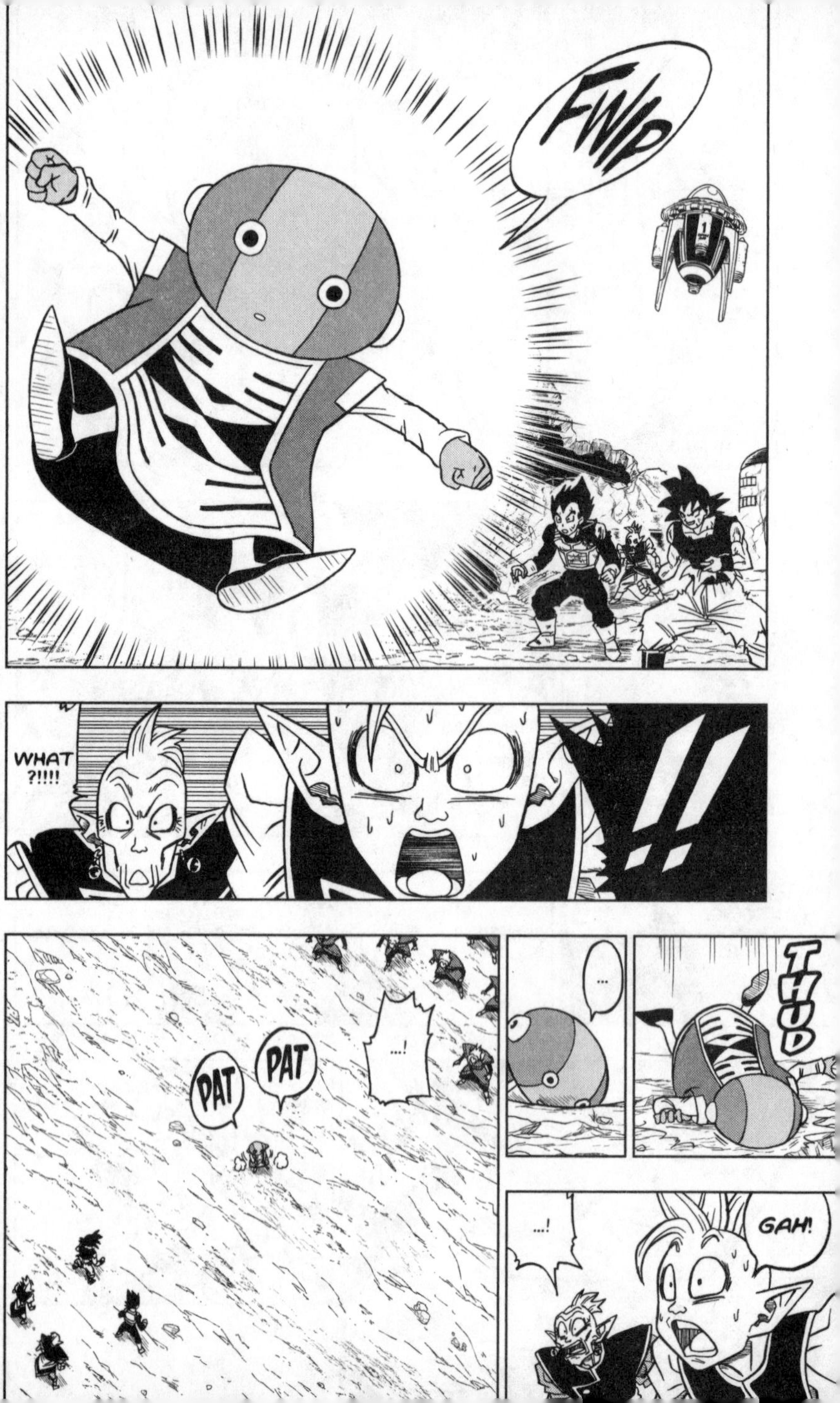
FWIP
!!
WHAT ?!!!!
THUD
...
GAH!
...!
...!
PAT
PAT

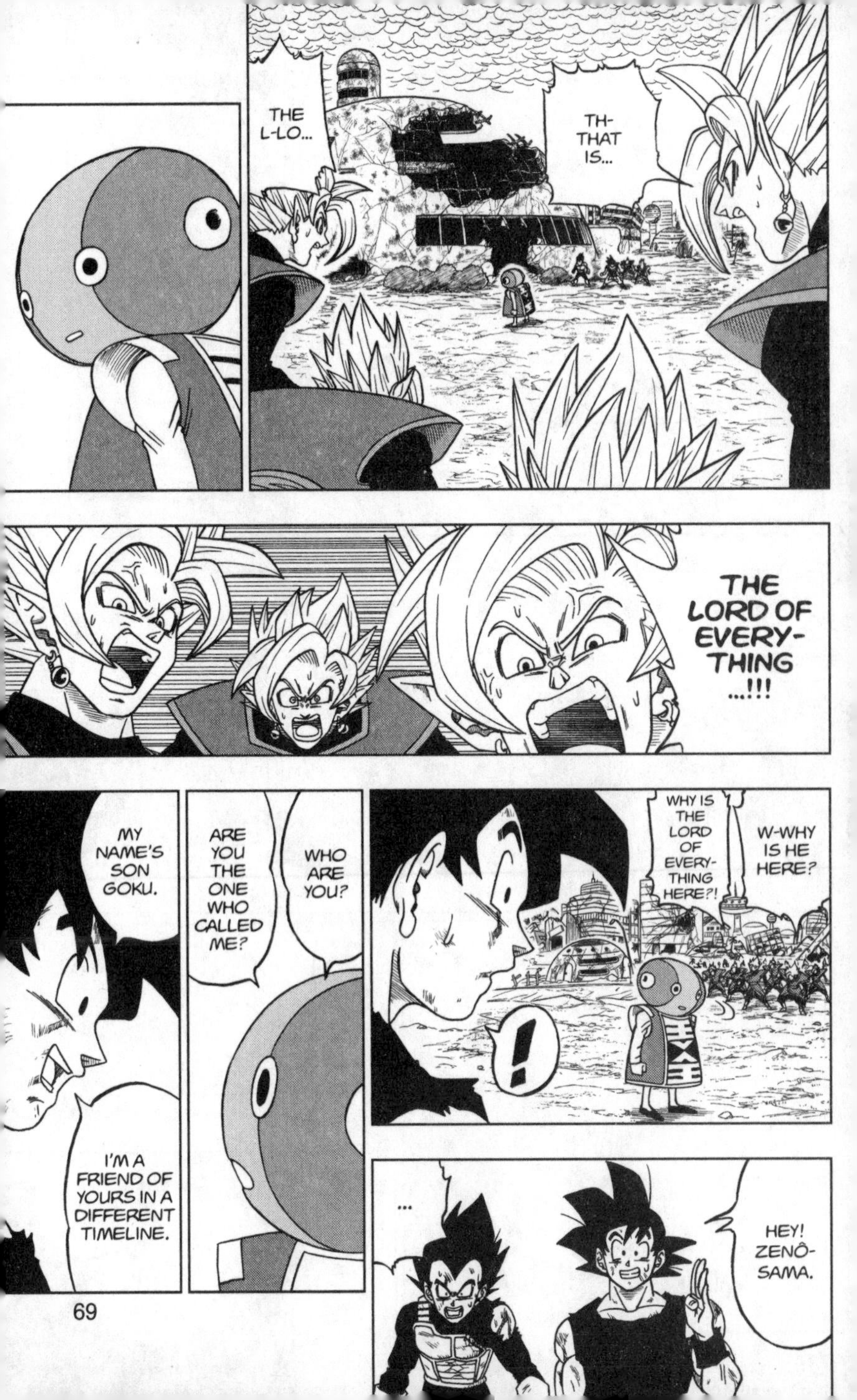
TH- THAT IS...
THE L-LO...
THE LORD OF EVERY-THING ...!!!
W-WHY IS HE HERE?
WHY IS THE LORD OF EVERY-THING HERE?!
!
HEY! ZENÔ-SAMA.
...
WHO ARE YOU?
ARE YOU THE ONE WHO CALLED ME?
MY NAME'S SON GOKU.
I'M A FRIEND OF YOURS IN A DIFFERENT TIMELINE.

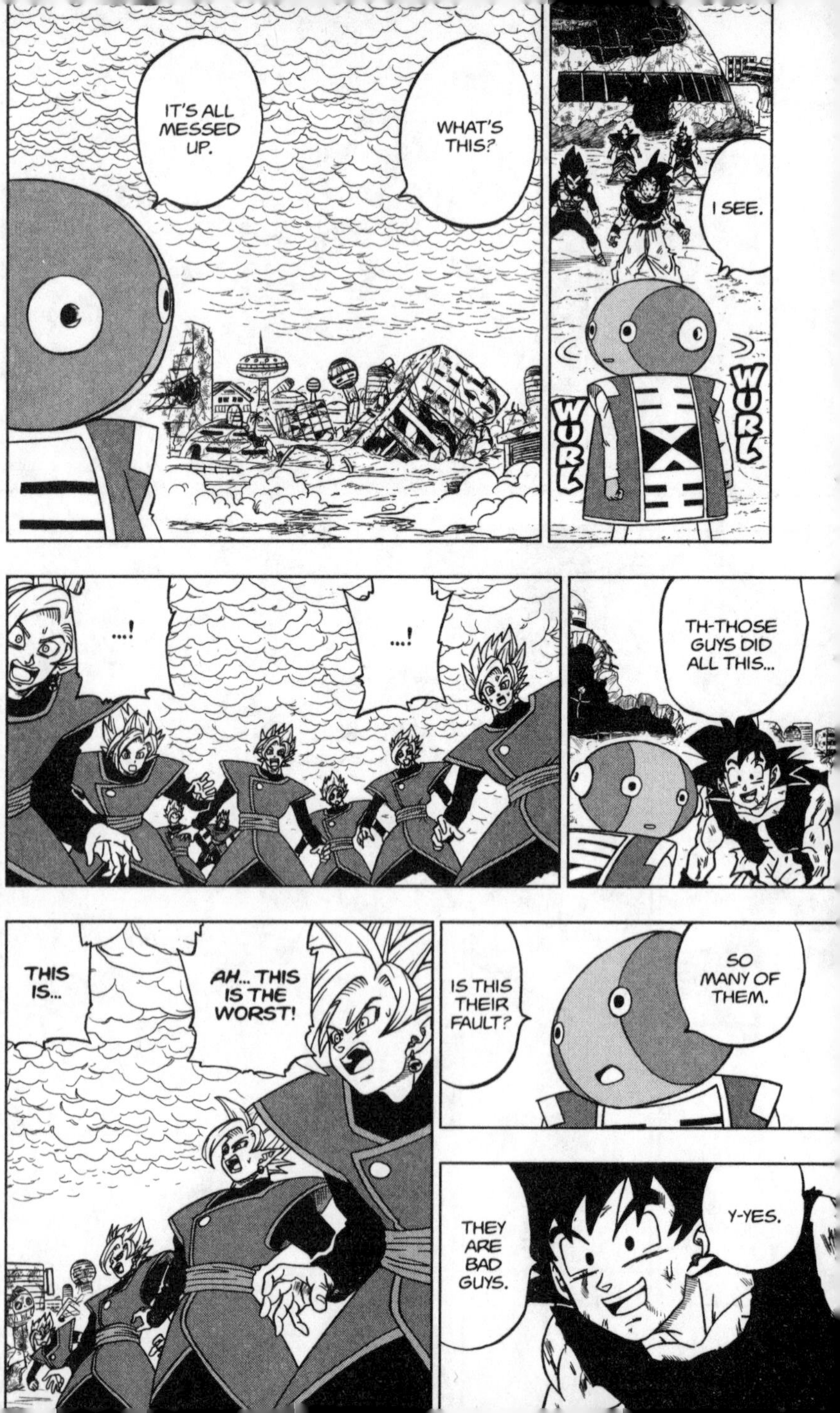
I SEE.
WURL
WURL
WHAT'S THIS?
IT'S ALL MESSED UP.
TH-THOSE GUYS DID ALL THIS...
...!
...!
SO MANY OF THEM.
IS THIS THEIR FAULT?
Y-YES.
THEY ARE BAD GUYS.
AH... THIS IS THE WORST!
THIS IS...

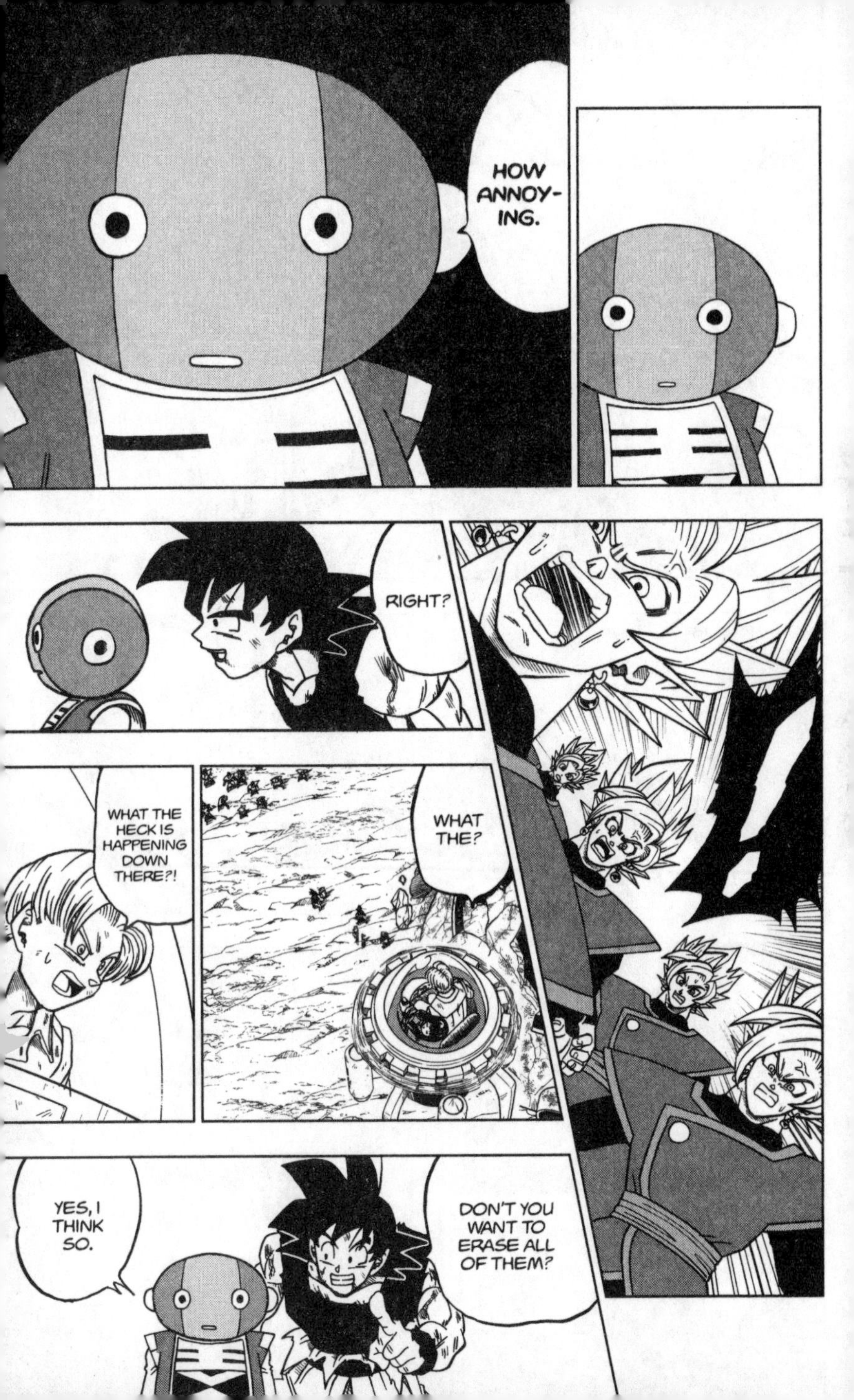
HOW ANNOY-ING.
RIGHT?
WHAT THE?
WHAT THE HECK IS HAPPENING DOWN THERE?!
DON'T YOU WANT TO ERASE ALL OF THEM?
YES, I THINK SO.

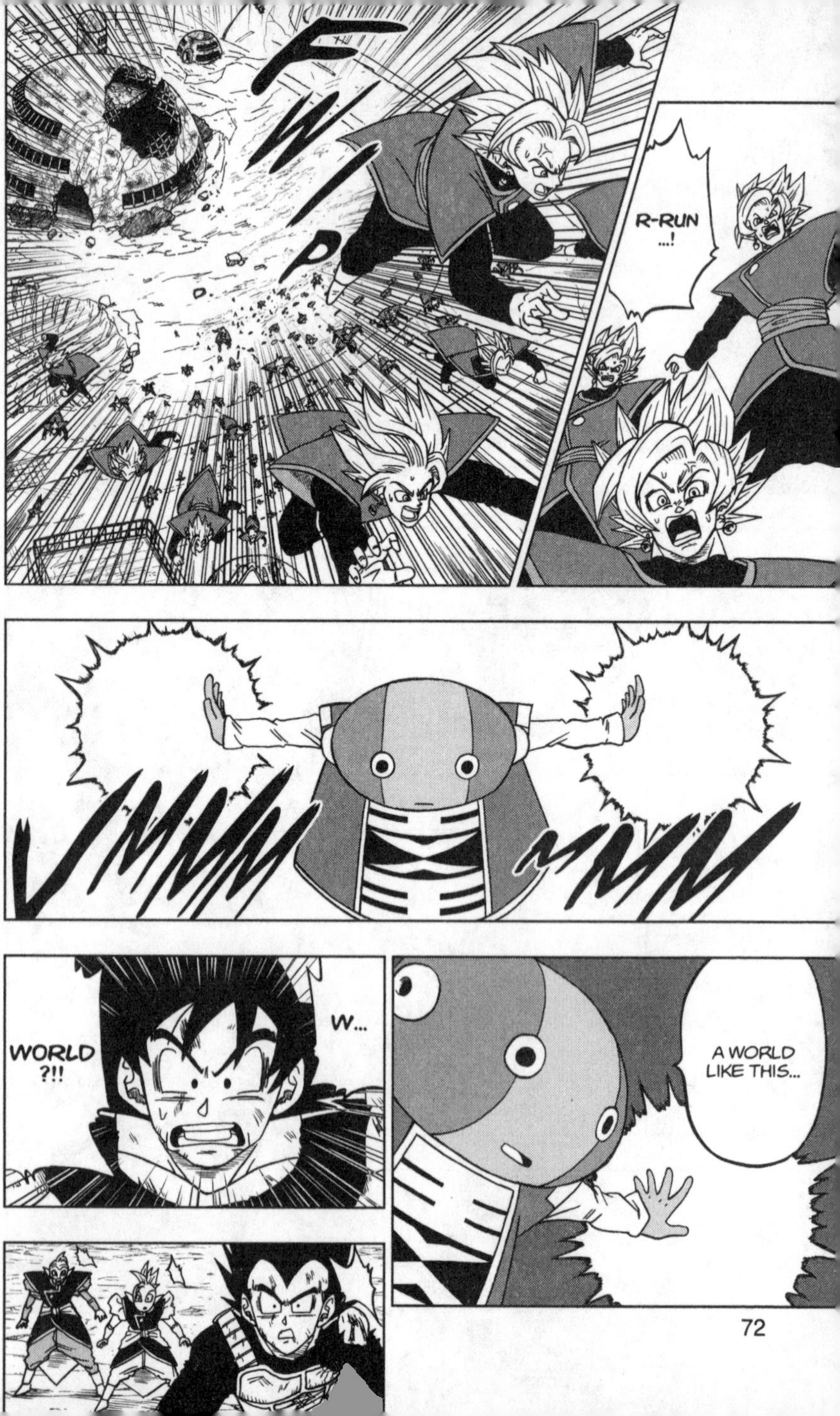
R-RUN ...!
FWIP
VMMMM
MMM
A WORLD LIKE THIS...
W...
WORLD ?!!

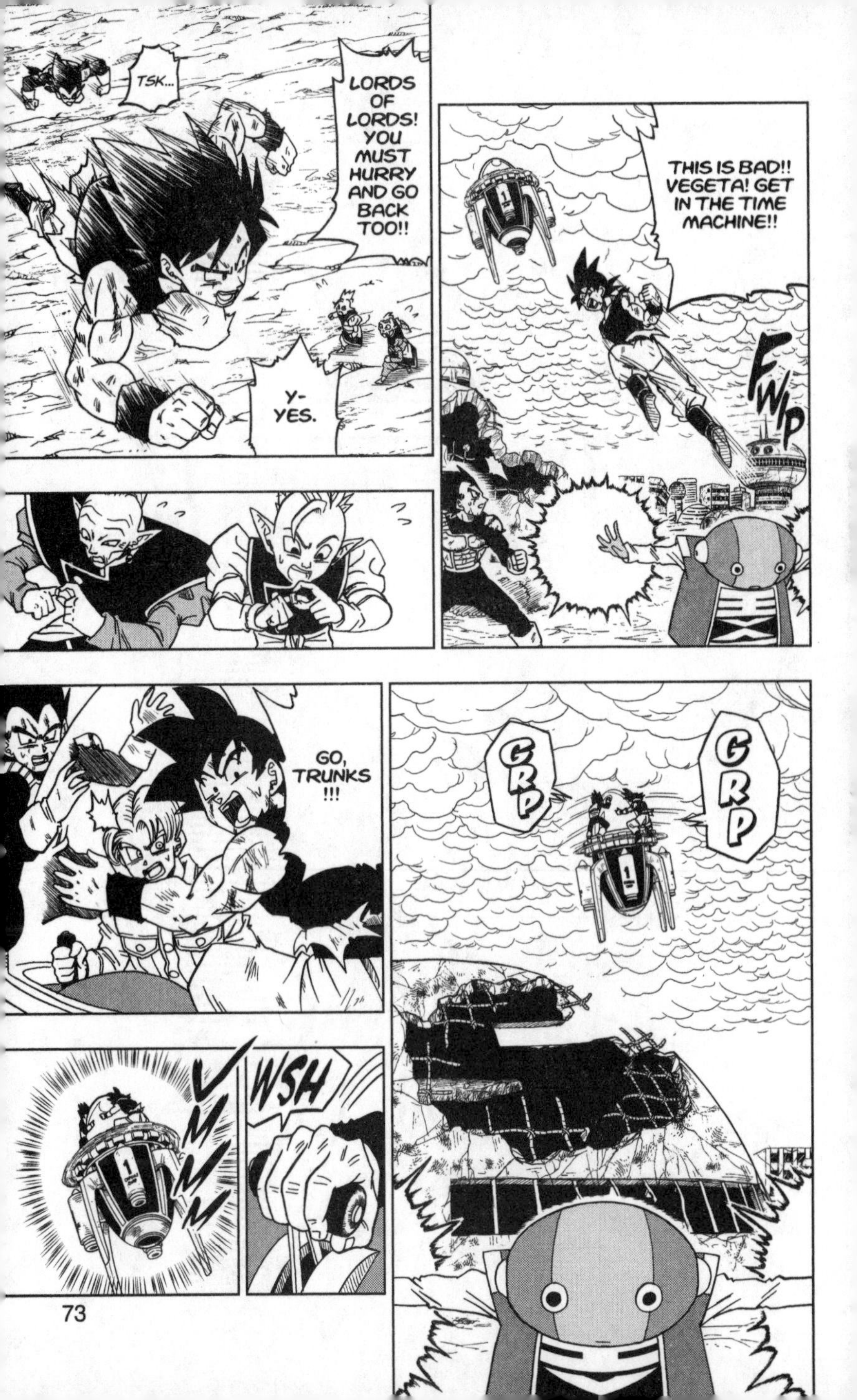
THIS IS BAD!! VEGETA! GET IN THE TIME MACHINE!!
FWIP
TSK...
LORDS OF LORDS! YOU MUST HURRY AND GO BACK TOO!!
Y- YES.
GRP GRP
GRP
GO, TRUNKS !!!
WSH
VMMMM

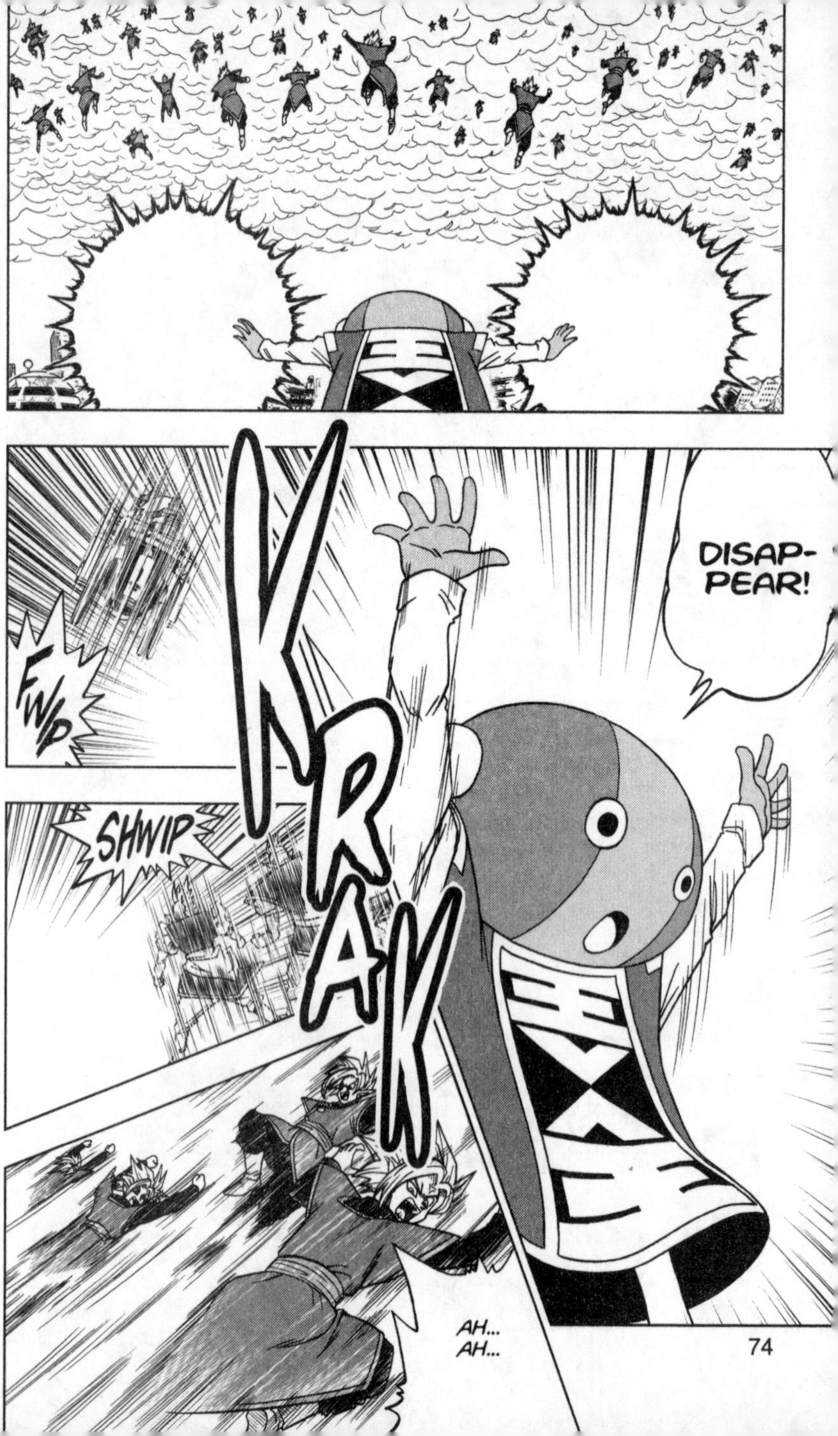
DISAP-
PEAR!
KRAK
FWIP
SHWIP
AH...
AH...

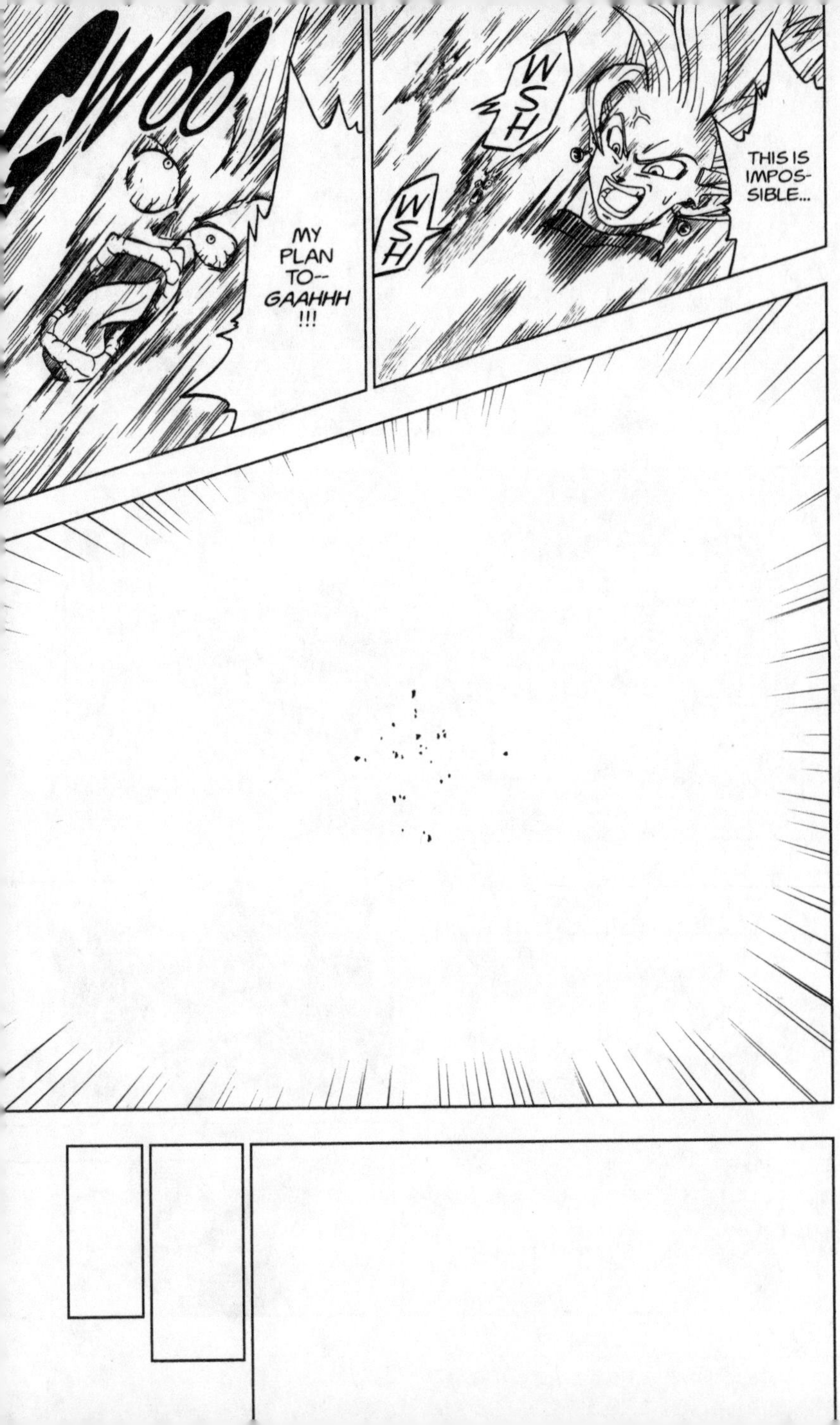
WSH
WSH
THIS IS IMPOSSIBLE...
MY PLAN TO-- GAAHHH!!!

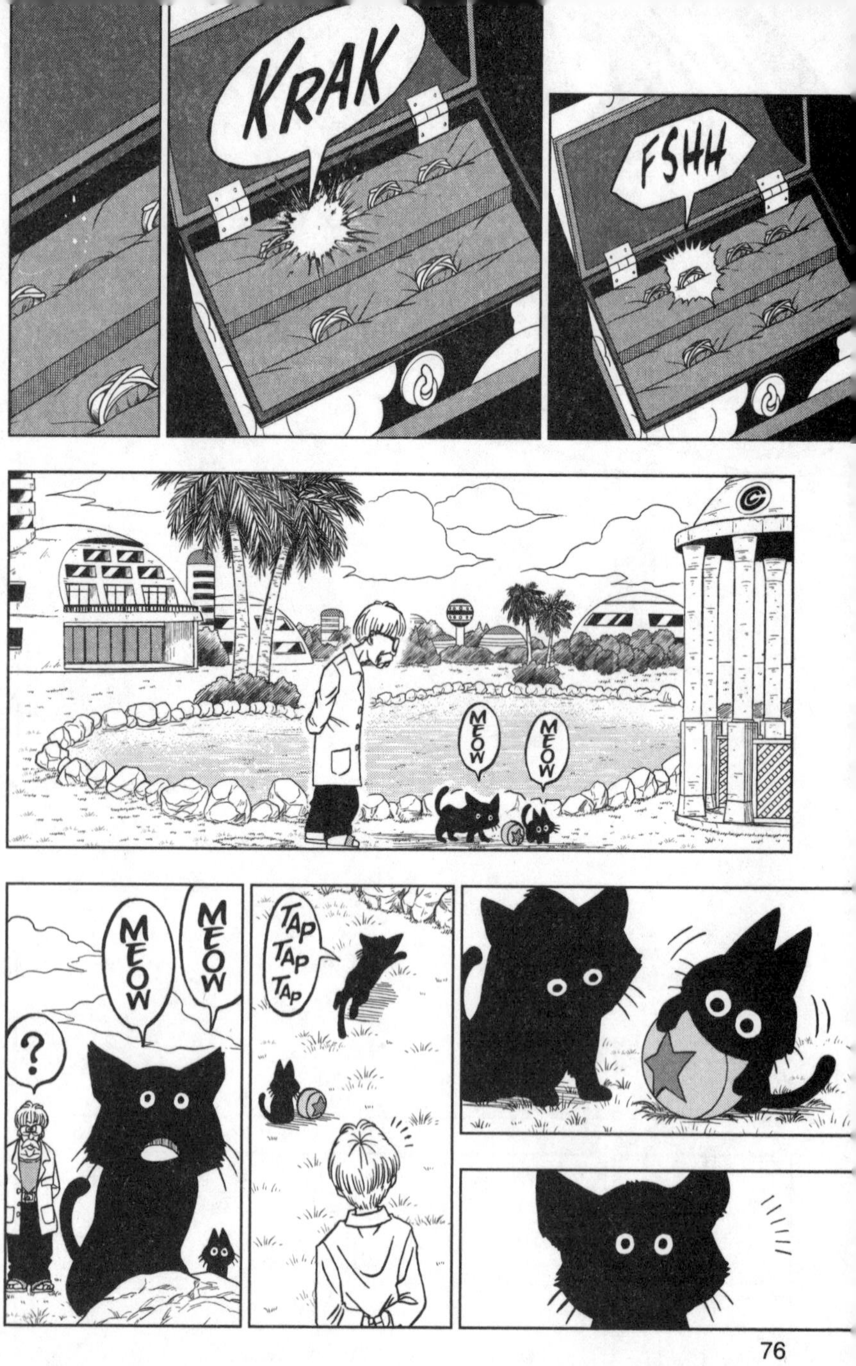
FSHH
KRAK
MEOW
MEOW
TAP TAP TAP
MEOW
MEOW
?

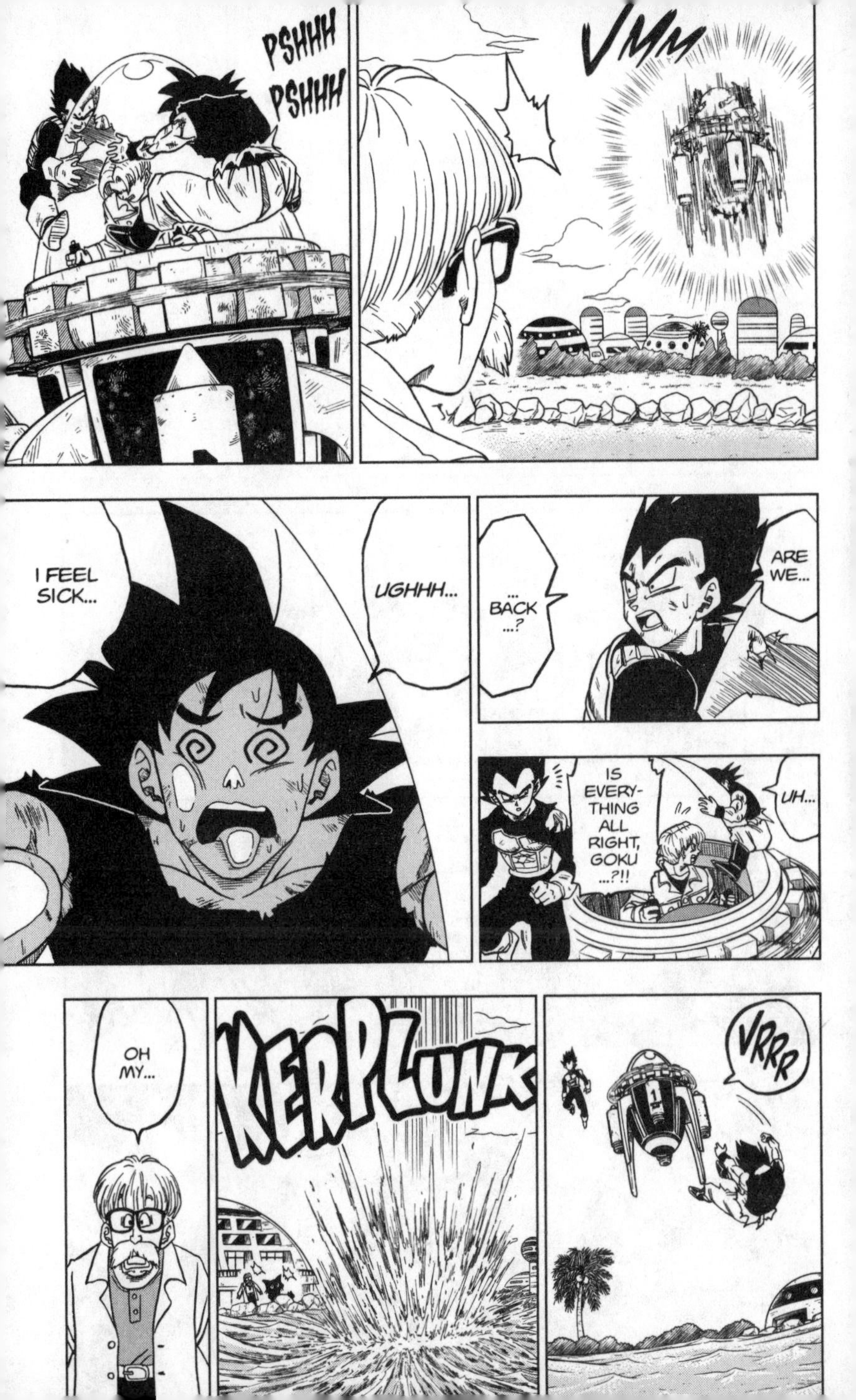
VMM
PSHHH PSHHH
ARE WE...
...BACK ...?
UH...
IS EVERYTHING ALL RIGHT, GOKU ...?!!
UGHHH...
I FEEL SICK...
VRRR
KERPLUNK
OH MY...

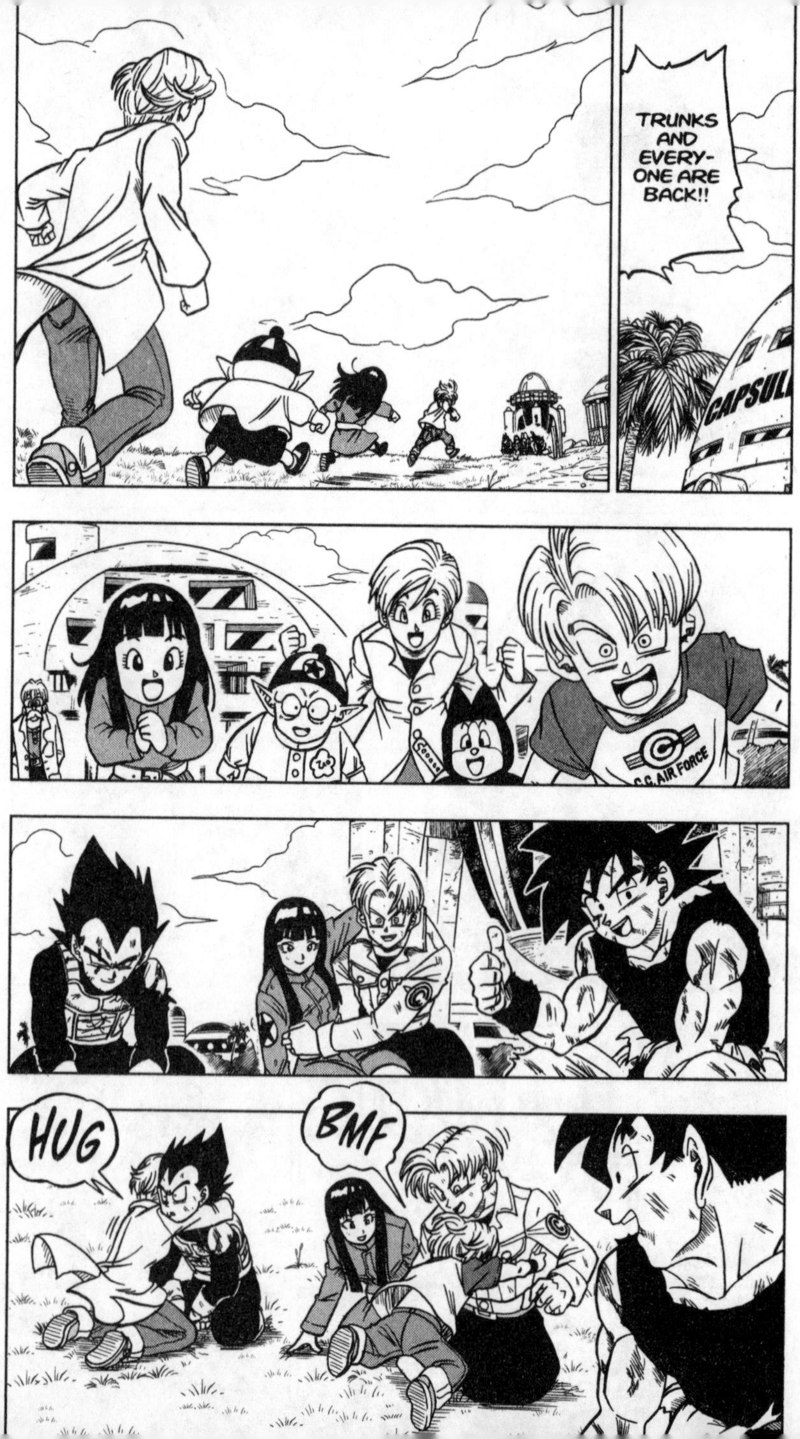
TRUNKS AND EVERY-ONE ARE BACK!!
BMF
HUG

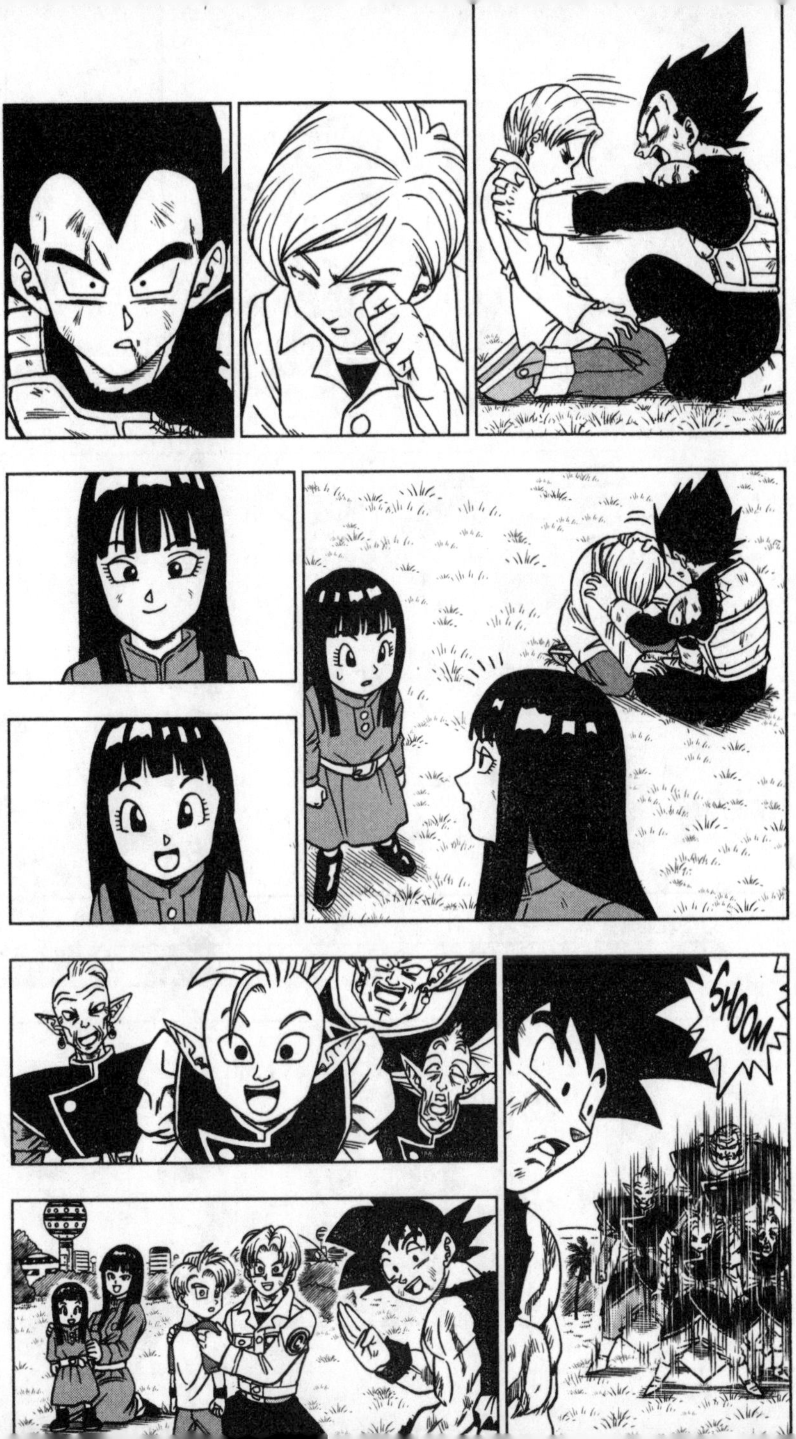
SHOOM

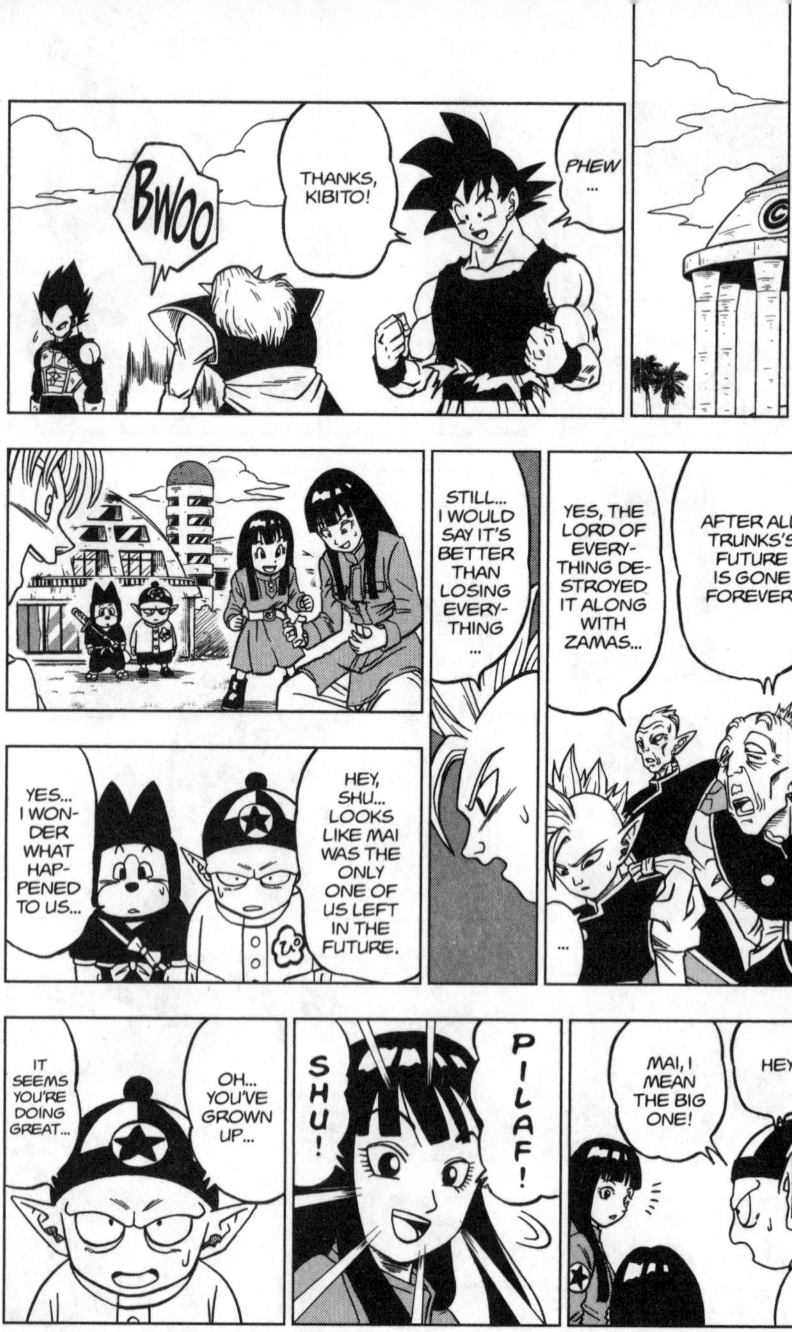
PHEW ...
THANKS, KIBITO!
BWOO
AFTER ALL, TRUNKS'S FUTURE IS GONE FOREVER.
YES, THE LORD OF EVERYTHING DESTROYED IT ALONG WITH ZAMAS...
...
STILL... I WOULD SAY IT'S BETTER THAN LOSING EVERYTHING ...
HEY, SHU... LOOKS LIKE MAI WAS THE ONLY ONE OF US LEFT IN THE FUTURE.
YES... I WONDER WHAT HAPPENED TO US...
HEY!
MAI, I MEAN THE BIG ONE!
PILAF!
SHU!
OH... YOU'VE GROWN UP...
IT SEEMS YOU'RE DOING GREAT...

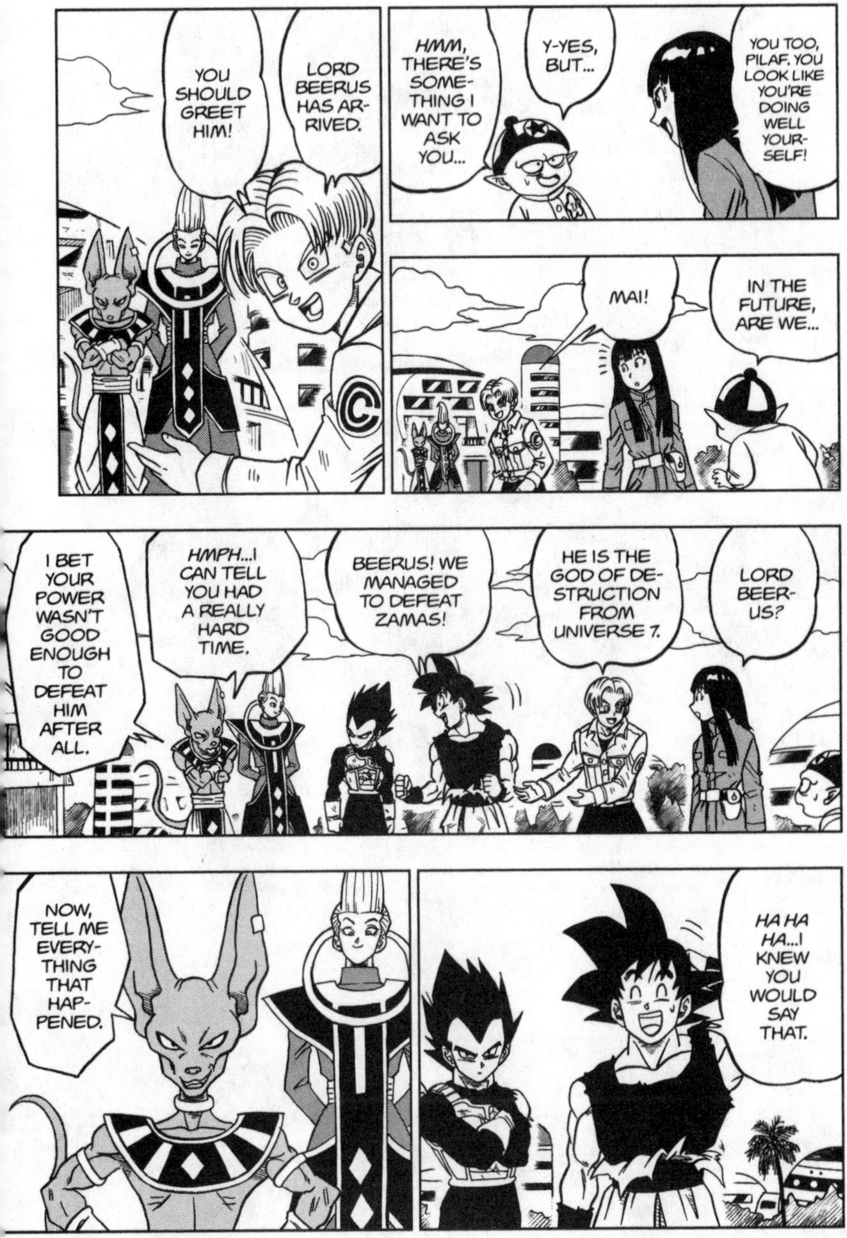
YOU TOO, PILAF. YOU LOOK LIKE YOU'RE DOING WELL YOURSELF!
Y-YES, BUT...
HMM, THERE'S SOMETHING I WANT TO ASK YOU...
IN THE FUTURE, ARE WE...
MAI!
LORD BEERUS HAS ARRIVED.
YOU SHOULD GREET HIM!
LORD BEERUS?
HE IS THE GOD OF DESTRUCTION FROM UNIVERSE 7.
BEERUS! WE MANAGED TO DEFEAT ZAMAS!
HMPH...I CAN TELL YOU HAD A REALLY HARD TIME.
I BET YOUR POWER WASN'T GOOD ENOUGH TO DEFEAT HIM AFTER ALL.
HA HA HA...I KNEW YOU WOULD SAY THAT.
NOW, TELL ME EVERYTHING THAT HAPPENED.

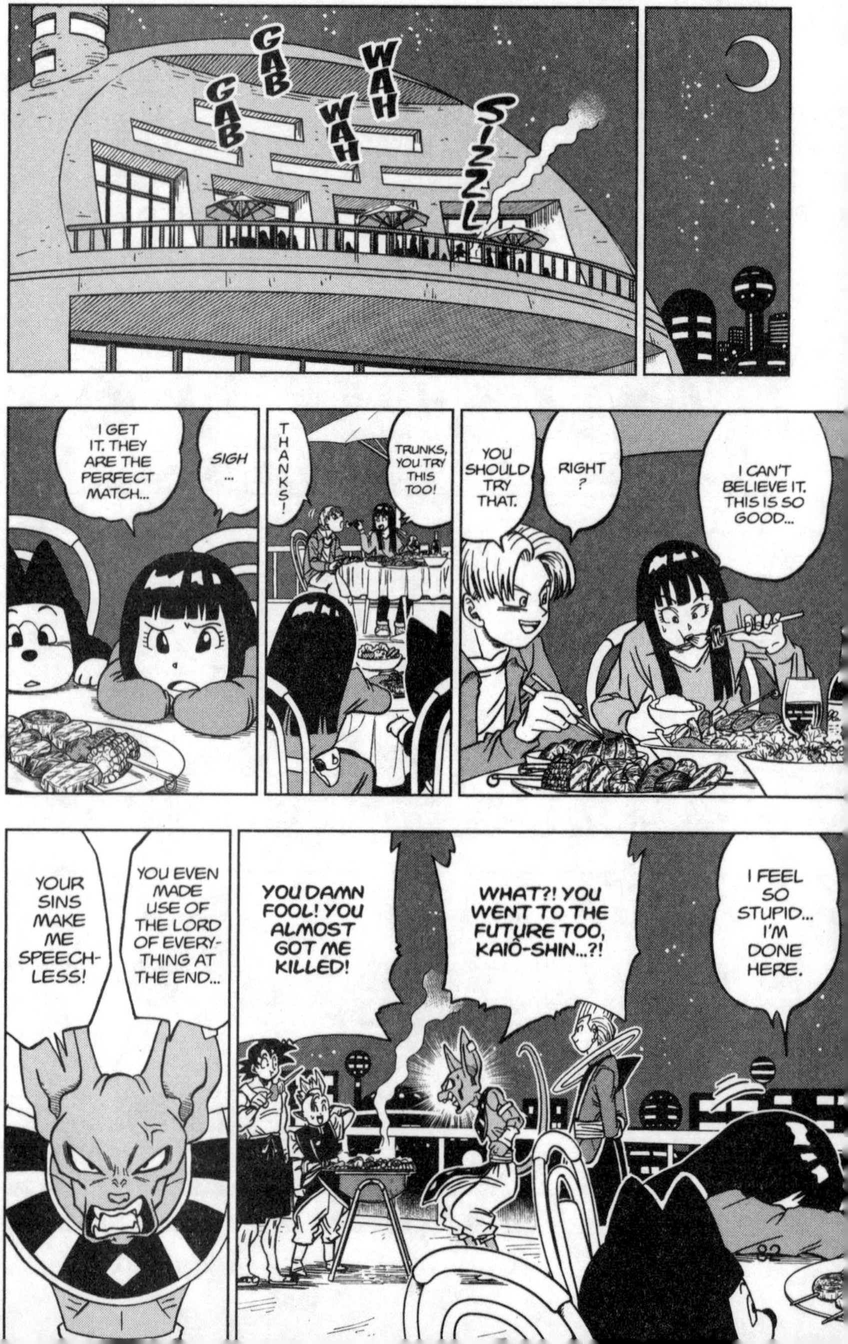
SIZZL
WAH WAH
GAB GAB
I CAN'T BELIEVE IT. THIS IS SO GOOD...
RIGHT?
YOU SHOULD TRY THAT.
TRUNKS, YOU TRY THIS TOO!
THANKS!
SIGH...
I GET IT. THEY ARE THE PERFECT MATCH...
I FEEL SO STUPID... I'M DONE HERE.
WHAT?! YOU WENT TO THE FUTURE TOO, KAIÔ-SHIN...?!
YOU DAMN FOOL! YOU ALMOST GOT ME KILLED!
YOU EVEN MADE USE OF THE LORD OF EVERYTHING AT THE END...
YOUR SINS MAKE ME SPEECHLESS!

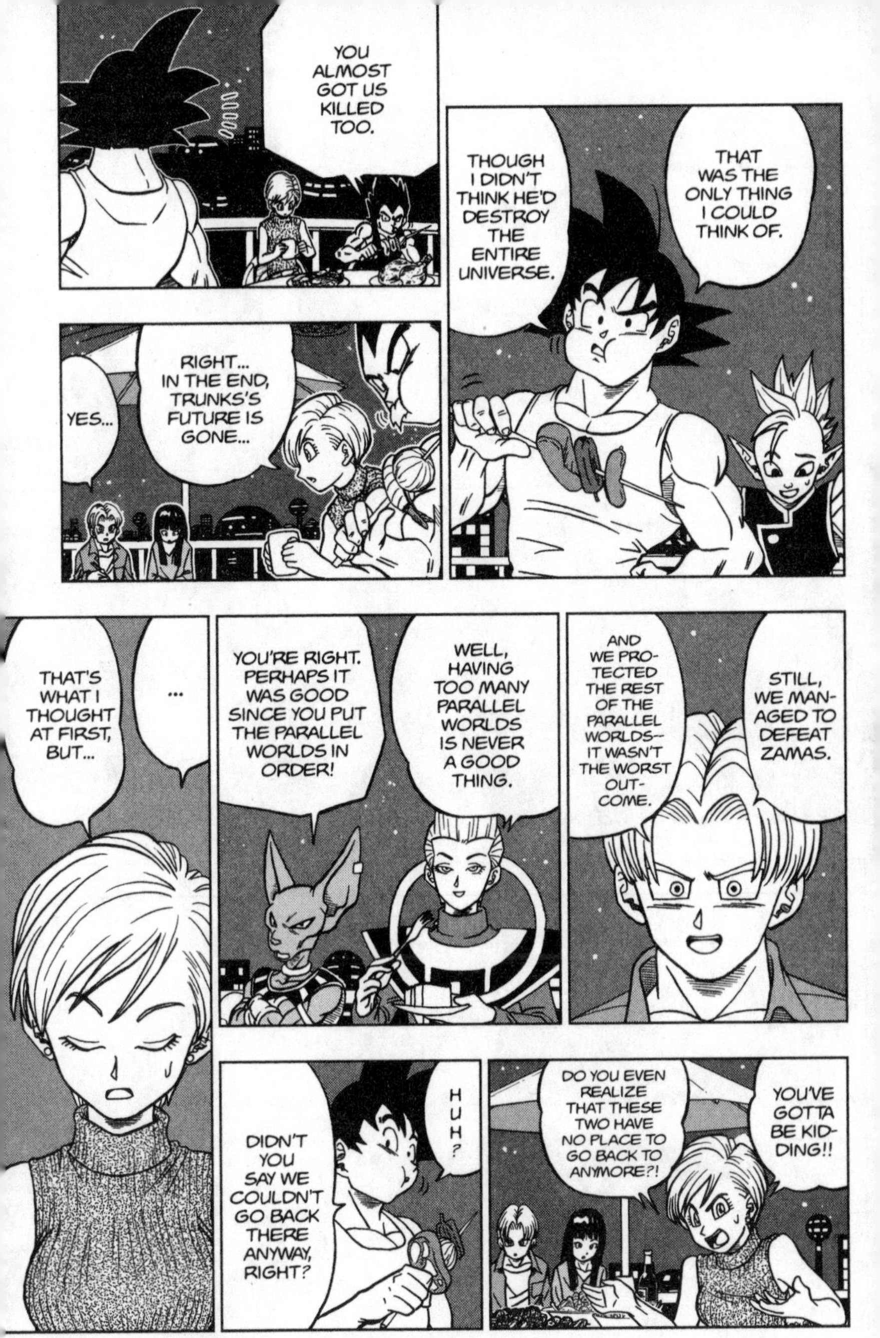
YOU ALMOST GOT US KILLED TOO.
THAT WAS THE ONLY THING I COULD THINK OF.
THOUGH I DIDN'T THINK HE'D DESTROY THE ENTIRE UNIVERSE.
RIGHT... IN THE END, TRUNKS'S FUTURE IS GONE...
YES...
STILL, WE MANAGED TO DEFEAT ZAMAS.
AND WE PROTECTED THE REST OF THE PARALLEL WORLDS-- IT WASN'T THE WORST OUTCOME.
WELL, HAVING TOO MANY PARALLEL WORLDS IS NEVER A GOOD THING.
YOU'RE RIGHT. PERHAPS IT WAS GOOD SINCE YOU PUT THE PARALLEL WORLDS IN ORDER!
...
THAT'S WHAT I THOUGHT AT FIRST, BUT...
YOU'VE GOTTA BE KIDDING!!
DO YOU EVEN REALIZE THAT THESE TWO HAVE NO PLACE TO GO BACK TO ANYMORE?!
HUH?
DIDN'T YOU SAY WE COULDN'T GO BACK THERE ANYWAY, RIGHT?

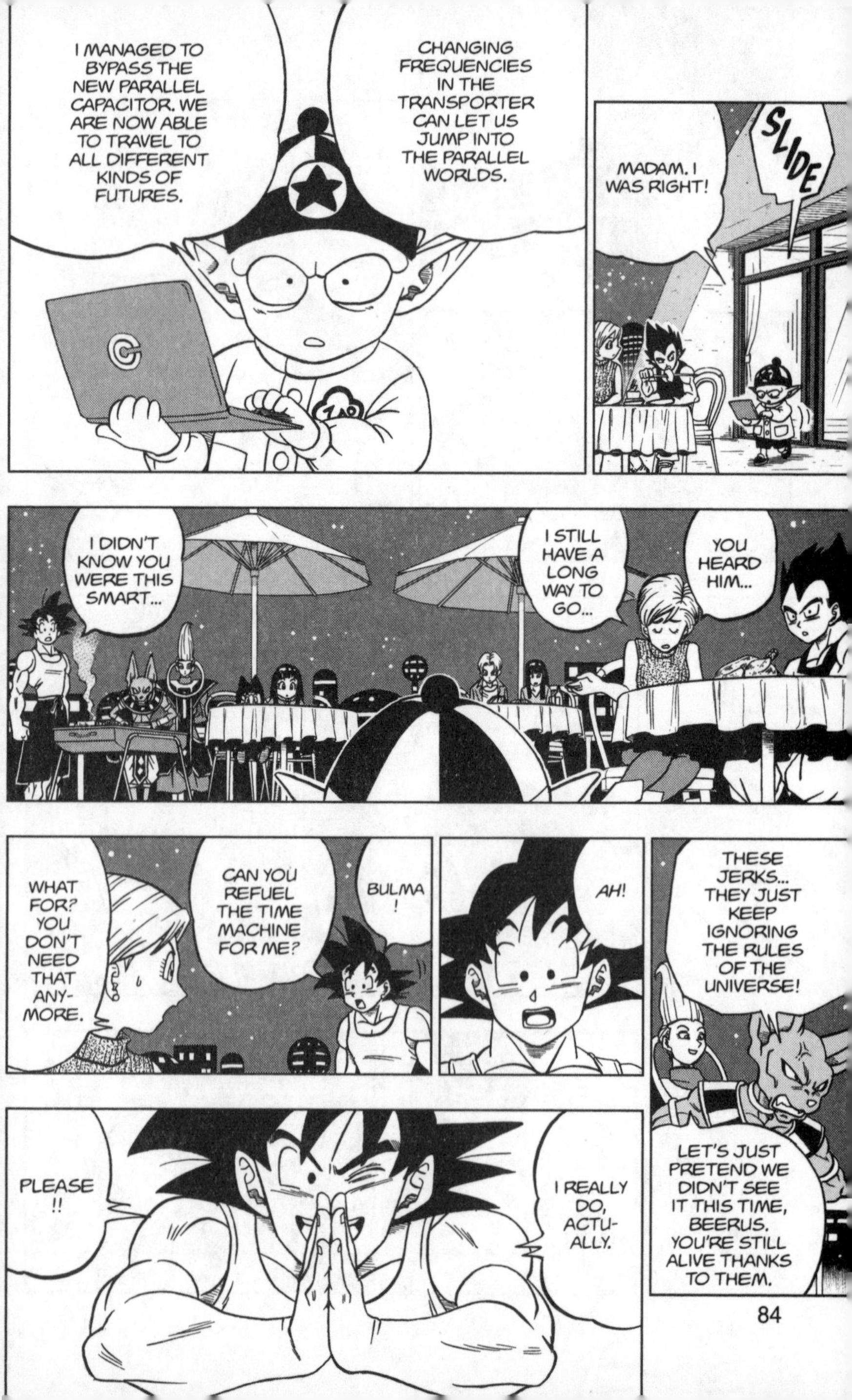

SLIDE
MADAM. I WAS RIGHT!
CHANGING FREQUENCIES IN THE TRANSPORTER CAN LET US JUMP INTO THE PARALLEL WORLDS.
I MANAGED TO BYPASS THE NEW PARALLEL CAPACITOR. WE ARE NOW ABLE TO TRAVEL TO ALL DIFFERENT KINDS OF FUTURES.
YOU HEARD HIM...
I STILL HAVE A LONG WAY TO GO...
I DIDN'T KNOW YOU WERE THIS SMART...
THESE JERKS... THEY JUST KEEP IGNORING THE RULES OF THE UNIVERSE!
LET'S JUST PRETEND WE DIDN'T SEE IT THIS TIME, BEERUS. YOU'RE STILL ALIVE THANKS TO THEM.
AH!
BULMA!
CAN YOU REFUEL THE TIME MACHINE FOR ME?
WHAT FOR? YOU DON'T NEED THAT ANY-MORE.
I REALLY DO, ACTU-ALLY.
PLEASE!!

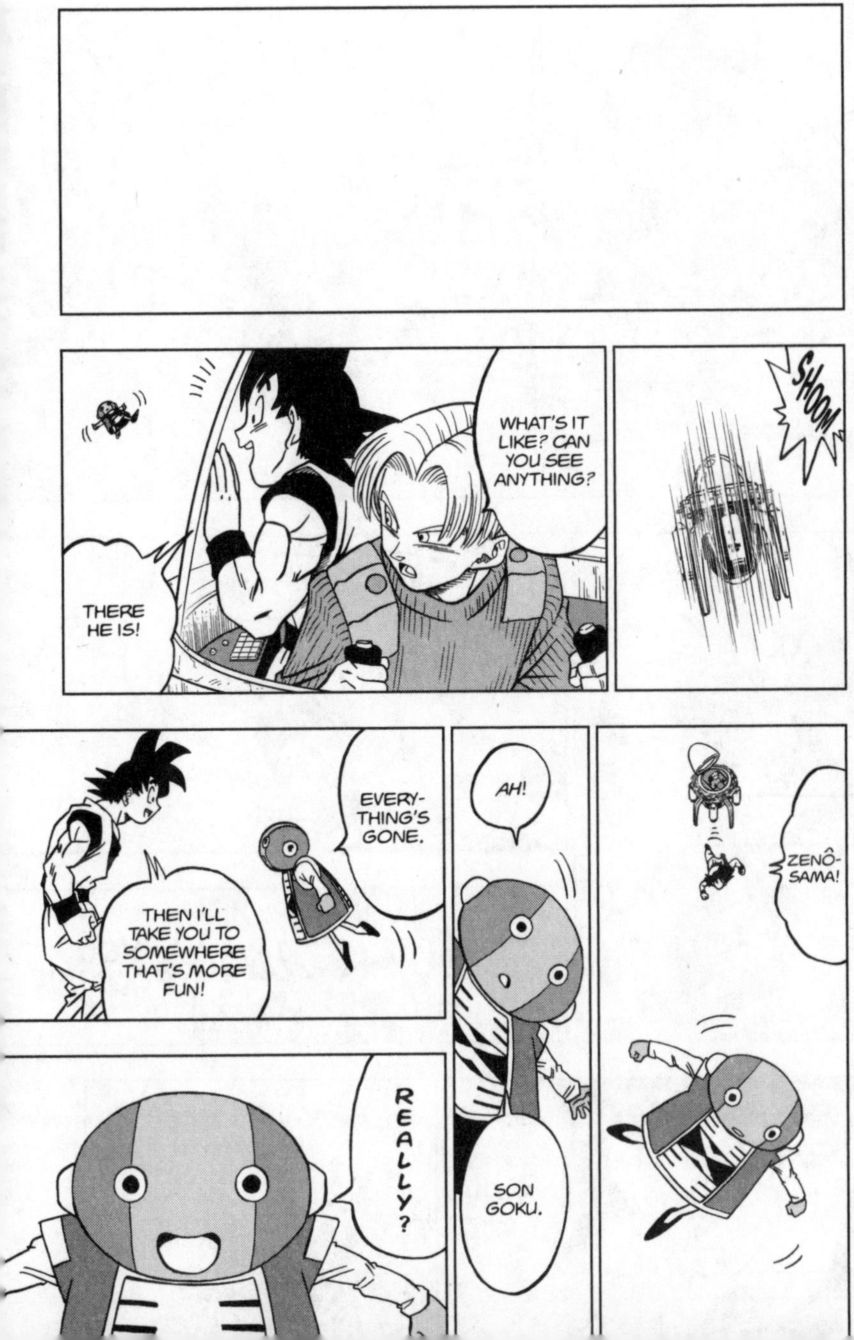
SHOOM
WHAT'S IT LIKE? CAN YOU SEE ANYTHING?
THERE HE IS!
ZENÔ-SAMA!
AH!
SON GOKU.
EVERY-THING'S GONE.
THEN I'LL TAKE YOU TO SOMEWHERE THAT'S MORE FUN!
REALLY?

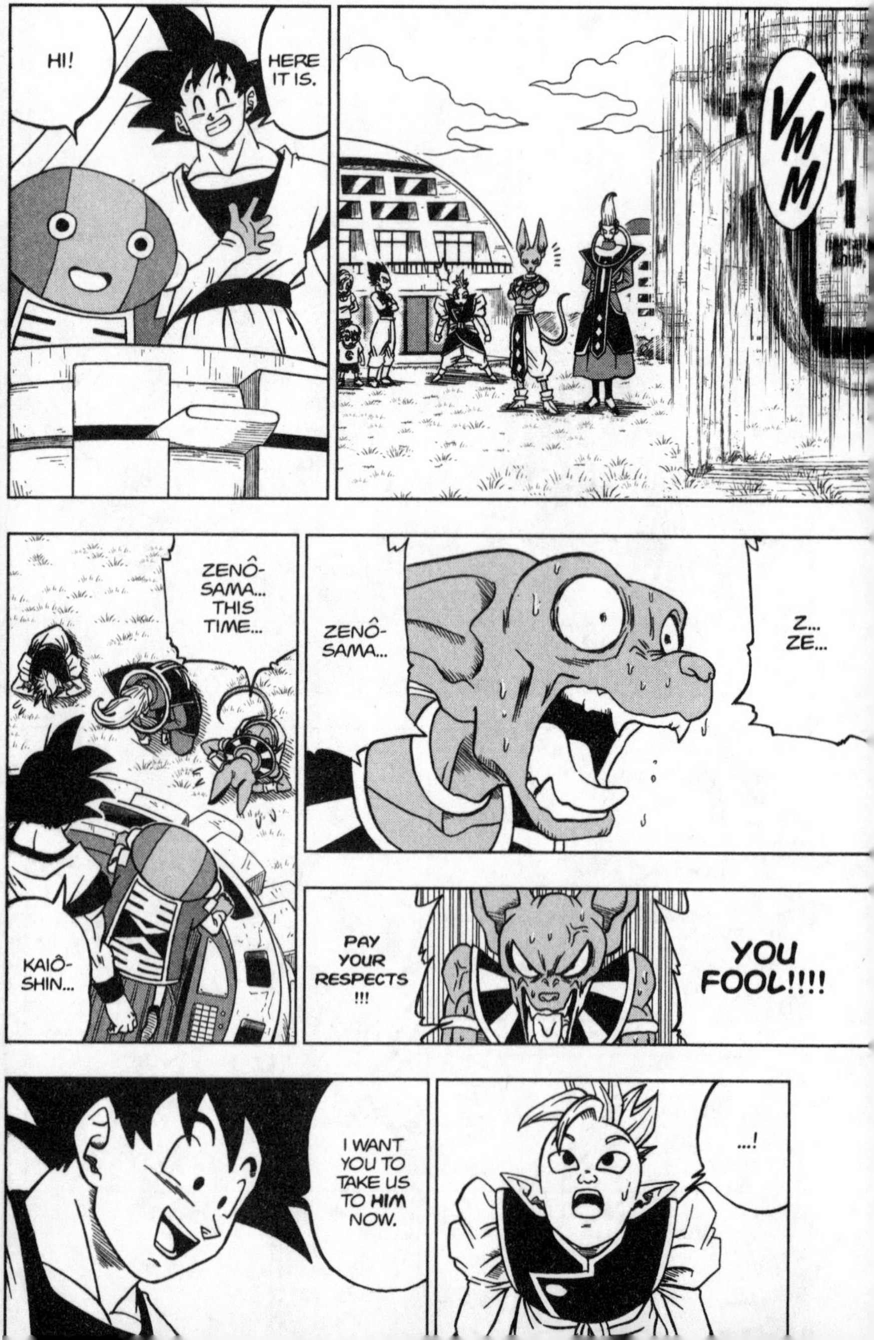
VMM
HERE IT IS.
HI!
Z... ZE...
ZENÔ-SAMA...
YOU FOOL!!!!
PAY YOUR RESPECTS !!!
ZENÔ-SAMA... THIS TIME...
KAIÔ-SHIN...
...!
I WANT YOU TO TAKE US TO HIM NOW.

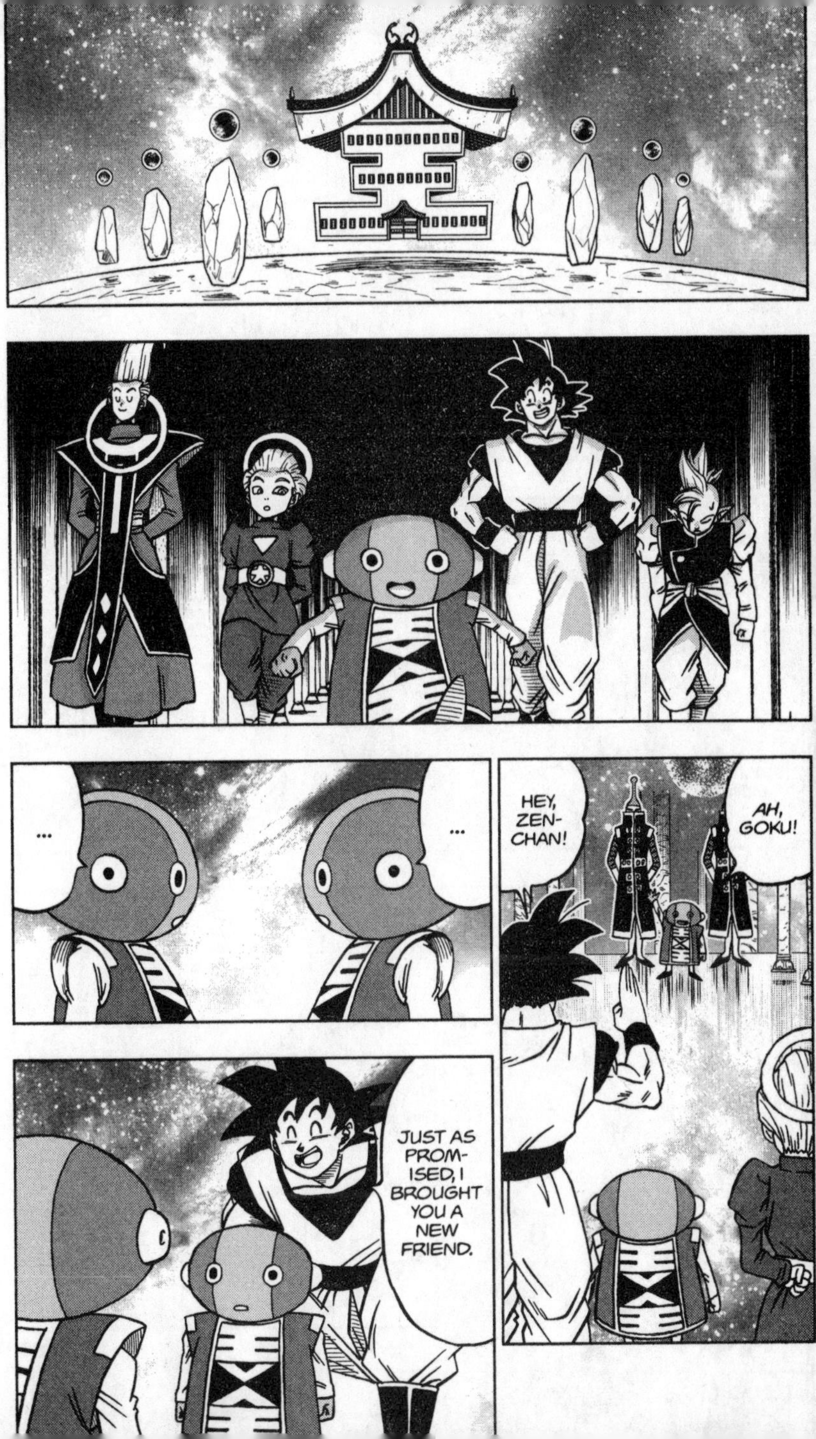
AH, GOKU!
HEY, ZEN-CHAN!
...
...
JUST AS PROMISED, I BROUGHT YOU A NEW FRIEND.

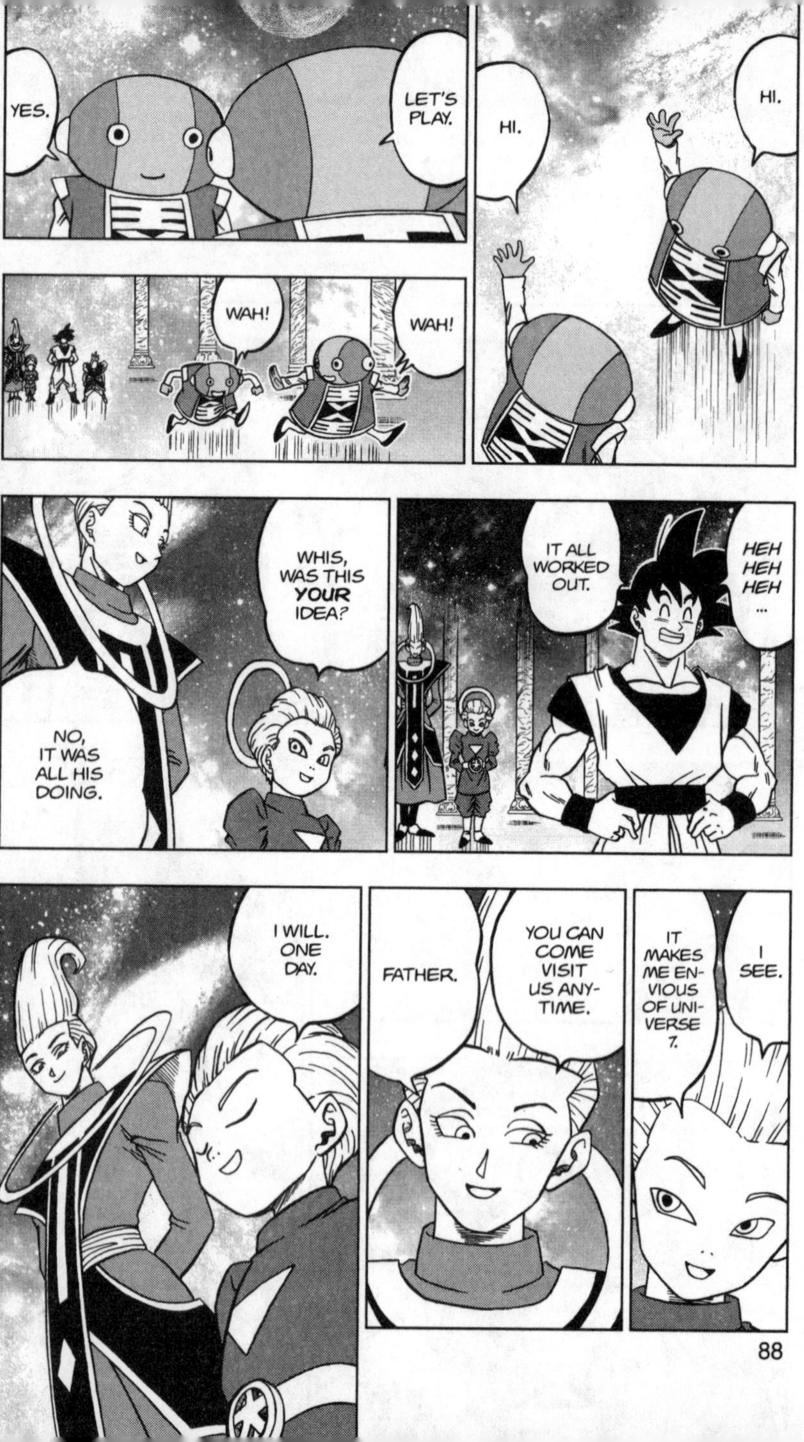
HI.
HI.
LET'S PLAY.
YES.
WAH!
WAH!
HEH HEH HEH ...
IT ALL WORKED OUT.
WHIS, WAS THIS YOUR IDEA?
NO, IT WAS ALL HIS DOING.
I SEE.
IT MAKES ME ENVIOUS OF UNIVERSE 7.
YOU CAN COME VISIT US ANYTIME.
FATHER.
I WILL. ONE DAY.

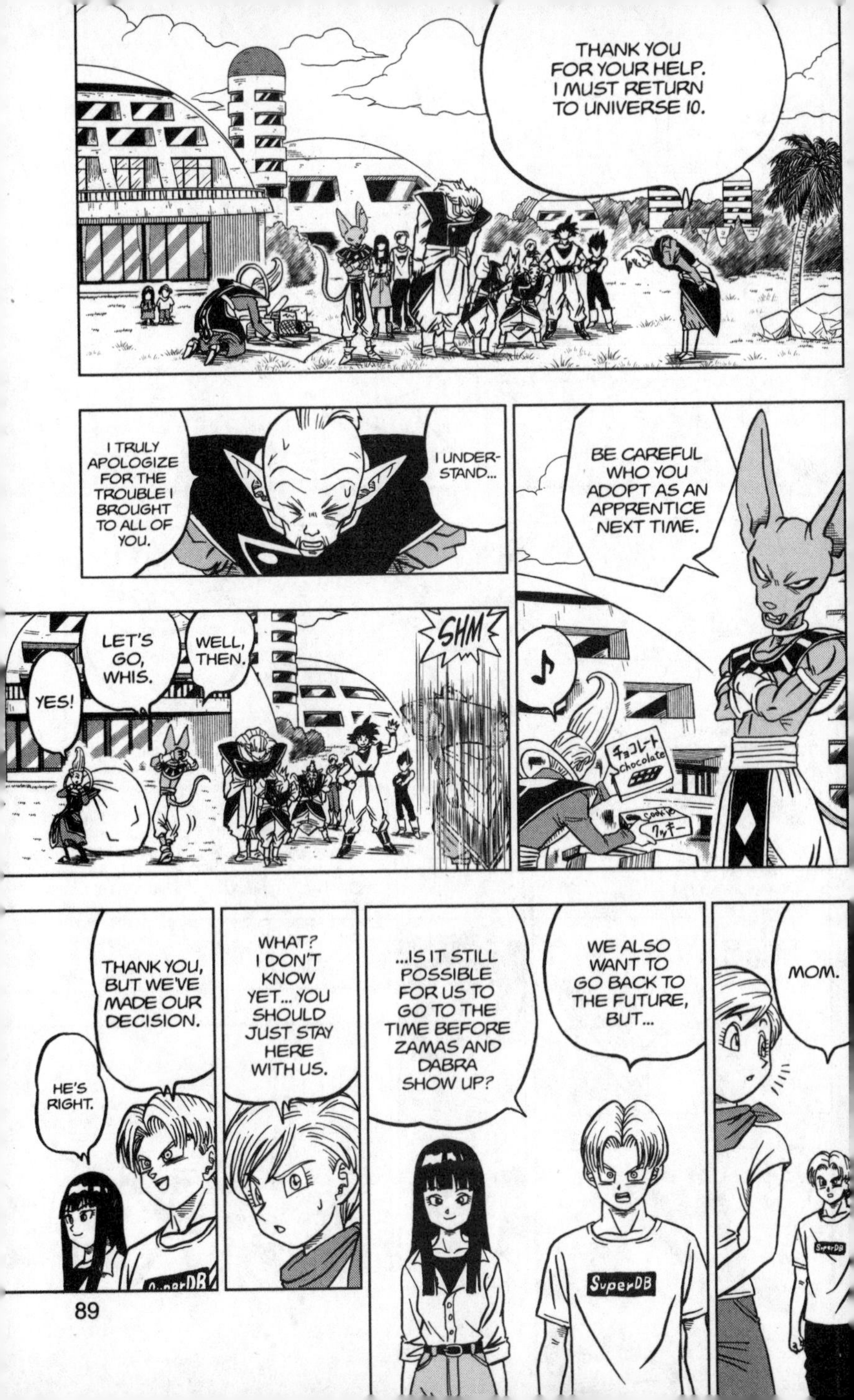
THANK YOU FOR YOUR HELP. I MUST RETURN TO UNIVERSE 10.
BE CAREFUL WHO YOU ADOPT AS AN APPRENTICE NEXT TIME.
♪
チョコレート Chocolate
クッキー
I UNDER-STAND...
I TRULY APOLOGIZE FOR THE TROUBLE I BROUGHT TO ALL OF YOU.
SHM
WELL, THEN.
LET'S GO, WHIS.
YES!
MOM.
WE ALSO WANT TO GO BACK TO THE FUTURE, BUT...
...IS IT STILL POSSIBLE FOR US TO GO TO THE TIME BEFORE ZAMAS AND DABRA SHOW UP?
SuperDB
WHAT? I DON'T KNOW YET... YOU SHOULD JUST STAY HERE WITH US.
THANK YOU, BUT WE'VE MADE OUR DECISION.
HE'S RIGHT.

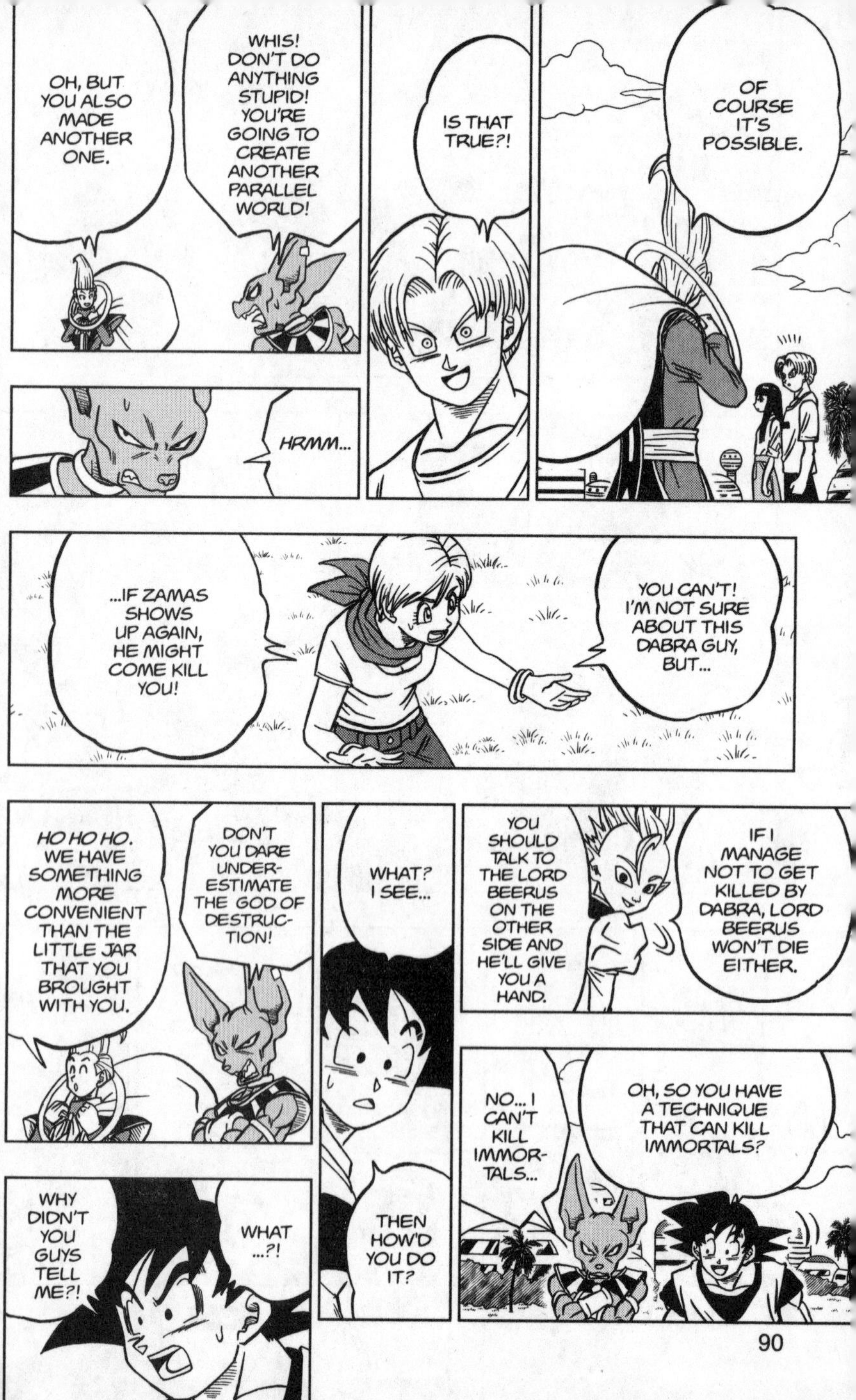
OF COURSE IT'S POSSIBLE.
IS THAT TRUE?!
WHIS! DON'T DO ANYTHING STUPID! YOU'RE GOING TO CREATE ANOTHER PARALLEL WORLD!
OH, BUT YOU ALSO MADE ANOTHER ONE.
HRMM...
YOU CAN'T! I'M NOT SURE ABOUT THIS DABRA GUY, BUT...
...IF ZAMAS SHOWS UP AGAIN, HE MIGHT COME KILL YOU!
IF I MANAGE NOT TO GET KILLED BY DABRA, LORD BEERUS WON'T DIE EITHER.
YOU SHOULD TALK TO THE LORD BEERUS ON THE OTHER SIDE AND HE'LL GIVE YOU A HAND.
OH, SO YOU HAVE A TECHNIQUE THAT CAN KILL IMMORTALS?
NO... I CAN'T KILL IMMORTALS...
WHAT? I SEE...
THEN HOW'D YOU DO IT?
DON'T YOU DARE UNDER-ESTIMATE THE GOD OF DESTRUCTION!
HO HO HO. WE HAVE SOMETHING MORE CONVENIENT THAN THE LITTLE JAR THAT YOU BROUGHT WITH YOU.
WHAT ...?!
WHY DIDN'T YOU GUYS TELL ME?!

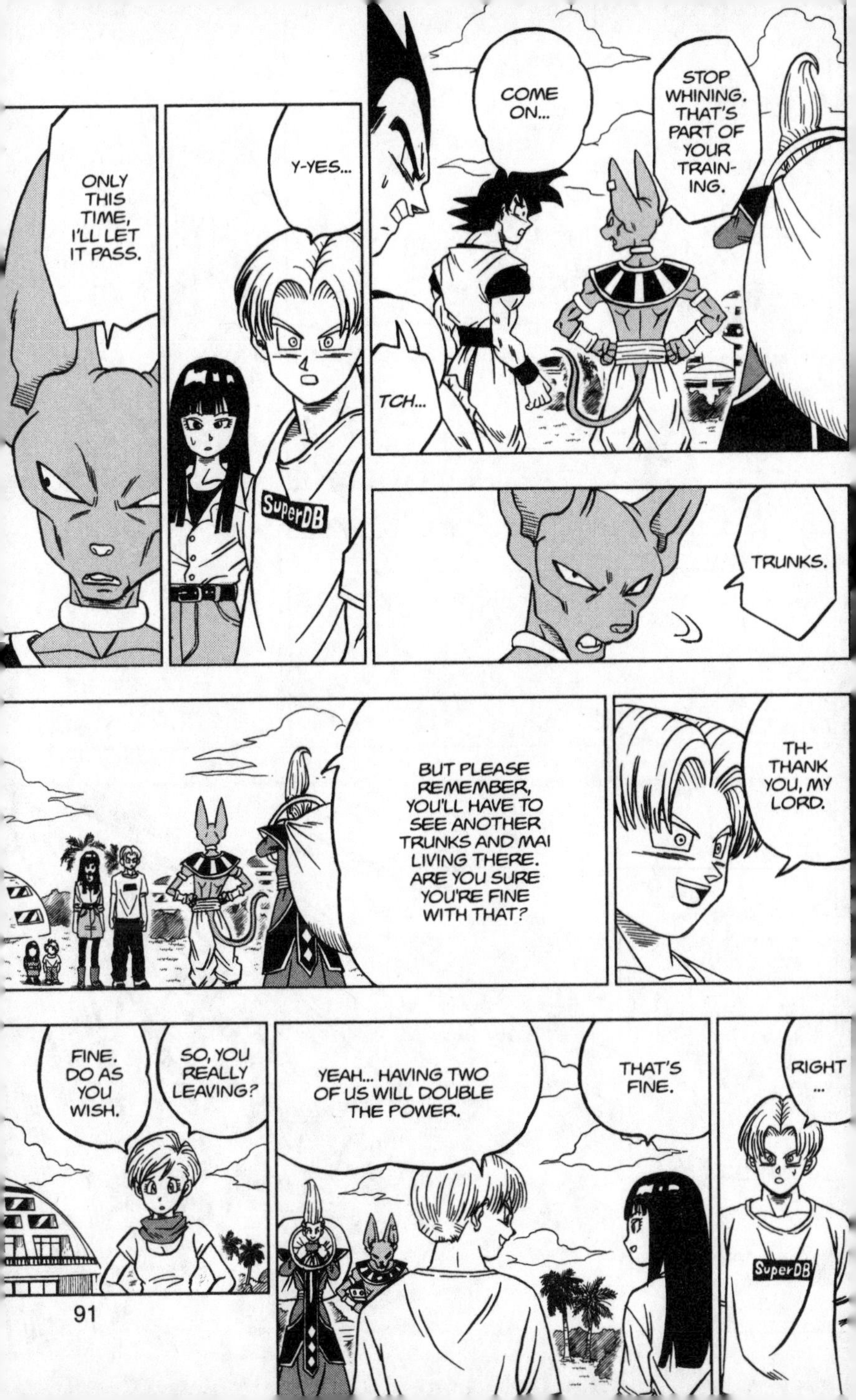
STOP WHINING. THAT'S PART OF YOUR TRAIN-ING.
COME ON...
TCH...
TRUNKS.
Y-YES...
ONLY THIS TIME, I'LL LET IT PASS.
TH-THANK YOU, MY LORD.
BUT PLEASE REMEMBER, YOU'LL HAVE TO SEE ANOTHER TRUNKS AND MAI LIVING THERE. ARE YOU SURE YOU'RE FINE WITH THAT?
RIGHT ...
THAT'S FINE.
YEAH... HAVING TWO OF US WILL DOUBLE THE POWER.
SO, YOU REALLY LEAVING?
FINE. DO AS YOU WISH.

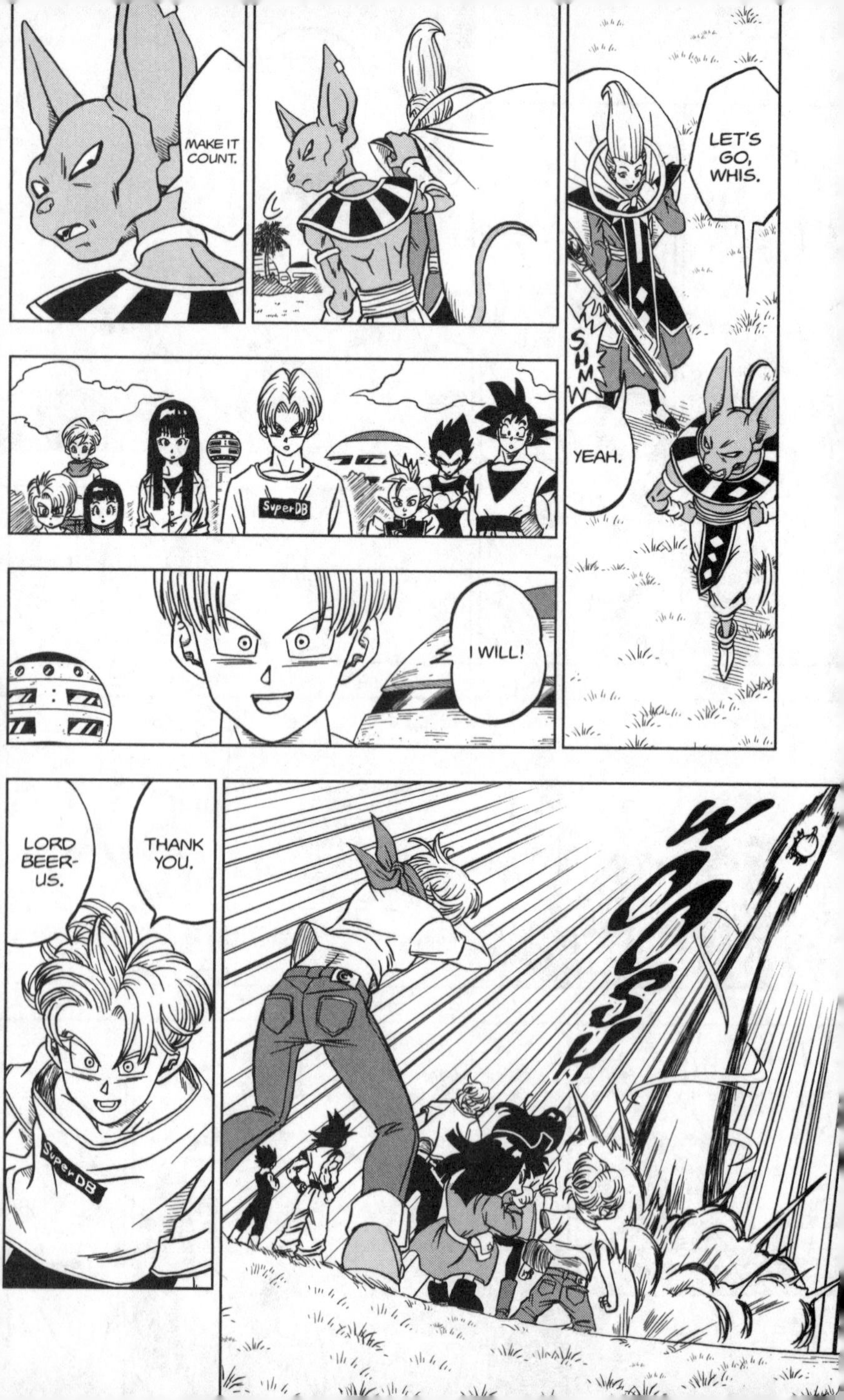
LET'S GO, WHIS.
SHM
YEAH.
MAKE IT COUNT.
SuperDB
I WILL!
WOOSH
THANK YOU.
LORD BEER-US.
SuperDB

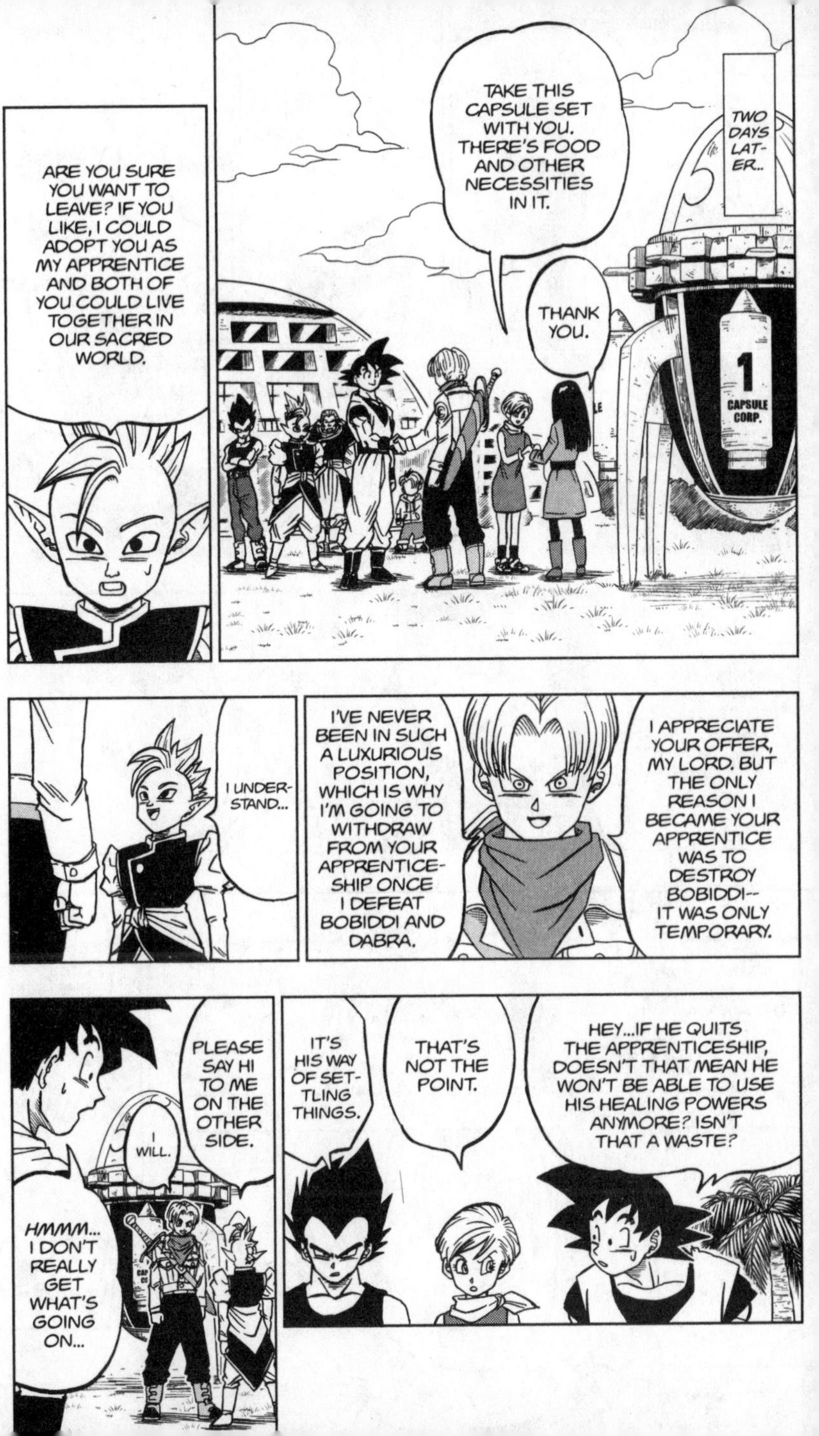
TWO DAYS LATER...
TAKE THIS CAPSULE SET WITH YOU. THERE'S FOOD AND OTHER NECESSITIES IN IT.
THANK YOU.
1 CAPSULE CORP.
ARE YOU SURE YOU WANT TO LEAVE? IF YOU LIKE, I COULD ADOPT YOU AS MY APPRENTICE AND BOTH OF YOU COULD LIVE TOGETHER IN OUR SACRED WORLD.
I APPRECIATE YOUR OFFER, MY LORD. BUT THE ONLY REASON I BECAME YOUR APPRENTICE WAS TO DESTROY BOBIDDI-- IT WAS ONLY TEMPORARY.
I'VE NEVER BEEN IN SUCH A LUXURIOUS POSITION, WHICH IS WHY I'M GOING TO WITHDRAW FROM YOUR APPRENTICE-SHIP ONCE I DEFEAT BOBIDDI AND DABRA.
I UNDER-STAND...
HEY...IF HE QUITS THE APPRENTICESHIP, DOESN'T THAT MEAN HE WON'T BE ABLE TO USE HIS HEALING POWERS ANYMORE? ISN'T THAT A WASTE?
THAT'S NOT THE POINT.
IT'S HIS WAY OF SET-TLING THINGS.
PLEASE SAY HI TO ME ON THE OTHER SIDE.
I WILL.
HMMM... I DON'T REALLY GET WHAT'S GOING ON...

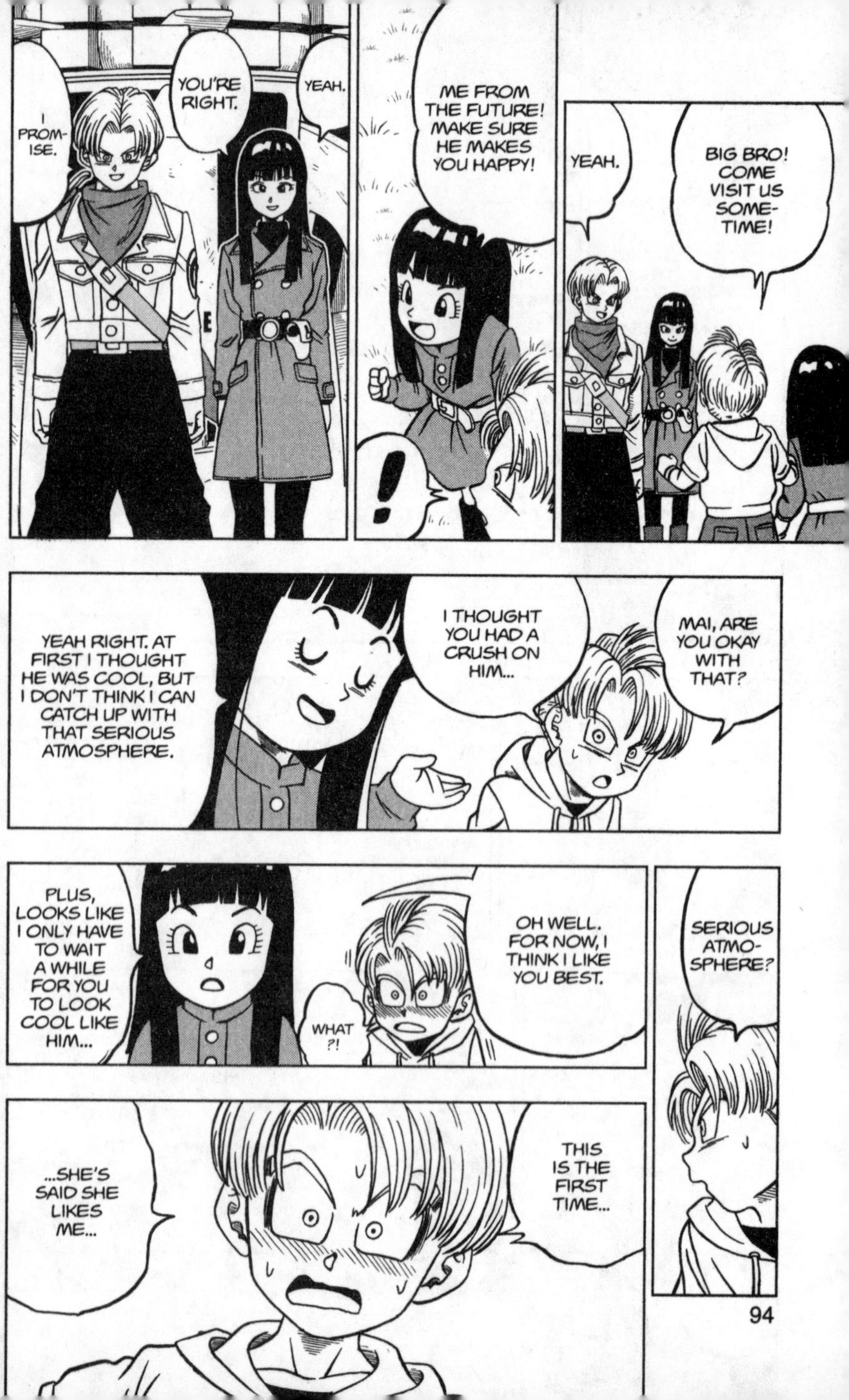
BIG BRO! COME VISIT US SOME-TIME!
YEAH.
ME FROM THE FUTURE! MAKE SURE HE MAKES YOU HAPPY!
!
YEAH.
YOU'RE RIGHT.
I PROM-ISE.
MAI, ARE YOU OKAY WITH THAT?
I THOUGHT YOU HAD A CRUSH ON HIM...
YEAH RIGHT. AT FIRST I THOUGHT HE WAS COOL, BUT I DON'T THINK I CAN CATCH UP WITH THAT SERIOUS ATMOSPHERE.
SERIOUS ATMO-SPHERE?
OH WELL. FOR NOW, I THINK I LIKE YOU BEST.
WHAT ?!
PLUS, LOOKS LIKE I ONLY HAVE TO WAIT A WHILE FOR YOU TO LOOK COOL LIKE HIM...
THIS IS THE FIRST TIME...
...SHE'S SAID SHE LIKES ME...

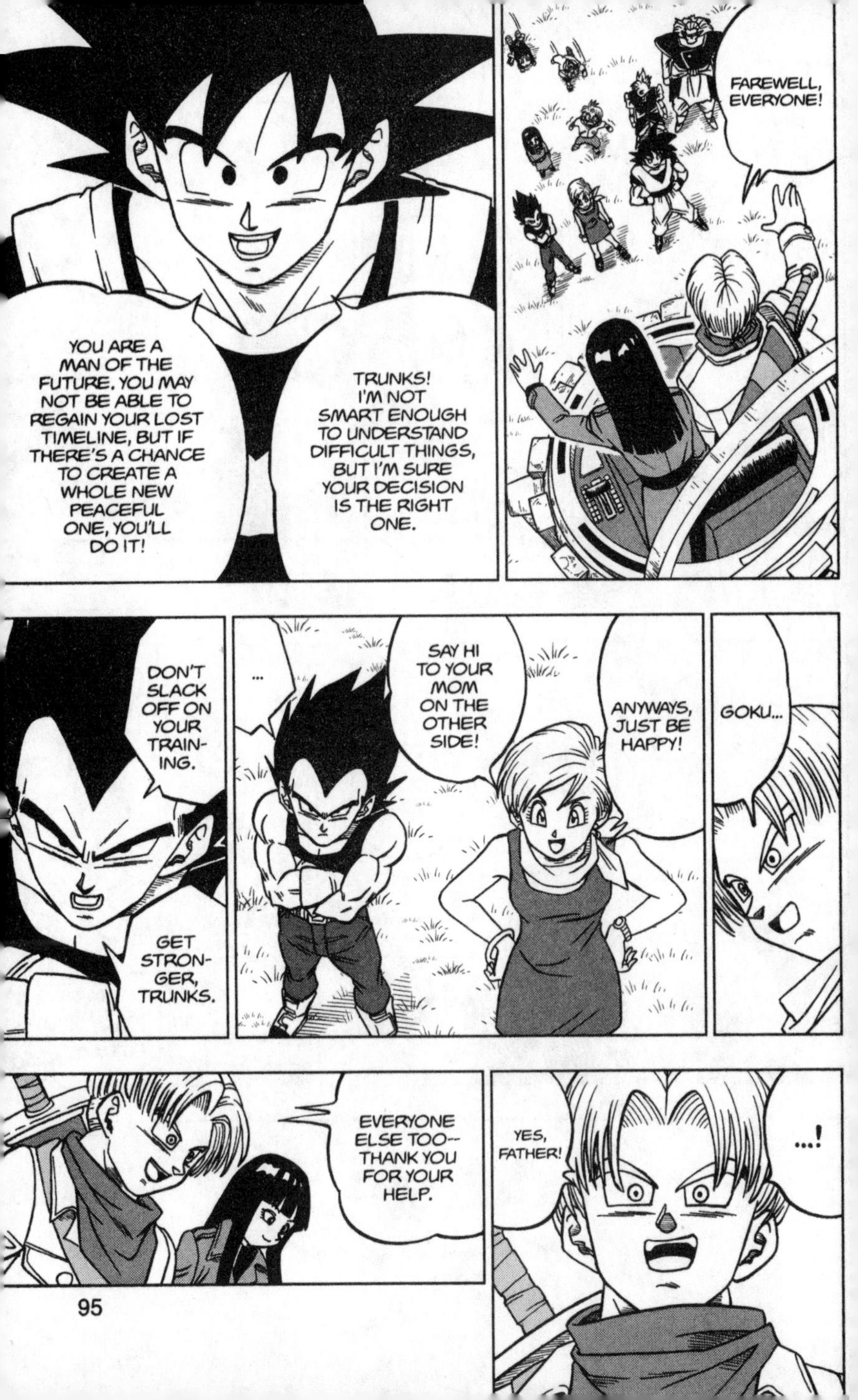
FAREWELL, EVERYONE!
TRUNKS! I'M NOT SMART ENOUGH TO UNDERSTAND DIFFICULT THINGS, BUT I'M SURE YOUR DECISION IS THE RIGHT ONE.
YOU ARE A MAN OF THE FUTURE. YOU MAY NOT BE ABLE TO REGAIN YOUR LOST TIMELINE, BUT IF THERE'S A CHANCE TO CREATE A WHOLE NEW PEACEFUL ONE, YOU'LL DO IT!
GOKU...
SAY HI TO YOUR MOM ON THE OTHER SIDE!
ANYWAYS, JUST BE HAPPY!
...
DON'T SLACK OFF ON YOUR TRAIN-ING.
GET STRON-GER, TRUNKS.
...!
YES, FATHER!
EVERYONE ELSE TOO-- THANK YOU FOR YOUR HELP.

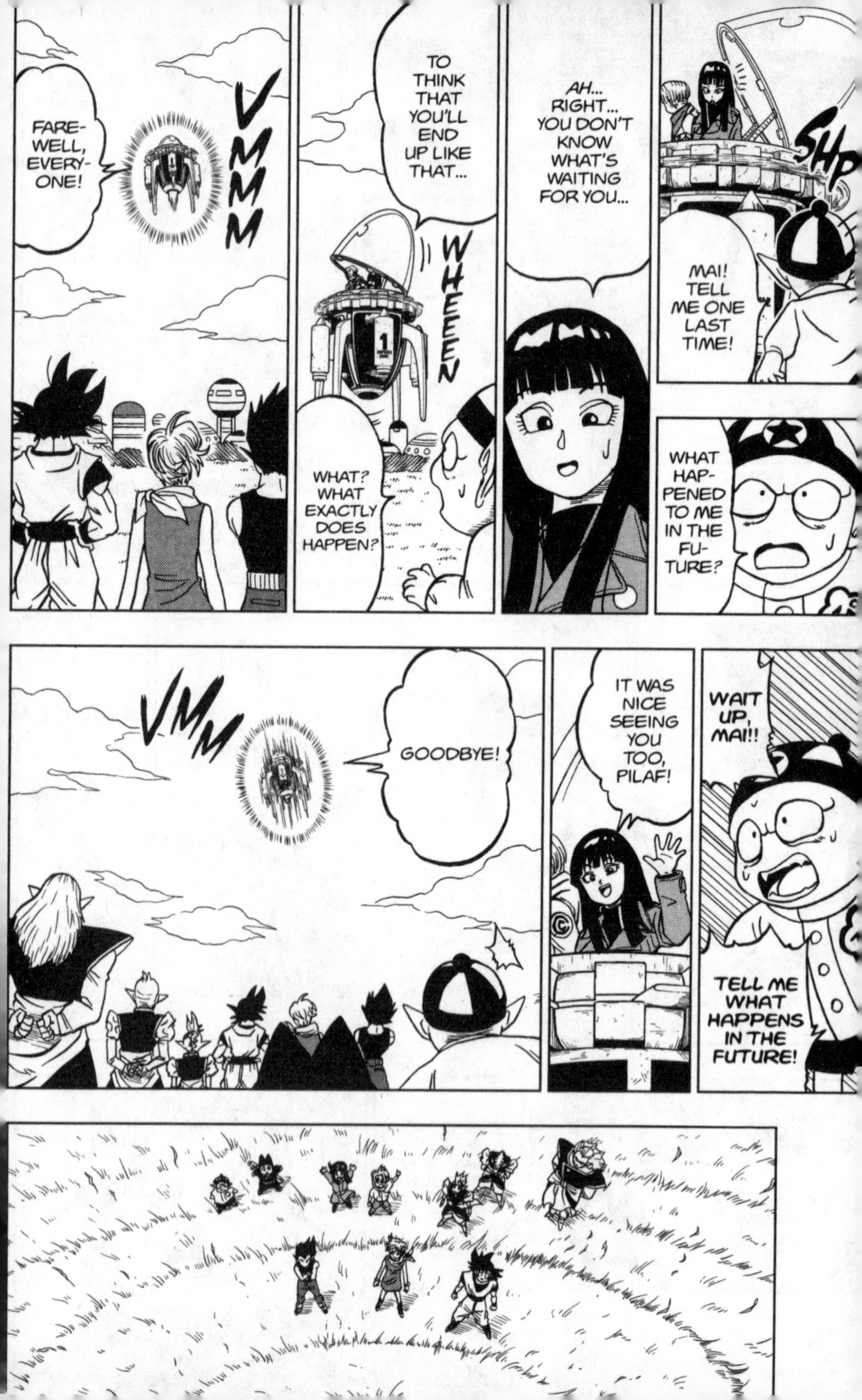
SHP
MAI! TELL ME ONE LAST TIME!
WHAT HAPPENED TO ME IN THE FUTURE?
AH... RIGHT... YOU DON'T KNOW WHAT'S WAITING FOR YOU...
TO THINK THAT YOU'LL END UP LIKE THAT...
WHEEEN
WHAT? WHAT EXACTLY DOES HAPPEN?
FAREWELL, EVERYONE!
VMMM
WAIT UP, MAI!!
TELL ME WHAT HAPPENS IN THE FUTURE!
IT WAS NICE SEEING YOU TOO, PILAF!
GOODBYE!
VMM

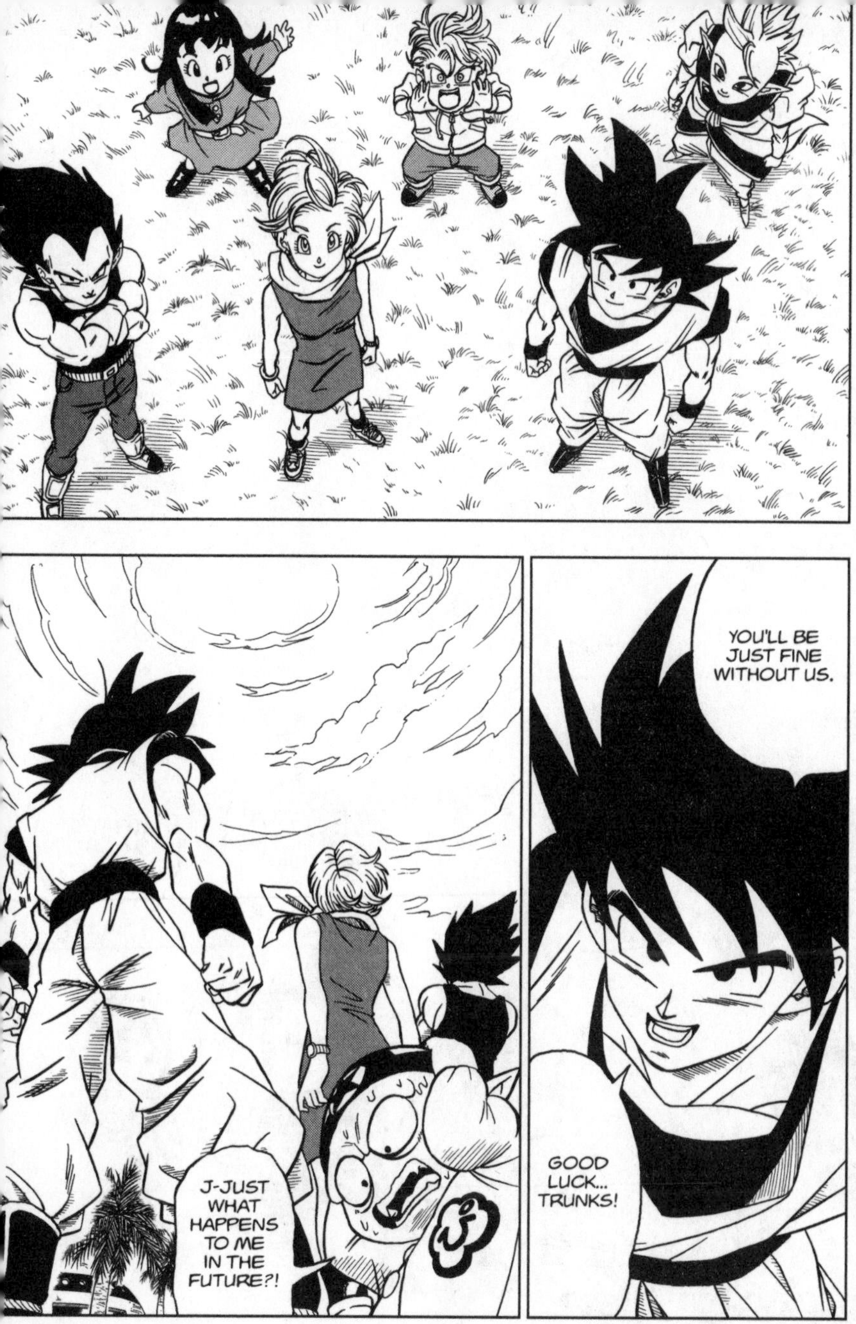
YOU'LL BE JUST FINE WITHOUT US.
GOOD LUCK... TRUNKS!
J-JUST WHAT HAPPENS TO ME IN THE FUTURE?!

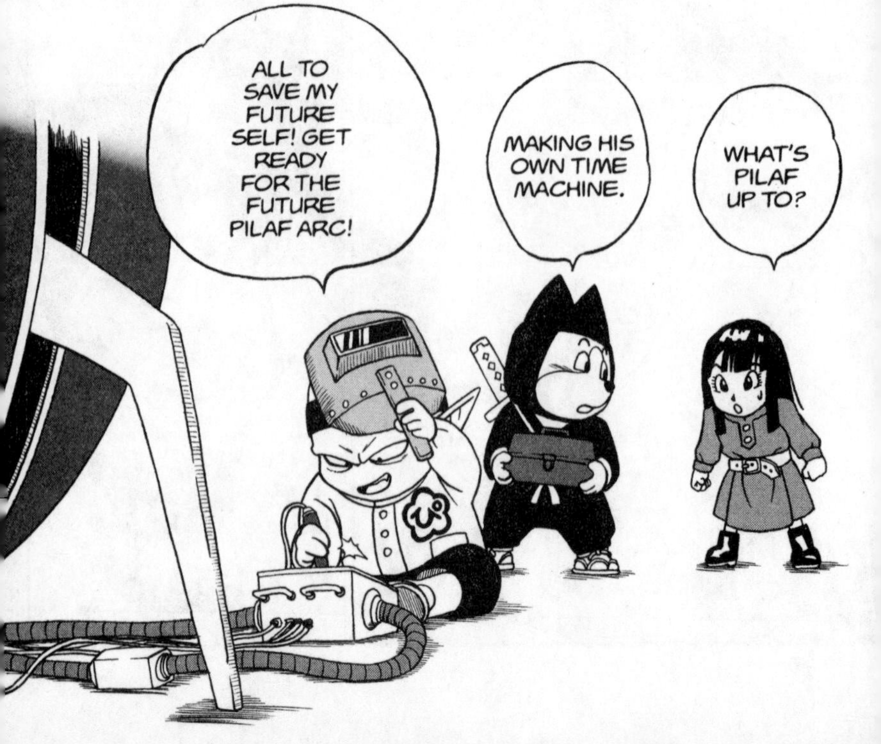
WHAT'S PILAF UP TO?
MAKING HIS OWN TIME MACHINE.
ALL TO SAVE MY FUTURE SELF! GET READY FOR THE FUTURE PILAF ARC!

DRAGON BALL SUPER

CHAPTER 27: LIFE, TRAINING AND MORE

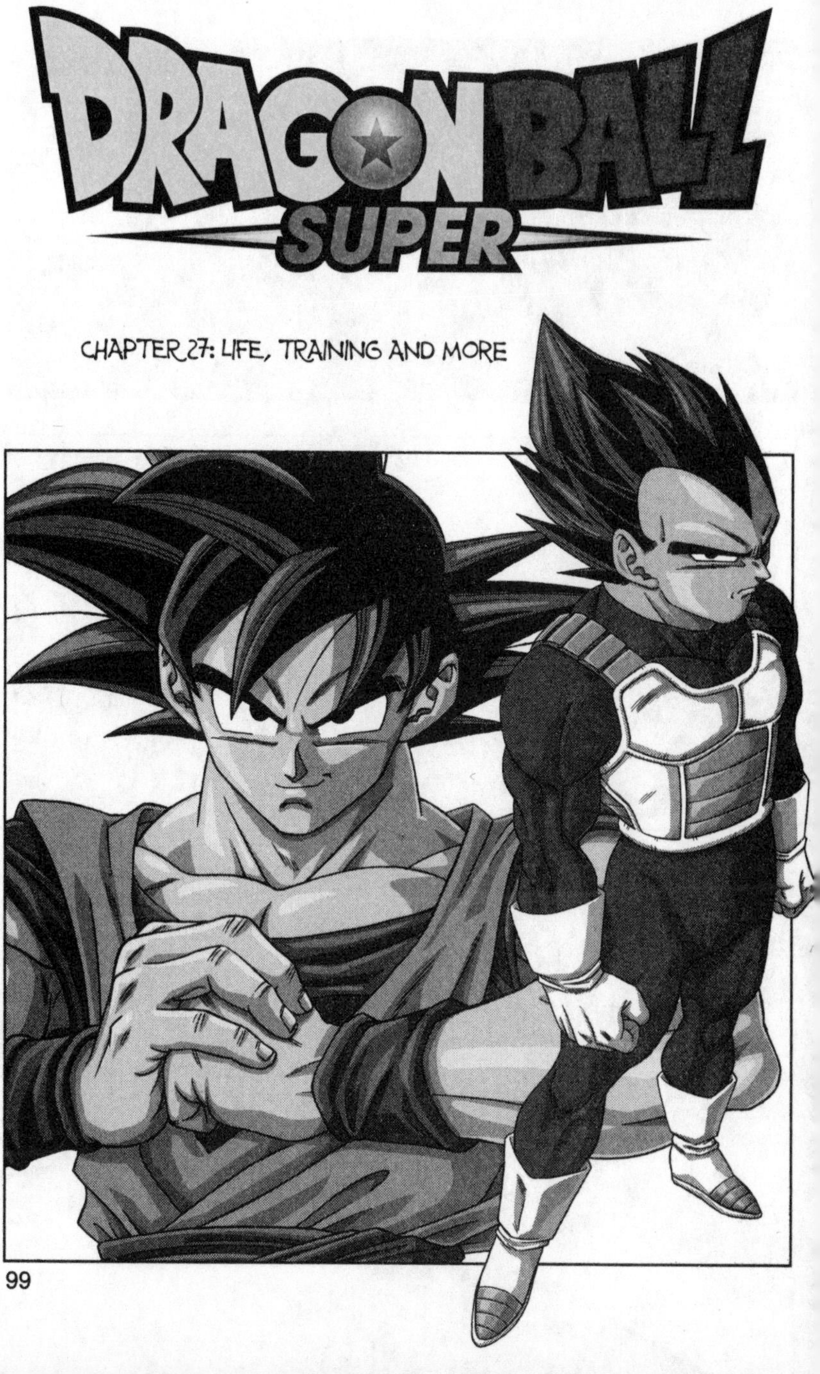

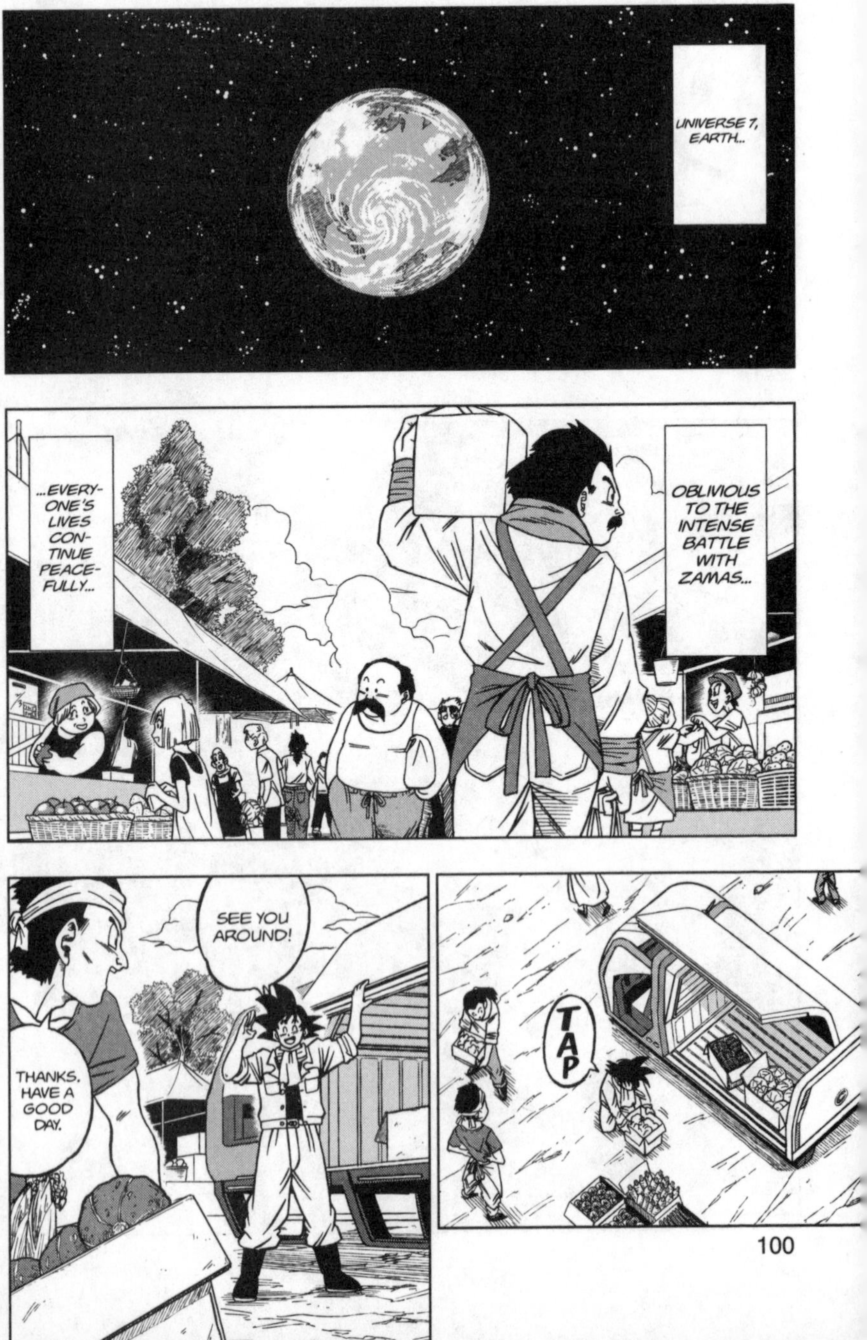
UNIVERSE 7, EARTH...
OBLIVIOUS TO THE INTENSE BATTLE WITH ZAMAS...
...EVERY-ONE'S LIVES CON-TINUE PEACE-FULLY...
TAP
SEE YOU AROUND!
THANKS. HAVE A GOOD DAY.

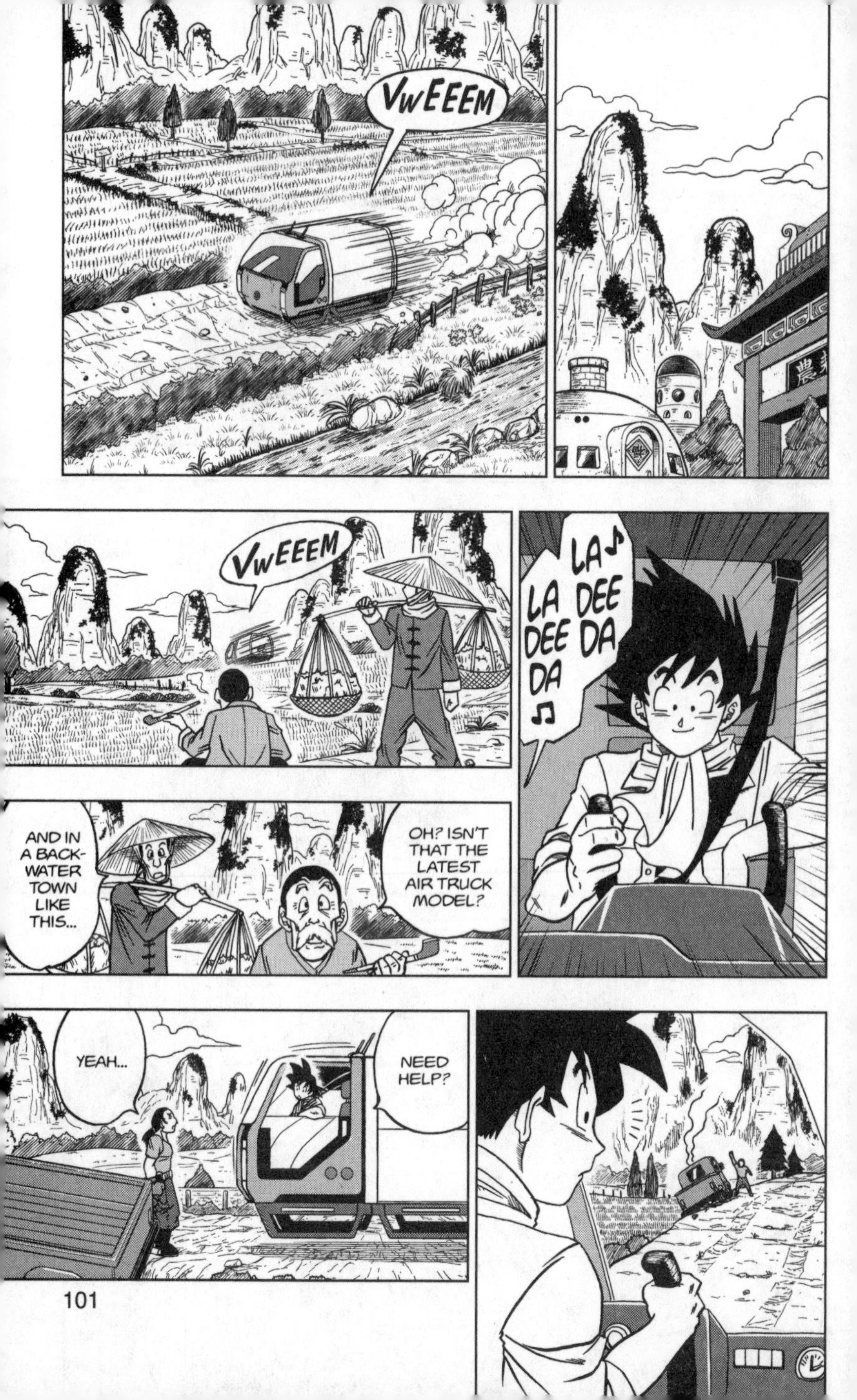

VWEEEM
LA♪ DEE DA LA DEE DA ♫
VWEEEM
OH? ISN'T THAT THE LATEST AIR TRUCK MODEL?
AND IN A BACK-WATER TOWN LIKE THIS...
NEED HELP?
YEAH...

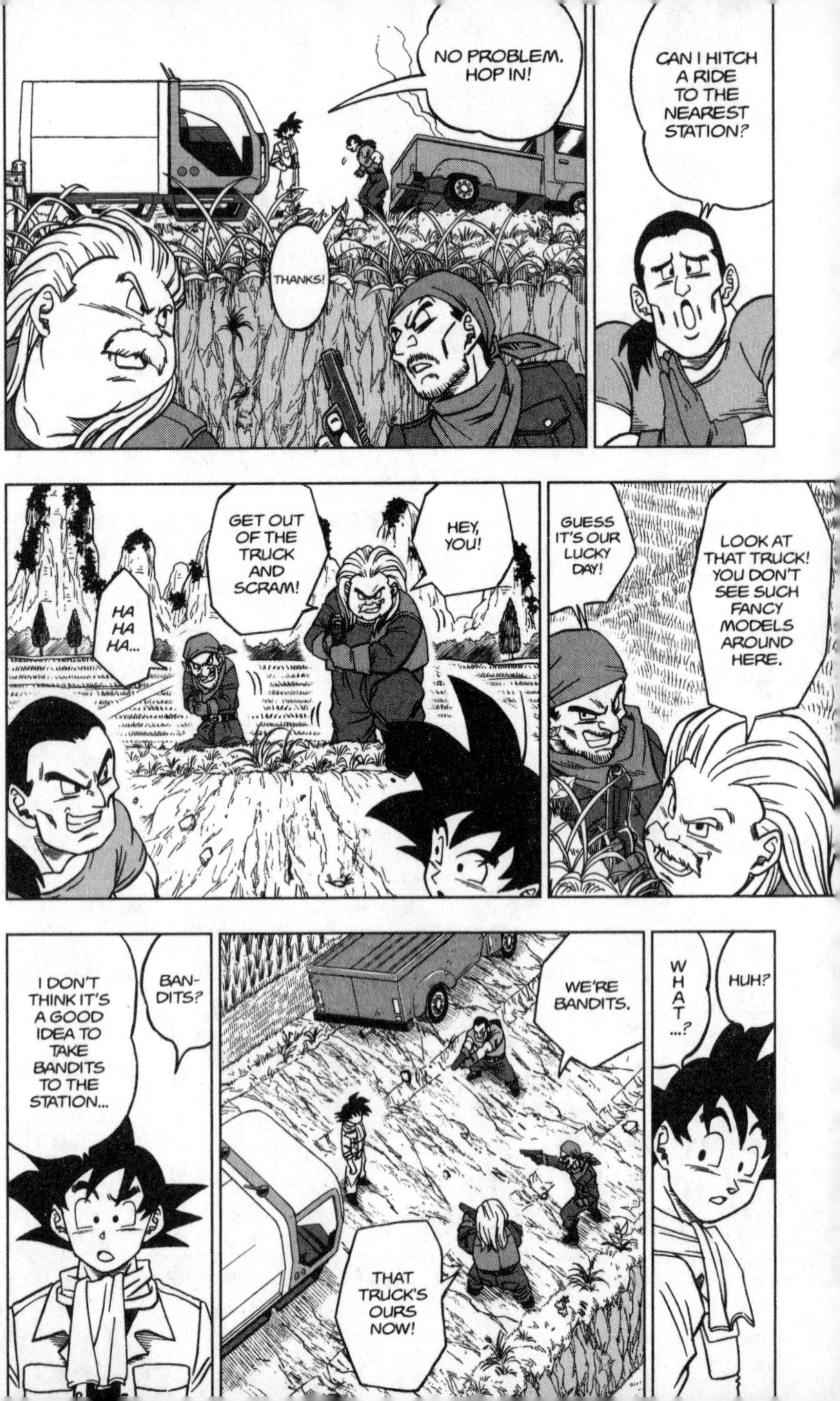
CAN I HITCH A RIDE TO THE NEAREST STATION?
NO PROBLEM. HOP IN!
THANKS!
LOOK AT THAT TRUCK! YOU DON'T SEE SUCH FANCY MODELS AROUND HERE.
GUESS IT'S OUR LUCKY DAY!
HEY, YOU!
GET OUT OF THE TRUCK AND SCRAM!
HA HA HA...
HUH?
WHAT...?
WE'RE BANDITS.
THAT TRUCK'S OURS NOW!
BAN-DITS?
I DON'T THINK IT'S A GOOD IDEA TO TAKE BANDITS TO THE STATION...

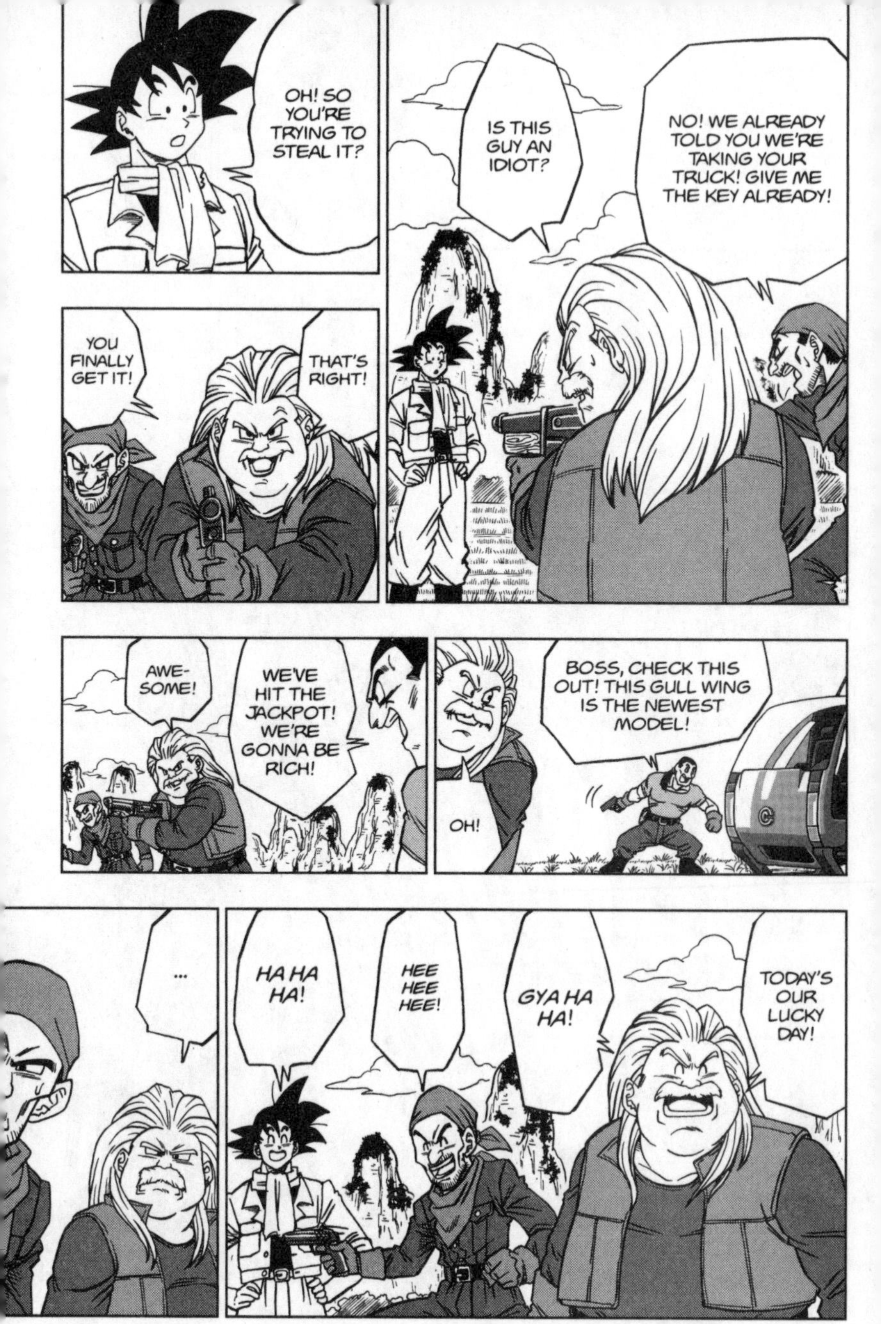
NO! WE ALREADY TOLD YOU WE'RE TAKING YOUR TRUCK! GIVE ME THE KEY ALREADY!
IS THIS GUY AN IDIOT?
OH! SO YOU'RE TRYING TO STEAL IT?
THAT'S RIGHT!
YOU FINALLY GET IT!
BOSS, CHECK THIS OUT! THIS GULL WING IS THE NEWEST MODEL!
OH!
WE'VE HIT THE JACKPOT! WE'RE GONNA BE RICH!
AWE-SOME!
TODAY'S OUR LUCKY DAY!
GYA HA HA!
HEE HEE HEE!
HA HA HA!
...

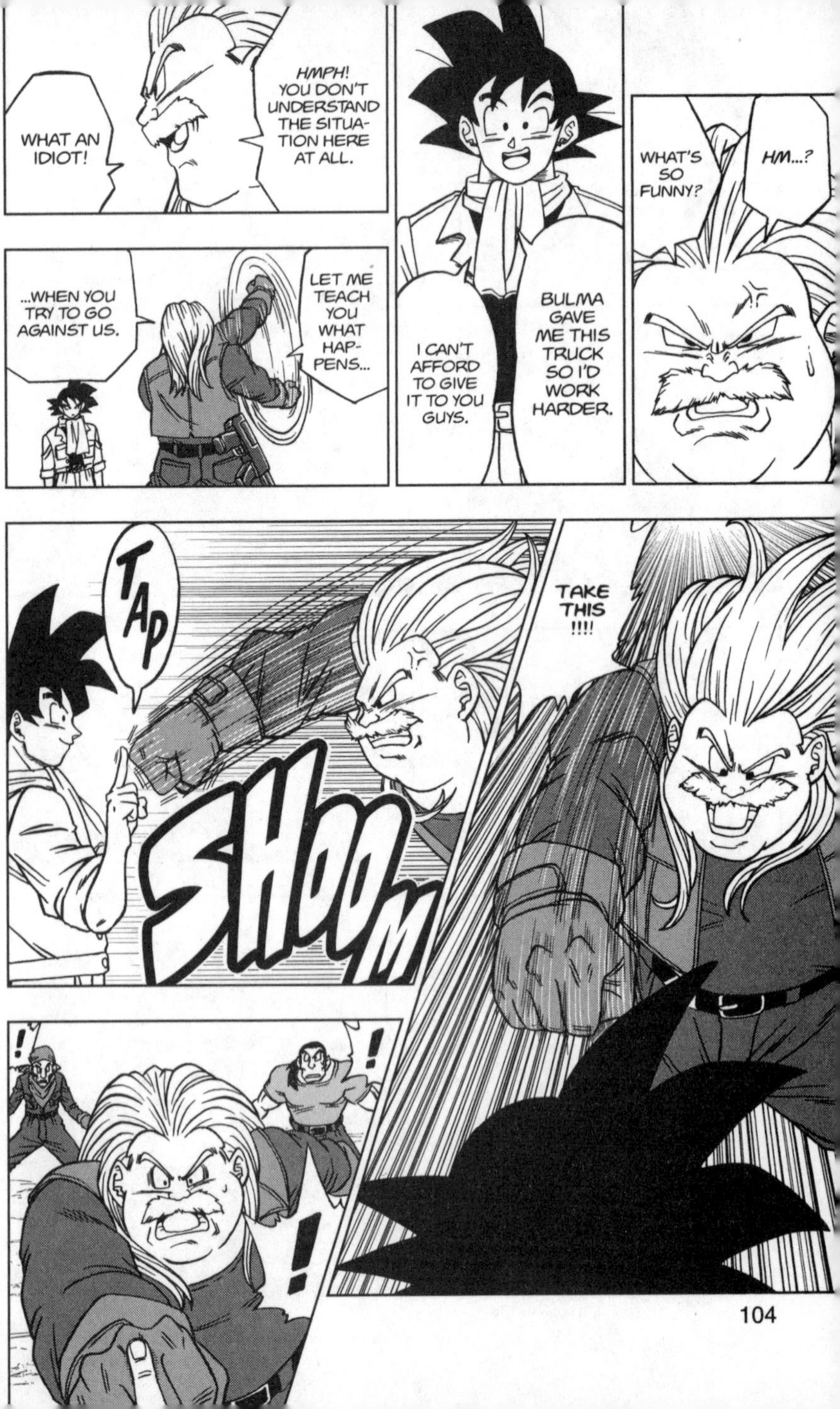
HM...?
WHAT'S SO FUNNY?
BULMA GAVE ME THIS TRUCK SO I'D WORK HARDER.
I CAN'T AFFORD TO GIVE IT TO YOU GUYS.
HMPH! YOU DON'T UNDERSTAND THE SITUATION HERE AT ALL.
WHAT AN IDIOT!
LET ME TEACH YOU WHAT HAPPENS...
...WHEN YOU TRY TO GO AGAINST US.
TAKE THIS!!!!
TAP
SHOOM
!
!
!

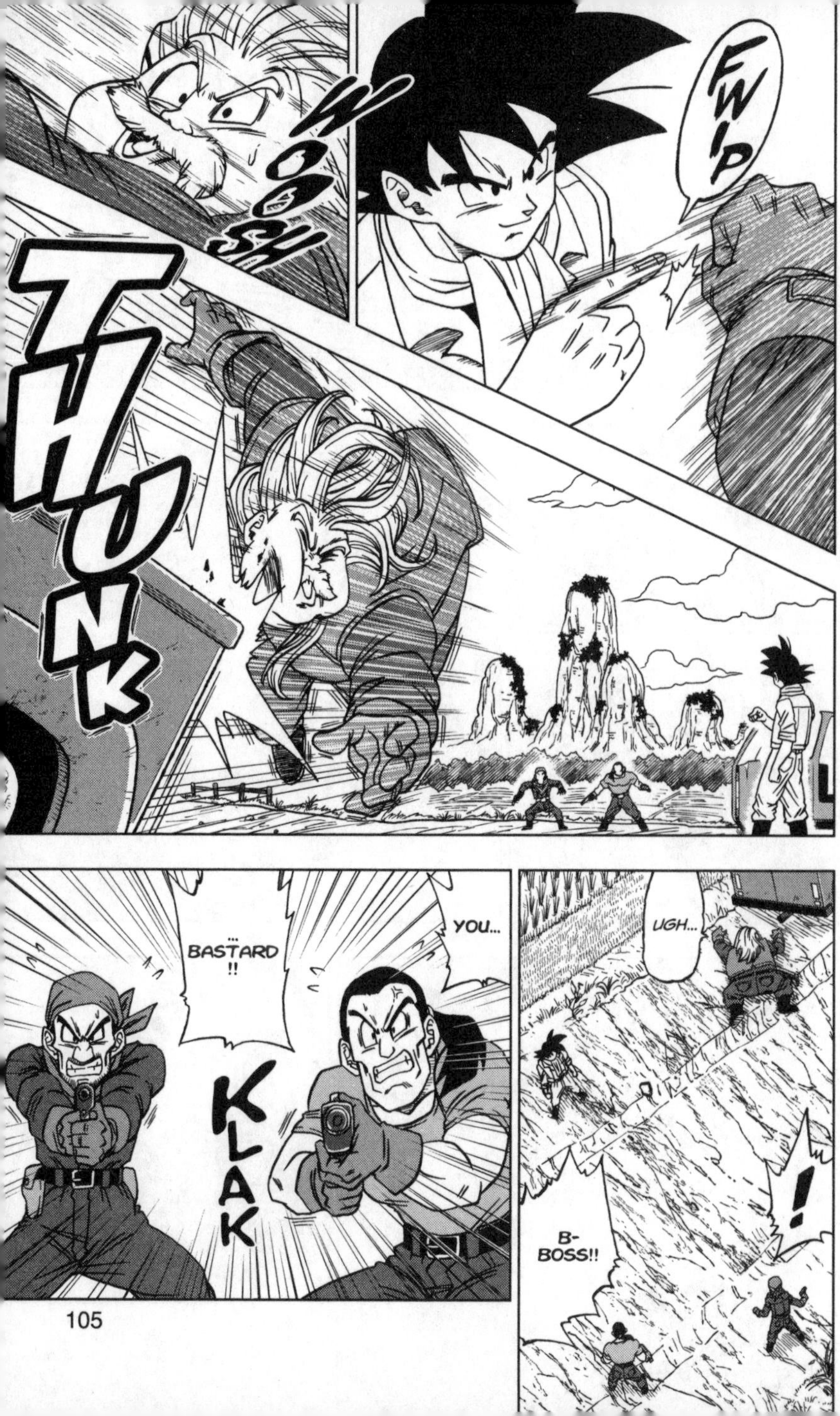
FWIP
WOOSH
THUNK
UGH...
!
B-BOSS!!
YOU...
... BASTARD !!
KLAK

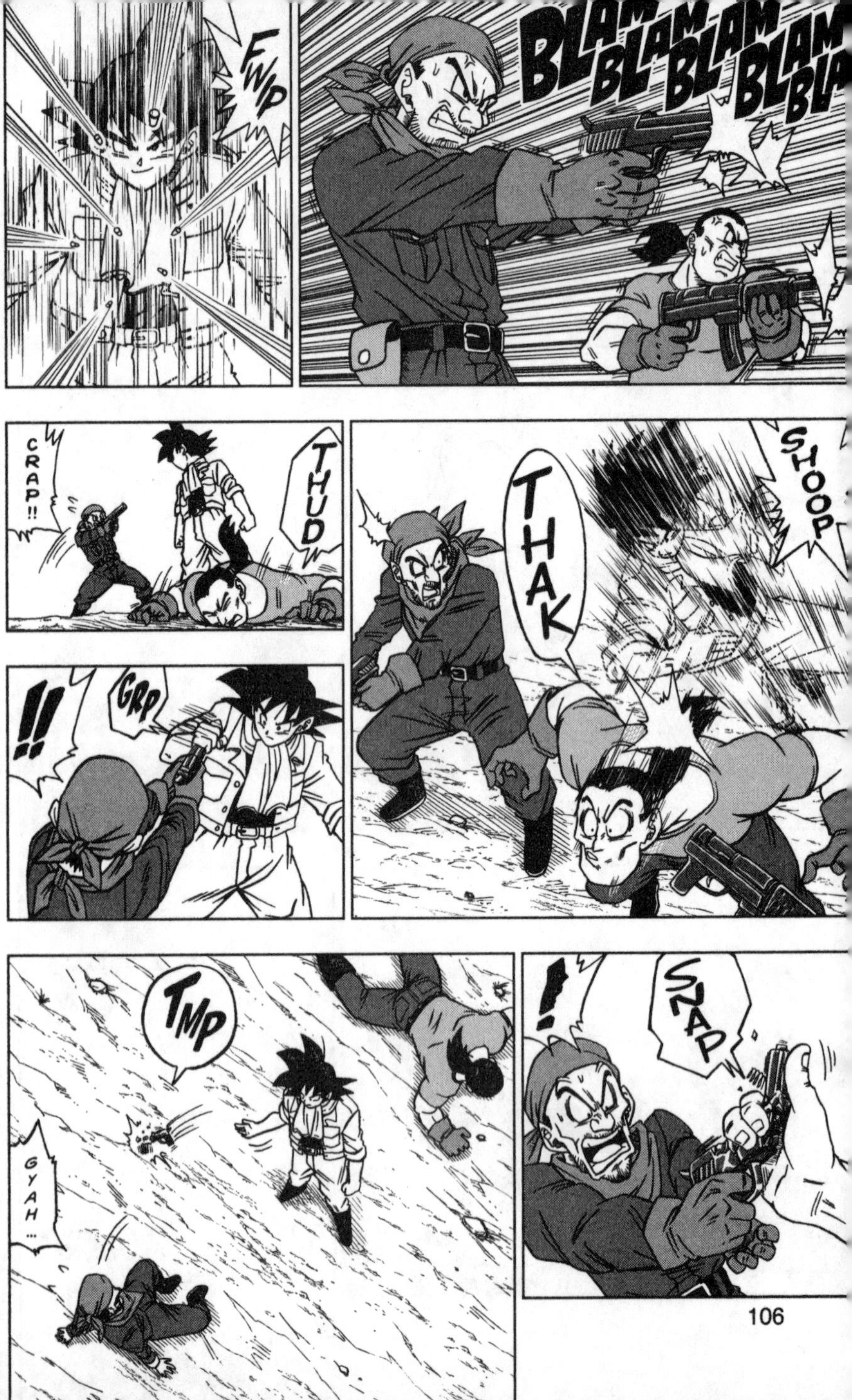
BLAM BLAM BLAM BLAM BLAM BLA
FWIP
SHOOP
THAK
THUD
CRAP!!
GRP
!!
SNAP
!
TMP
GYAH...

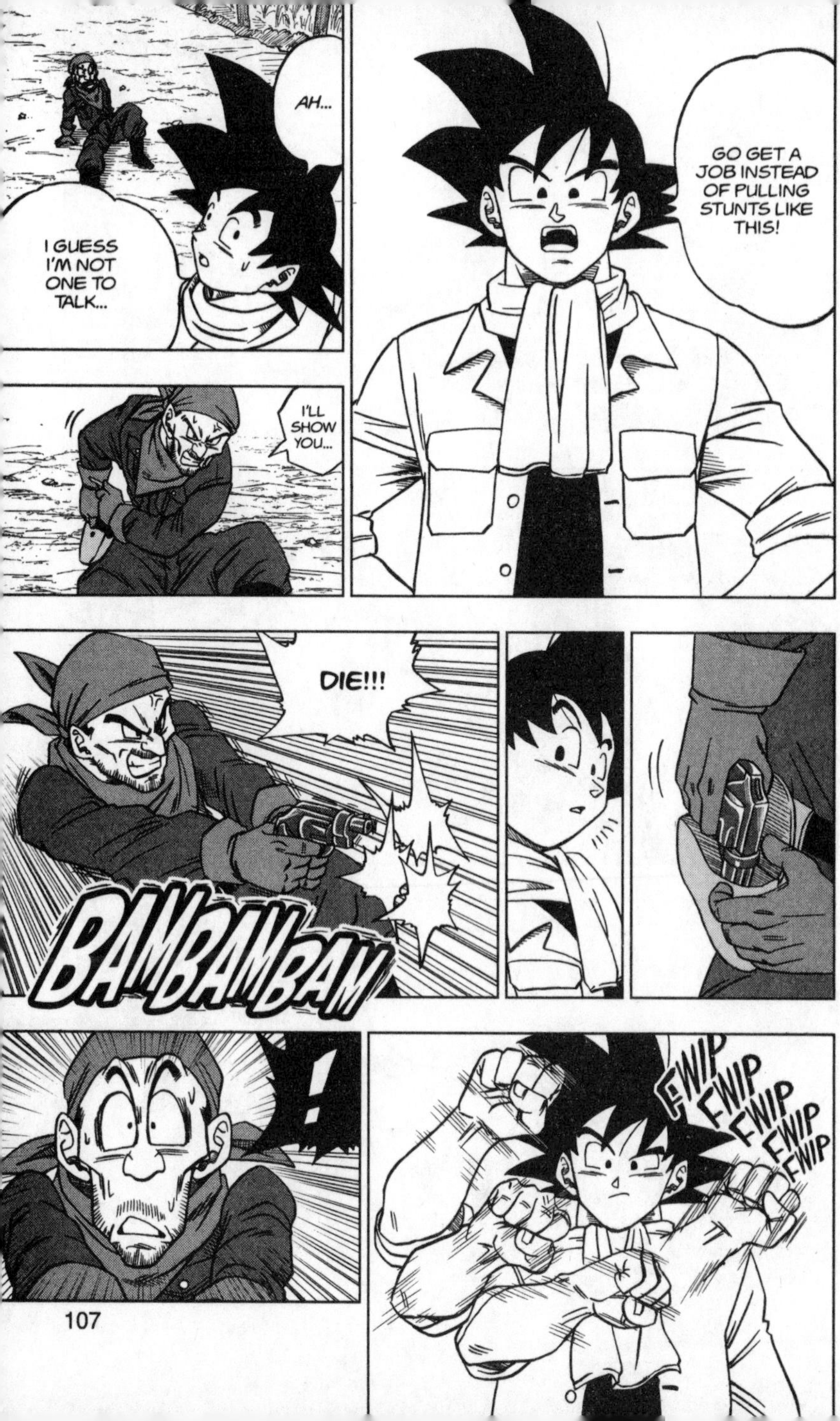
GO GET A JOB INSTEAD OF PULLING STUNTS LIKE THIS!
AH...
I GUESS I'M NOT ONE TO TALK...
I'LL SHOW YOU...
DIE!!!
BAMBAMBAM
FWIP FWIP FWIP FWIP FWIP
!

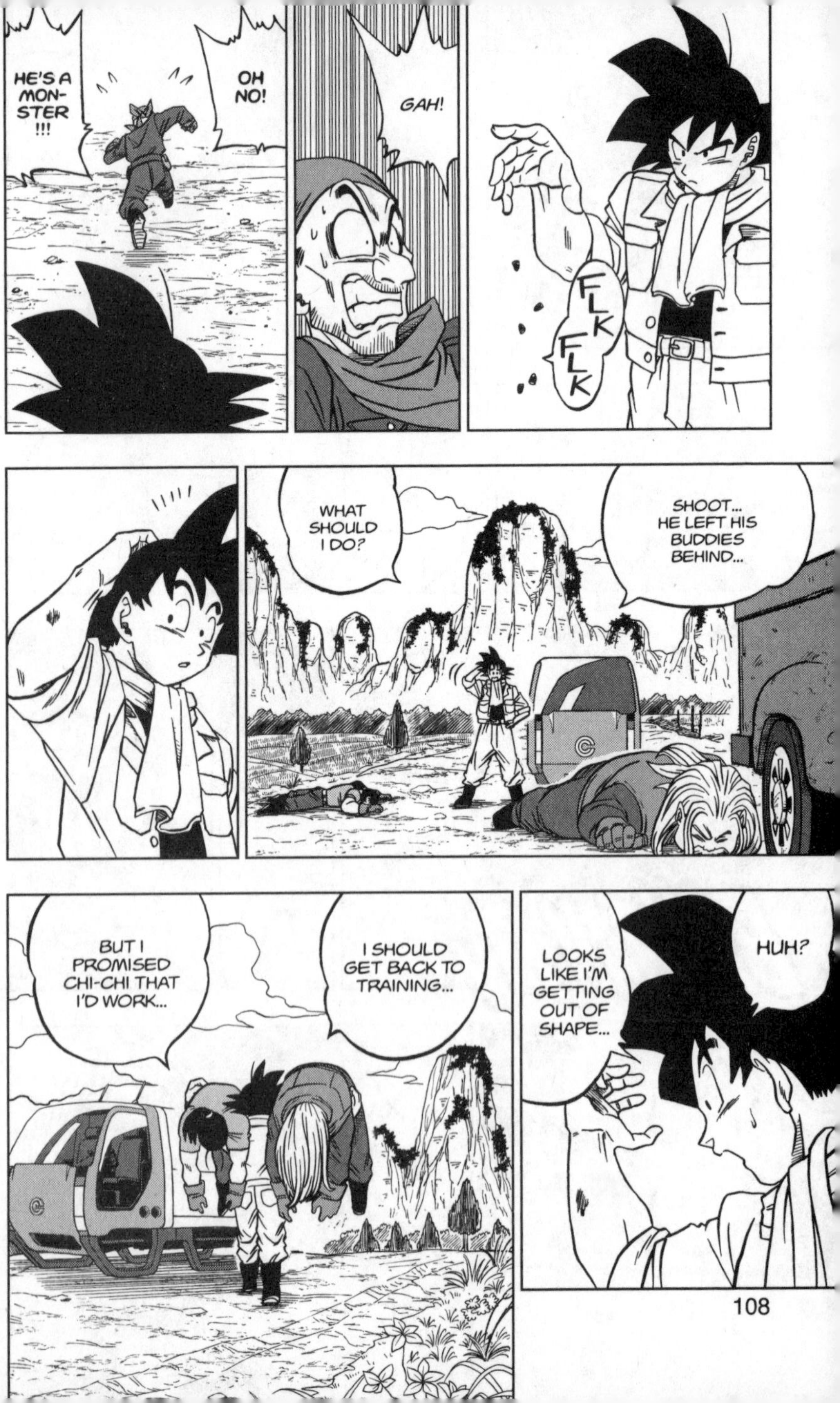
FLK
FLK
GAH!
OH NO!
HE'S A MONSTER!!!
SHOOT... HE LEFT HIS BUDDIES BEHIND...
WHAT SHOULD I DO?
HUH?
LOOKS LIKE I'M GETTING OUT OF SHAPE...
I SHOULD GET BACK TO TRAINING...
BUT I PROMISED CHI-CHI THAT I'D WORK...

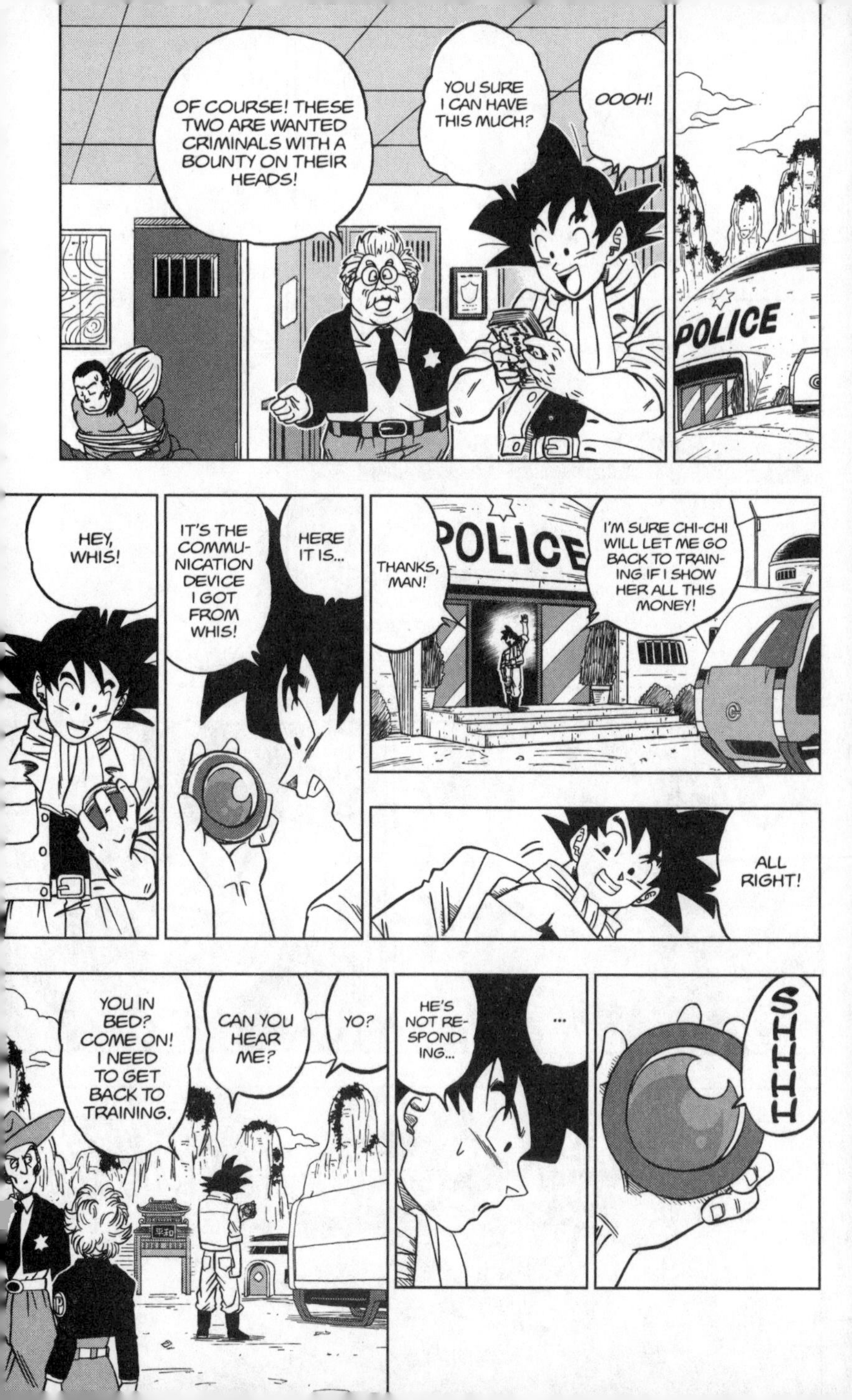
OOOH!
YOU SURE I CAN HAVE THIS MUCH?
OF COURSE! THESE TWO ARE WANTED CRIMINALS WITH A BOUNTY ON THEIR HEADS!
POLICE
I'M SURE CHI-CHI WILL LET ME GO BACK TO TRAIN-ING IF I SHOW HER ALL THIS MONEY!
POLICE
THANKS, MAN!
ALL RIGHT!
HERE IT IS...
IT'S THE COMMU-NICATION DEVICE I GOT FROM WHIS!
HEY, WHIS!
SHHHH
...
HE'S NOT RE-SPOND-ING...
YO?
CAN YOU HEAR ME?
YOU IN BED? COME ON! I NEED TO GET BACK TO TRAINING.

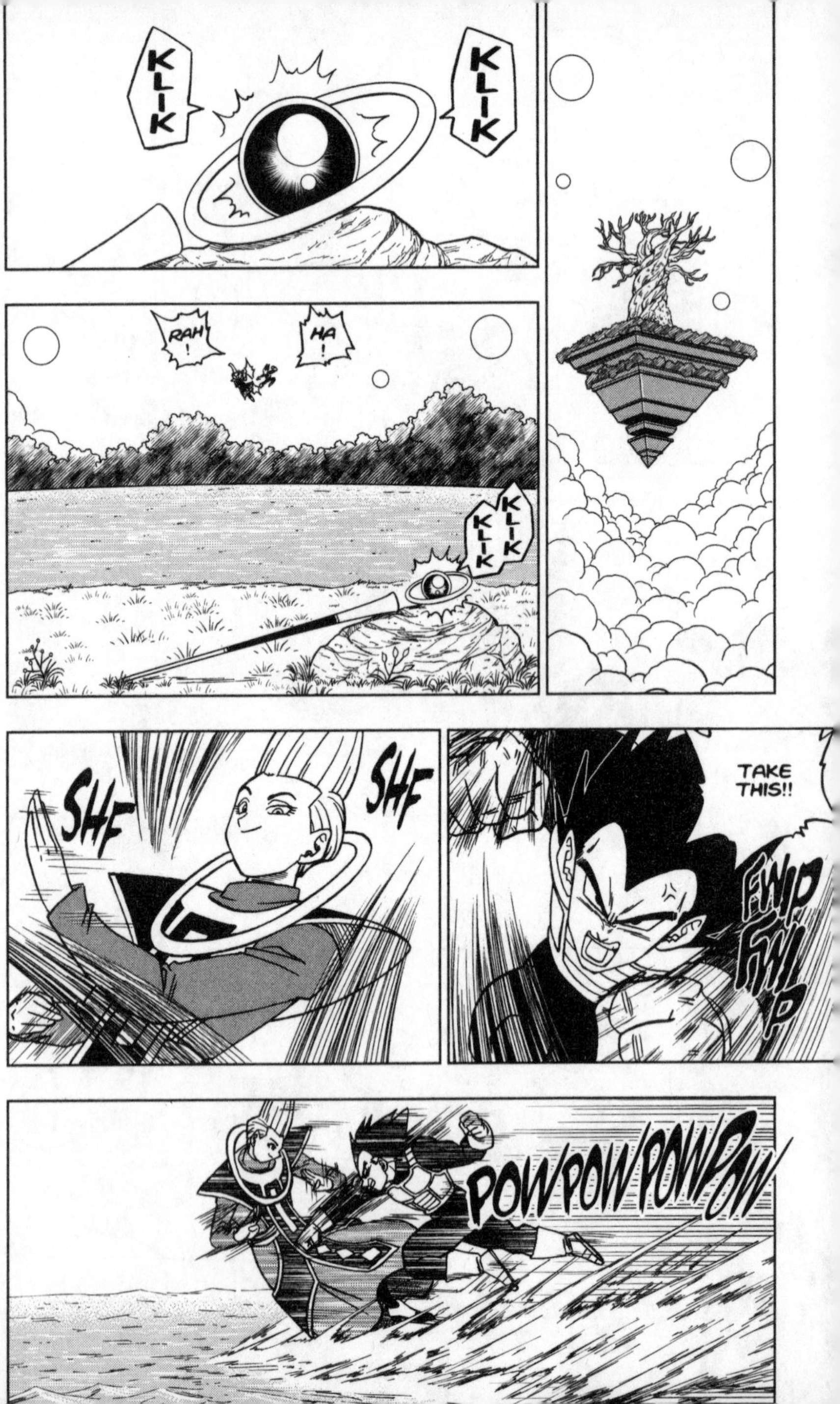
KLIK
KLIK
RAH!
HA!
KLIK
KLIK
TAKE THIS!!
FWIP
FWIP
SHF
SHF
POW POW POW POW

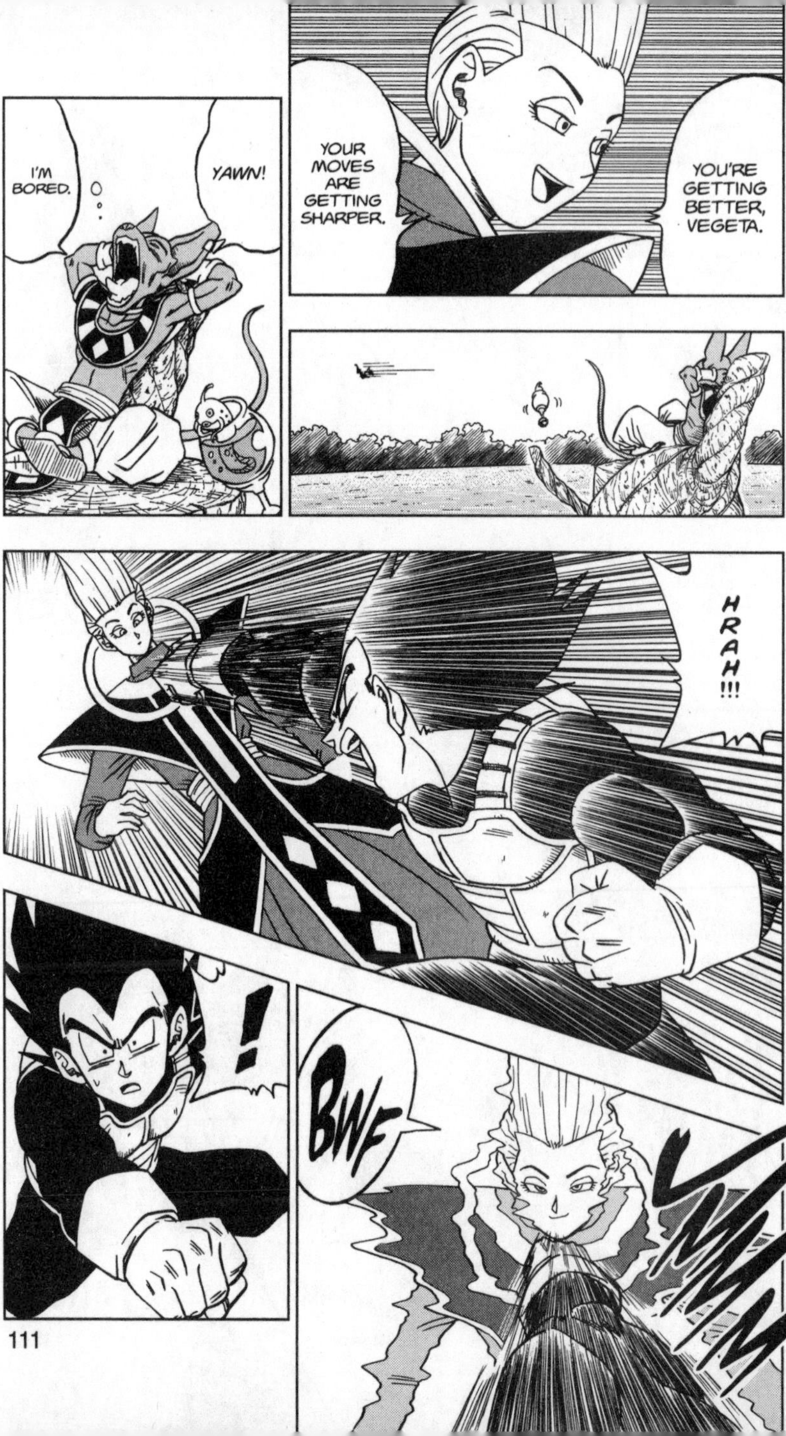
YOU'RE GETTING BETTER, VEGETA.
YOUR MOVES ARE GETTING SHARPER.
YAWN!
I'M BORED.
HRAH!!!
BWF
!

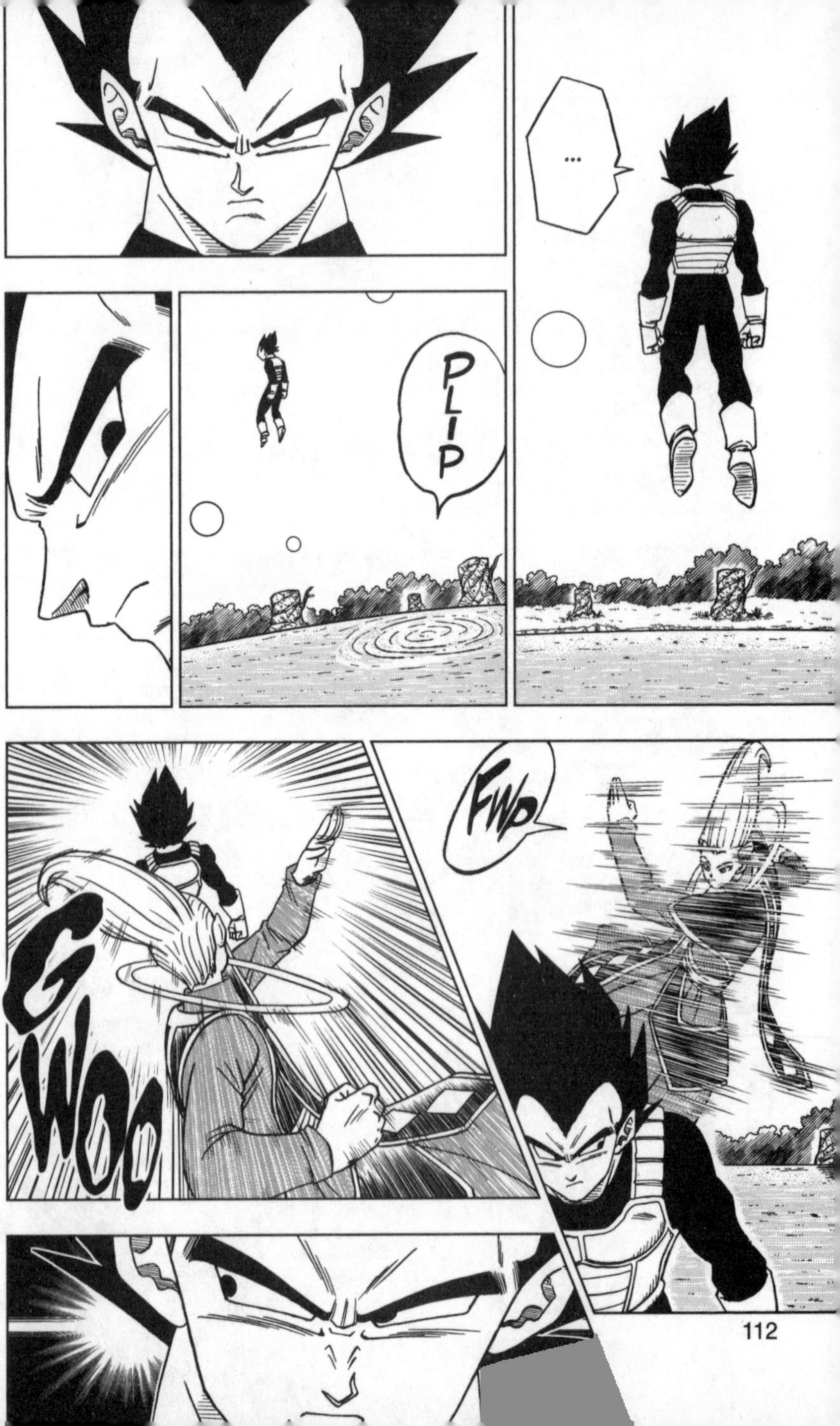
...
PLIP
FWP
GWOO

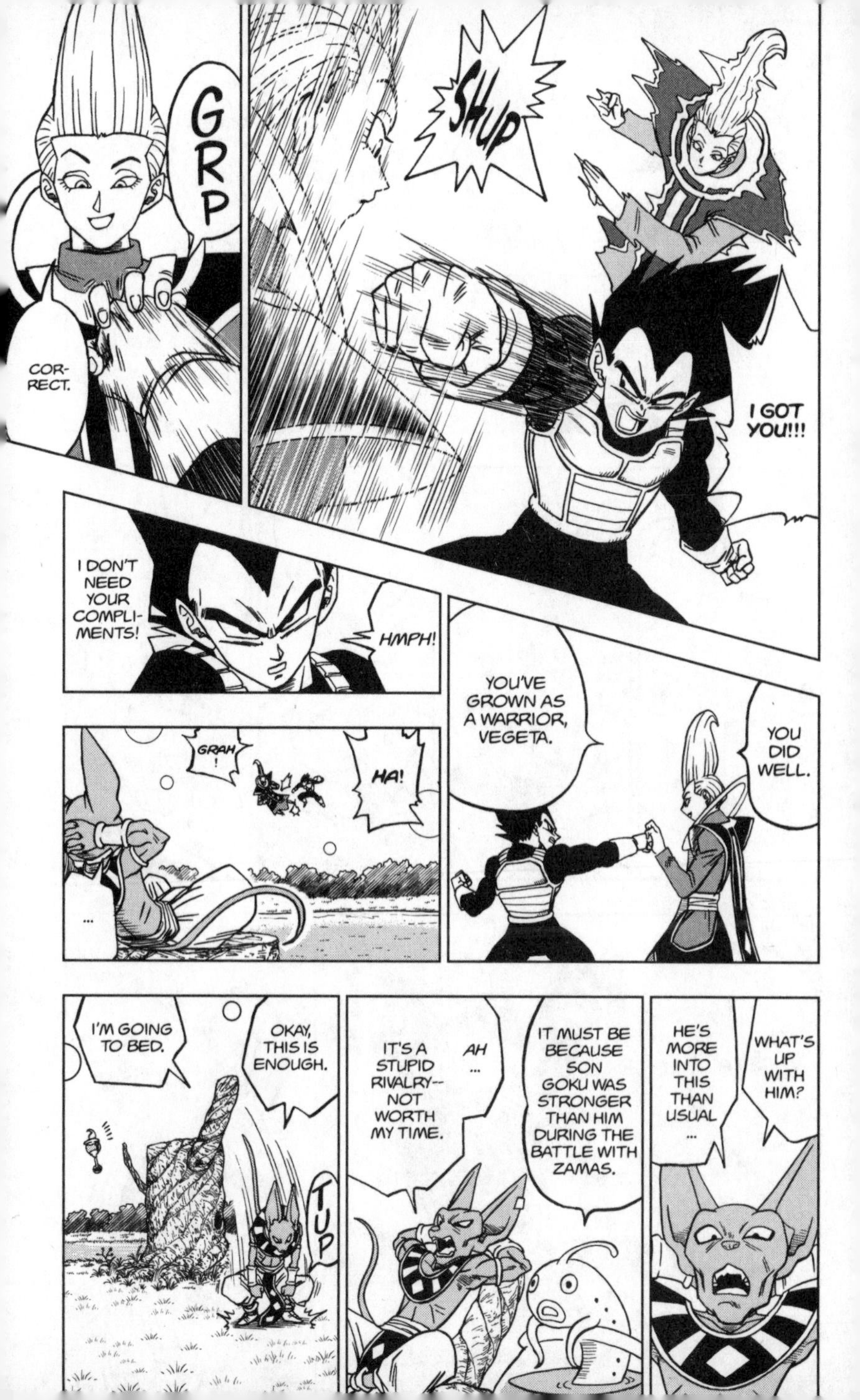
SHUP
I GOT YOU!!!
GRP
COR-RECT.
HMPH!
I DON'T NEED YOUR COMPLI-MENTS!
YOU DID WELL.
YOU'VE GROWN AS A WARRIOR, VEGETA.
HA!
GRAH!
...
WHAT'S UP WITH HIM?
HE'S MORE INTO THIS THAN USUAL...
IT MUST BE BECAUSE SON GOKU WAS STRONGER THAN HIM DURING THE BATTLE WITH ZAMAS.
AH...
IT'S A STUPID RIVALRY-- NOT WORTH MY TIME.
OKAY, THIS IS ENOUGH.
I'M GOING TO BED.
TUP

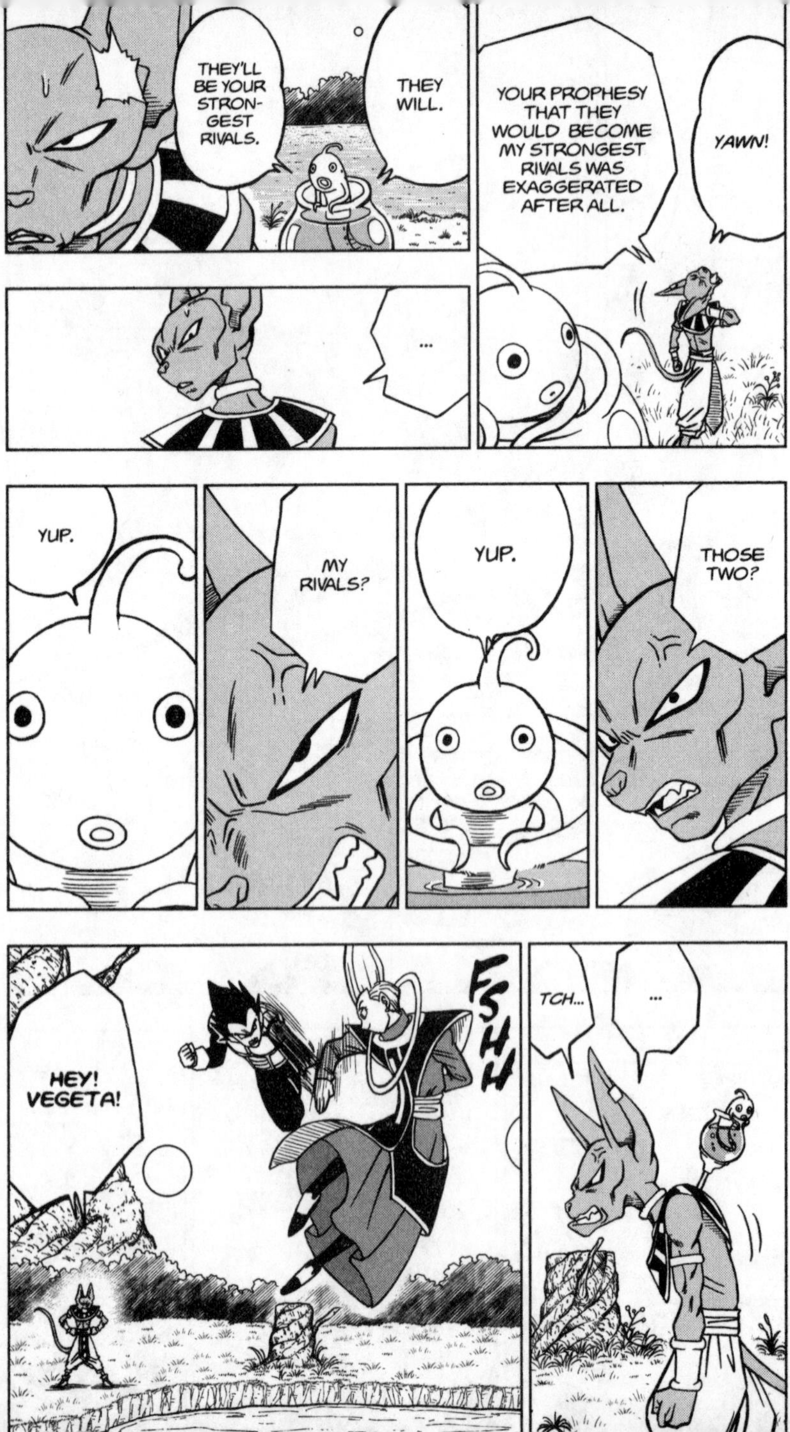
YOUR PROPHESY THAT THEY WOULD BECOME MY STRONGEST RIVALS WAS EXAGGERATED AFTER ALL.
YAWN!
THEY WILL.
THEY'LL BE YOUR STRONGEST RIVALS.
...
THOSE TWO?
YUP.
MY RIVALS?
YUP.
...
TCH...
FSHH
HEY! VEGETA!

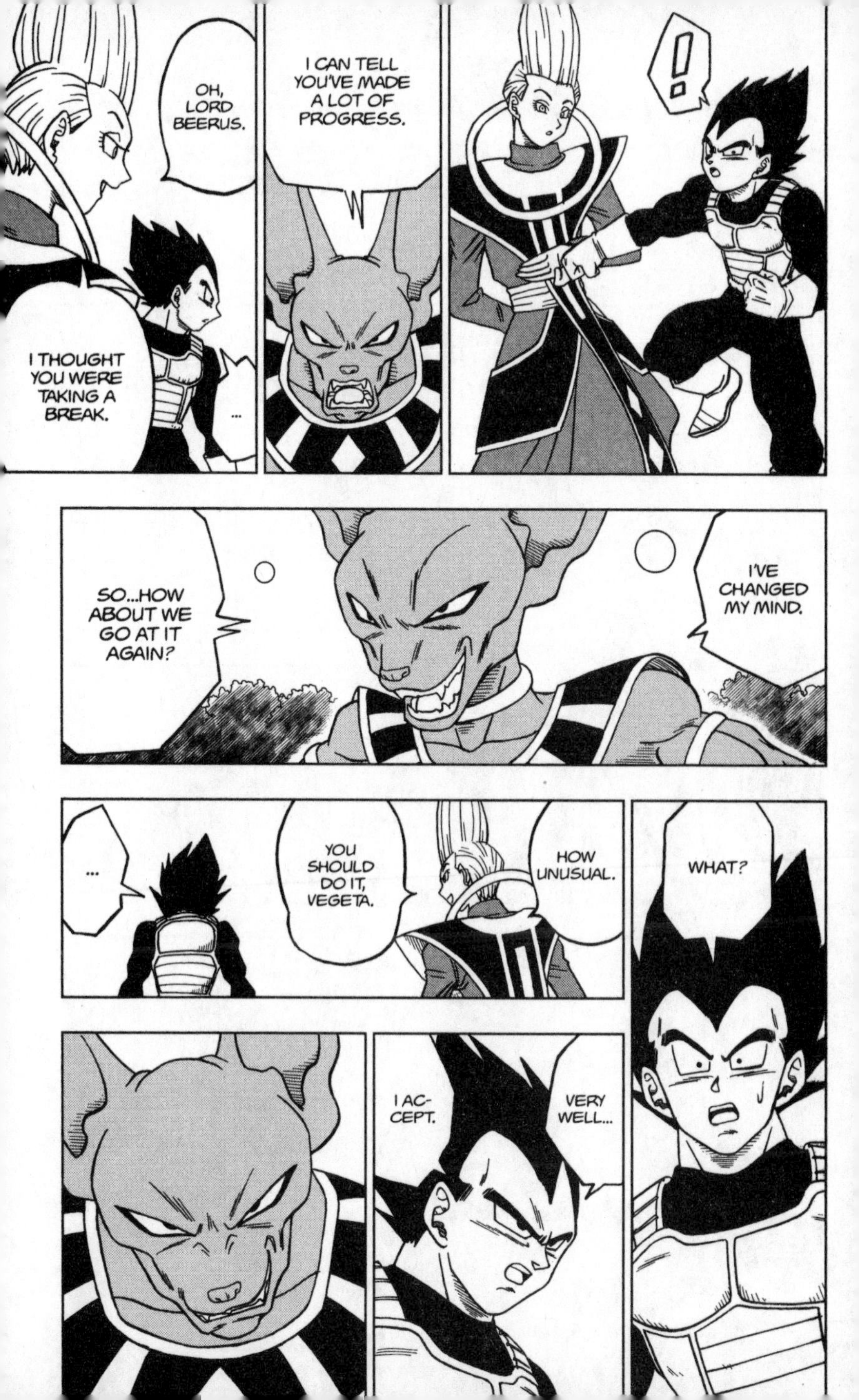
!
I CAN TELL YOU'VE MADE A LOT OF PROGRESS.
OH, LORD BEERUS.
I THOUGHT YOU WERE TAKING A BREAK.
...
I'VE CHANGED MY MIND.
SO...HOW ABOUT WE GO AT IT AGAIN?
WHAT?
HOW UNUSUAL.
YOU SHOULD DO IT, VEGETA.
...
VERY WELL...
I AC-CEPT.

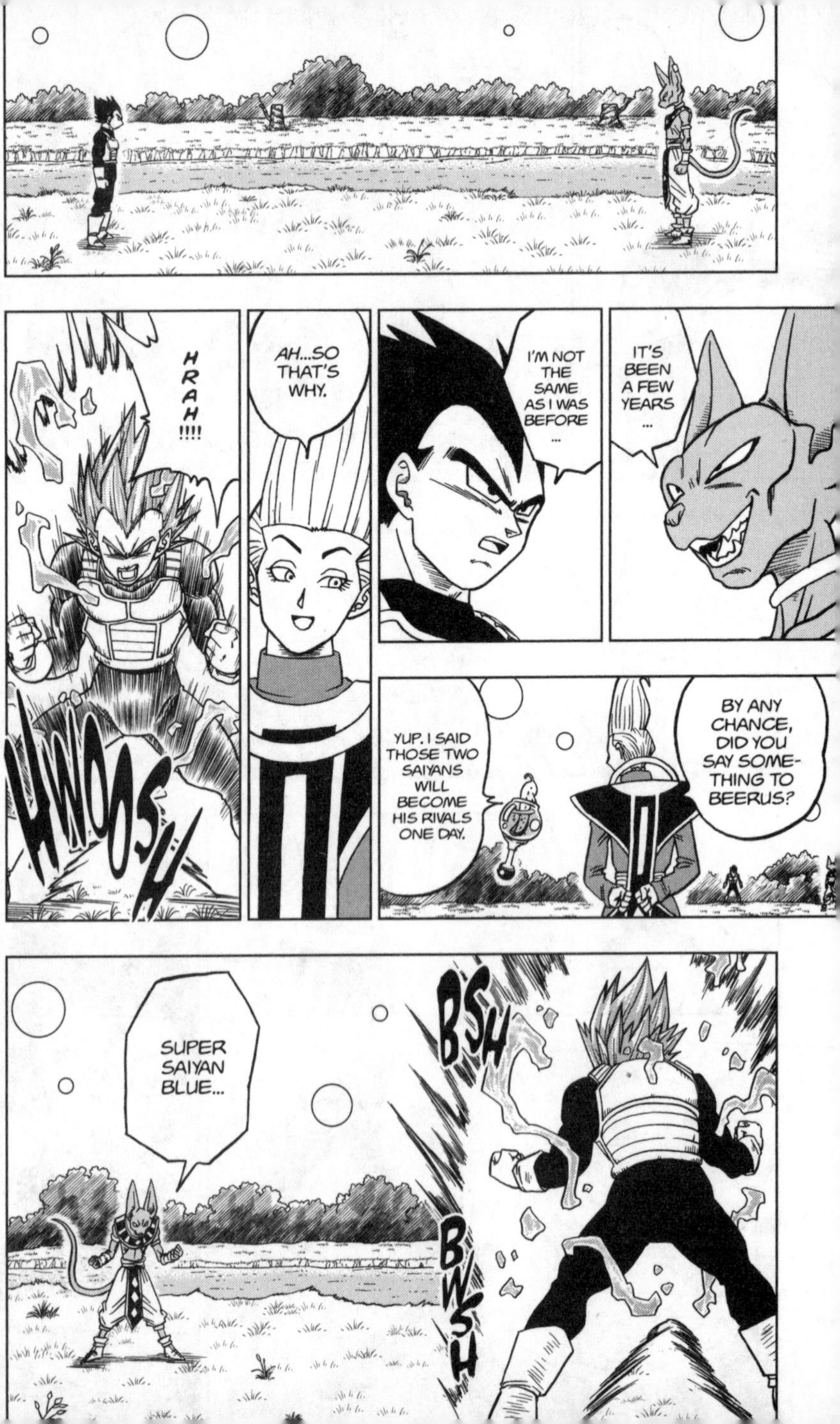
IT'S BEEN A FEW YEARS...
I'M NOT THE SAME AS I WAS BEFORE...
BY ANY CHANCE, DID YOU SAY SOME-THING TO BEERUS?
YUP. I SAID THOSE TWO SAIYANS WILL BECOME HIS RIVALS ONE DAY.
AH...SO THAT'S WHY.
HRAH!!!!
HWOOSH
BSH
SUPER SAIYAN BLUE...
BWSH

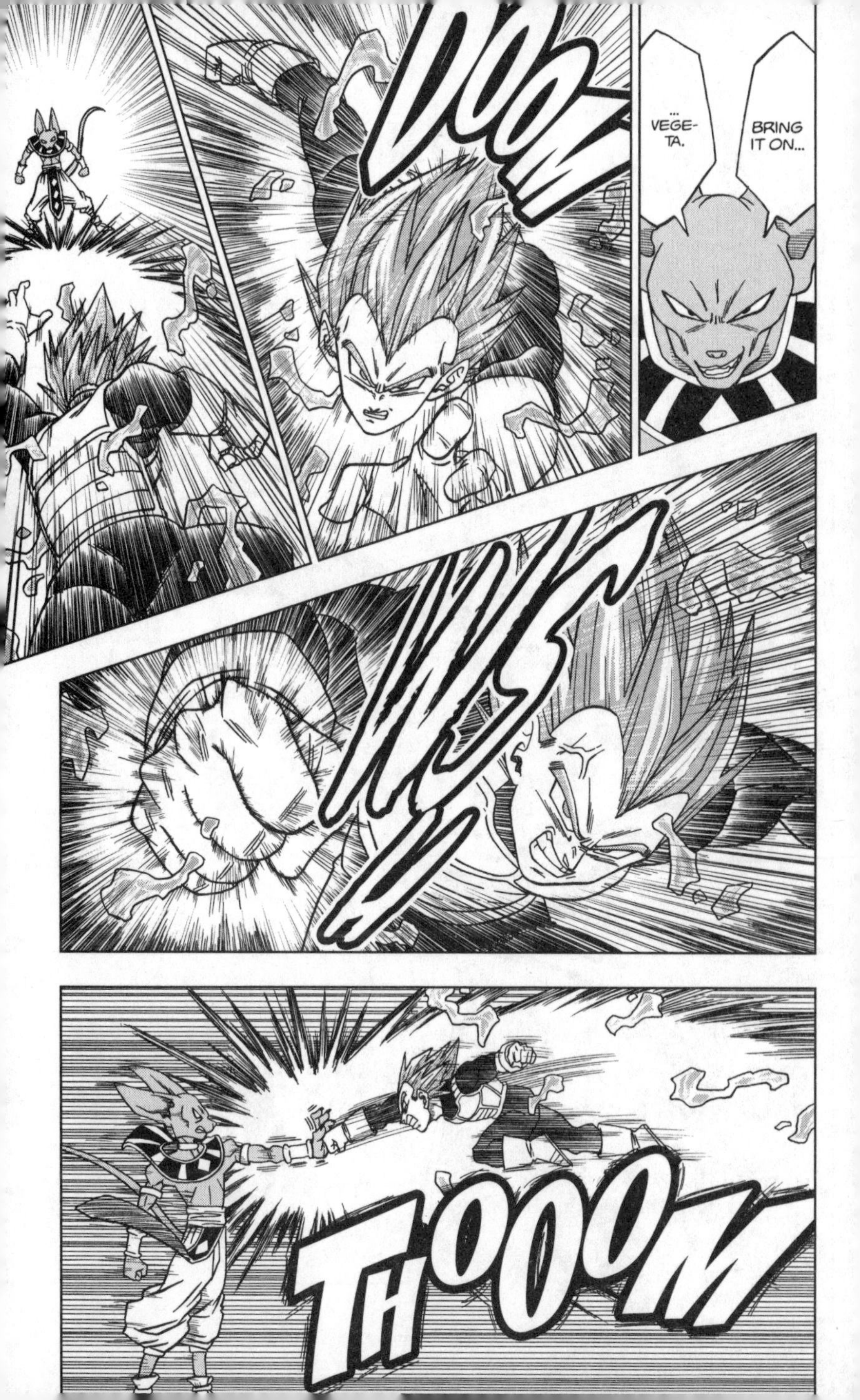
BRING IT ON...
... VEGE- TA.
THOOOM

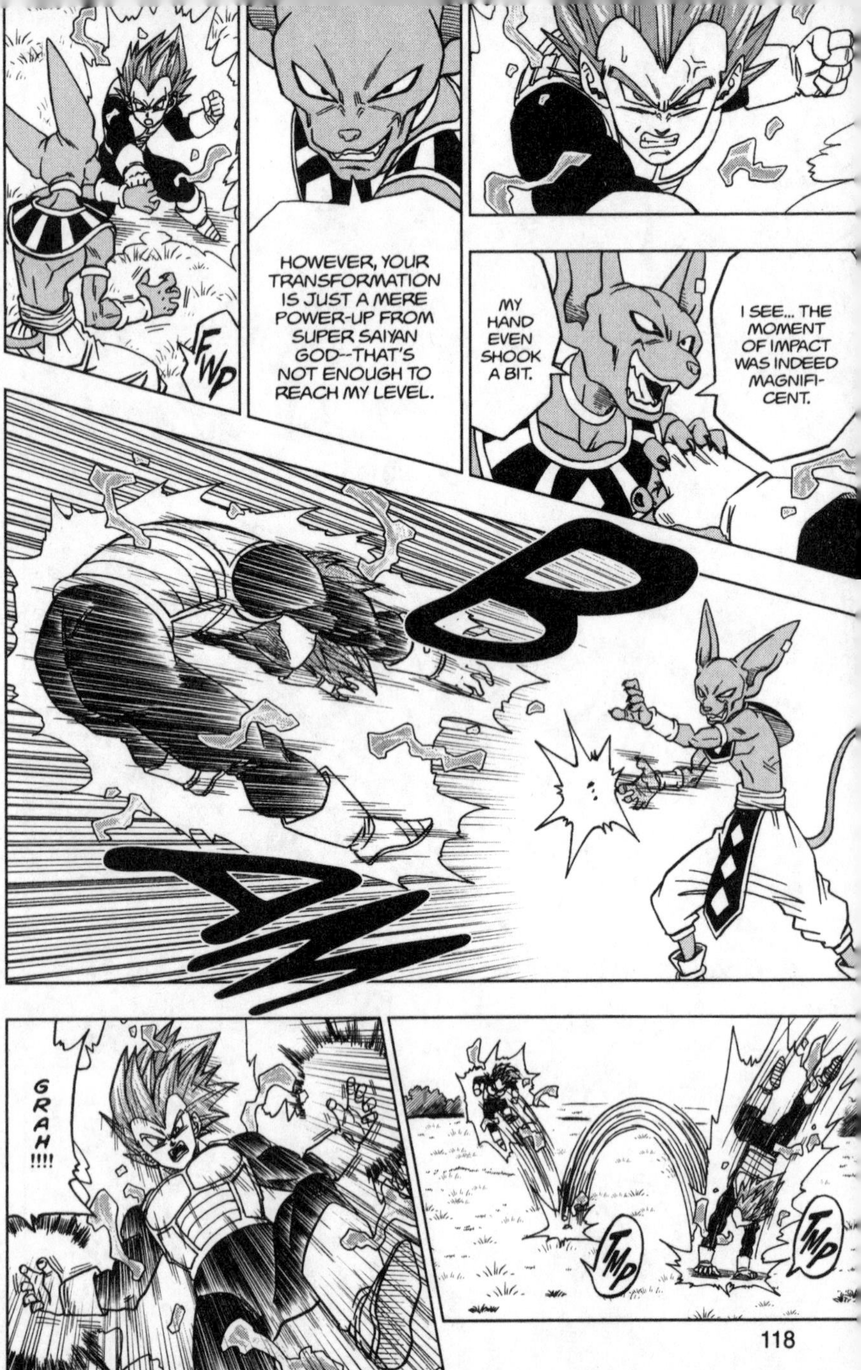
I SEE... THE MOMENT OF IMPACT WAS INDEED MAGNIFI-CENT.
MY HAND EVEN SHOOK A BIT.
HOWEVER, YOUR TRANSFORMATION IS JUST A MERE POWER-UP FROM SUPER SAIYAN GOD--THAT'S NOT ENOUGH TO REACH MY LEVEL.
FWP
BAM
TMP
TMP
GRAH!!!!

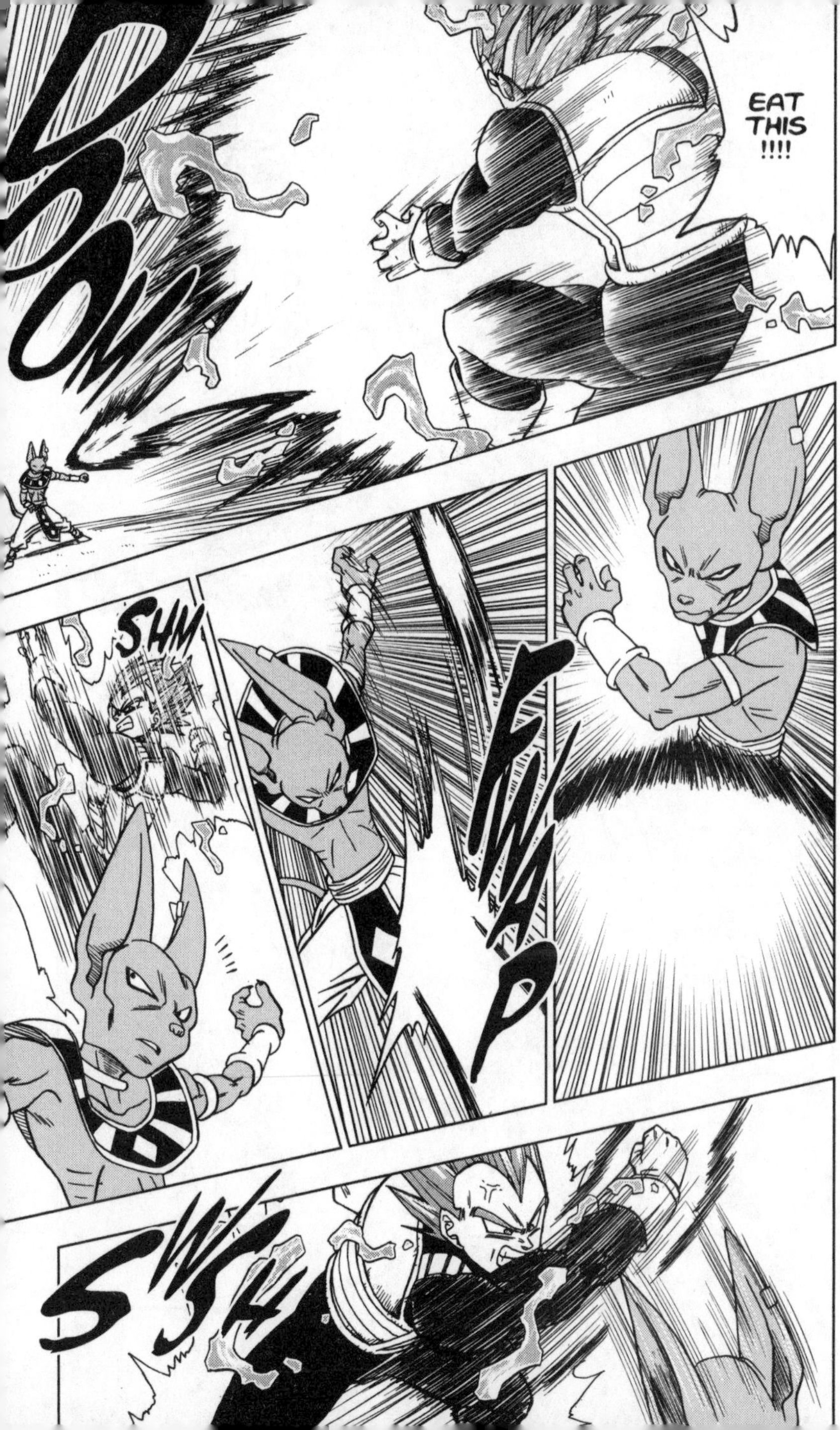
EAT THIS !!!!
VOOM
SHM
SWSH

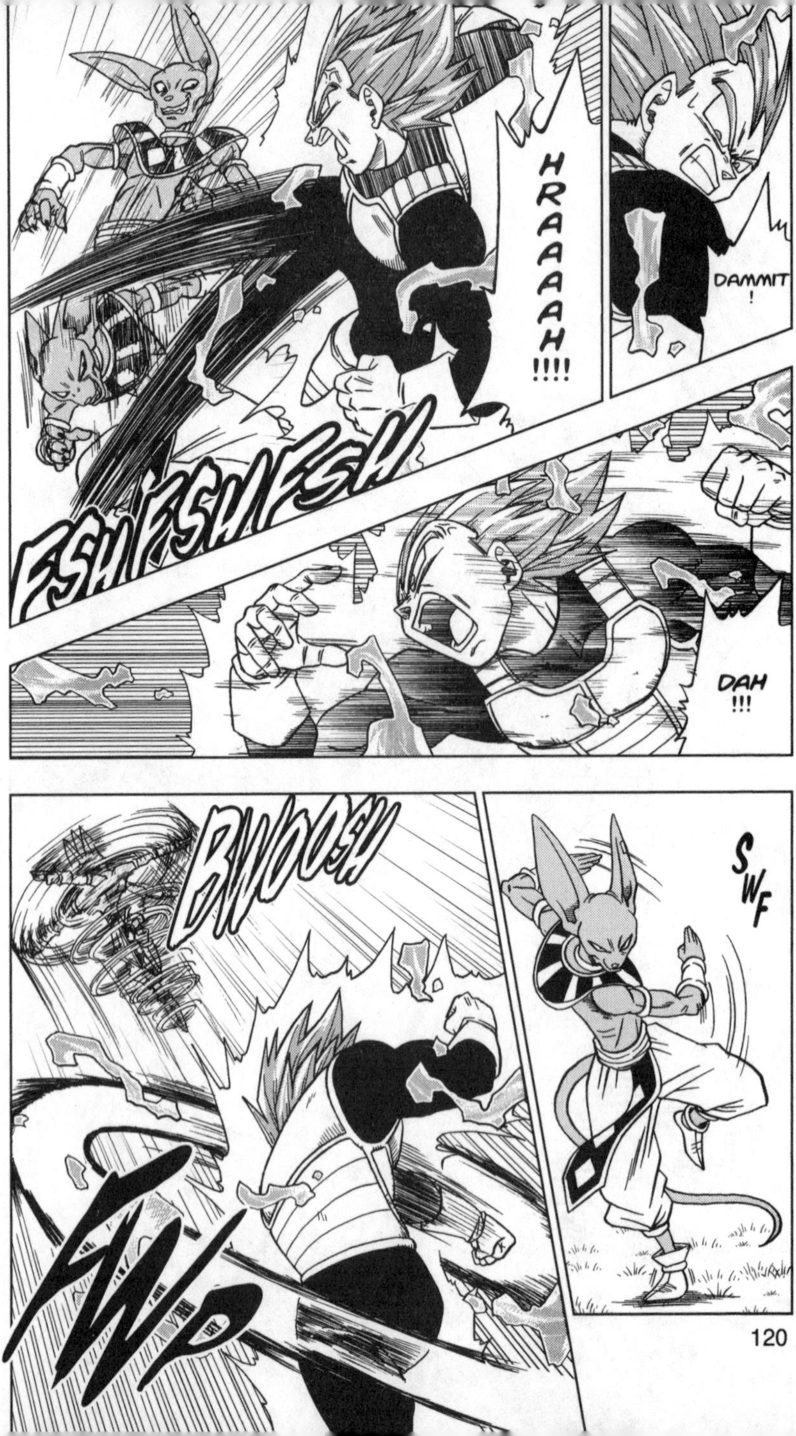
DAMMIT!
HRAAAAAH!!!!
FSHFSHFSH
DAH!!!
SWF
BWOOSH
FWIP

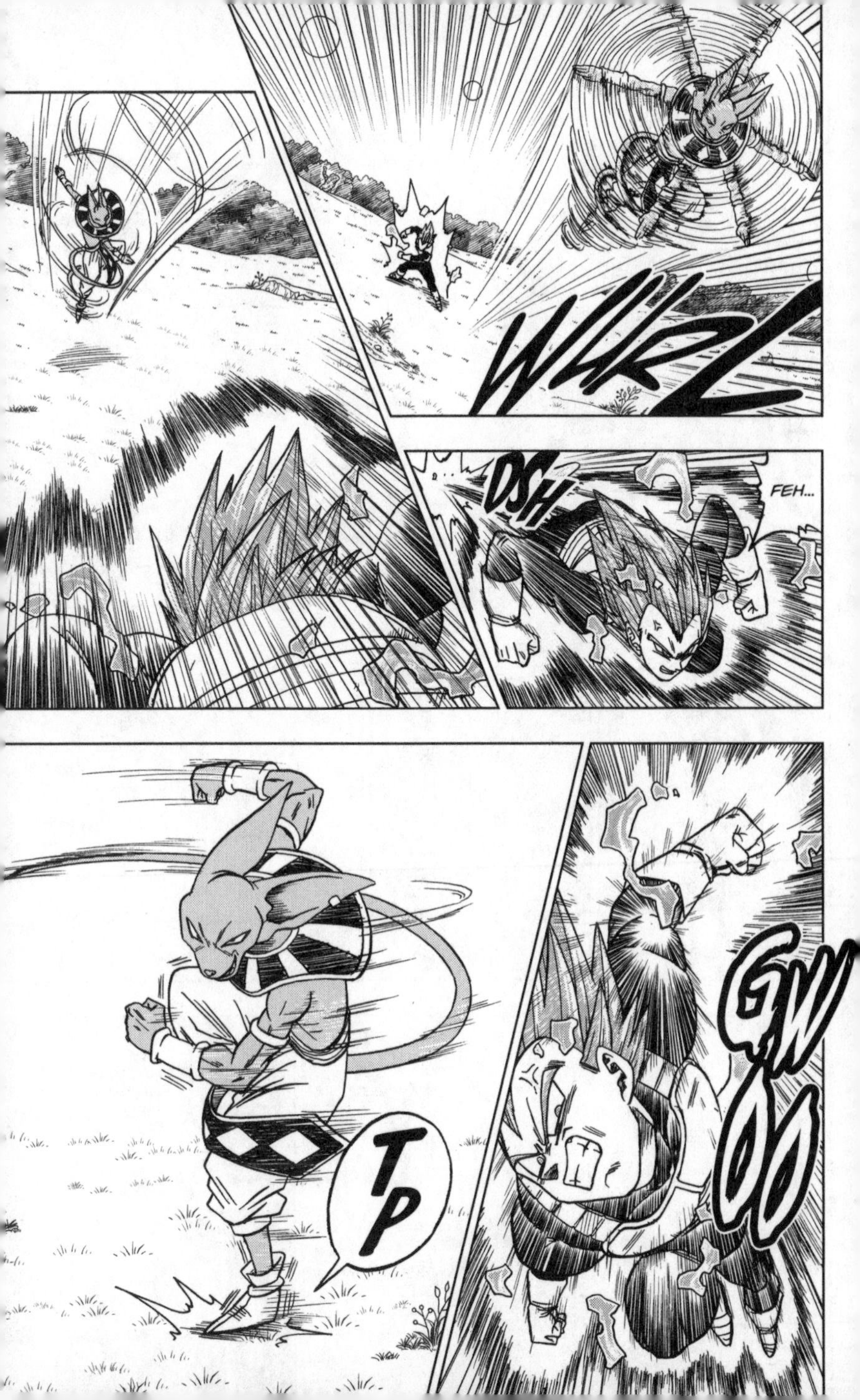
WURZ
FEH...
DSH
?...
GWOO
TP

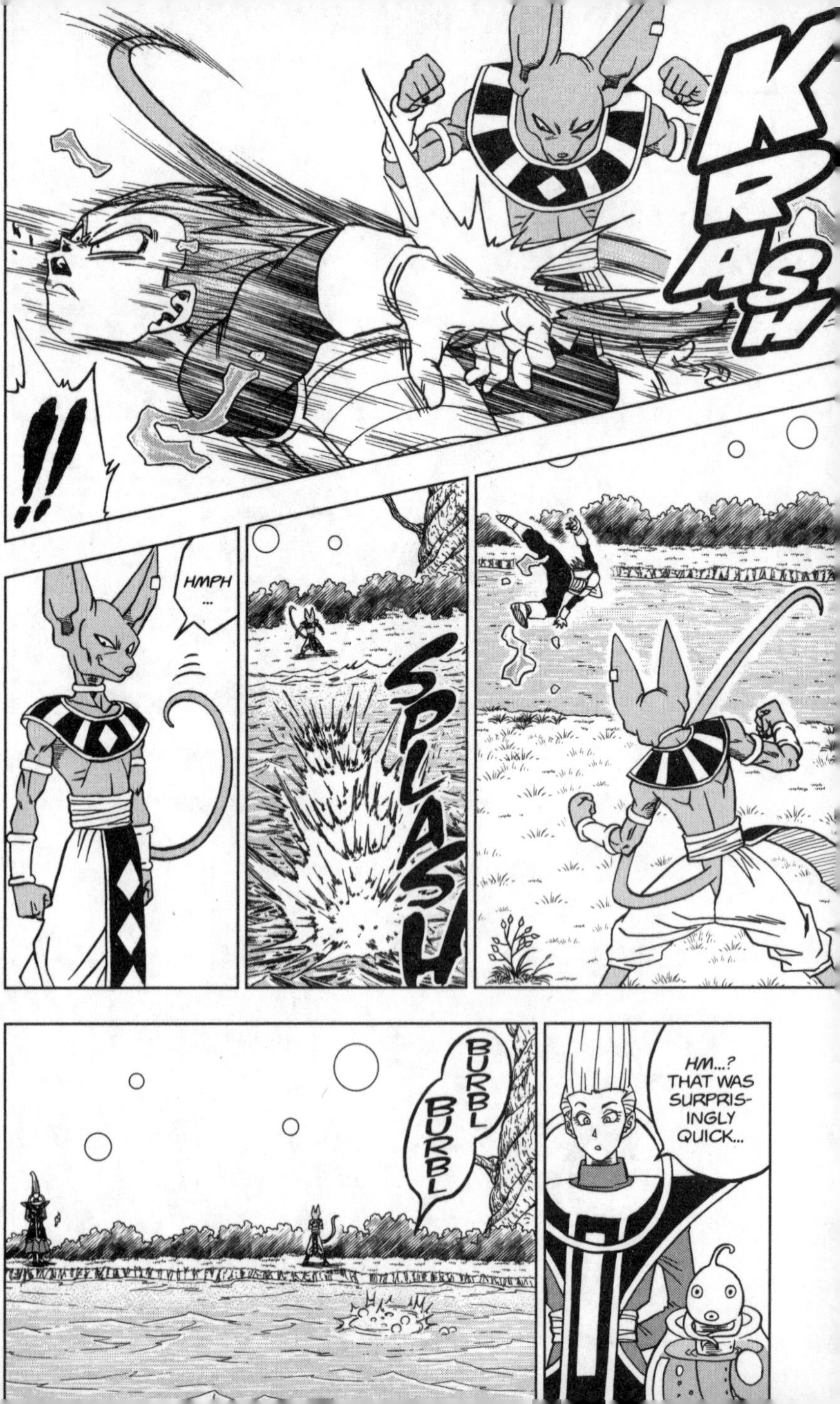
KRASH
!!
SPLASH
HMPH ...
HM...? THAT WAS SURPRIS-INGLY QUICK...
BURBL BURBL

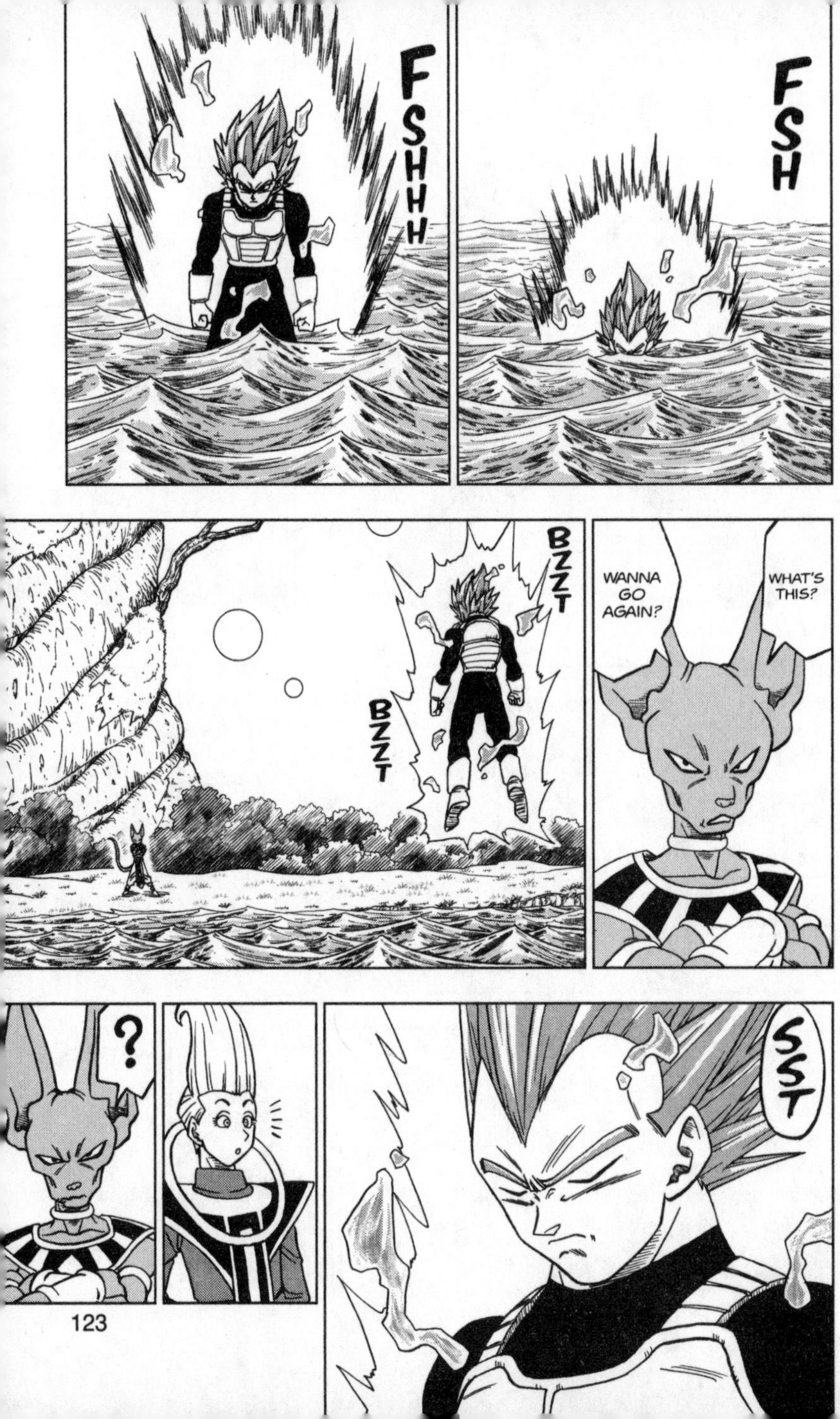
FSH
FSHHH
WHAT'S THIS?
WANNA GO AGAIN?
BZZT
BZZT
SST
?

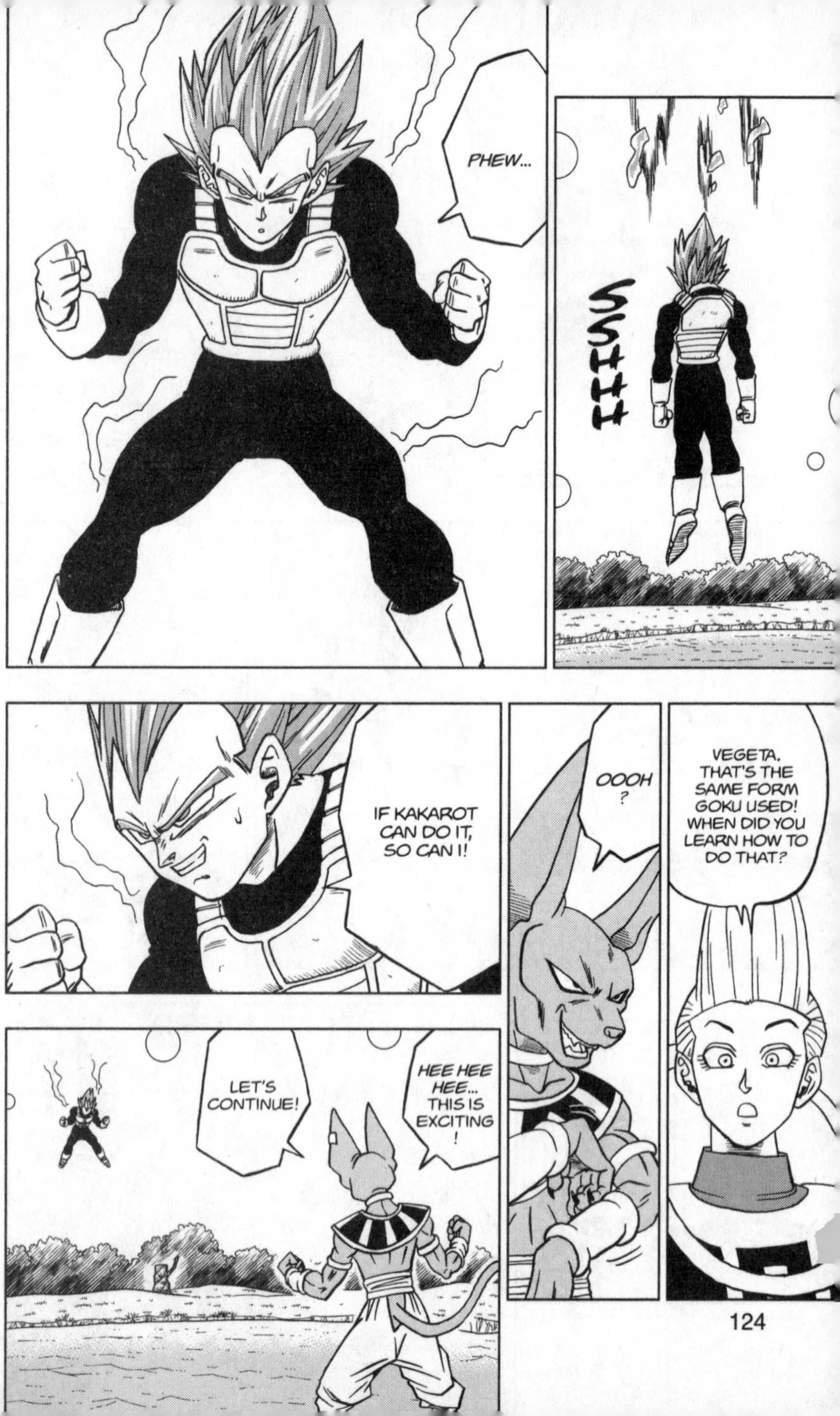
SSHHH
PHEW...
VEGETA. THAT'S THE SAME FORM GOKU USED! WHEN DID YOU LEARN HOW TO DO THAT?
OOOH?
IF KAKAROT CAN DO IT, SO CAN I!
HEE HEE HEE... THIS IS EXCITING!
LET'S CONTINUE!

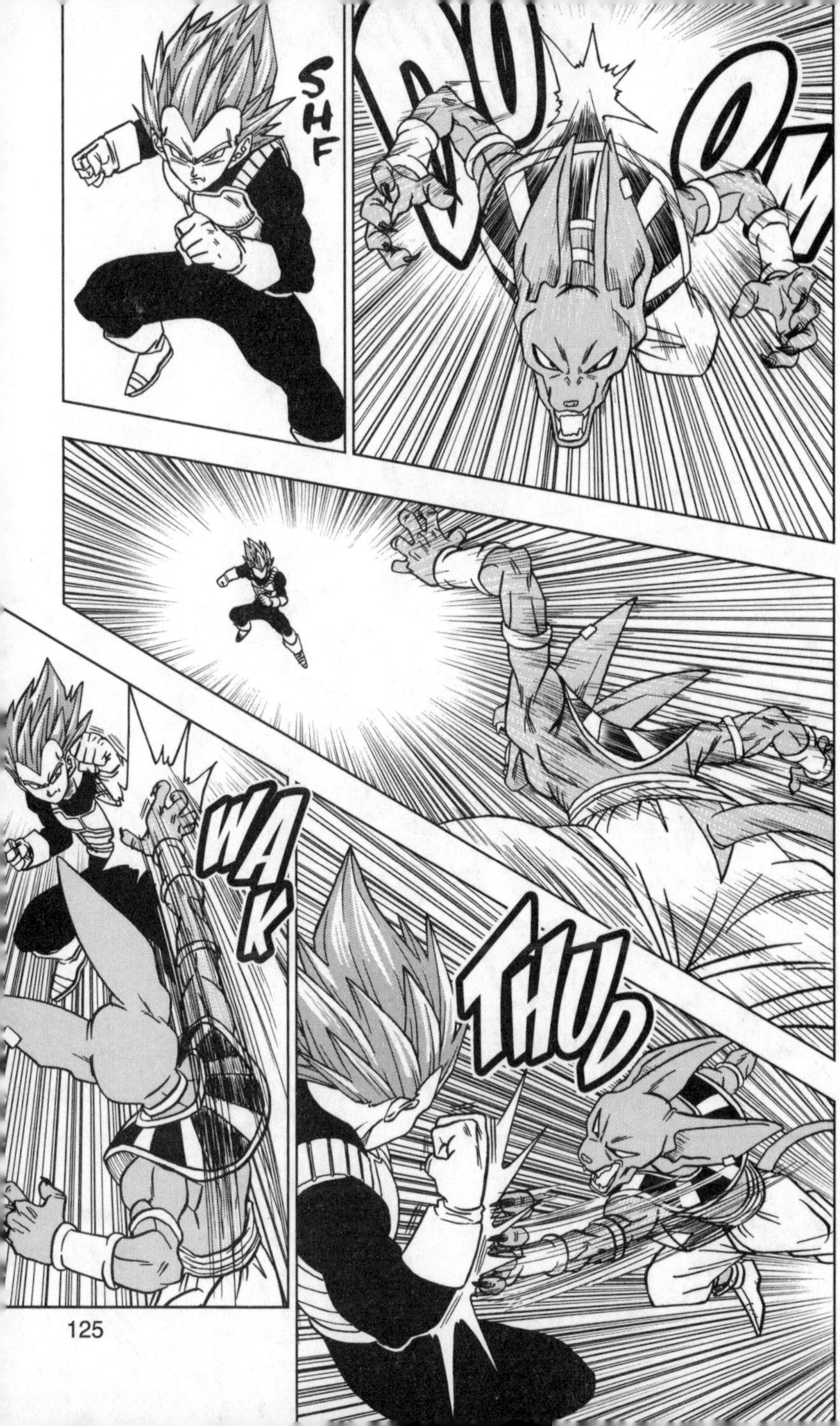
DOOM
SHF
THUD
WAK

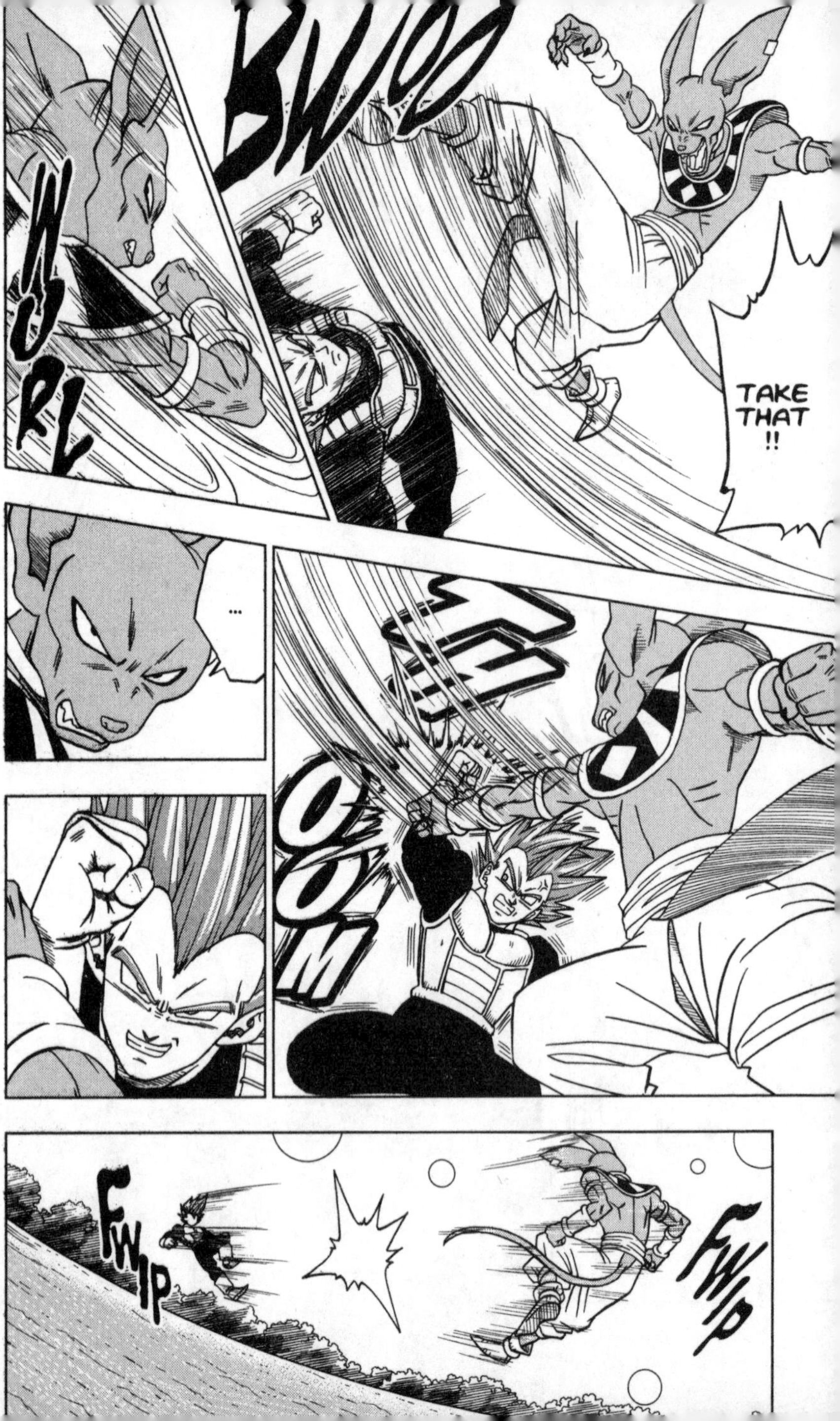

TAKE THAT!!
BWOO
WHIRL
WHOOOM
...
FWIP
FWIP

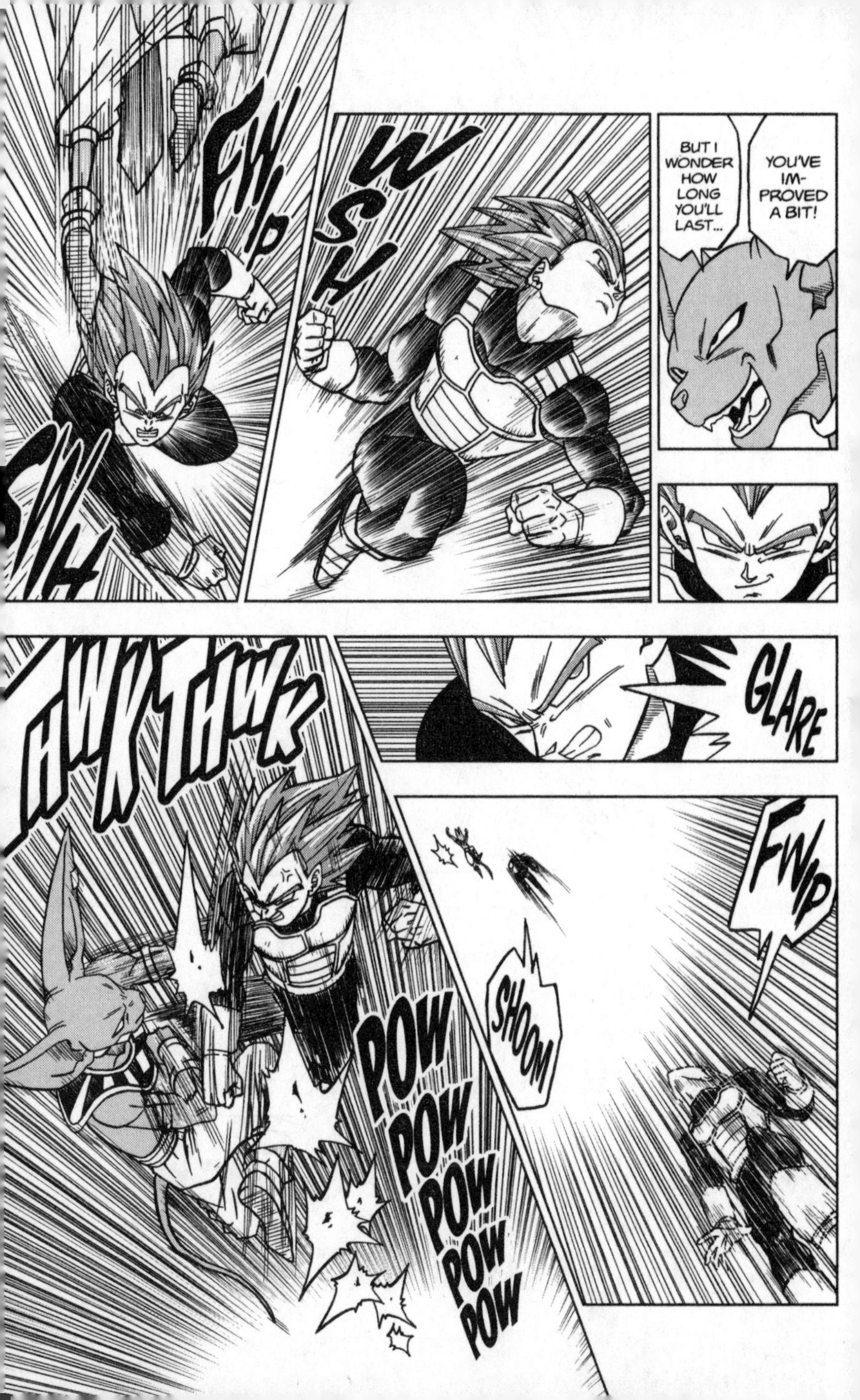
YOU'VE IM-PROVED A BIT!
BUT I WONDER HOW LONG YOU'LL LAST...
WSH
FWIP
GLARE
FWIP
SHOOM
THWK
POW
POW
POW
POW
POW

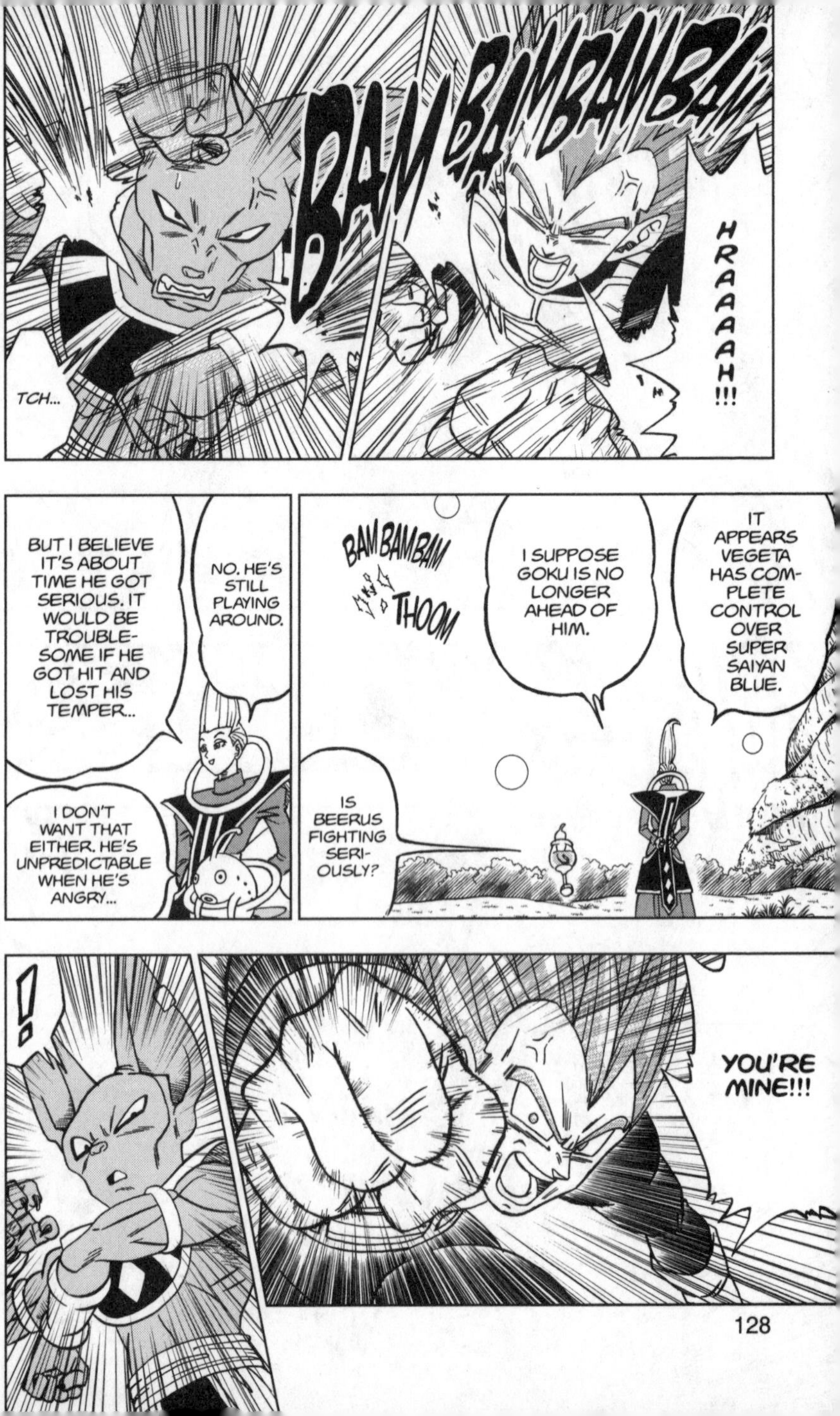
HRAAAAAH!!!
BAM BAM BAM BAM BAM
TCH...
IT APPEARS VEGETA HAS COMPLETE CONTROL OVER SUPER SAIYAN BLUE.
I SUPPOSE GOKU IS NO LONGER AHEAD OF HIM.
BAM BAM BAM
THOOM
IS BEERUS FIGHTING SERIOUSLY?
NO. HE'S STILL PLAYING AROUND.
BUT I BELIEVE IT'S ABOUT TIME HE GOT SERIOUS. IT WOULD BE TROUBLESOME IF HE GOT HIT AND LOST HIS TEMPER...
I DON'T WANT THAT EITHER. HE'S UNPREDICTABLE WHEN HE'S ANGRY...
YOU'RE MINE!!!
!

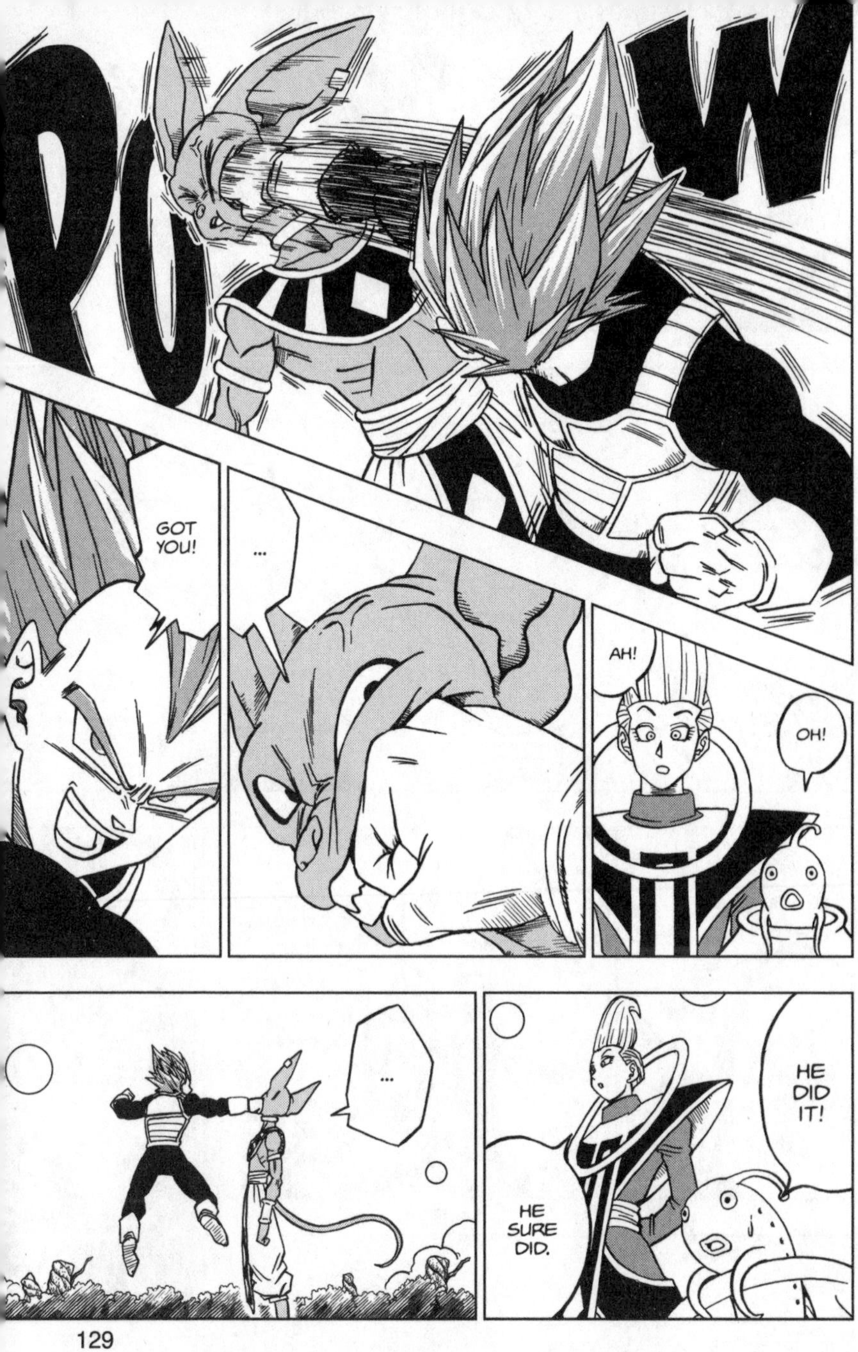
POW
AH!
OH!
...
GOT YOU!
HE DID IT!
HE SURE DID.
...

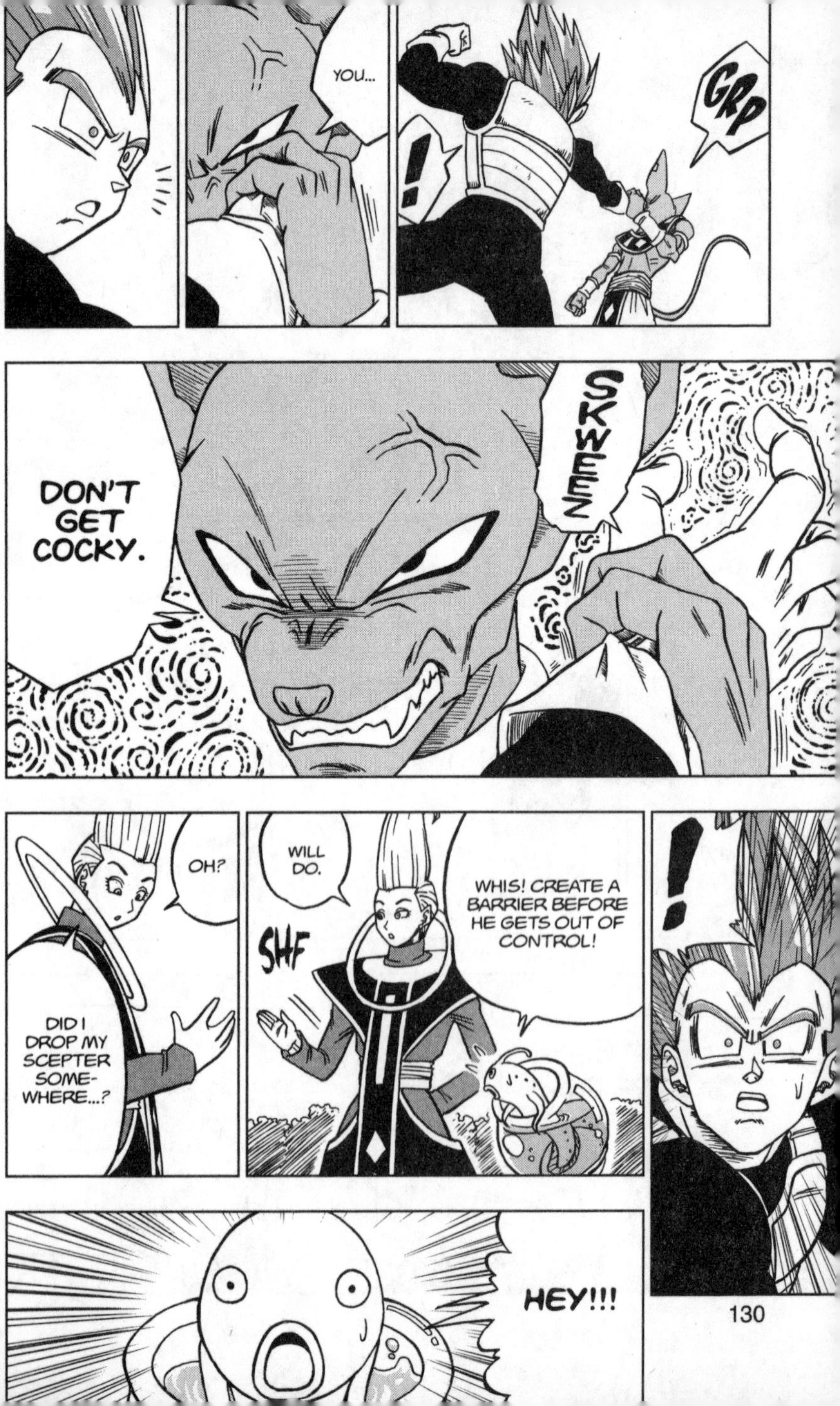
GRP
!
YOU...
SKWEEN
DON'T GET COCKY.
!
WHIS! CREATE A BARRIER BEFORE HE GETS OUT OF CONTROL!
WILL DO.
SHF
OH?
DID I DROP MY SCEPTER SOME-WHERE...?
HEY!!!

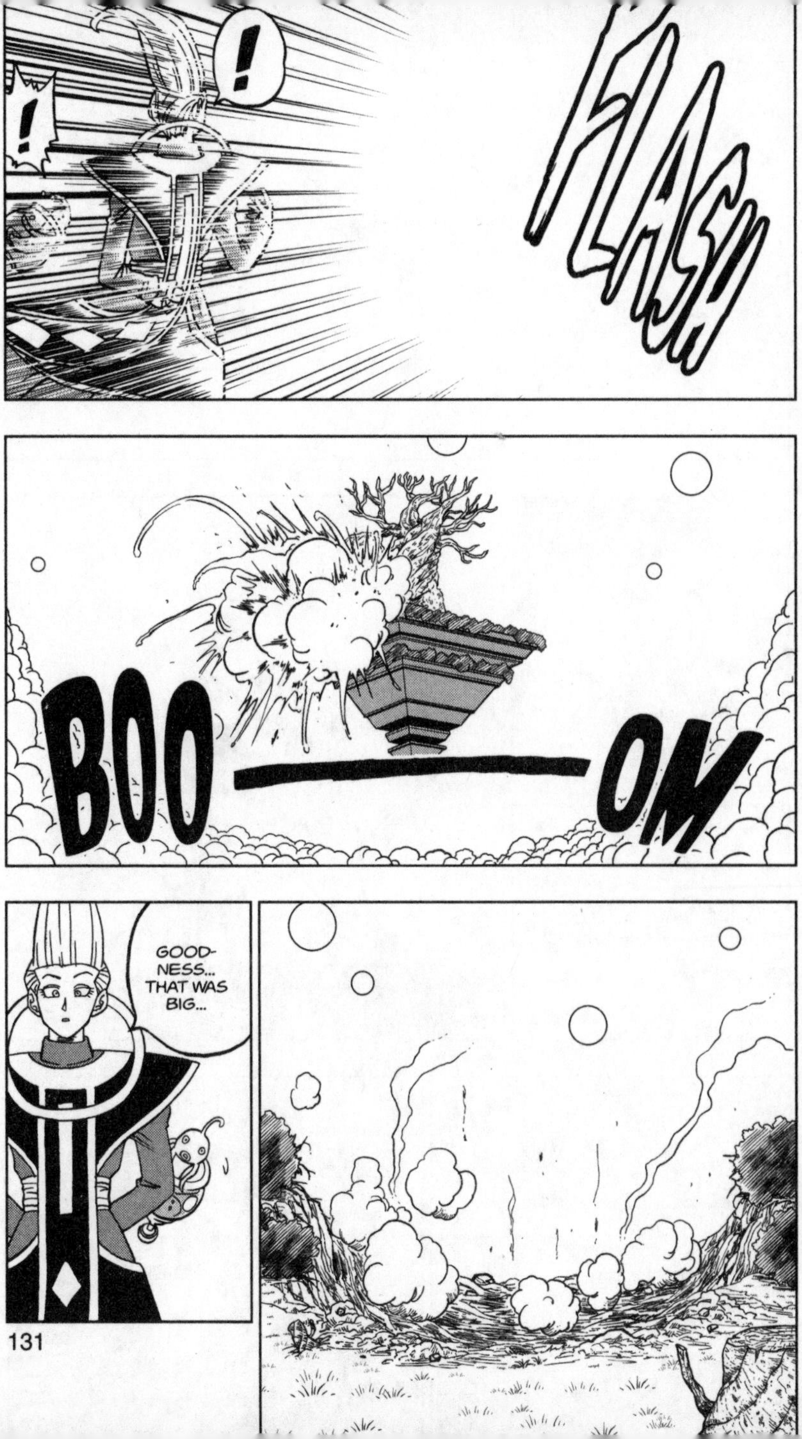
FLASH!
!
!
BOO—OM
GOOD-NESS... THAT WAS BIG...

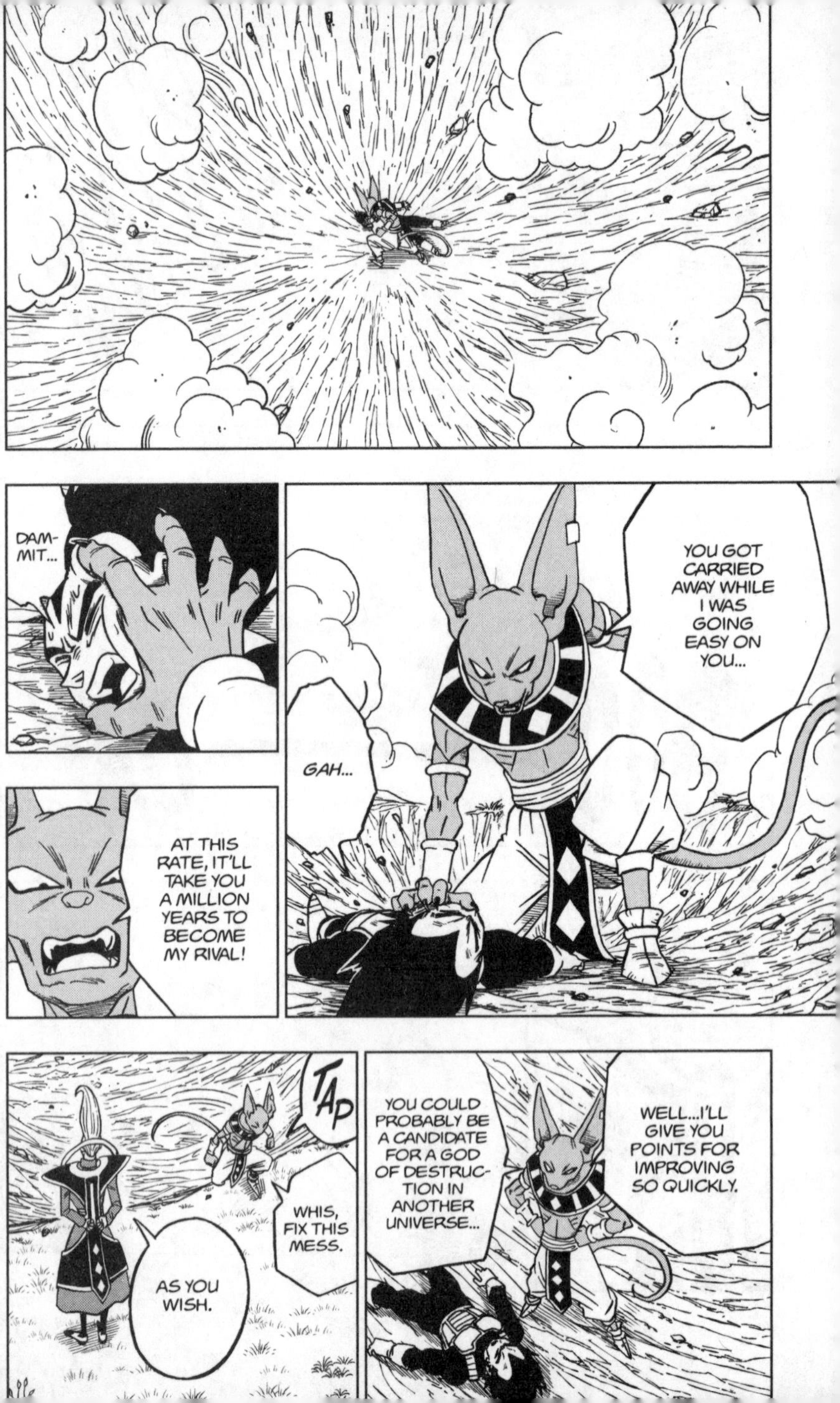
YOU GOT CARRIED AWAY WHILE I WAS GOING EASY ON YOU...
GAH...
DAM-MIT...
AT THIS RATE, IT'LL TAKE YOU A MILLION YEARS TO BECOME MY RIVAL!
WELL...I'LL GIVE YOU POINTS FOR IMPROVING SO QUICKLY.
YOU COULD PROBABLY BE A CANDIDATE FOR A GOD OF DESTRUCTION IN ANOTHER UNIVERSE...
TAP
WHIS, FIX THIS MESS.
AS YOU WISH.

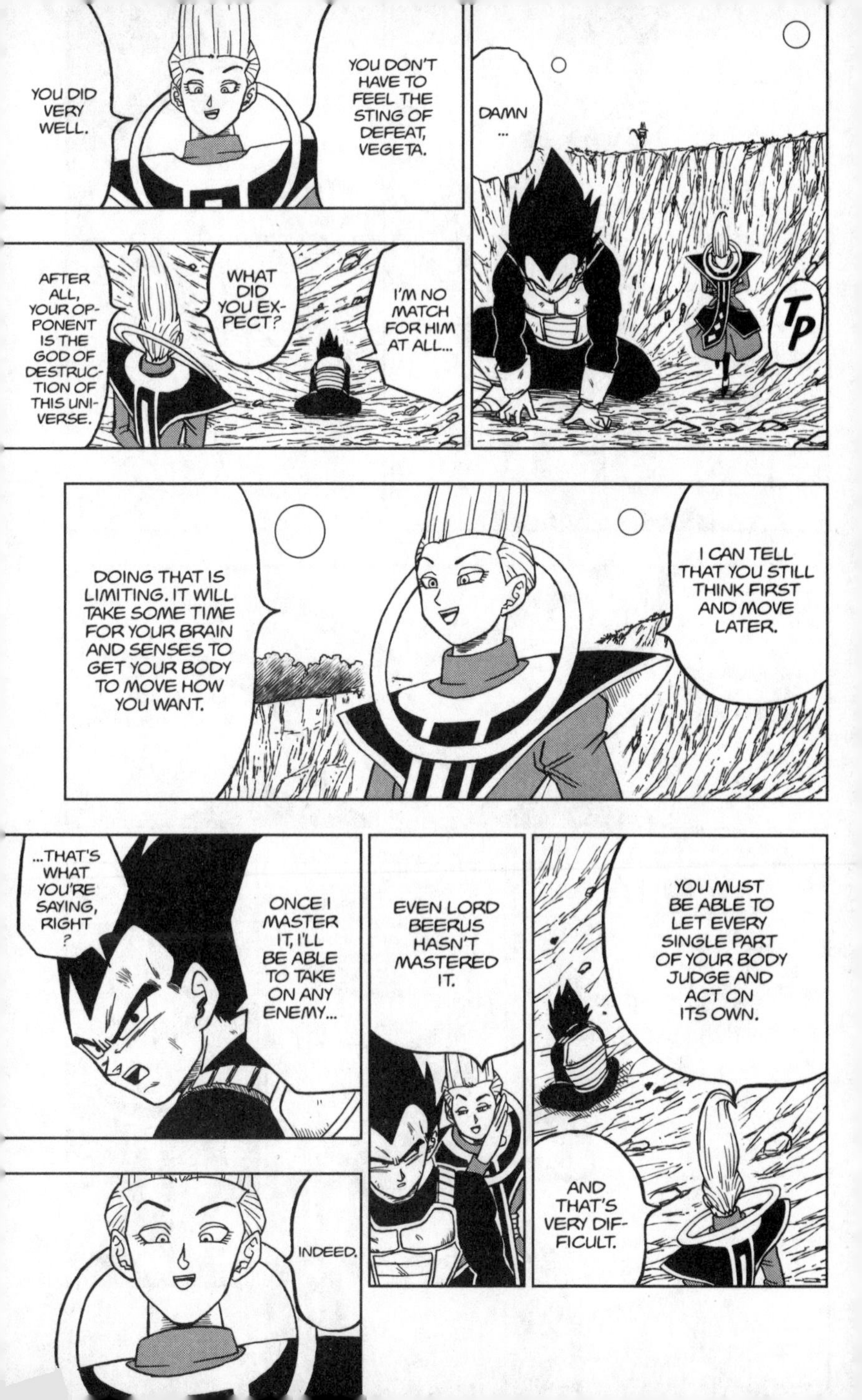
DAMN ...
TP
YOU DON'T HAVE TO FEEL THE STING OF DEFEAT, VEGETA.
YOU DID VERY WELL.
I'M NO MATCH FOR HIM AT ALL...
WHAT DID YOU EXPECT?
AFTER ALL, YOUR OPPONENT IS THE GOD OF DESTRUCTION OF THIS UNIVERSE.
I CAN TELL THAT YOU STILL THINK FIRST AND MOVE LATER.
DOING THAT IS LIMITING. IT WILL TAKE SOME TIME FOR YOUR BRAIN AND SENSES TO GET YOUR BODY TO MOVE HOW YOU WANT.
YOU MUST BE ABLE TO LET EVERY SINGLE PART OF YOUR BODY JUDGE AND ACT ON ITS OWN.
AND THAT'S VERY DIFFICULT.
EVEN LORD BEERUS HASN'T MASTERED IT.
ONCE I MASTER IT, I'LL BE ABLE TO TAKE ON ANY ENEMY...
...THAT'S WHAT YOU'RE SAYING, RIGHT?
INDEED.

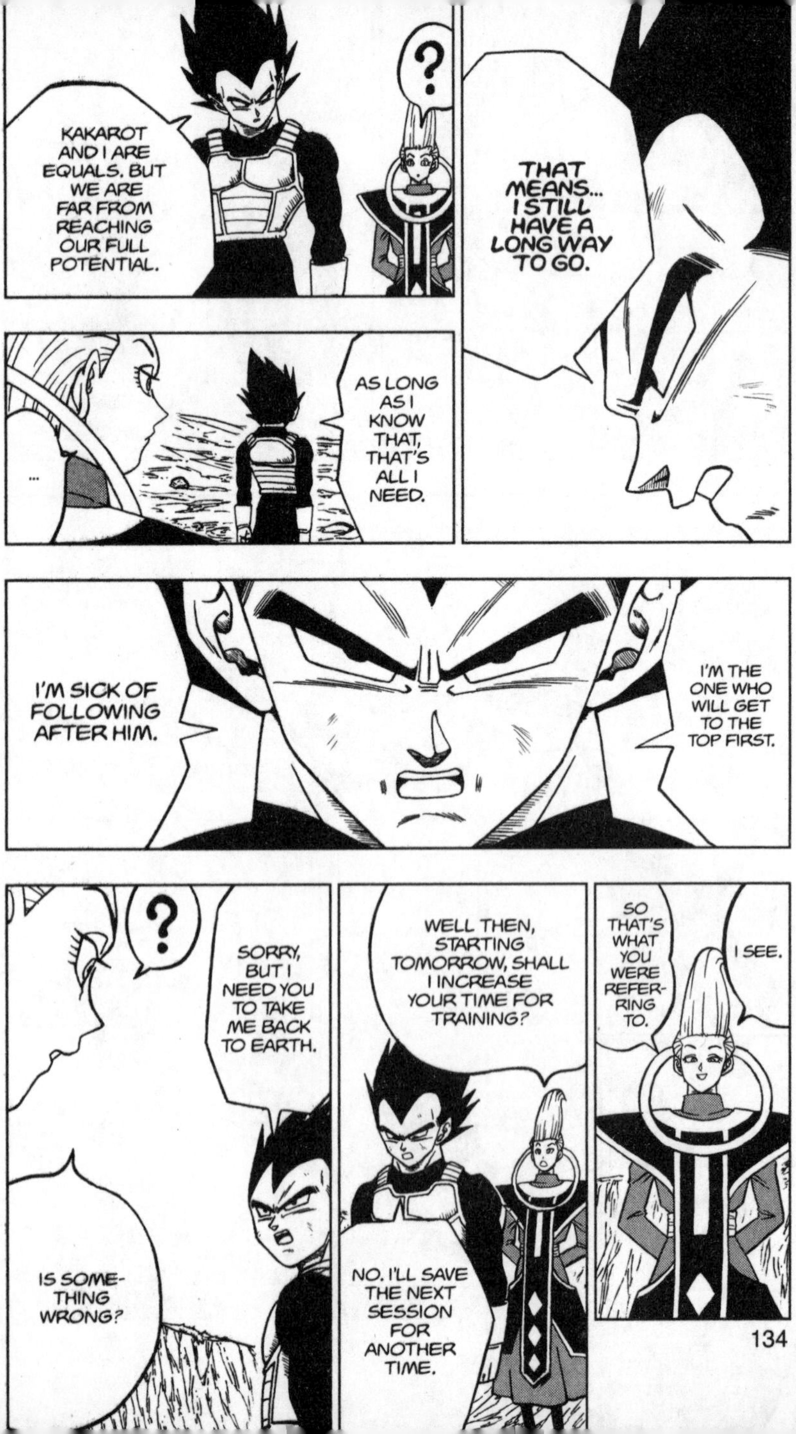
THAT MEANS... I STILL HAVE A LONG WAY TO GO.
KAKAROT AND I ARE EQUALS. BUT WE ARE FAR FROM REACHING OUR FULL POTENTIAL.
?
AS LONG AS I KNOW THAT, THAT'S ALL I NEED.
...
I'M THE ONE WHO WILL GET TO THE TOP FIRST.
I'M SICK OF FOLLOWING AFTER HIM.
I SEE.
SO THAT'S WHAT YOU WERE REFERRING TO.
WELL THEN, STARTING TOMORROW, SHALL I INCREASE YOUR TIME FOR TRAINING?
NO. I'LL SAVE THE NEXT SESSION FOR ANOTHER TIME.
SORRY, BUT I NEED YOU TO TAKE ME BACK TO EARTH.
?
IS SOMETHING WRONG?

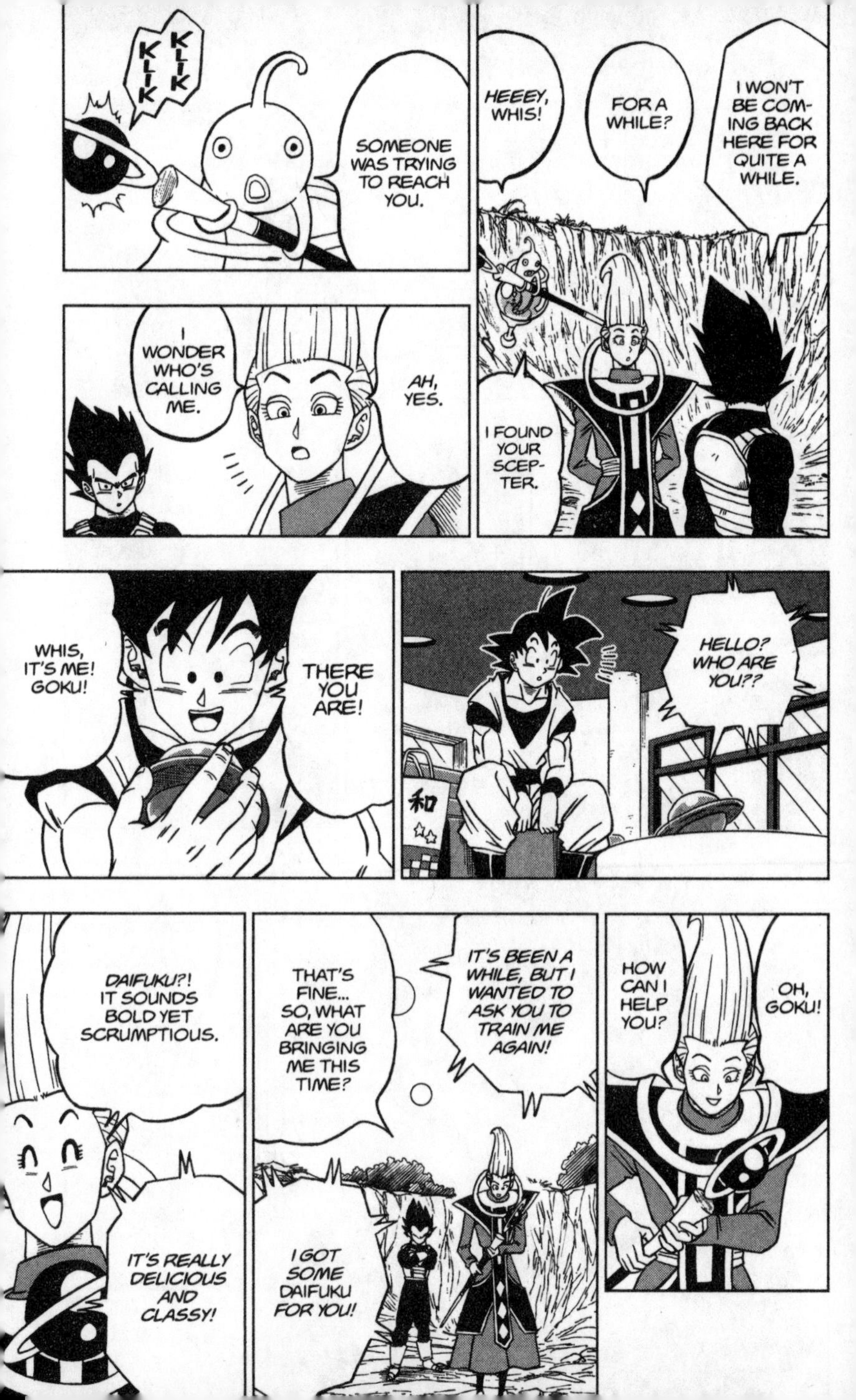
I WON'T BE COMING BACK HERE FOR QUITE A WHILE.
FOR A WHILE?
HEEEY, WHIS!
I FOUND YOUR SCEPTER.
SOMEONE WAS TRYING TO REACH YOU.
KLIK KLIK
AH, YES.
I WONDER WHO'S CALLING ME.
HELLO? WHO ARE YOU??
和
THERE YOU ARE!
WHIS, IT'S ME! GOKU!
OH, GOKU!
HOW CAN I HELP YOU?
IT'S BEEN A WHILE, BUT I WANTED TO ASK YOU TO TRAIN ME AGAIN!
THAT'S FINE... SO, WHAT ARE YOU BRINGING ME THIS TIME?
I GOT SOME DAIFUKU FOR YOU!
DAIFUKU?! IT SOUNDS BOLD YET SCRUMPTIOUS.
IT'S REALLY DELICIOUS AND CLASSY!

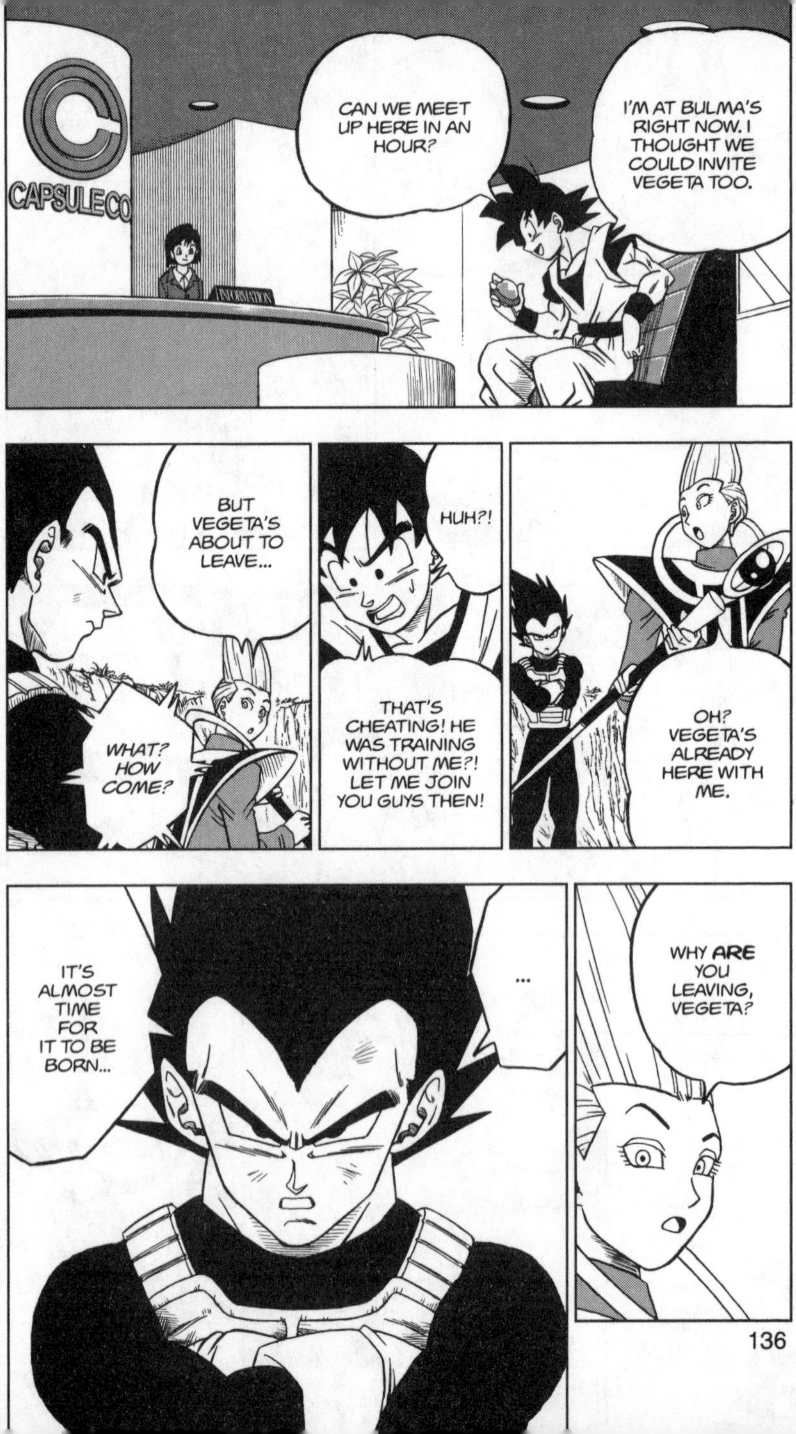
I'M AT BULMA'S RIGHT NOW. I THOUGHT WE COULD INVITE VEGETA TOO.
CAN WE MEET UP HERE IN AN HOUR?
CAPSULE CO
INFORMATION
OH? VEGETA'S ALREADY HERE WITH ME.
HUH?!
THAT'S CHEATING! HE WAS TRAINING WITHOUT ME?! LET ME JOIN YOU GUYS THEN!
BUT VEGETA'S ABOUT TO LEAVE...
WHAT? HOW COME?
WHY **ARE** YOU LEAVING, VEGETA?
...
IT'S ALMOST TIME FOR IT TO BE BORN...

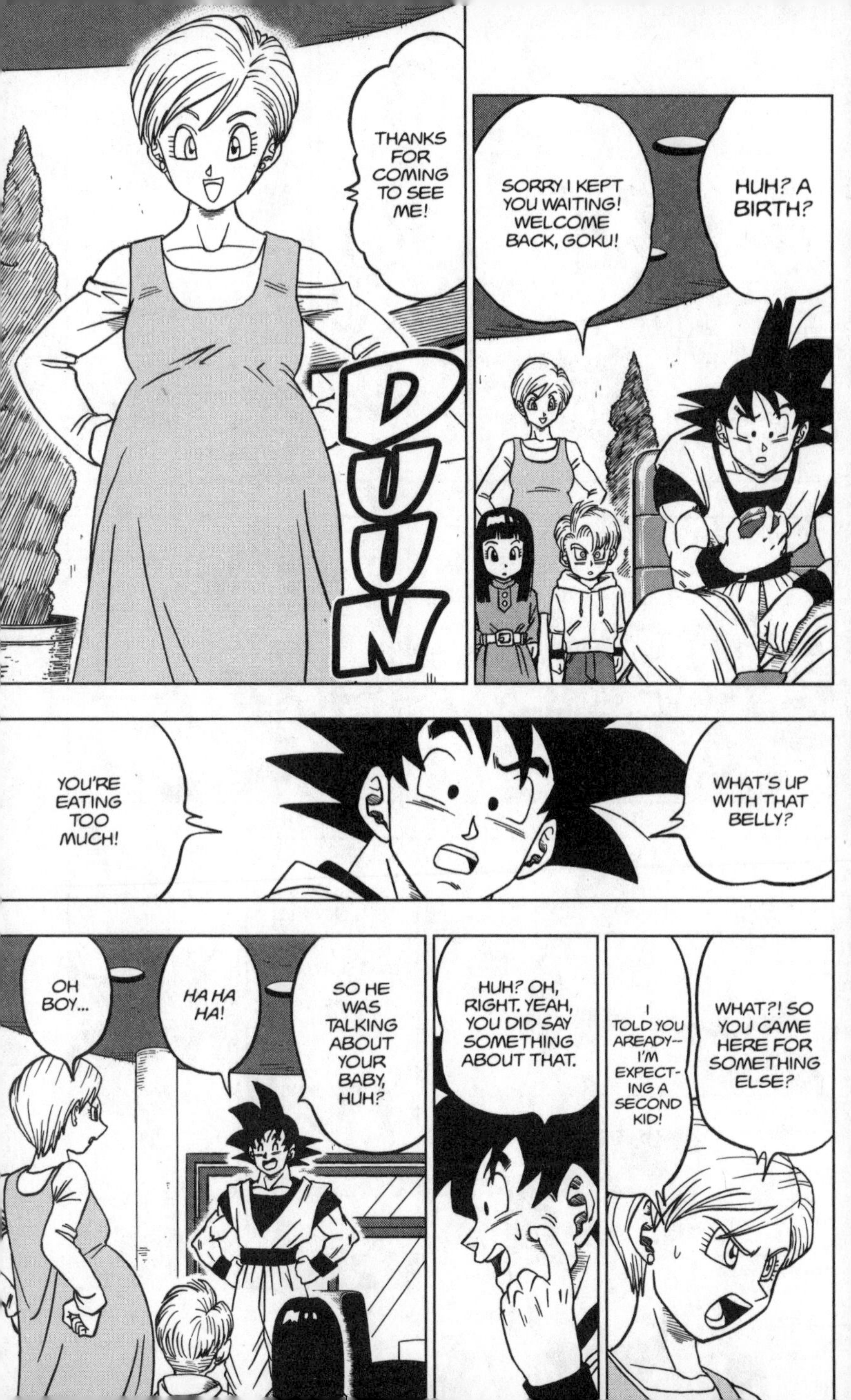
HUH? A BIRTH?
SORRY I KEPT YOU WAITING! WELCOME BACK, GOKU!
THANKS FOR COMING TO SEE ME!
DUUN
WHAT'S UP WITH THAT BELLY?
YOU'RE EATING TOO MUCH!
WHAT?! SO YOU CAME HERE FOR SOMETHING ELSE?
I TOLD YOU AREADY-- I'M EXPECTING A SECOND KID!
HUH? OH, RIGHT. YEAH, YOU DID SAY SOMETHING ABOUT THAT.
SO HE WAS TALKING ABOUT YOUR BABY, HUH?
HA HA HA!
OH BOY...

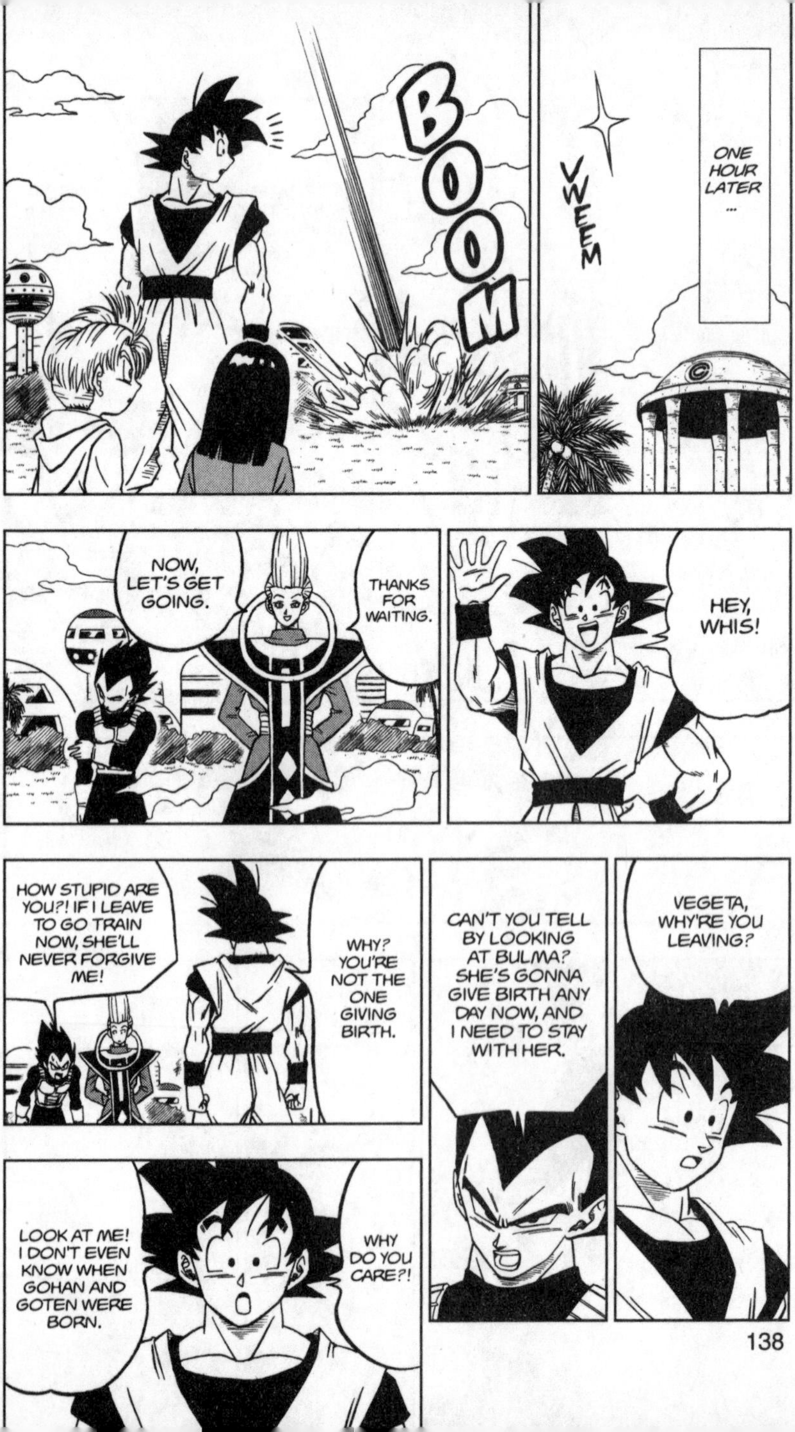
ONE HOUR LATER ...
VWEEM
BOOM
HEY, WHIS!
THANKS FOR WAITING.
NOW, LET'S GET GOING.
VEGETA, WHY'RE YOU LEAVING?
CAN'T YOU TELL BY LOOKING AT BULMA? SHE'S GONNA GIVE BIRTH ANY DAY NOW, AND I NEED TO STAY WITH HER.
WHY? YOU'RE NOT THE ONE GIVING BIRTH.
HOW STUPID ARE YOU?! IF I LEAVE TO GO TRAIN NOW, SHE'LL NEVER FORGIVE ME!
WHY DO YOU CARE?!
LOOK AT ME! I DON'T EVEN KNOW WHEN GOHAN AND GOTEN WERE BORN.

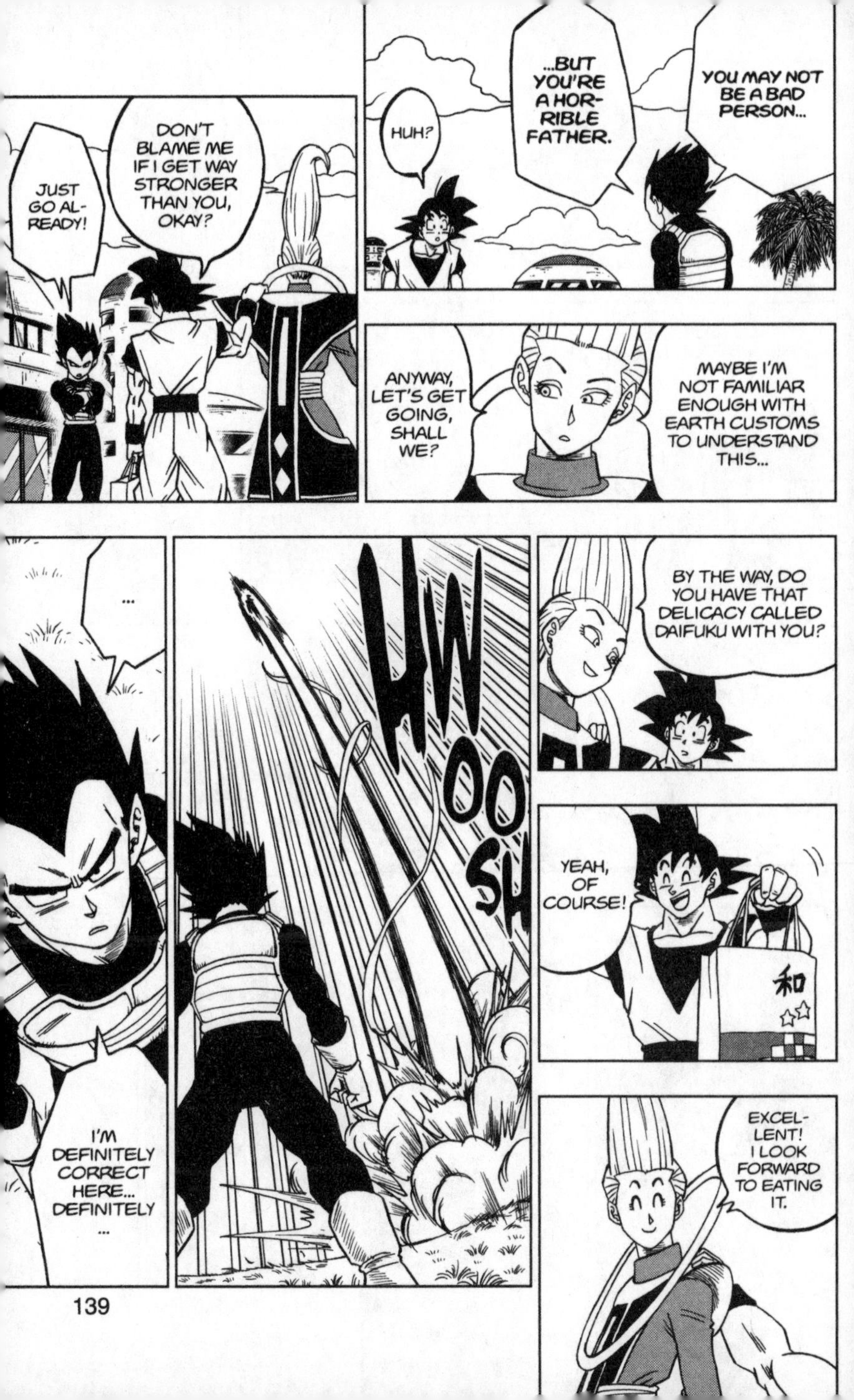
YOU MAY NOT BE A BAD PERSON...
...BUT YOU'RE A HOR-RIBLE FATHER.
HUH?
MAYBE I'M NOT FAMILIAR ENOUGH WITH EARTH CUSTOMS TO UNDERSTAND THIS...
ANYWAY, LET'S GET GOING, SHALL WE?
DON'T BLAME ME IF I GET WAY STRONGER THAN YOU, OKAY?
JUST GO AL-READY!
BY THE WAY, DO YOU HAVE THAT DELICACY CALLED DAIFUKU WITH YOU?
YEAH, OF COURSE!
和
EXCEL-LENT! I LOOK FORWARD TO EATING IT.
HWOOSH
...
I'M DEFINITELY CORRECT HERE... DEFINITELY...

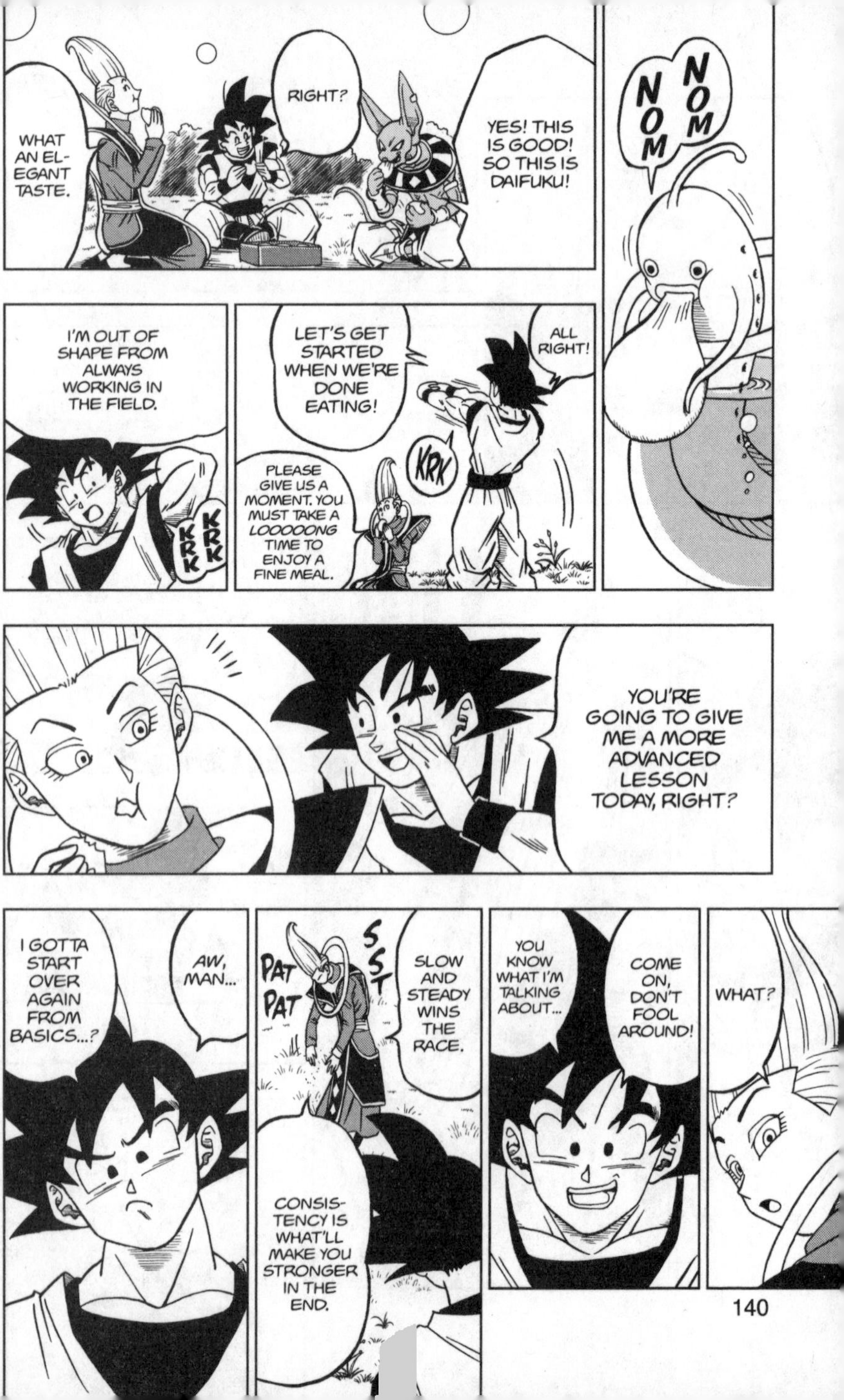

NOM NOM NOM NOM
YES! THIS IS GOOD! SO THIS IS DAIFUKU!
RIGHT?
WHAT AN EL-EGANT TASTE.
ALL RIGHT!
LET'S GET STARTED WHEN WE'RE DONE EATING!
KRK
PLEASE GIVE US A MOMENT. YOU MUST TAKE A *LOOOOONG* TIME TO ENJOY A FINE MEAL.
I'M OUT OF SHAPE FROM ALWAYS WORKING IN THE FIELD.
KRK KRK
YOU'RE GOING TO GIVE ME A MORE ADVANCED LESSON TODAY, RIGHT?
WHAT?
COME ON, DON'T FOOL AROUND!
YOU KNOW WHAT I'M TALKING ABOUT...
SST
SLOW AND STEADY WINS THE RACE.
PAT PAT
CONSIS-TENCY IS WHAT'LL MAKE YOU STRONGER IN THE END.
AW, MAN...
I GOTTA START OVER AGAIN FROM BASICS...?

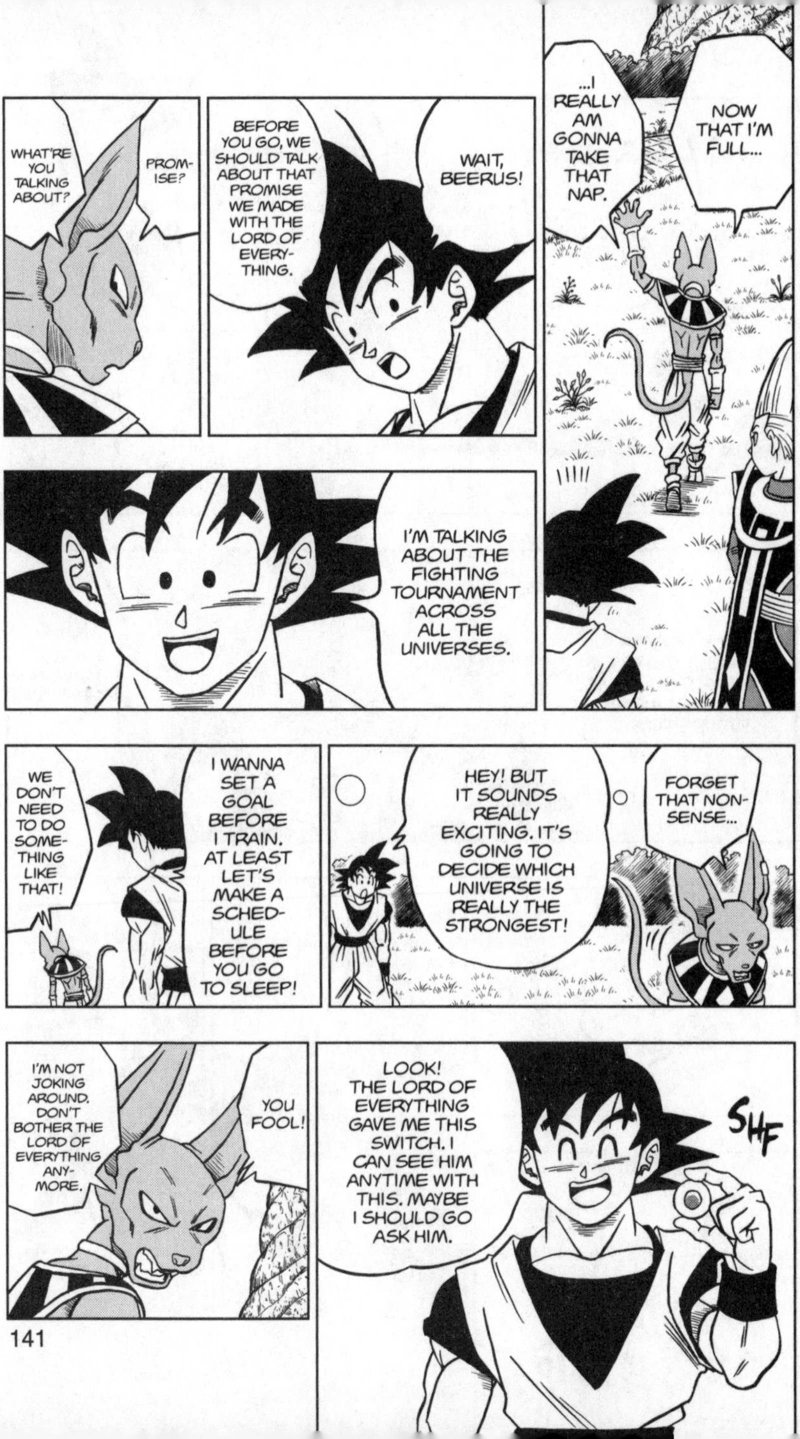
NOW THAT I'M FULL...
...I REALLY AM GONNA TAKE THAT NAP.
WAIT, BEERUS!
BEFORE YOU GO, WE SHOULD TALK ABOUT THAT PROMISE WE MADE WITH THE LORD OF EVERY-THING.
PROM-ISE?
WHAT'RE YOU TALKING ABOUT?
I'M TALKING ABOUT THE FIGHTING TOURNAMENT ACROSS ALL THE UNIVERSES.
FORGET THAT NON-SENSE...
HEY! BUT IT SOUNDS REALLY EXCITING. IT'S GOING TO DECIDE WHICH UNIVERSE IS REALLY THE STRONGEST!
WE DON'T NEED TO DO SOME-THING LIKE THAT!
I WANNA SET A GOAL BEFORE I TRAIN. AT LEAST LET'S MAKE A SCHED-ULE BEFORE YOU GO TO SLEEP!
SHF
LOOK! THE LORD OF EVERYTHING GAVE ME THIS SWITCH. I CAN SEE HIM ANYTIME WITH THIS. MAYBE I SHOULD GO ASK HIM.
YOU FOOL!
I'M NOT JOKING AROUND. DON'T BOTHER THE LORD OF EVERYTHING ANY-MORE.

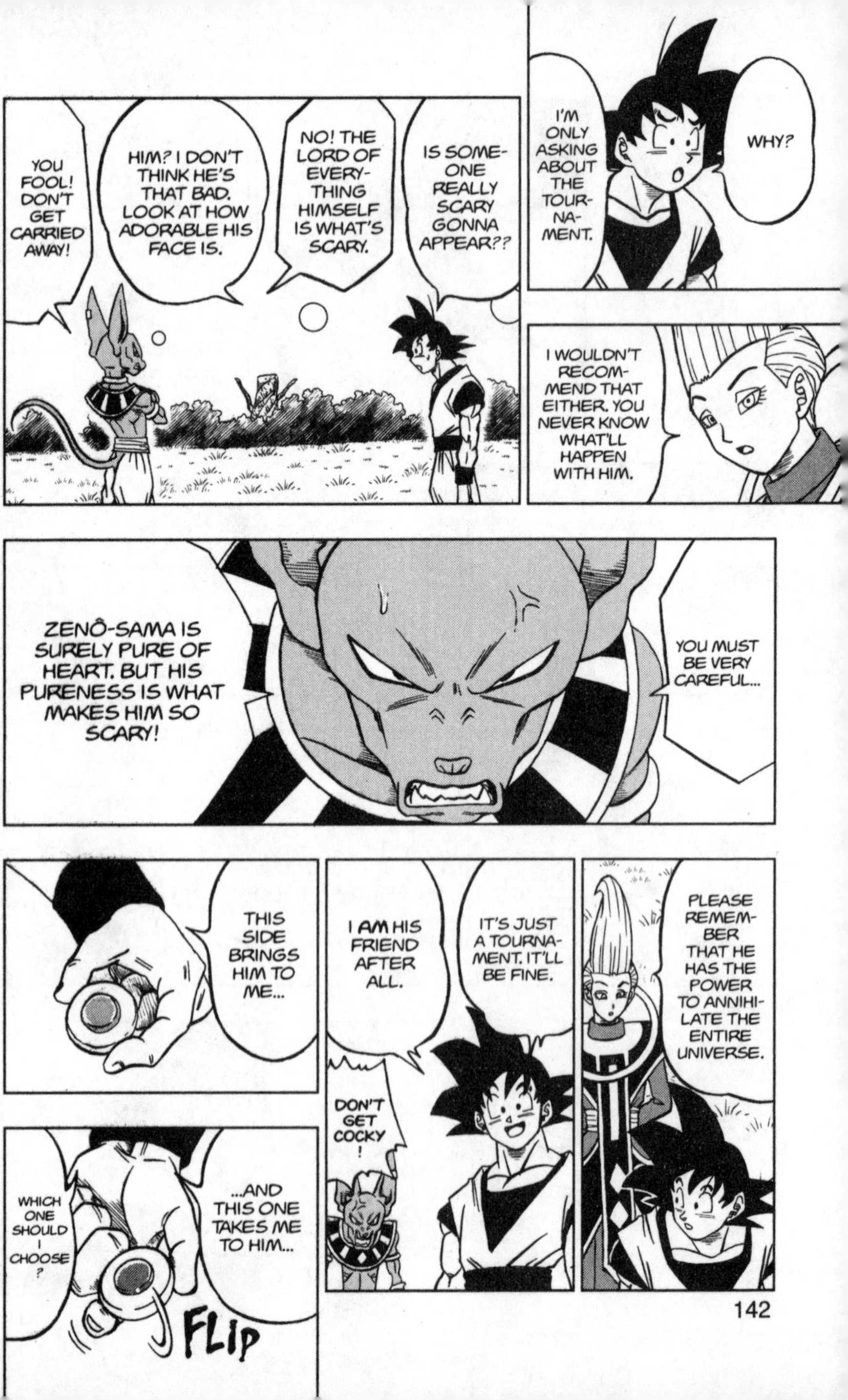
WHY?
I'M ONLY ASKING ABOUT THE TOURNAMENT.
I WOULDN'T RECOMMEND THAT EITHER. YOU NEVER KNOW WHAT'LL HAPPEN WITH HIM.
IS SOMEONE REALLY SCARY GONNA APPEAR??
NO! THE LORD OF EVERYTHING HIMSELF IS WHAT'S SCARY.
HIM? I DON'T THINK HE'S THAT BAD. LOOK AT HOW ADORABLE HIS FACE IS.
YOU FOOL! DON'T GET CARRIED AWAY!
YOU MUST BE VERY CAREFUL...
ZENÔ-SAMA IS SURELY PURE OF HEART. BUT HIS PURENESS IS WHAT MAKES HIM SO SCARY!
PLEASE REMEMBER THAT HE HAS THE POWER TO ANNIHILATE THE ENTIRE UNIVERSE.
IT'S JUST A TOURNAMENT. IT'LL BE FINE.
I AM HIS FRIEND AFTER ALL.
DON'T GET COCKY!
THIS SIDE BRINGS HIM TO ME...
...AND THIS ONE TAKES ME TO HIM...
WHICH ONE SHOULD I CHOOSE?
FLIP

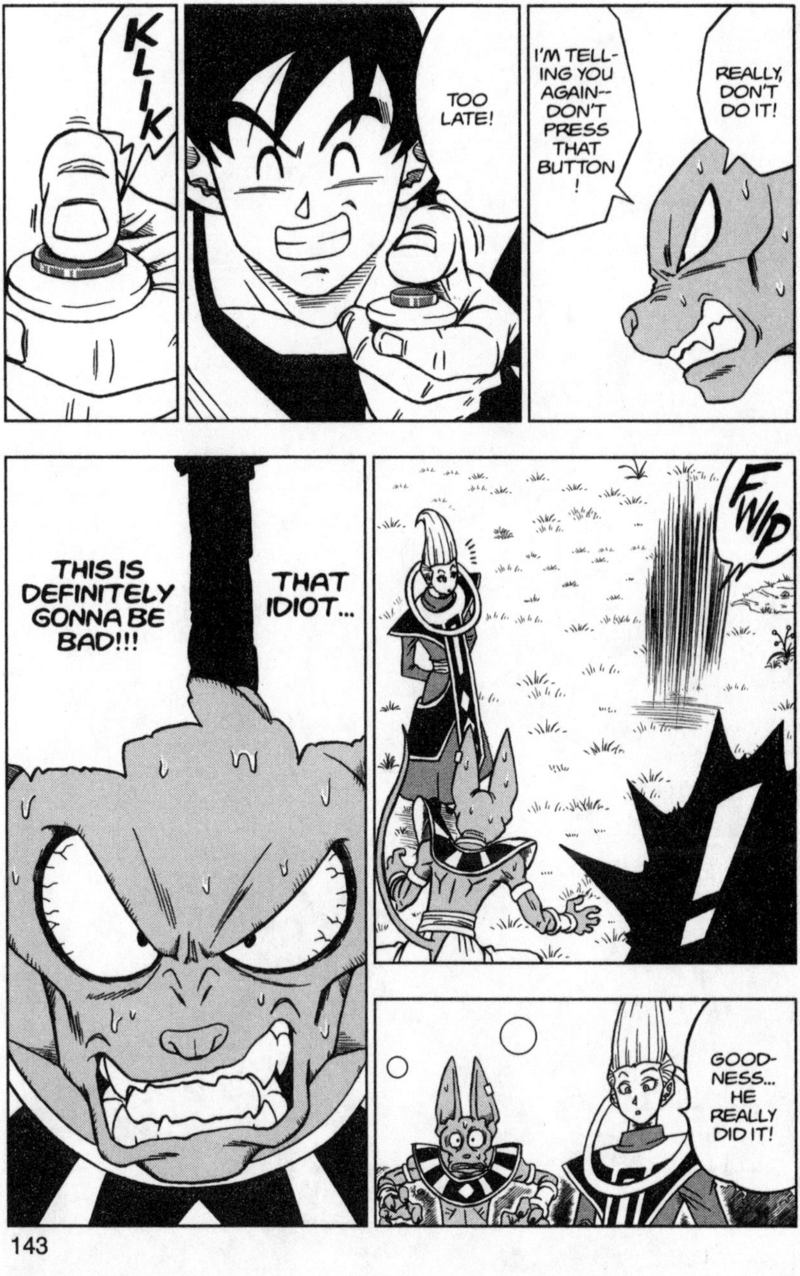
REALLY, DON'T DO IT!
I'M TELLING YOU AGAIN-- DON'T PRESS THAT BUTTON!
TOO LATE!
KLIK
FWIP
GOODNESS... HE REALLY DID IT!
THAT IDIOT...
THIS IS DEFINITELY GONNA BE BAD!!!

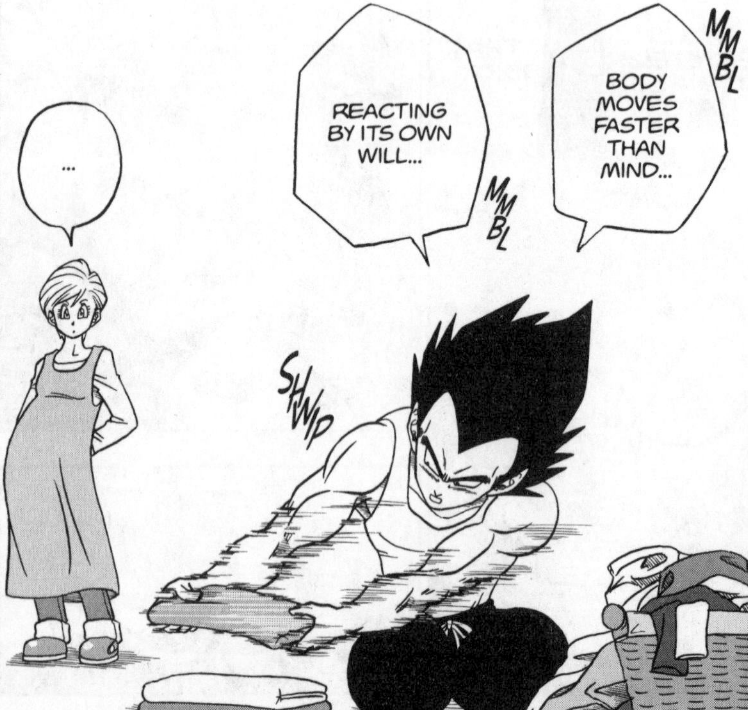
MMBL
BODY MOVES FASTER THAN MIND...
REACTING BY ITS OWN WILL...
MMBL
SHNIP
...

DRAGON BALL SUPER

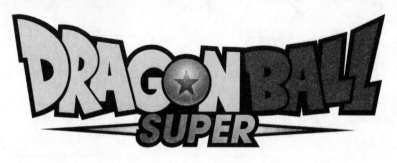

CHAPTER 28: THE GODS OF DESTRUCTION FROM ALL 12 UNIVERSES

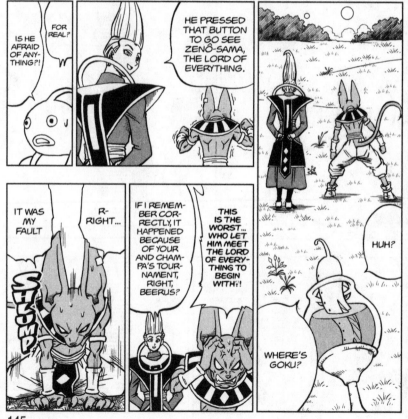

HUH?
WHERE'S GOKU?
HE PRESSED THAT BUTTON TO GO SEE ZENÔ-SAMA, THE LORD OF EVERYTHING.
FOR REAL?
IS HE AFRAID OF ANYTHING?!
THIS IS THE WORST... WHO LET HIM MEET THE LORD OF EVERYTHING TO BEGIN WITH?!
IF I REMEMBER CORRECTLY, IT HAPPENED BECAUSE OF YOUR AND CHAMPA'S TOURNAMENT, RIGHT, BEERUS?
R-RIGHT...
IT WAS MY FAULT
SHLUMP

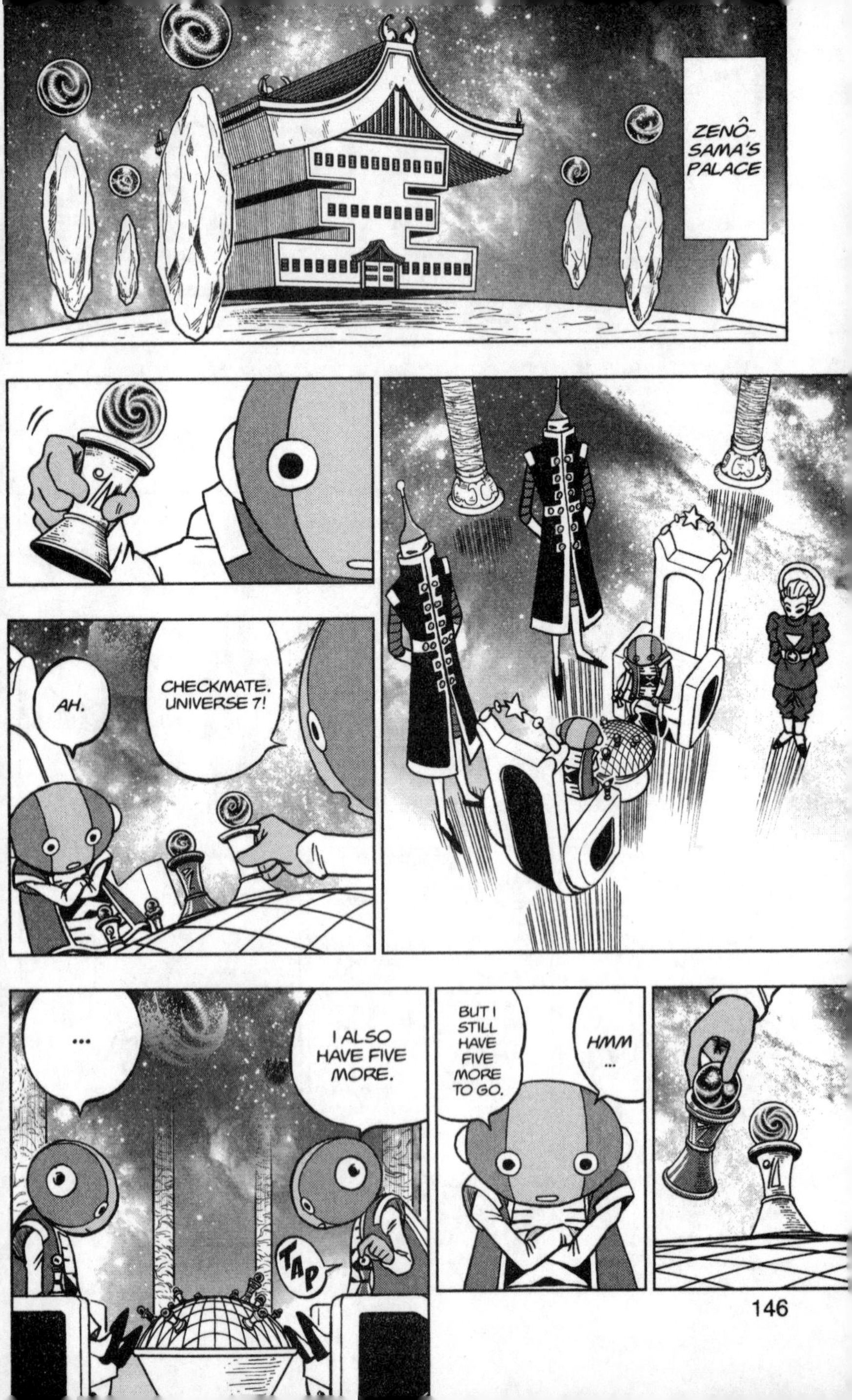
ZENÔ-SAMA'S PALACE
CHECKMATE. UNIVERSE 7!
AH.
HMM ...
BUT I STILL HAVE FIVE MORE TO GO.
I ALSO HAVE FIVE MORE.
...
TAP

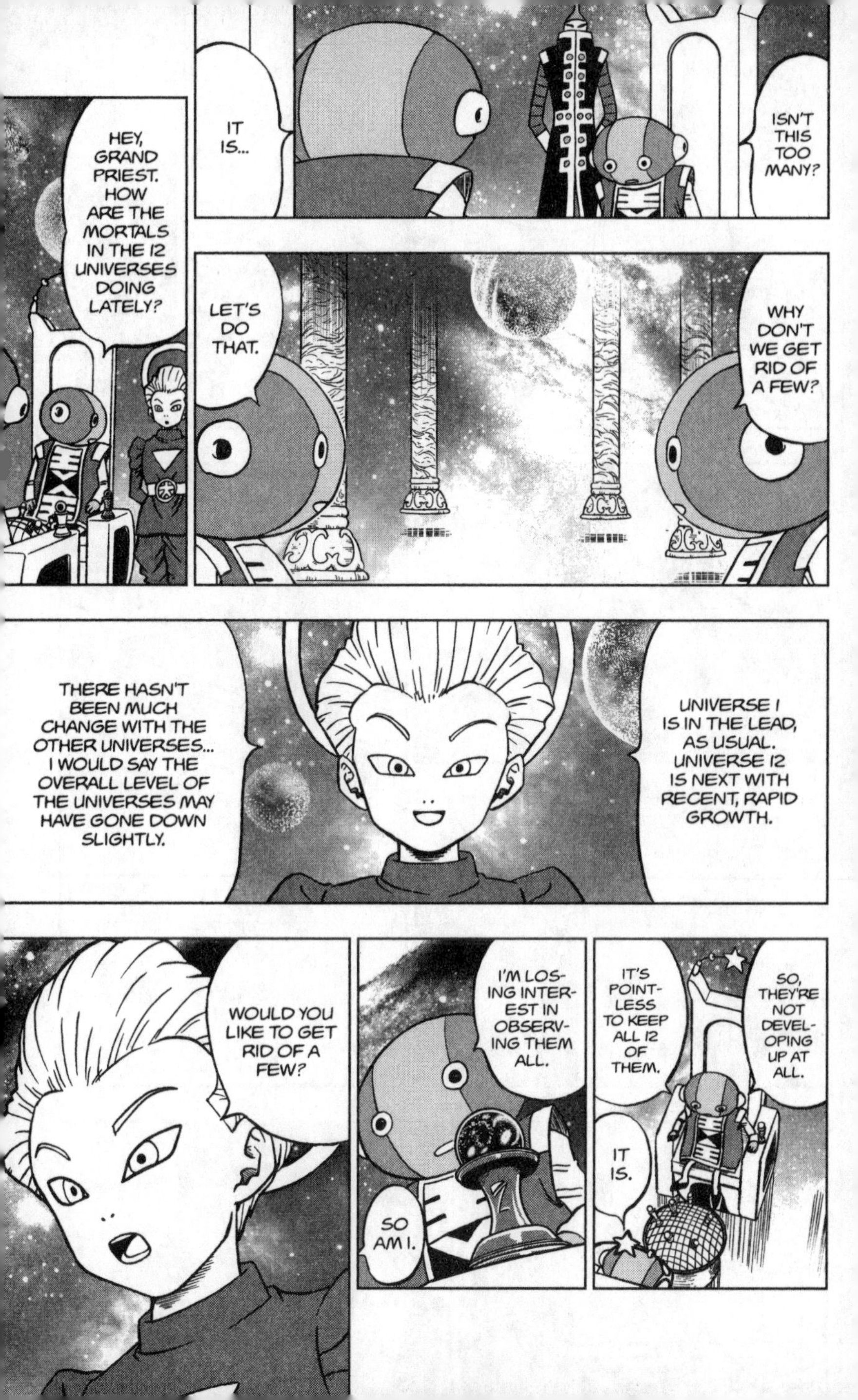
ISN'T THIS TOO MANY?
IT IS...
WHY DON'T WE GET RID OF A FEW?
LET'S DO THAT.
HEY, GRAND PRIEST. HOW ARE THE MORTALS IN THE 12 UNIVERSES DOING LATELY?
UNIVERSE 1 IS IN THE LEAD, AS USUAL. UNIVERSE 12 IS NEXT WITH RECENT, RAPID GROWTH.
THERE HASN'T BEEN MUCH CHANGE WITH THE OTHER UNIVERSES... I WOULD SAY THE OVERALL LEVEL OF THE UNIVERSES MAY HAVE GONE DOWN SLIGHTLY.
SO, THEY'RE NOT DEVEL-OPING UP AT ALL.
IT'S POINT-LESS TO KEEP ALL 12 OF THEM.
IT IS.
I'M LOS-ING INTER-EST IN OBSERV-ING THEM ALL.
SO AM I.
WOULD YOU LIKE TO GET RID OF A FEW?

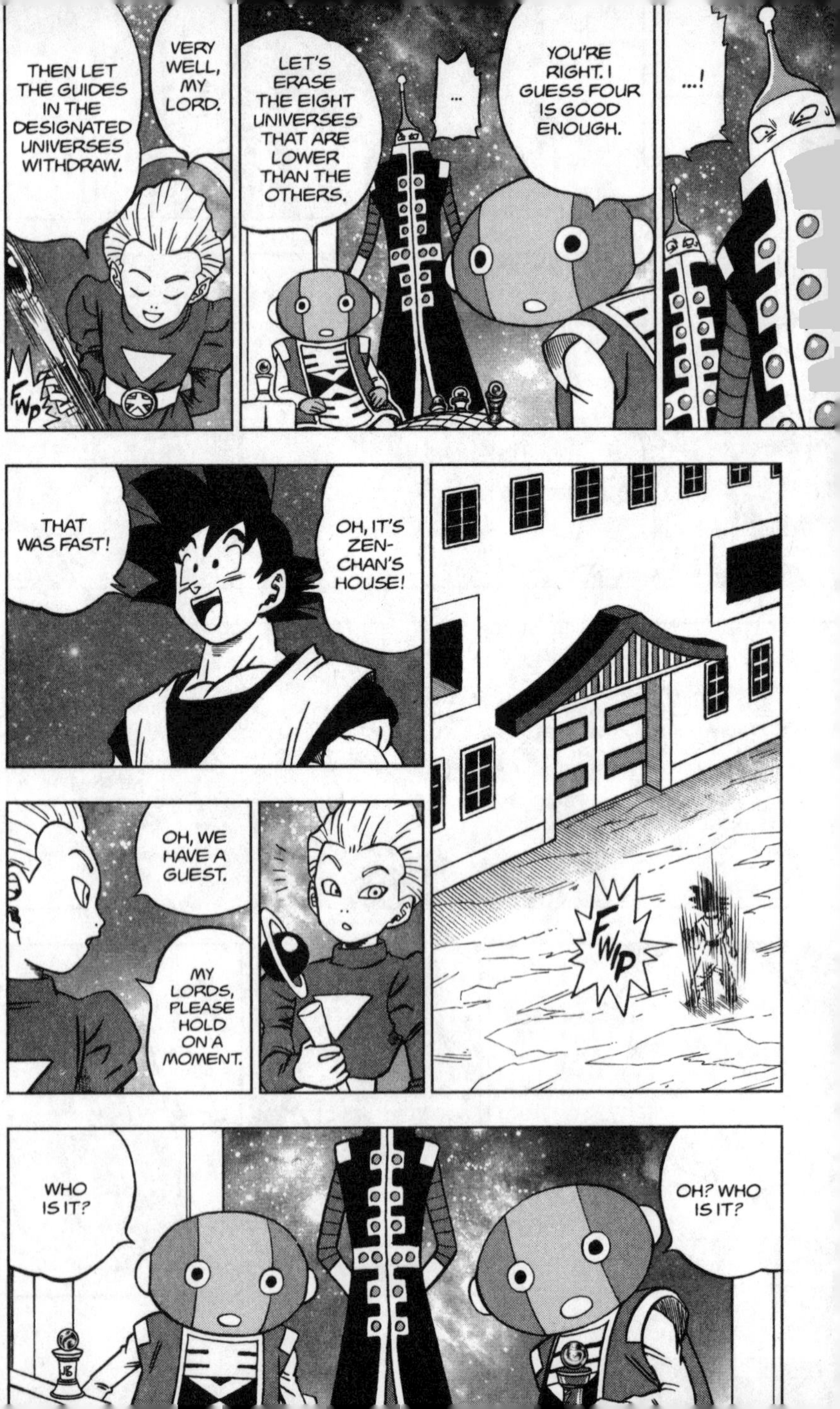
...!
YOU'RE RIGHT. I GUESS FOUR IS GOOD ENOUGH.
...
LET'S ERASE THE EIGHT UNIVERSES THAT ARE LOWER THAN THE OTHERS.
VERY WELL, MY LORD.
THEN LET THE GUIDES IN THE DESIGNATED UNIVERSES WITHDRAW.
FWP
FWIP
OH, IT'S ZEN-CHAN'S HOUSE!
THAT WAS FAST!
OH, WE HAVE A GUEST.
MY LORDS, PLEASE HOLD ON A MOMENT.
OH? WHO IS IT?
WHO IS IT?

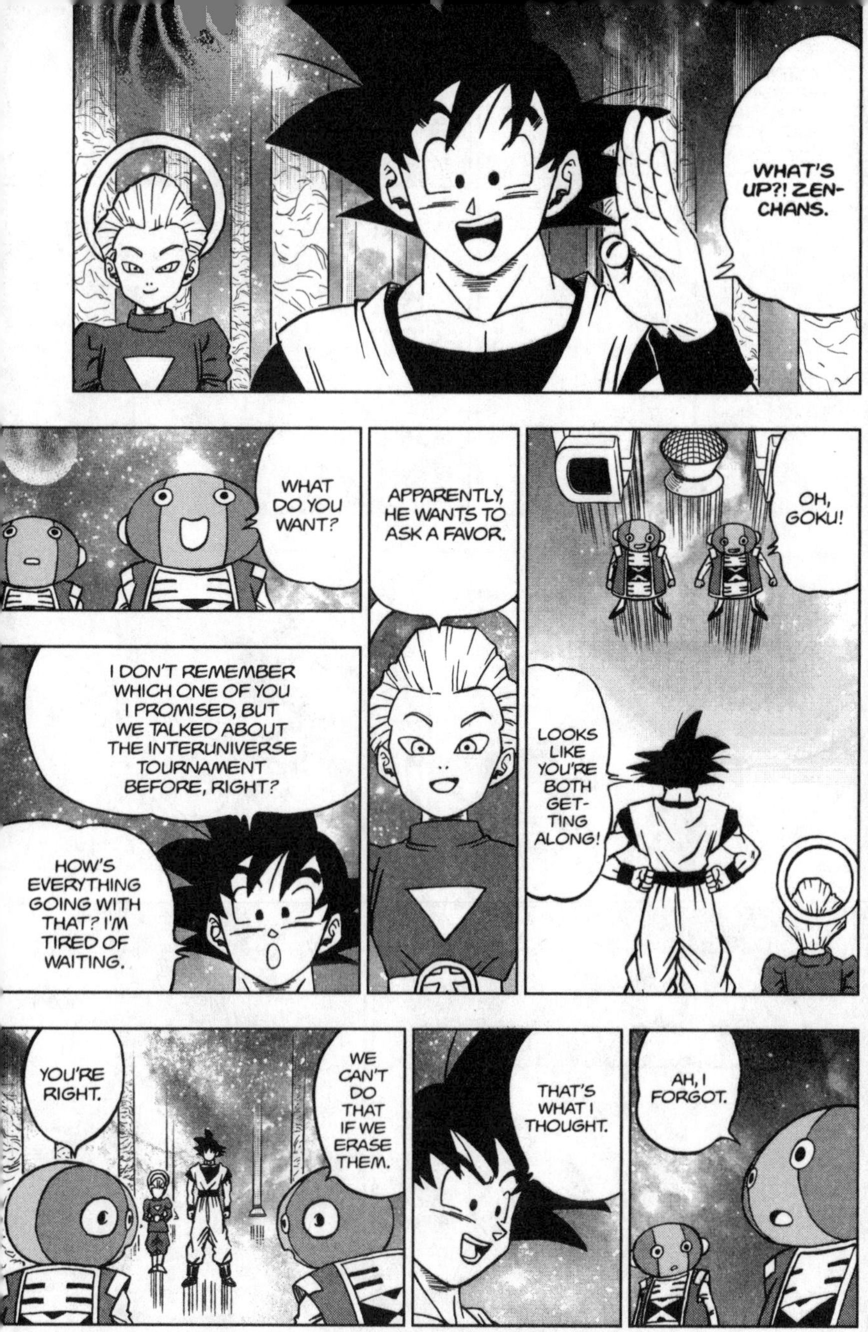
WHAT'S UP?! ZEN-CHANS.
OH, GOKU!
LOOKS LIKE YOU'RE BOTH GETTING ALONG!
APPARENTLY, HE WANTS TO ASK A FAVOR.
WHAT DO YOU WANT?
I DON'T REMEMBER WHICH ONE OF YOU I PROMISED, BUT WE TALKED ABOUT THE INTERUNIVERSE TOURNAMENT BEFORE, RIGHT?
HOW'S EVERYTHING GOING WITH THAT? I'M TIRED OF WAITING.
AH, I FORGOT.
THAT'S WHAT I THOUGHT.
WE CAN'T DO THAT IF WE ERASE THEM.
YOU'RE RIGHT.

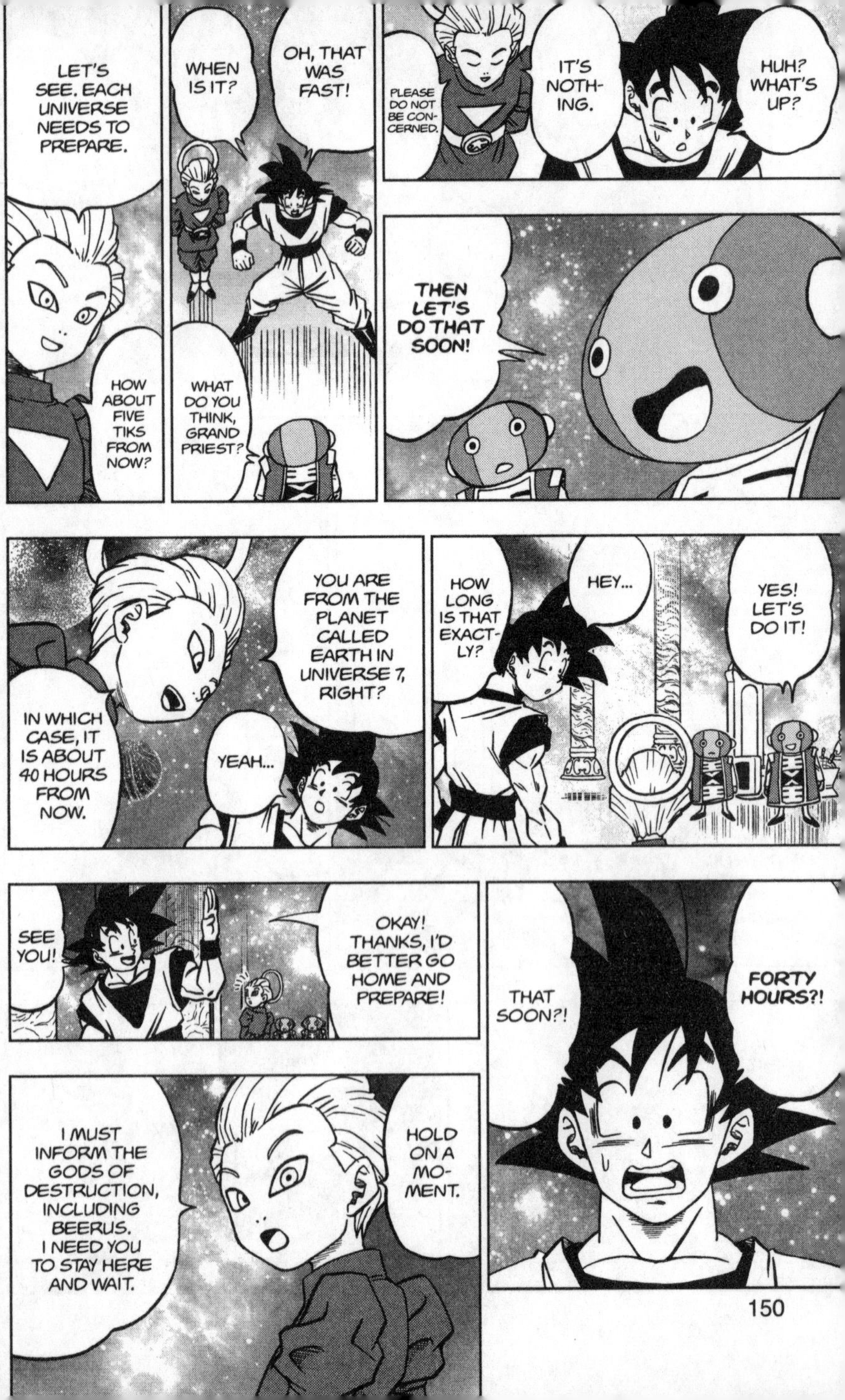
HUH? WHAT'S UP?
IT'S NOTHING.
PLEASE DO NOT BE CONCERNED.
THEN LET'S DO THAT SOON!
OH, THAT WAS FAST!
WHEN IS IT?
WHAT DO YOU THINK, GRAND PRIEST?
LET'S SEE. EACH UNIVERSE NEEDS TO PREPARE.
HOW ABOUT FIVE TIKS FROM NOW?
YES! LET'S DO IT!
HEY...
HOW LONG IS THAT EXACTLY?
YOU ARE FROM THE PLANET CALLED EARTH IN UNIVERSE 7, RIGHT?
YEAH...
IN WHICH CASE, IT IS ABOUT 40 HOURS FROM NOW.
FORTY HOURS?!
THAT SOON?!
OKAY! THANKS, I'D BETTER GO HOME AND PREPARE!
SEE YOU!
HOLD ON A MOMENT.
I MUST INFORM THE GODS OF DESTRUCTION, INCLUDING BEERUS. I NEED YOU TO STAY HERE AND WAIT.

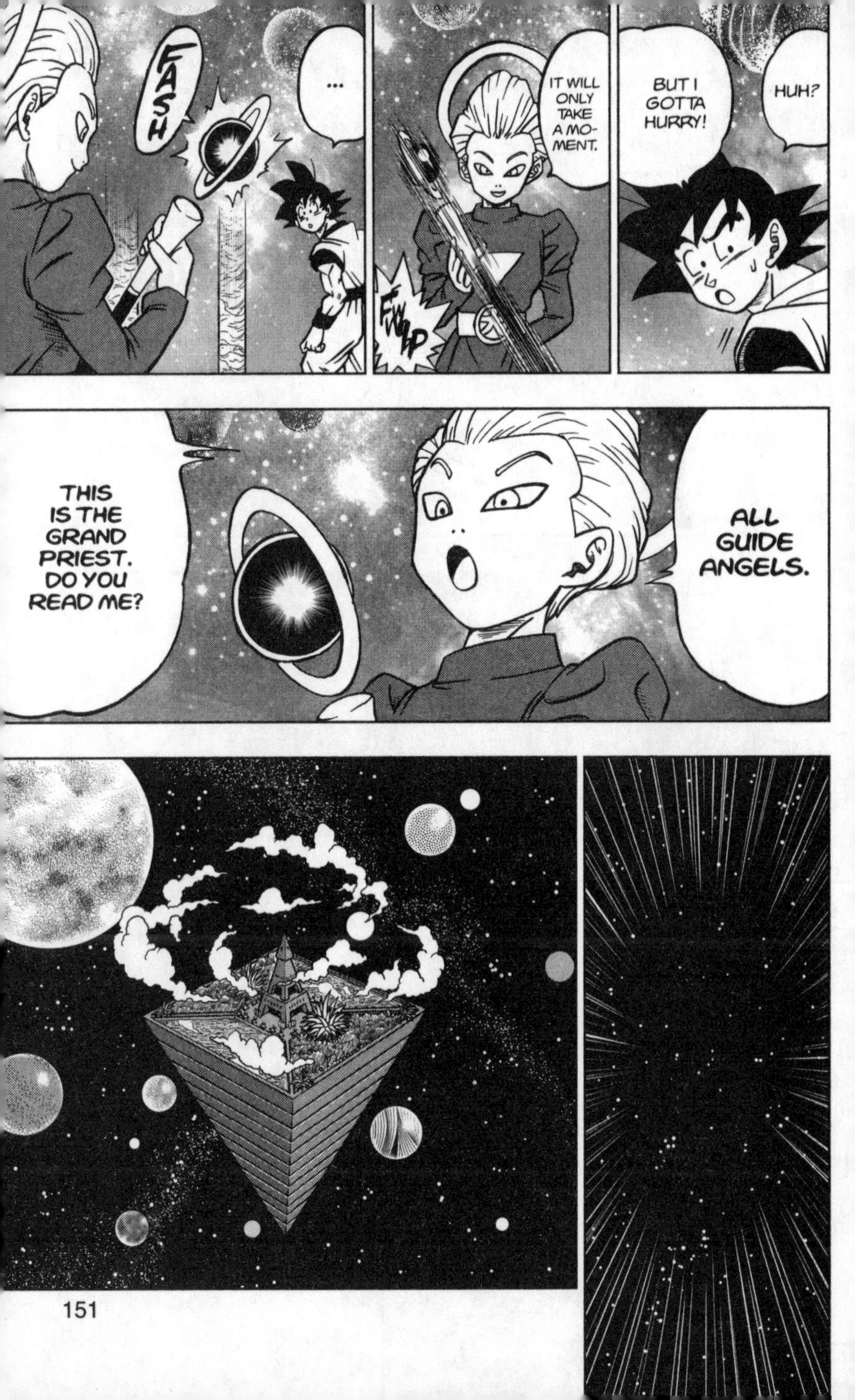
HUH?
BUT I GOTTA HURRY!
IT WILL ONLY TAKE A MOMENT.
...
FASH
ALL GUIDE ANGELS.
THIS IS THE GRAND PRIEST. DO YOU READ ME?

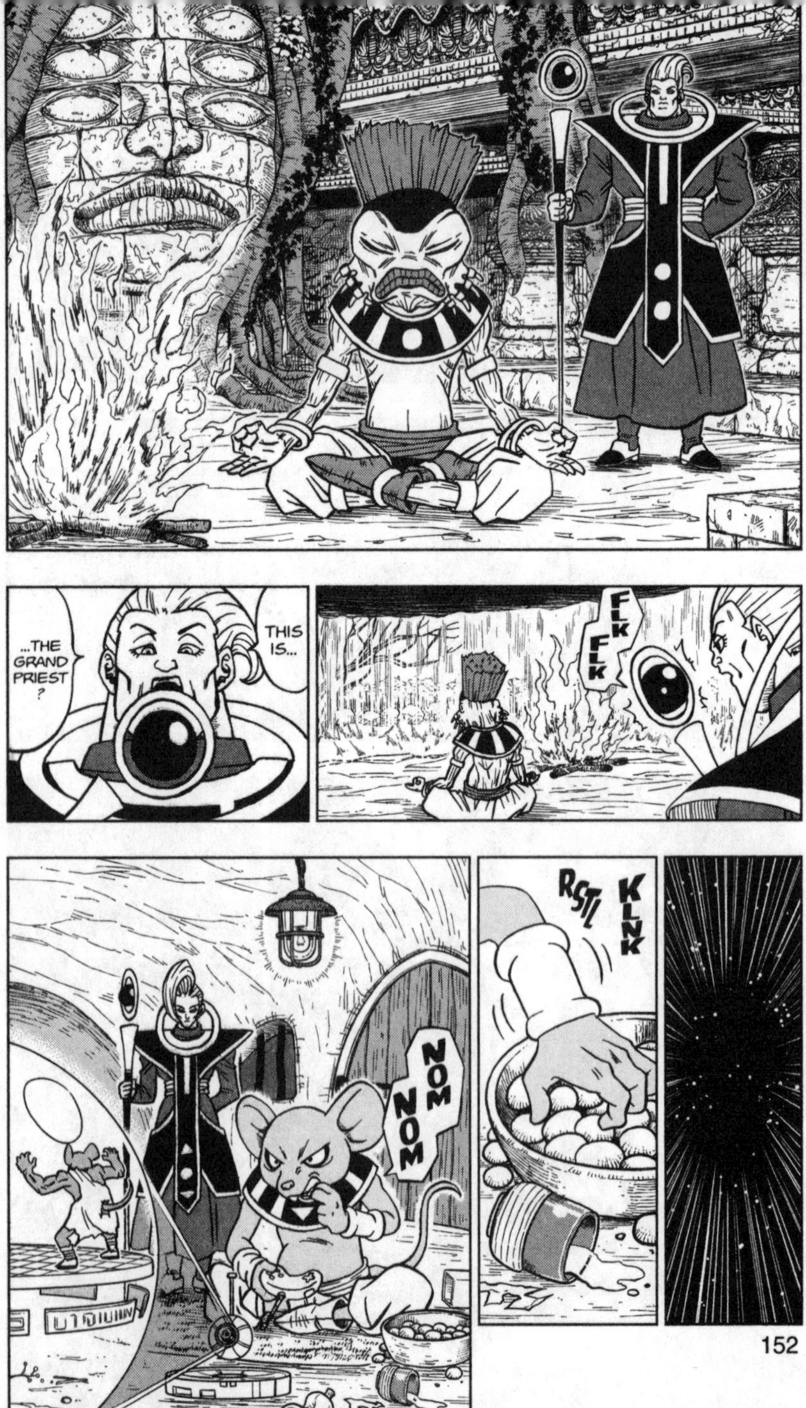
FLK
FLK
THIS IS...
...THE GRAND PRIEST?
KLNK
RSTL
NOM NOM NOM

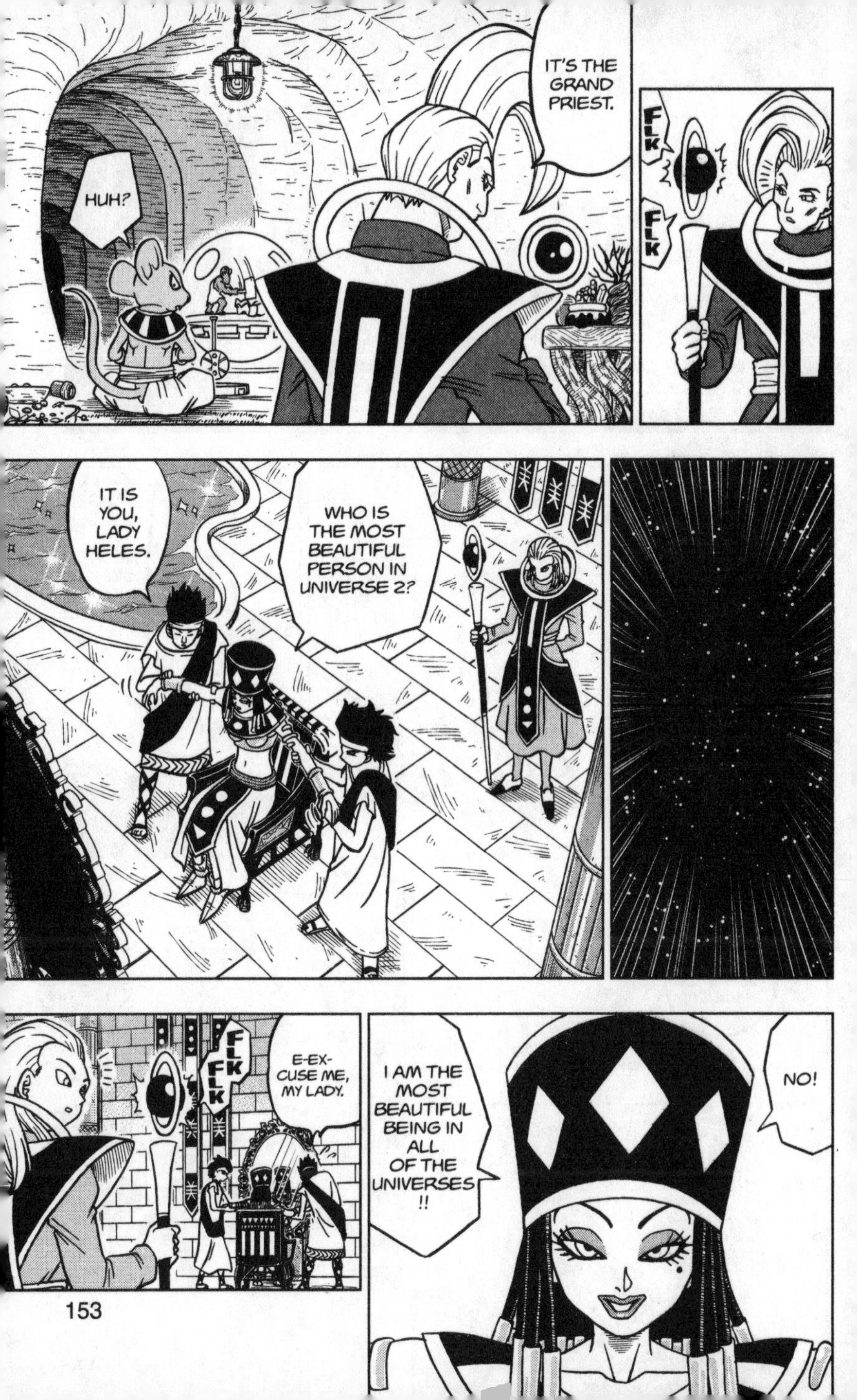
FLK
FLK
IT'S THE GRAND PRIEST.
HUH?
WHO IS THE MOST BEAUTIFUL PERSON IN UNIVERSE 2?
IT IS YOU, LADY HELES.
NO!
I AM THE MOST BEAUTIFUL BEING IN ALL OF THE UNIVERSES!!
E-EX-CUSE ME, MY LADY.
FLK
FLK

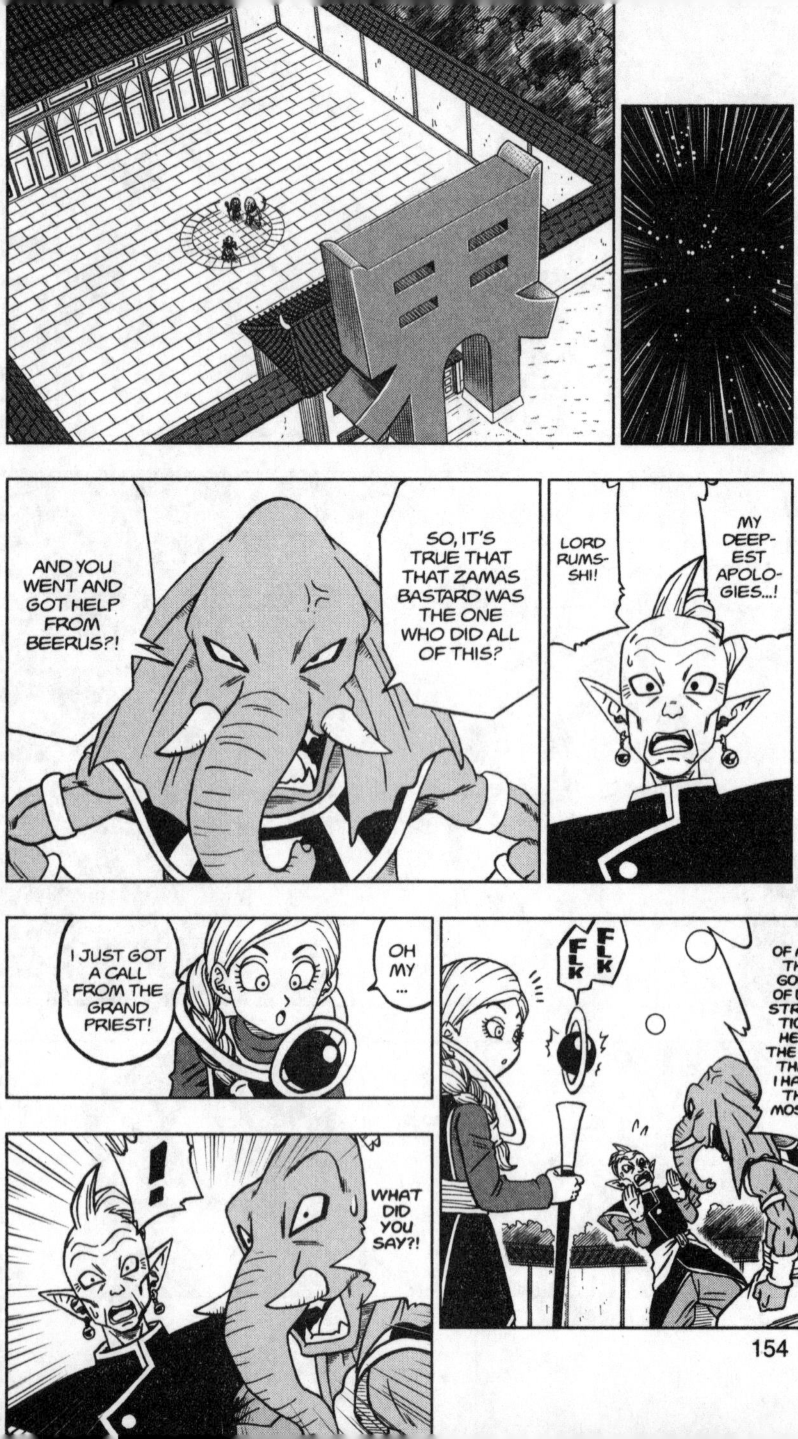
MY DEEP-EST APOLO-GIES...!
LORD RUMS-SHI!
SO, IT'S TRUE THAT THAT ZAMAS BASTARD WAS THE ONE WHO DID ALL OF THIS?
AND YOU WENT AND GOT HELP FROM BEERUS?!
OF ALL THE GODS OF DE-STRUC-TION, HE IS THE ONE THAT I HATE THE MOST!!
FLK FLK
OH MY ...
I JUST GOT A CALL FROM THE GRAND PRIEST!
WHAT DID YOU SAY?!
!

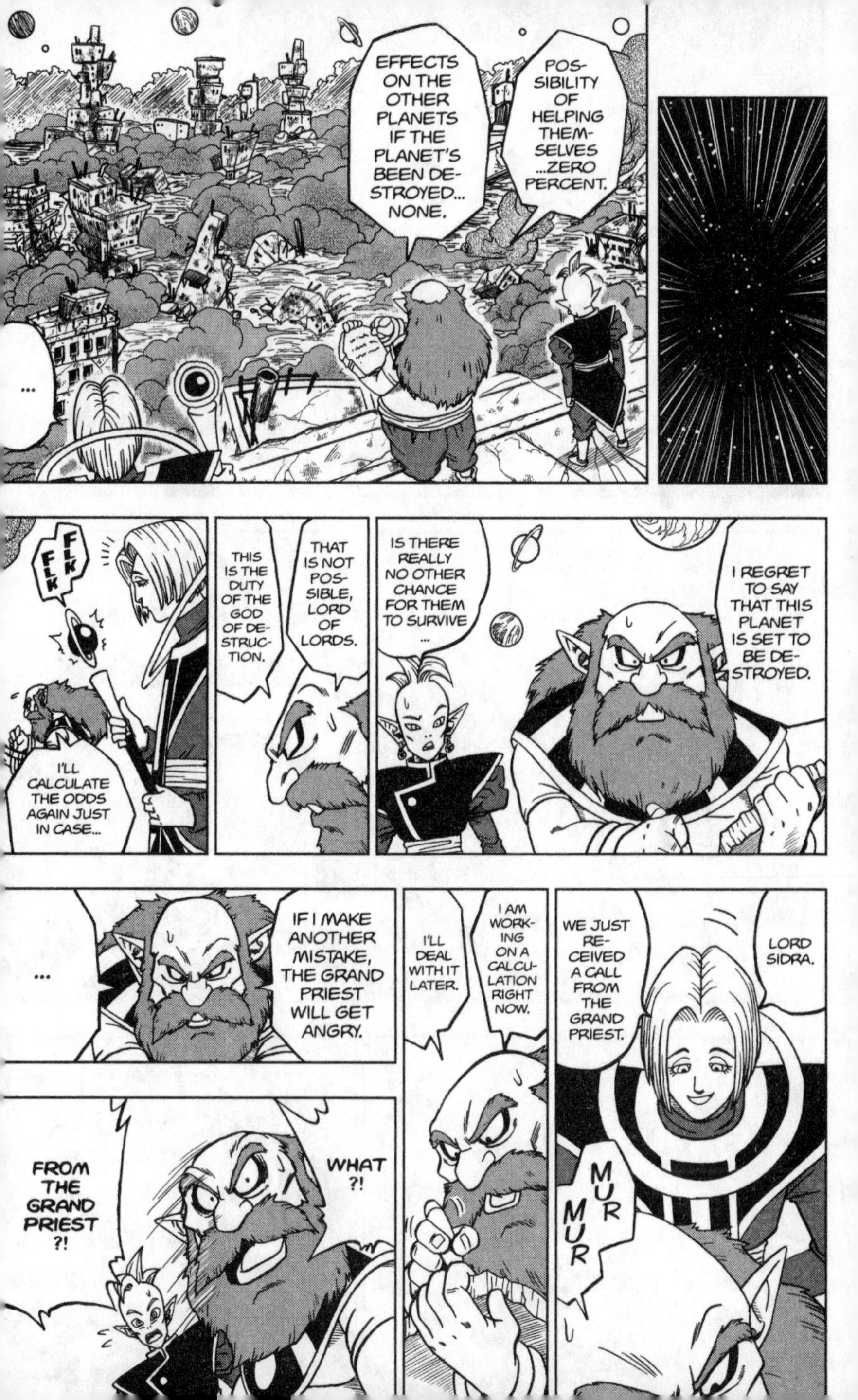
POSSIBILITY OF HELPING THEMSELVES ...ZERO PERCENT.
EFFECTS ON THE OTHER PLANETS IF THE PLANET'S BEEN DESTROYED... NONE.
...
I REGRET TO SAY THAT THIS PLANET IS SET TO BE DESTROYED.
IS THERE REALLY NO OTHER CHANCE FOR THEM TO SURVIVE ...
THAT IS NOT POSSIBLE, LORD OF LORDS.
THIS IS THE DUTY OF THE GOD OF DESTRUCTION.
FLK FLK
I'LL CALCULATE THE ODDS AGAIN JUST IN CASE...
LORD SIDRA.
WE JUST RECEIVED A CALL FROM THE GRAND PRIEST.
MUR MUR
MUR MUR
I AM WORKING ON A CALCULATION RIGHT NOW.
I'LL DEAL WITH IT LATER.
IF I MAKE ANOTHER MISTAKE, THE GRAND PRIEST WILL GET ANGRY.
...
WHAT?!
FROM THE GRAND PRIEST?!

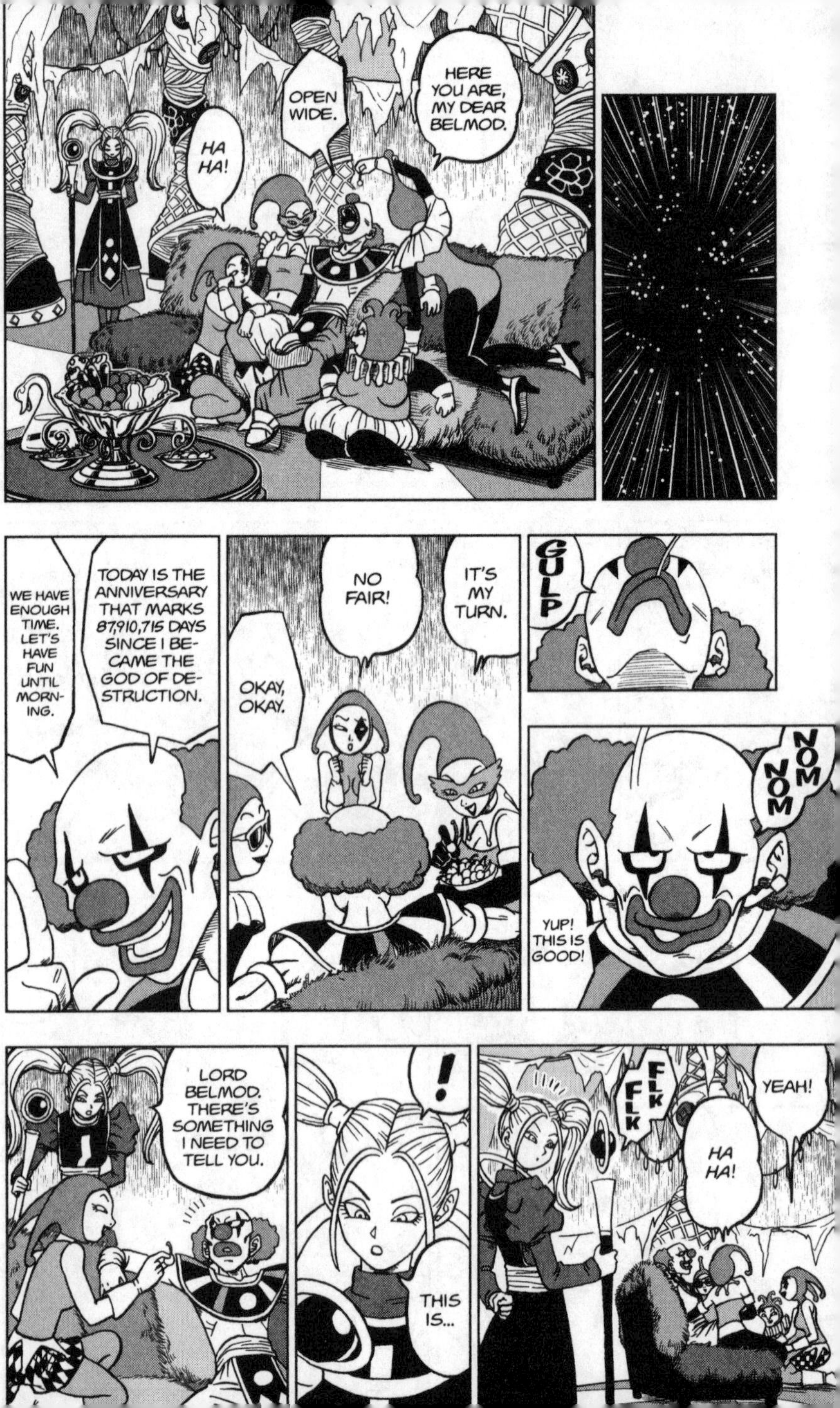
HERE YOU ARE, MY DEAR BELMOD.
OPEN WIDE.
HA HA!
GULP
NOM NOM
YUP! THIS IS GOOD!
IT'S MY TURN.
NO FAIR!
OKAY, OKAY.
TODAY IS THE ANNIVERSARY THAT MARKS 87,910,715 DAYS SINCE I BE-CAME THE GOD OF DE-STRUCTION.
WE HAVE ENOUGH TIME. LET'S HAVE FUN UNTIL MORN-ING.
YEAH!
HA HA!
FLK FLK
!
THIS IS...
LORD BELMOD. THERE'S SOMETHING I NEED TO TELL YOU.

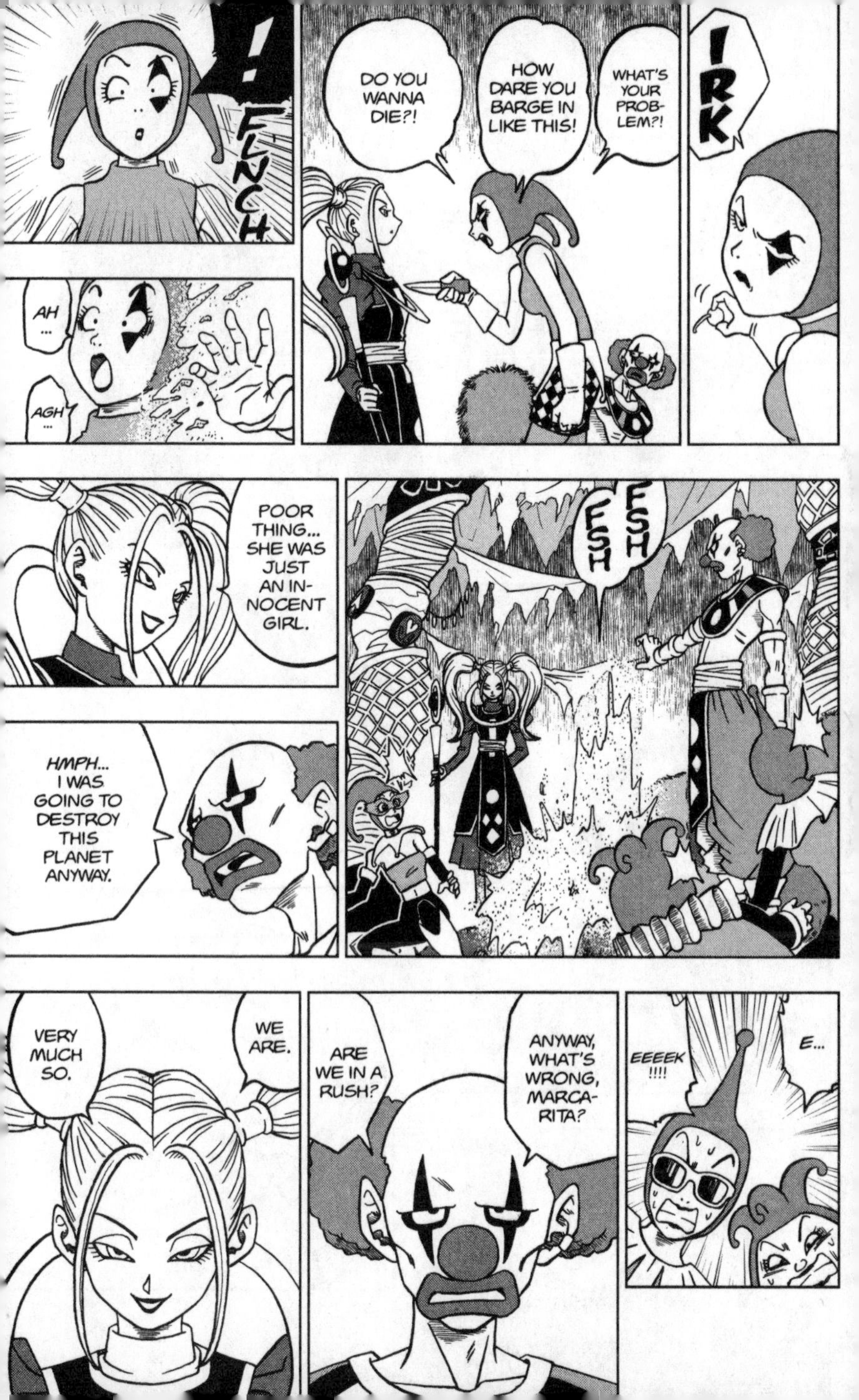
IRK
WHAT'S YOUR PROB-LEM?!
HOW DARE YOU BARGE IN LIKE THIS!
DO YOU WANNA DIE?!
!
FLINCH
AH ...
AGH ...
FSH FSH
POOR THING... SHE WAS JUST AN IN-NOCENT GIRL.
HMPH... I WAS GOING TO DESTROY THIS PLANET ANYWAY.
E...
EEEEK !!!!
ANYWAY, WHAT'S WRONG, MARCA-RITA?
ARE WE IN A RUSH?
WE ARE.
VERY MUCH SO.

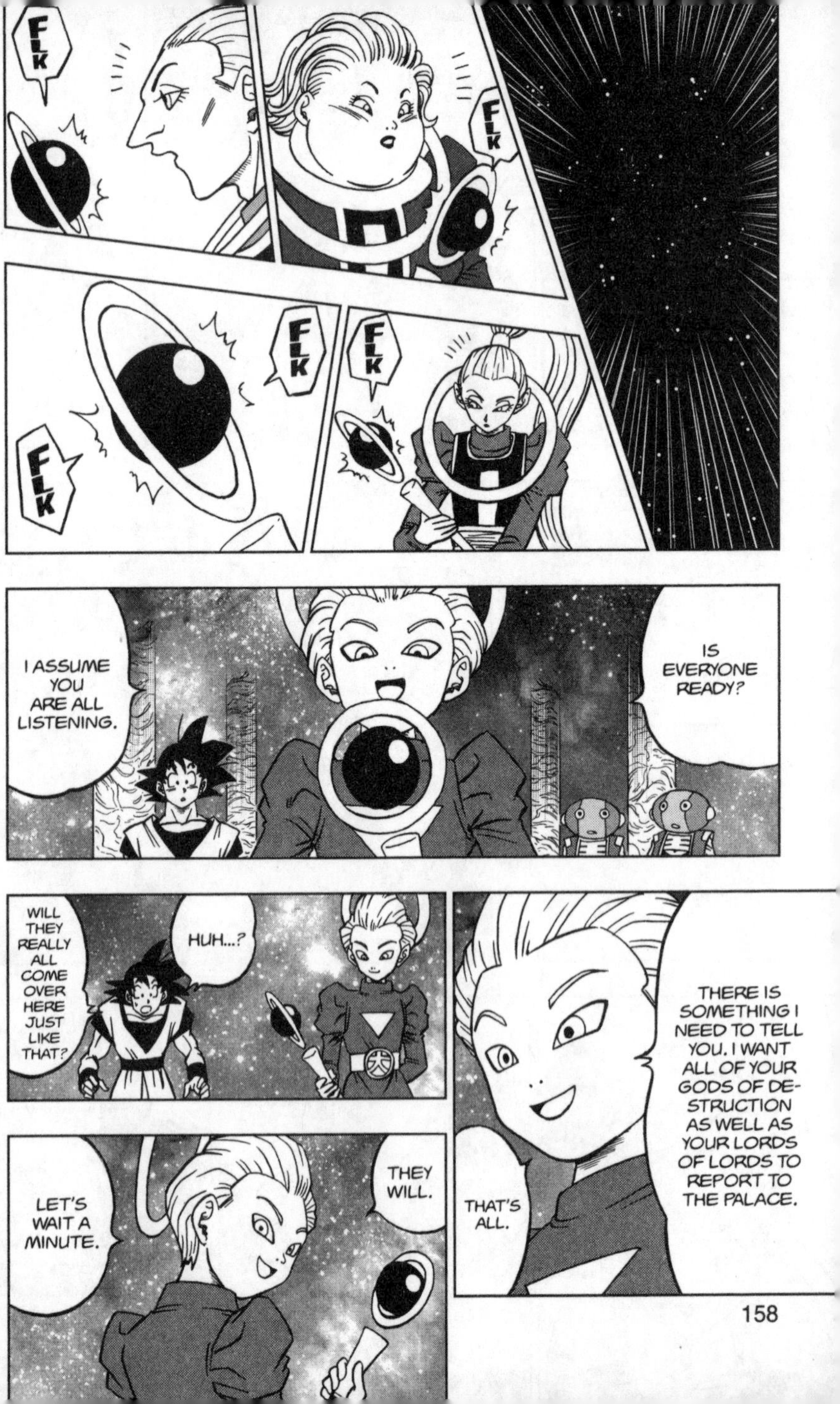
FLK
FLK
FLK
FLK
FLK
IS EVERYONE READY?
I ASSUME YOU ARE ALL LISTENING.
THERE IS SOMETHING I NEED TO TELL YOU. I WANT ALL OF YOUR GODS OF DE-STRUCTION AS WELL AS YOUR LORDS OF LORDS TO REPORT TO THE PALACE.
THAT'S ALL.
HUH...?
WILL THEY REALLY ALL COME OVER HERE JUST LIKE THAT?
THEY WILL.
LET'S WAIT A MINUTE.

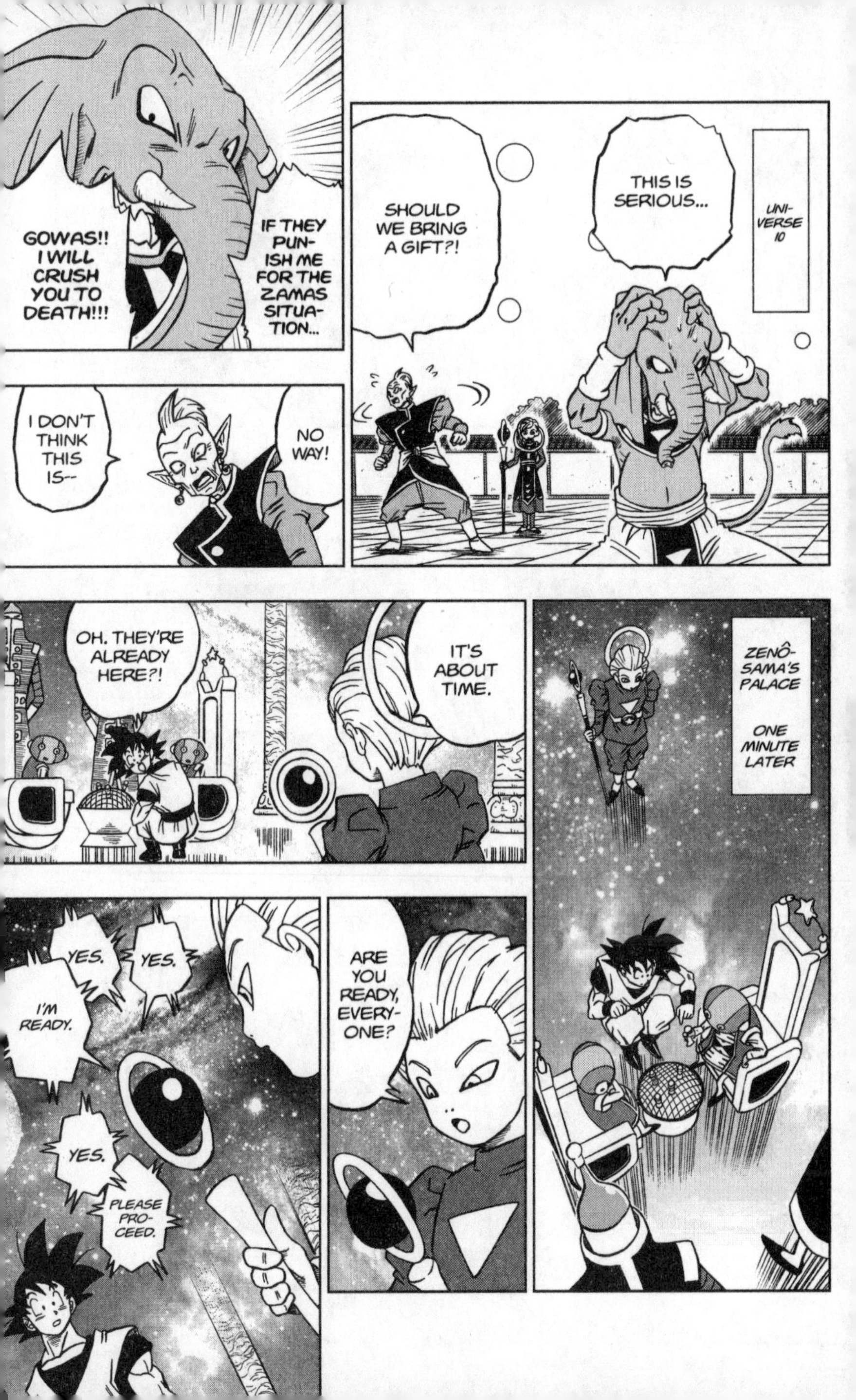
UNIVERSE 10
THIS IS SERIOUS...
SHOULD WE BRING A GIFT?!
IF THEY PUNISH ME FOR THE ZAMAS SITUATION...
GOWAS!! I WILL CRUSH YOU TO DEATH!!!
NO WAY!
I DON'T THINK THIS IS--
ZENÔ-SAMA'S PALACE
ONE MINUTE LATER
IT'S ABOUT TIME.
OH. THEY'RE ALREADY HERE?!
ARE YOU READY, EVERYONE?
YES.
YES.
I'M READY.
YES.
PLEASE PROCEED.

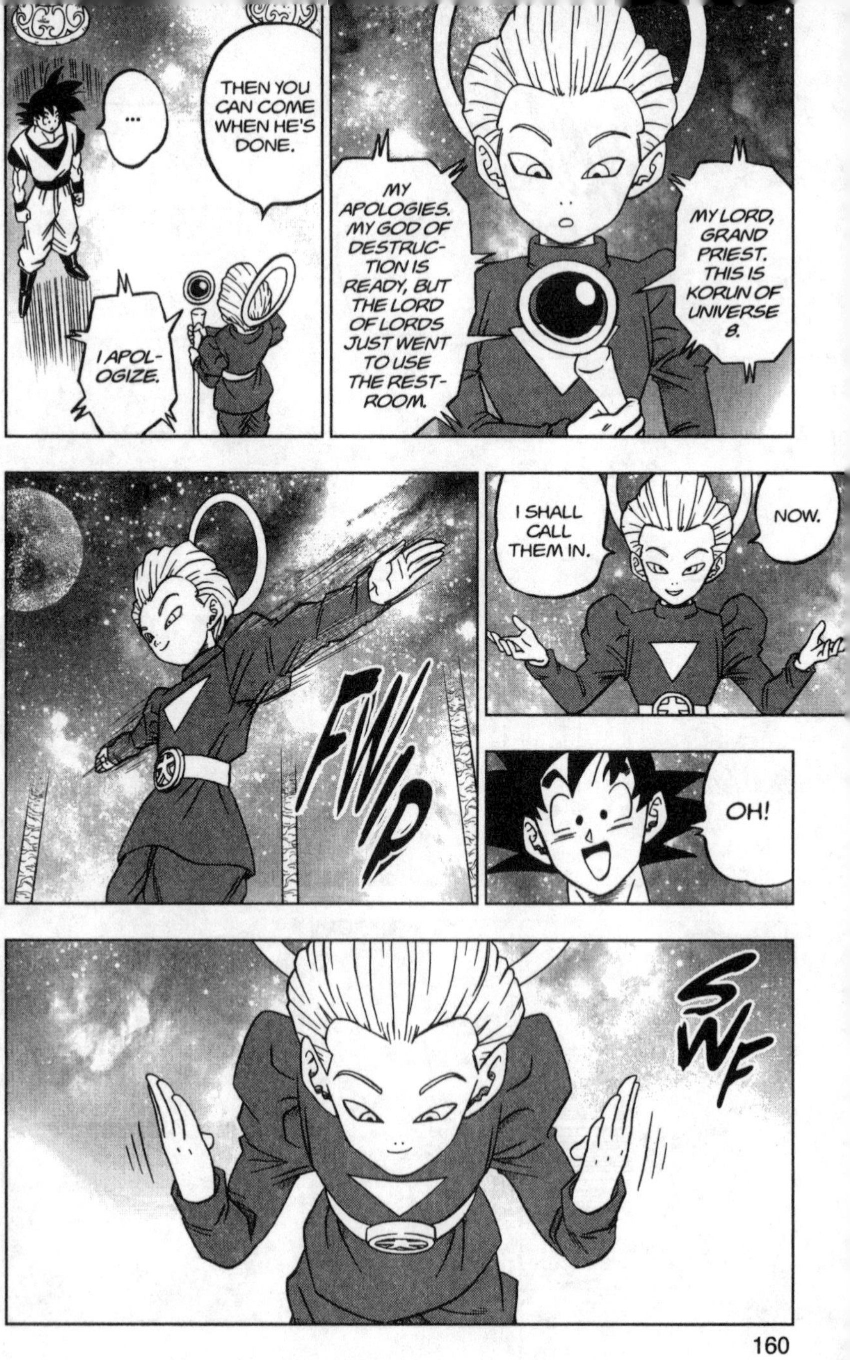
MY LORD, GRAND PRIEST. THIS IS KORUN OF UNIVERSE 8.
MY APOLOGIES. MY GOD OF DESTRUCTION IS READY, BUT THE LORD OF LORDS JUST WENT TO USE THE RESTROOM.
THEN YOU CAN COME WHEN HE'S DONE.
...
I APOLOGIZE.
NOW.
I SHALL CALL THEM IN.
OH!
FWIP
SWF

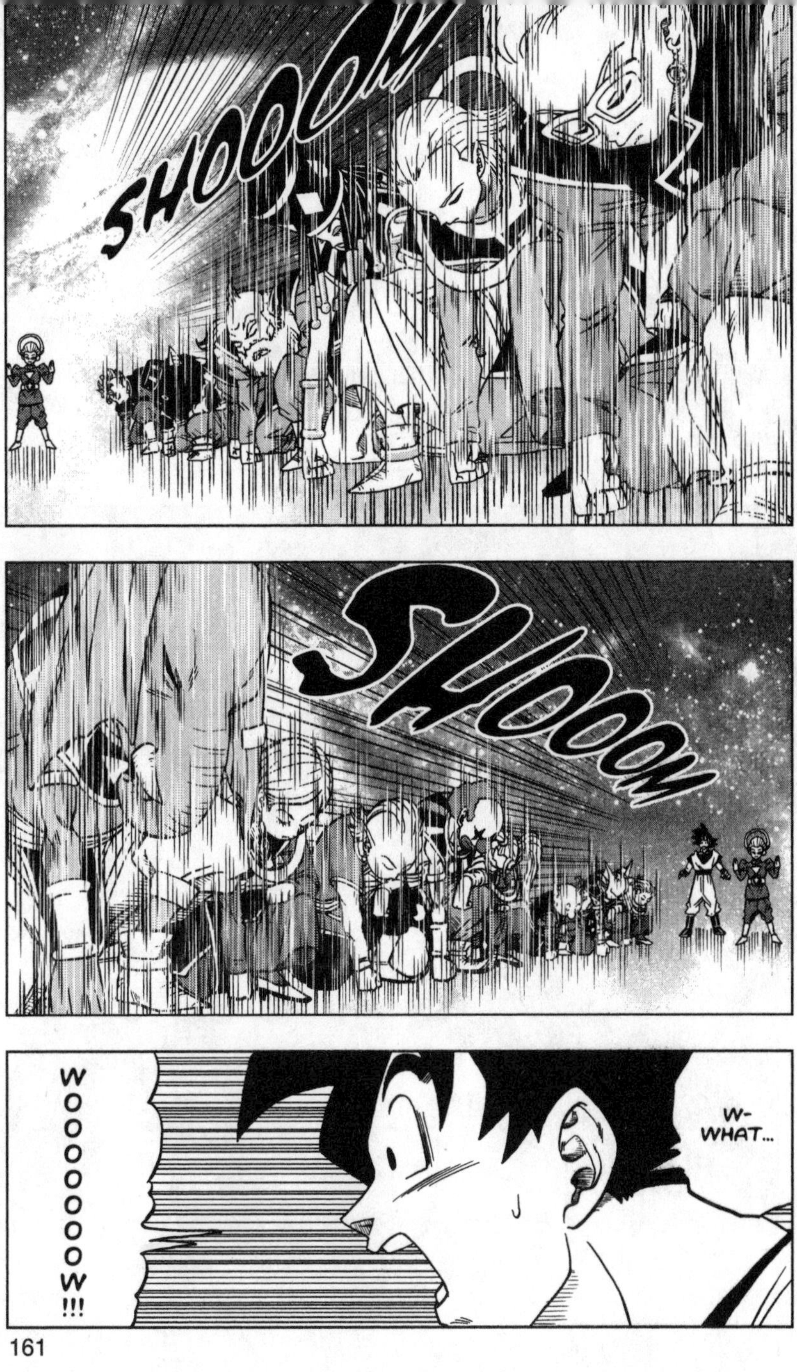
SHOOOM
SHOOOM
W-
WHAT...
WOOOOOOOW
!!!

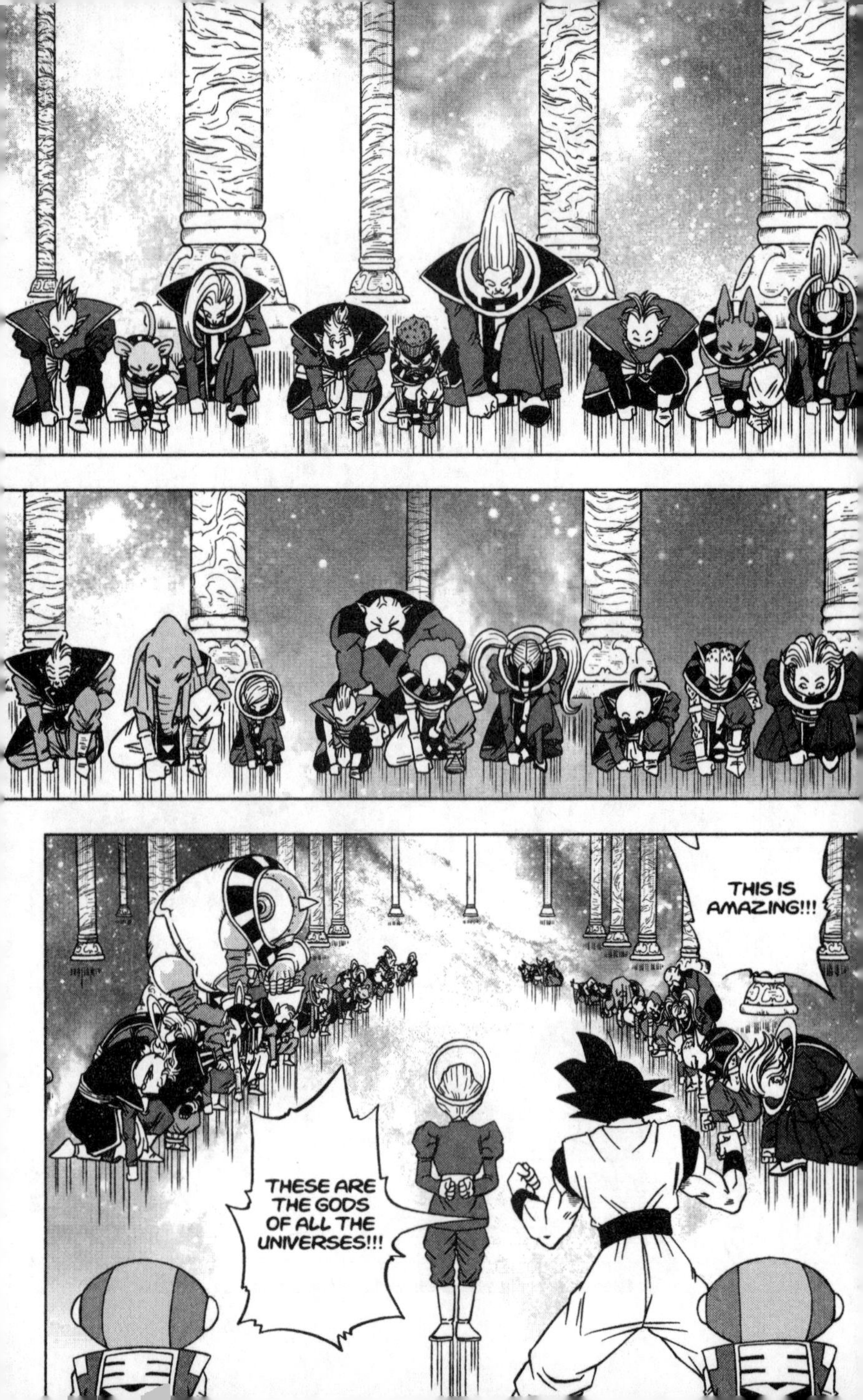
THIS IS AMAZING!!!
THESE ARE THE GODS OF ALL THE UNIVERSES!!!

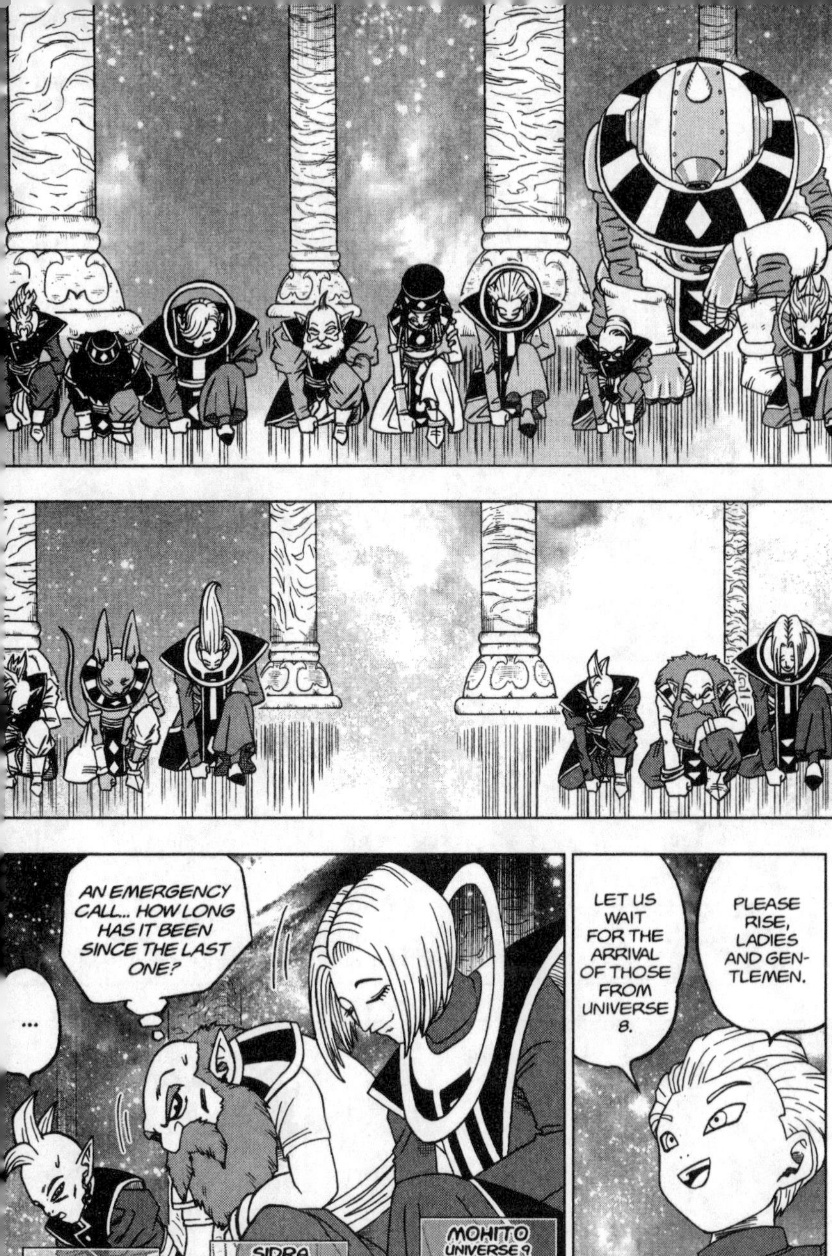
PLEASE RISE, LADIES AND GEN- TLEMEN.
LET US WAIT FOR THE ARRIVAL OF THOSE FROM UNIVERSE 8.
AN EMERGENCY CALL... HOW LONG HAS IT BEEN SINCE THE LAST ONE?
...
MOHITO UNIVERSE 9 GUIDE ANGEL
SIDRA UNIVERSE 9 GOD OF DESTRUCTION
ROH UNIVERSE 9 LORD OF LORDS

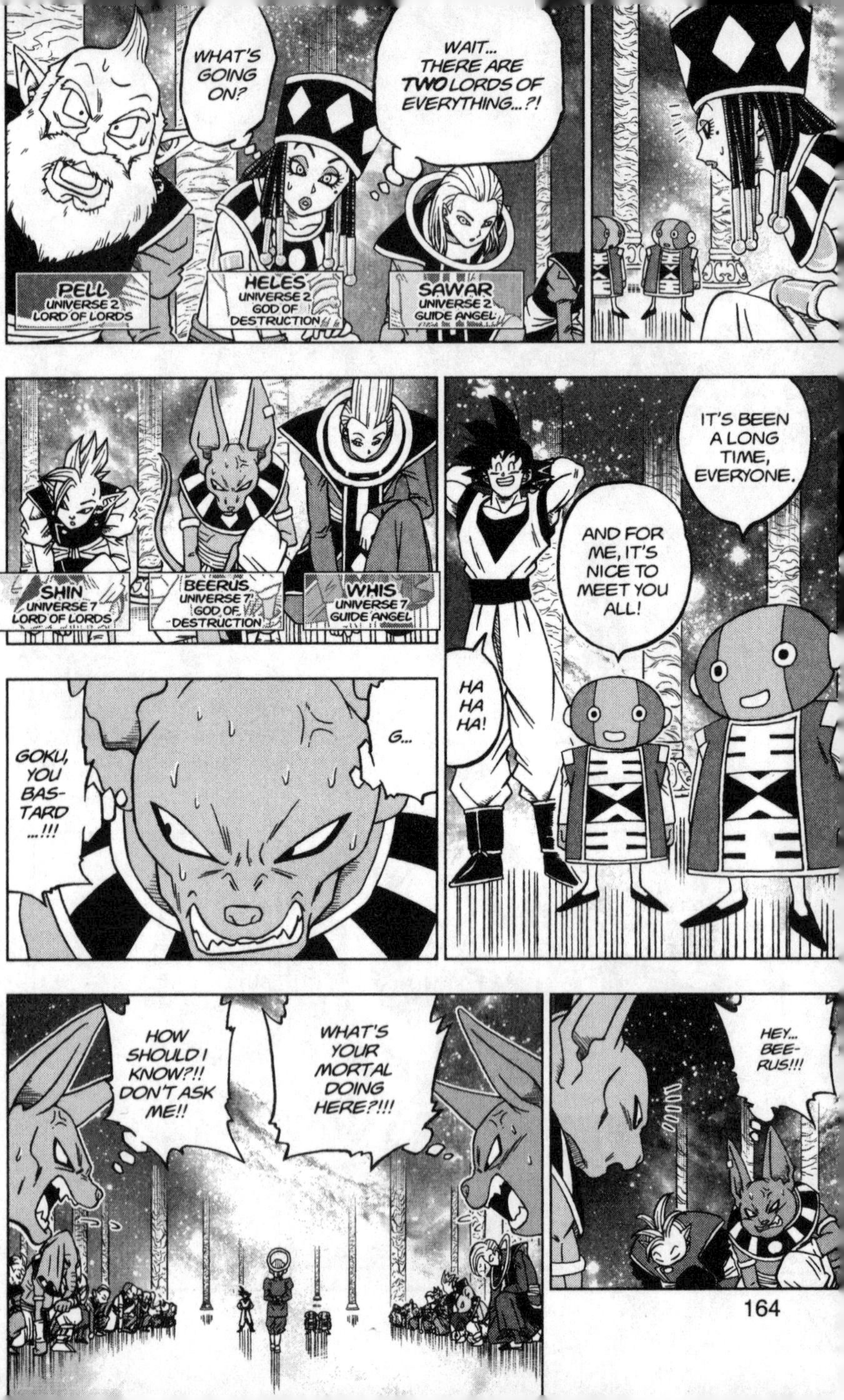
WAIT... THERE ARE TWO LORDS OF EVERYTHING...?!
WHAT'S GOING ON?
SAWAR
UNIVERSE 2
GUIDE ANGEL
HELES
UNIVERSE 2
GOD OF DESTRUCTION
PELL
UNIVERSE 2
LORD OF LORDS
IT'S BEEN A LONG TIME, EVERYONE.
AND FOR ME, IT'S NICE TO MEET YOU ALL!
HA HA HA!
WHIS
UNIVERSE 7
GUIDE ANGEL
BEERUS
UNIVERSE 7
GOD OF DESTRUCTION
SHIN
UNIVERSE 7
LORD OF LORDS
G...
GOKU, YOU BAS-TARD...!!!
HEY... BEE-RUS!!!
WHAT'S YOUR MORTAL DOING HERE?!!!
HOW SHOULD I KNOW?!! DON'T ASK ME!!

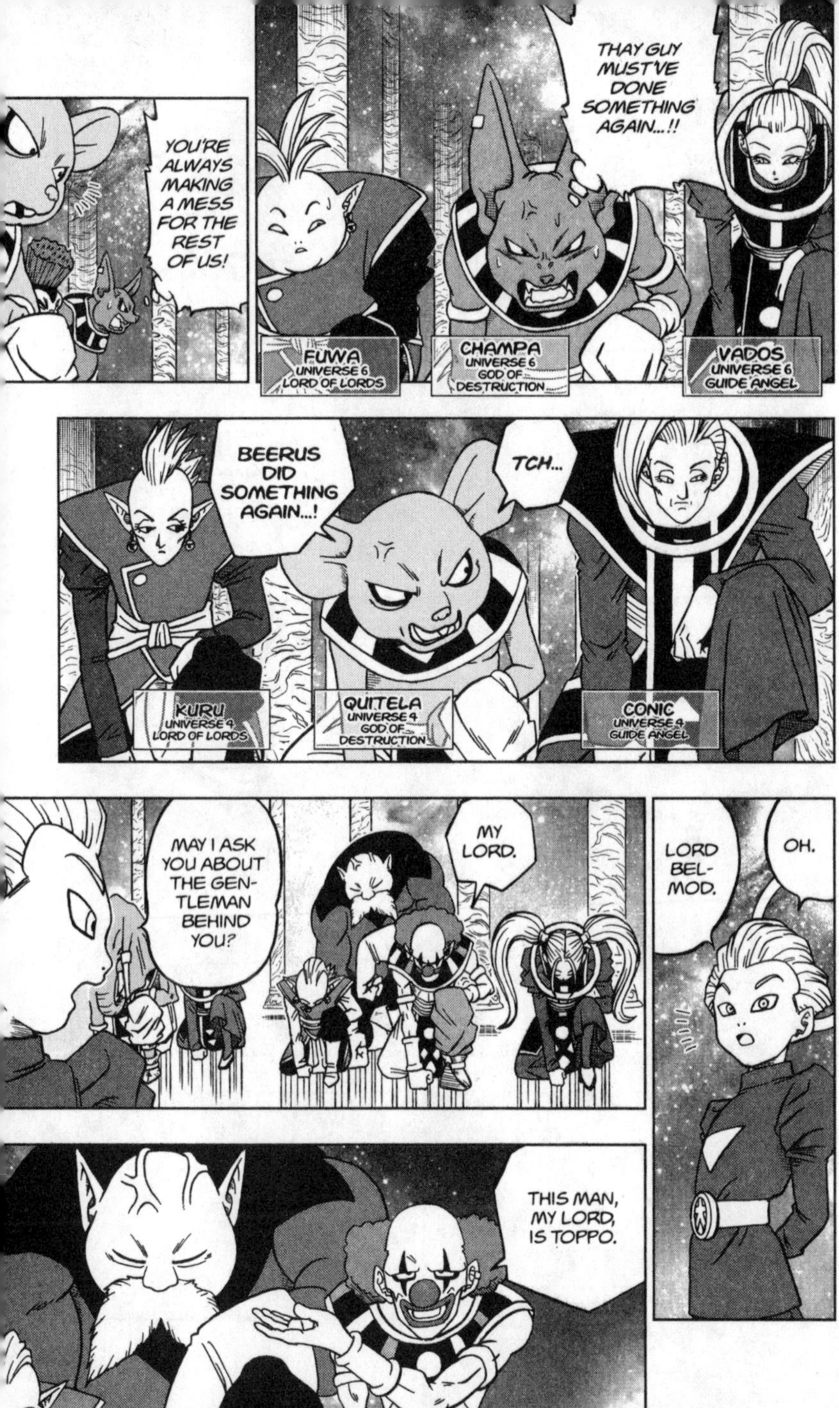
THAY GUY MUST'VE DONE SOMETHING AGAIN...!!
VADOS UNIVERSE 6 GUIDE ANGEL
CHAMPA UNIVERSE 6 GOD OF DESTRUCTION
FUWA UNIVERSE 6 LORD OF LORDS
YOU'RE ALWAYS MAKING A MESS FOR THE REST OF US!
TCH...
BEERUS DID SOMETHING AGAIN...!
CONIC UNIVERSE 4 GUIDE ANGEL
QUITELA UNIVERSE 4 GOD OF DESTRUCTION
KURU UNIVERSE 4 LORD OF LORDS
OH.
LORD BEL-MOD.
MY LORD.
MAY I ASK YOU ABOUT THE GEN-TLEMAN BEHIND YOU?
THIS MAN, MY LORD, IS TOPPO.

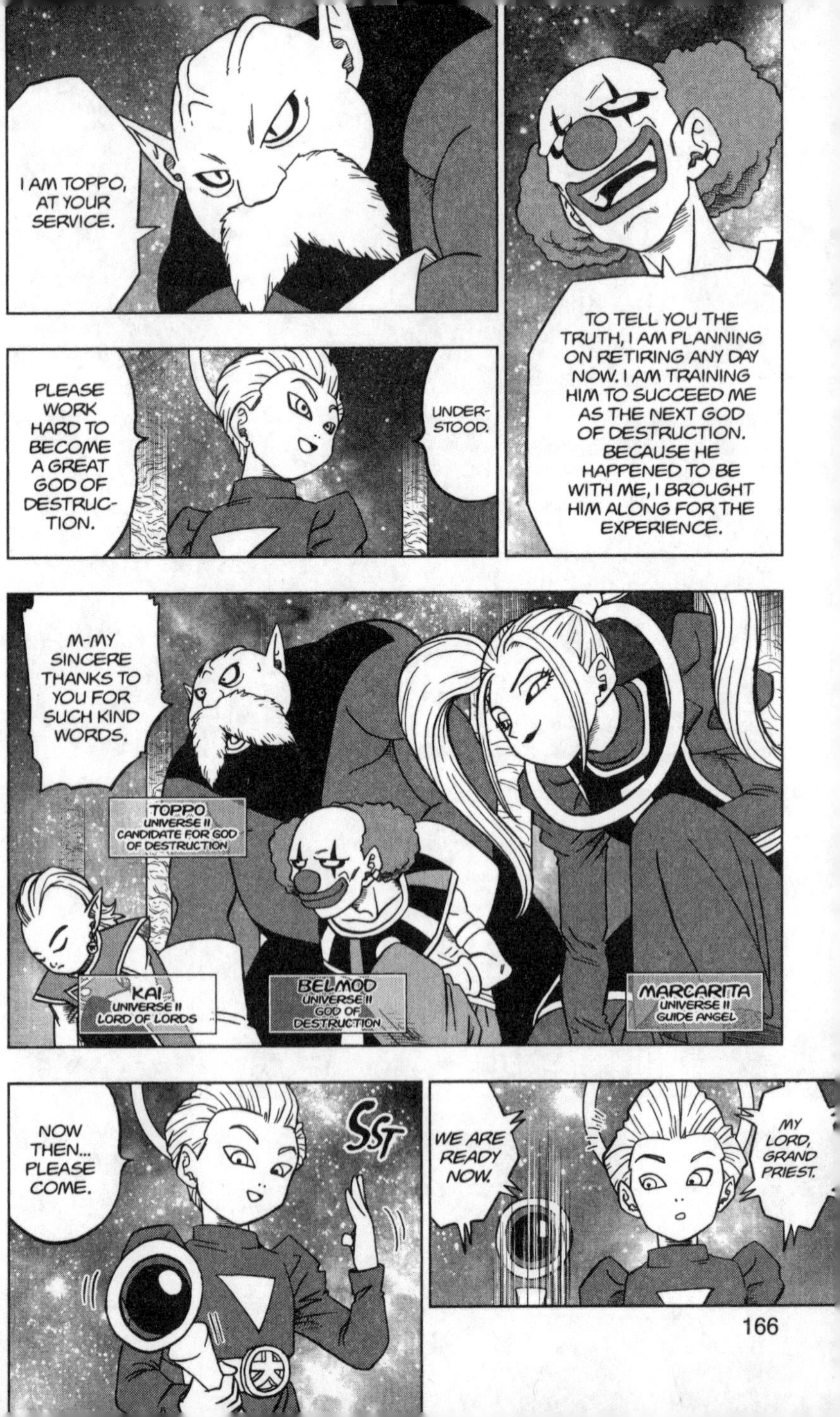
TO TELL YOU THE TRUTH, I AM PLANNING ON RETIRING ANY DAY NOW. I AM TRAINING HIM TO SUCCEED ME AS THE NEXT GOD OF DESTRUCTION. BECAUSE HE HAPPENED TO BE WITH ME, I BROUGHT HIM ALONG FOR THE EXPERIENCE.
I AM TOPPO, AT YOUR SERVICE.
PLEASE WORK HARD TO BECOME A GREAT GOD OF DESTRUCTION.
UNDERSTOOD.
M-MY SINCERE THANKS TO YOU FOR SUCH KIND WORDS.
MARCARITA UNIVERSE 11 GUIDE ANGEL
TOPPO UNIVERSE 11 CANDIDATE FOR GOD OF DESTRUCTION
BELMOD UNIVERSE 11 GOD OF DESTRUCTION
KAI UNIVERSE 11 LORD OF LORDS
MY LORD, GRAND PRIEST.
WE ARE READY NOW.
SST
NOW THEN... PLEASE COME.

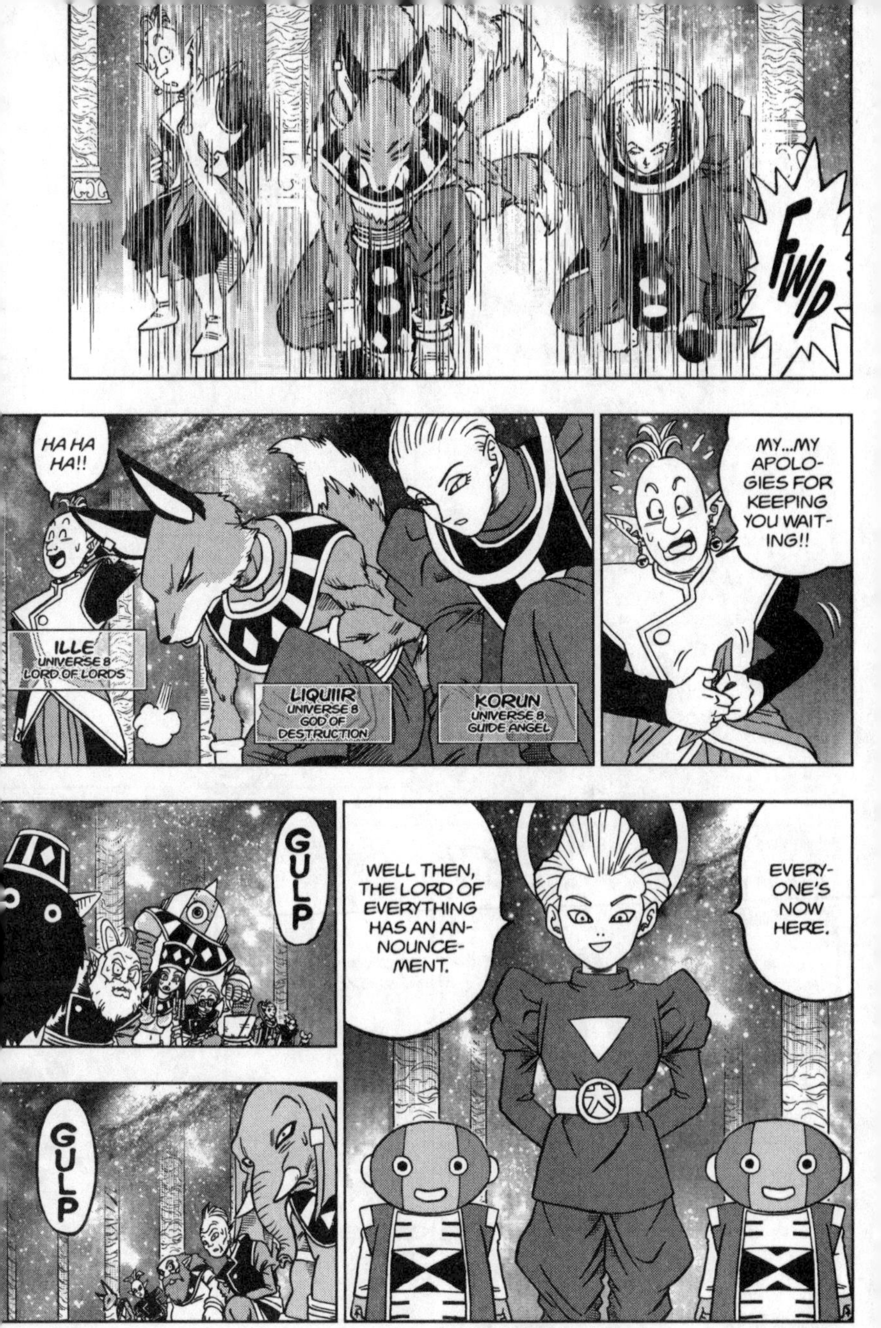
FWIP
MY...MY APOLOGIES FOR KEEPING YOU WAITING!!
HA HA HA!!
KORUN UNIVERSE 8 GUIDE ANGEL
LIQUIIR UNIVERSE 8 GOD OF DESTRUCTION
ILLE UNIVERSE 8 LORD OF LORDS
EVERYONE'S NOW HERE.
WELL THEN, THE LORD OF EVERYTHING HAS AN ANNOUNCEMENT.
GULP
GULP

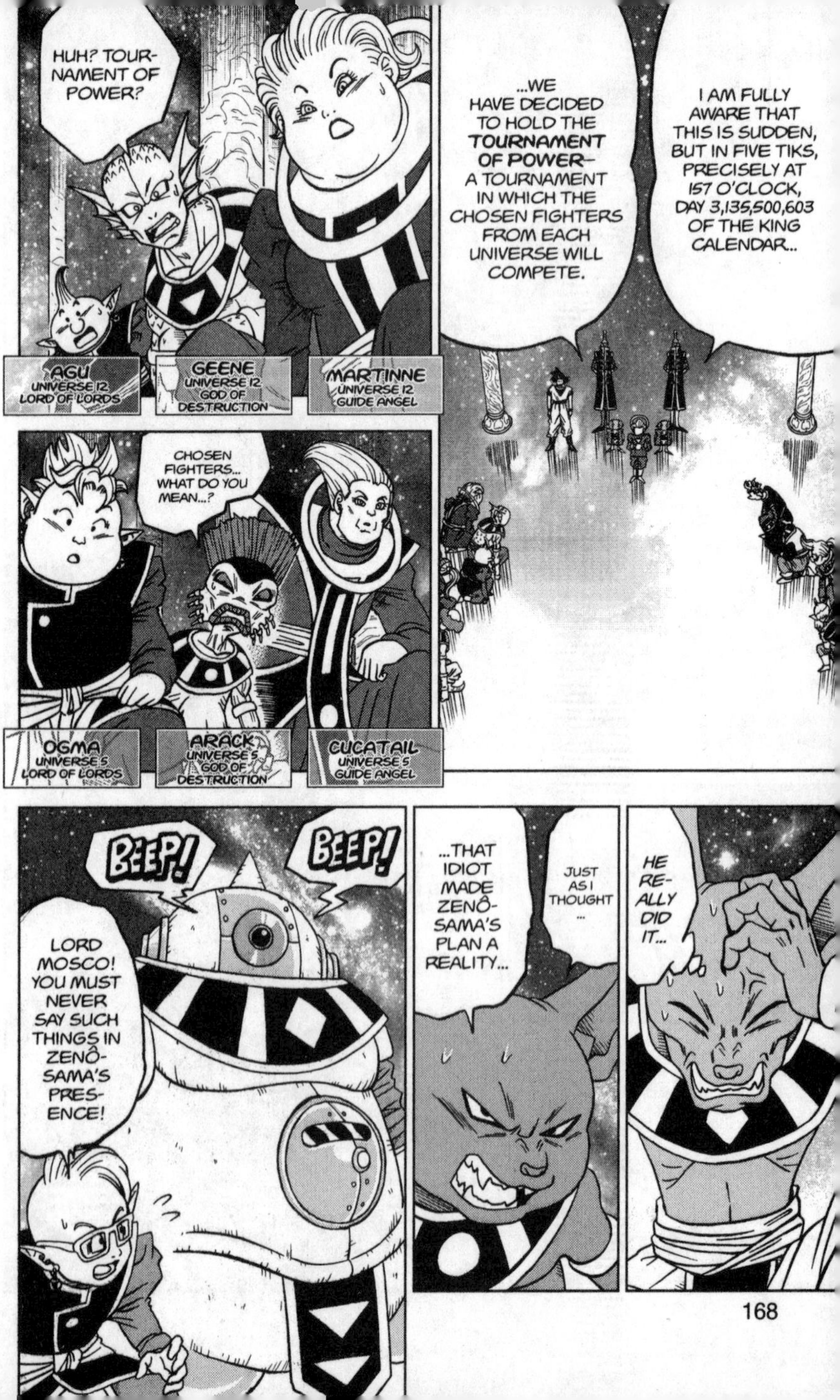
I AM FULLY AWARE THAT THIS IS SUDDEN, BUT IN FIVE TIKS, PRECISELY AT 157 O'CLOCK, DAY 3,135,500,603 OF THE KING CALENDAR...
...WE HAVE DECIDED TO HOLD THE TOURNAMENT OF POWER— A TOURNAMENT IN WHICH THE CHOSEN FIGHTERS FROM EACH UNIVERSE WILL COMPETE.
HUH? TOURNAMENT OF POWER?
MARTINNE UNIVERSE 12 GUIDE ANGEL
GEENE UNIVERSE 12 GOD OF DESTRUCTION
AGU UNIVERSE 12 LORD OF LORDS
CHOSEN FIGHTERS... WHAT DO YOU MEAN...?
CUCATAIL UNIVERSE 5 GUIDE ANGEL
ARACK UNIVERSE 5 GOD OF DESTRUCTION
OGMA UNIVERSE 5 LORD OF LORDS
HE REALLY DID IT...
JUST AS I THOUGHT...
...THAT IDIOT MADE ZENÔ-SAMA'S PLAN A REALITY...
BEEP!
BEEP!
LORD MOSCO! YOU MUST NEVER SAY SUCH THINGS IN ZENÔ-SAMA'S PRESENCE!

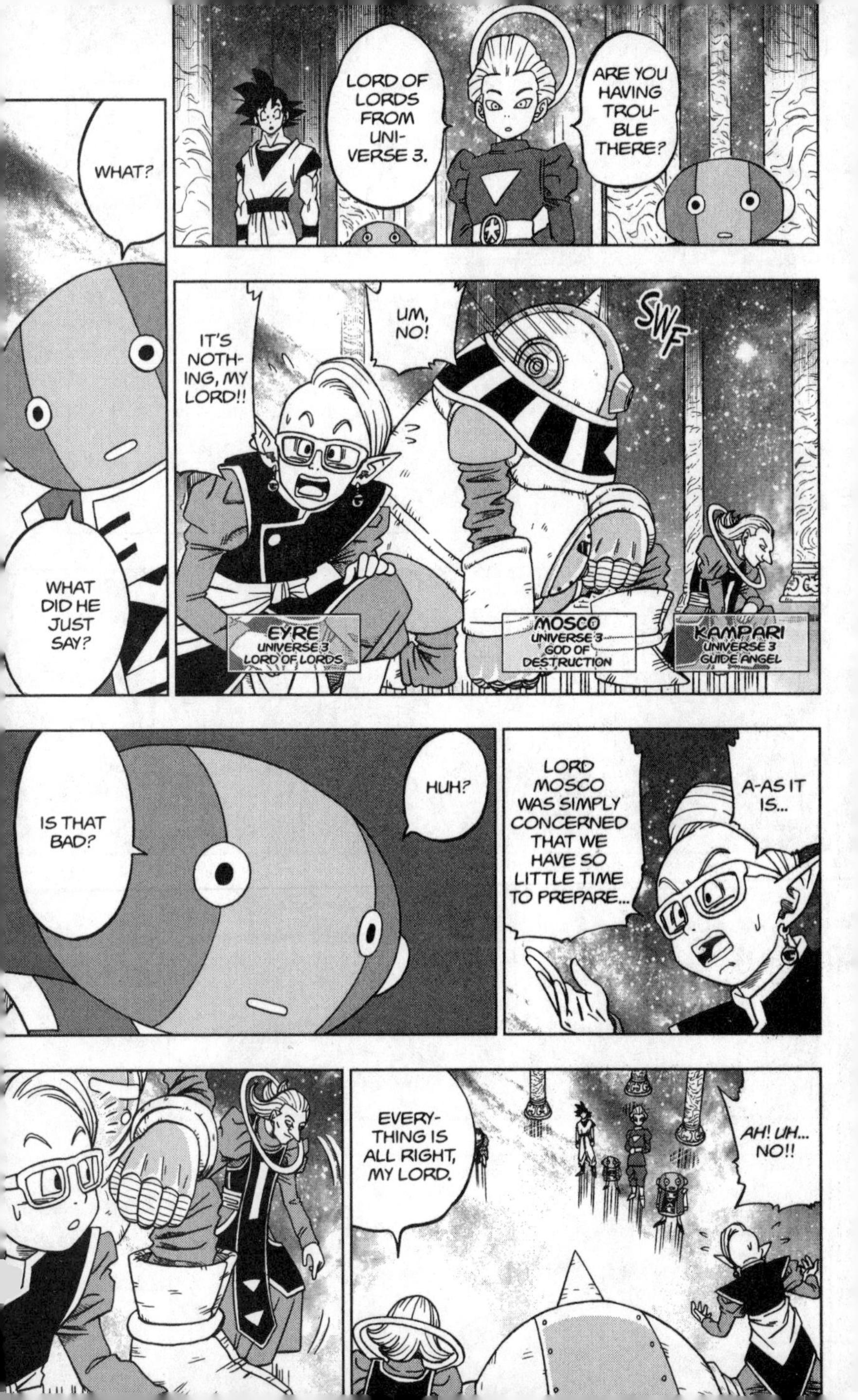
ARE YOU HAVING TROU-BLE THERE?
LORD OF LORDS FROM UNI-VERSE 3.
SWF
UM, NO!
IT'S NOTH-ING, MY LORD!!
KAMPARI UNIVERSE 3 GUIDE ANGEL
MOSCO UNIVERSE 3 GOD OF DESTRUCTION
EYRE UNIVERSE 3 LORD OF LORDS
WHAT?
WHAT DID HE JUST SAY?
A-AS IT IS...
LORD MOSCO WAS SIMPLY CONCERNED THAT WE HAVE SO LITTLE TIME TO PREPARE...
HUH?
IS THAT BAD?
AH! UH... NO!!
EVERY-THING IS ALL RIGHT, MY LORD.

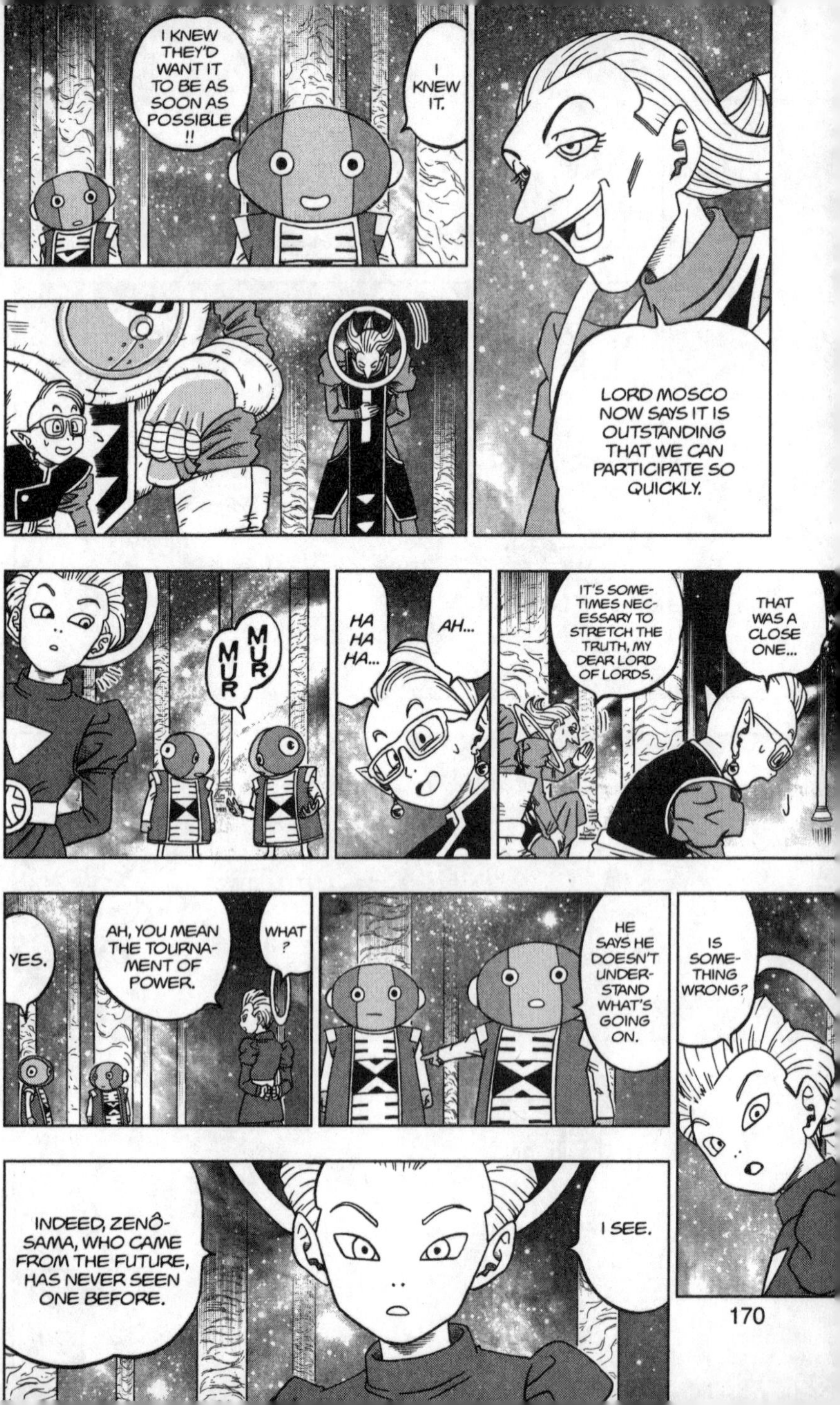

LORD MOSCO NOW SAYS IT IS OUTSTANDING THAT WE CAN PARTICIPATE SO QUICKLY.
I KNEW IT.
I KNEW THEY'D WANT IT TO BE AS SOON AS POSSIBLE!!
THAT WAS A CLOSE ONE...
IT'S SOMETIMES NECESSARY TO STRETCH THE TRUTH, MY DEAR LORD OF LORDS.
AH...
HA HA HA...
MUR MUR
IS SOMETHING WRONG?
HE SAYS HE DOESN'T UNDERSTAND WHAT'S GOING ON.
WHAT?
AH, YOU MEAN THE TOURNAMENT OF POWER.
YES.
I SEE.
INDEED, ZENÔ-SAMA, WHO CAME FROM THE FUTURE, HAS NEVER SEEN ONE BEFORE.

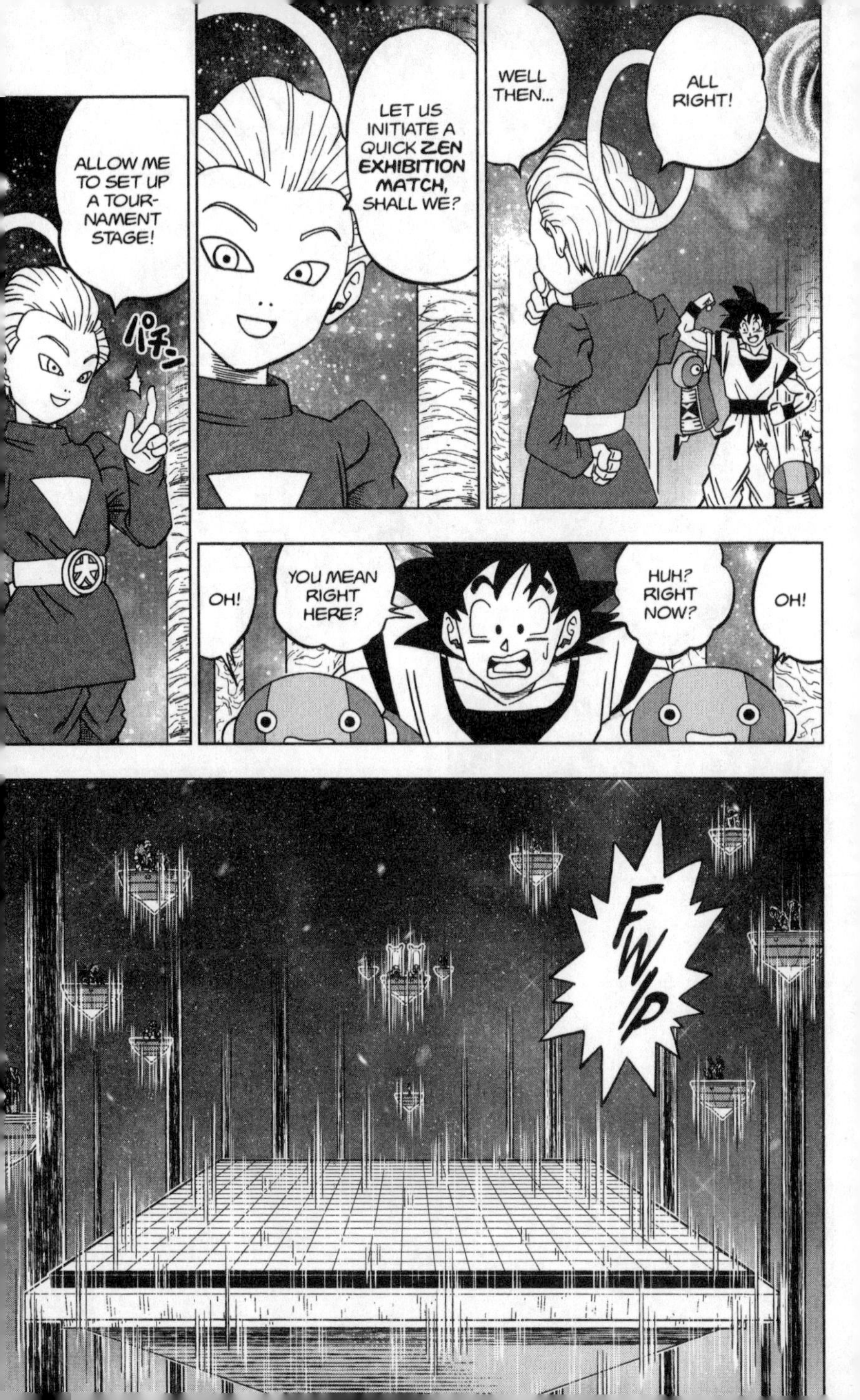
ALL RIGHT!
WELL THEN...
LET US INITIATE A QUICK **ZEN EXHIBITION MATCH,** SHALL WE?
OH!
HUH? RIGHT NOW?
YOU MEAN RIGHT HERE?
OH!
ALLOW ME TO SET UP A TOUR-NAMENT STAGE!
パチン
FWIP

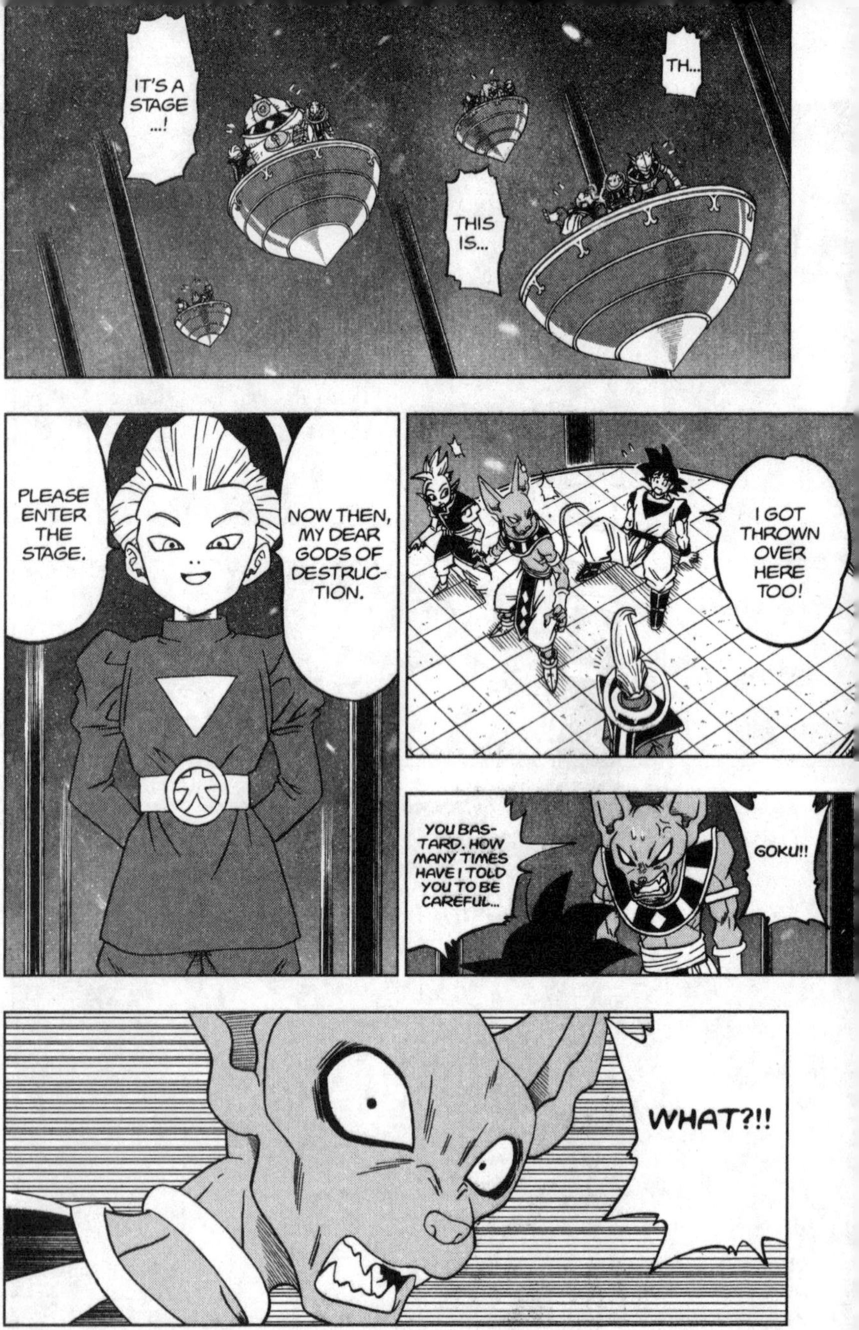
TH...
THIS IS...
IT'S A STAGE ...!
I GOT THROWN OVER HERE TOO!
GOKU!!
YOU BASTARD. HOW MANY TIMES HAVE I TOLD YOU TO BE CAREFUL...
NOW THEN, MY DEAR GODS OF DESTRUCTION.
PLEASE ENTER THE STAGE.
WHAT?!!

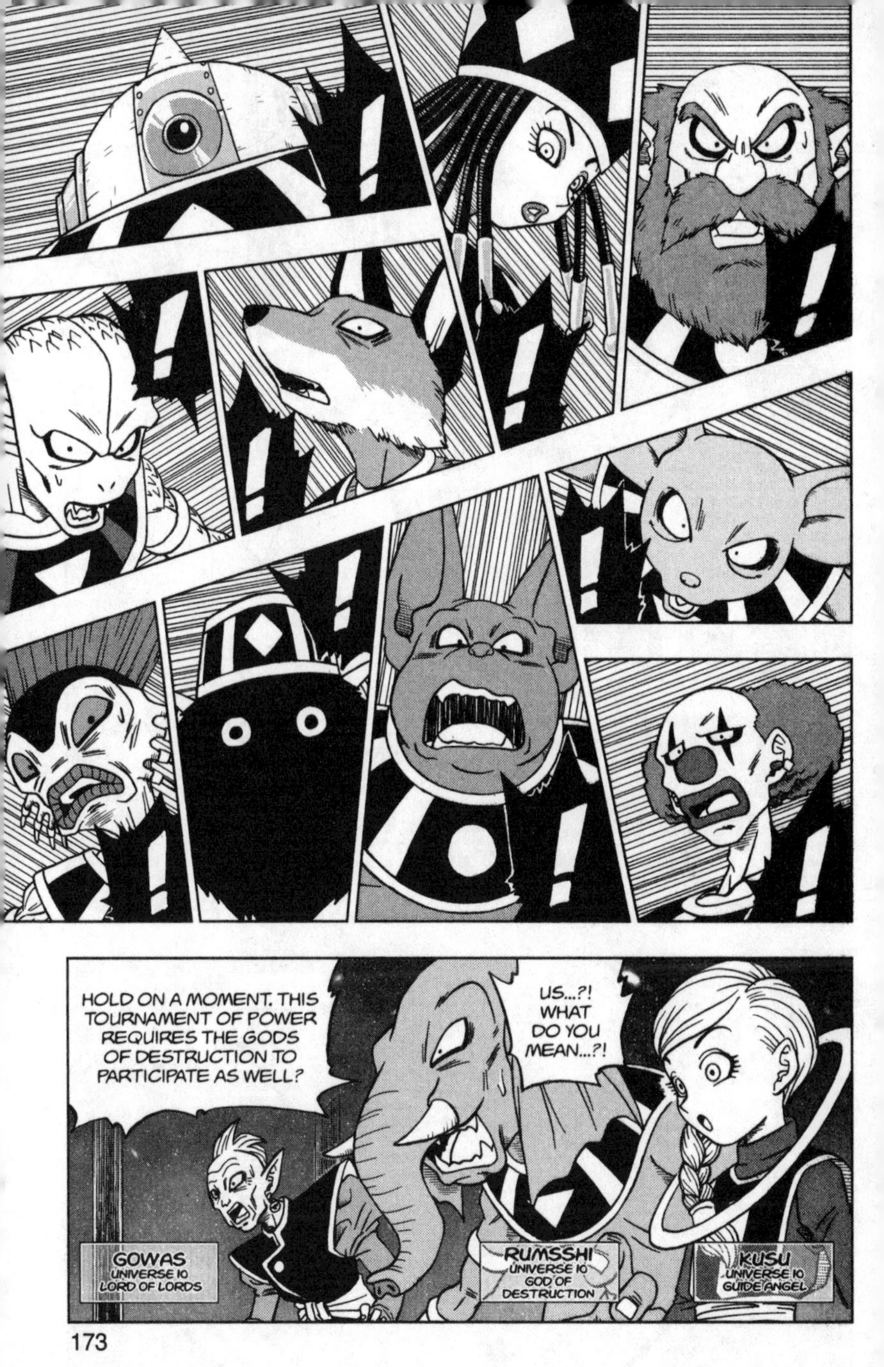
US...?! WHAT DO YOU MEAN...?!
HOLD ON A MOMENT. THIS TOURNAMENT OF POWER REQUIRES THE GODS OF DESTRUCTION TO PARTICIPATE AS WELL?
KUSU UNIVERSE 10 GUIDE ANGEL
RUMSSHI UNIVERSE 10 GOD OF DESTRUCTION
GOWAS UNIVERSE 10 LORD OF LORDS

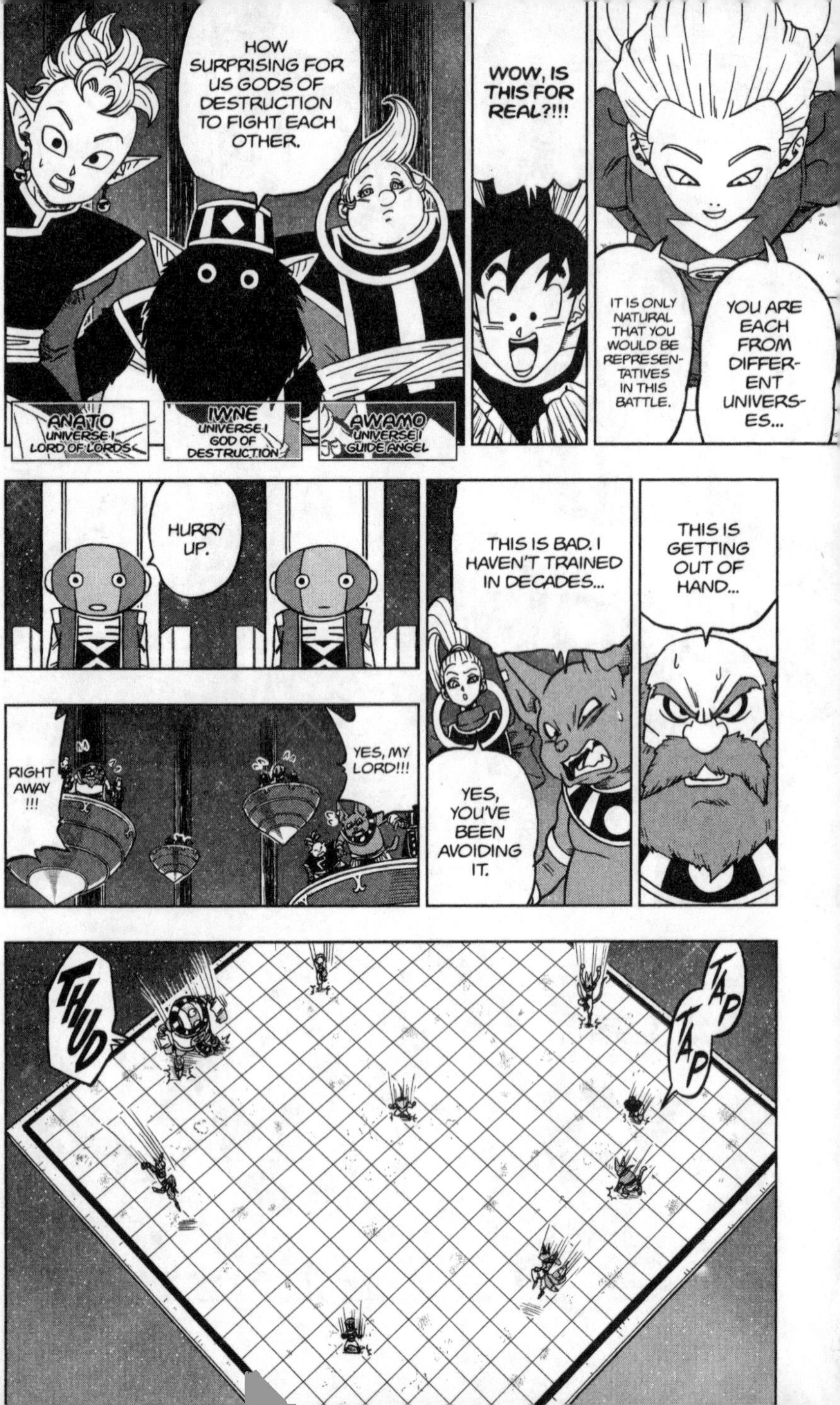
YOU ARE EACH FROM DIFFERENT UNIVERSES...
IT IS ONLY NATURAL THAT YOU WOULD BE REPRESENTATIVES IN THIS BATTLE.
WOW, IS THIS FOR REAL?!!!
AWAMO UNIVERSE 1 GUIDE ANGEL
HOW SURPRISING FOR US GODS OF DESTRUCTION TO FIGHT EACH OTHER.
IWNE UNIVERSE 1 GOD OF DESTRUCTION
ANATO UNIVERSE 1 LORD OF LORDS
THIS IS GETTING OUT OF HAND...
THIS IS BAD. I HAVEN'T TRAINED IN DECADES...
YES, YOU'VE BEEN AVOIDING IT.
HURRY UP.
YES, MY LORD!!!
RIGHT AWAY!!!
TAP TAP
THUD

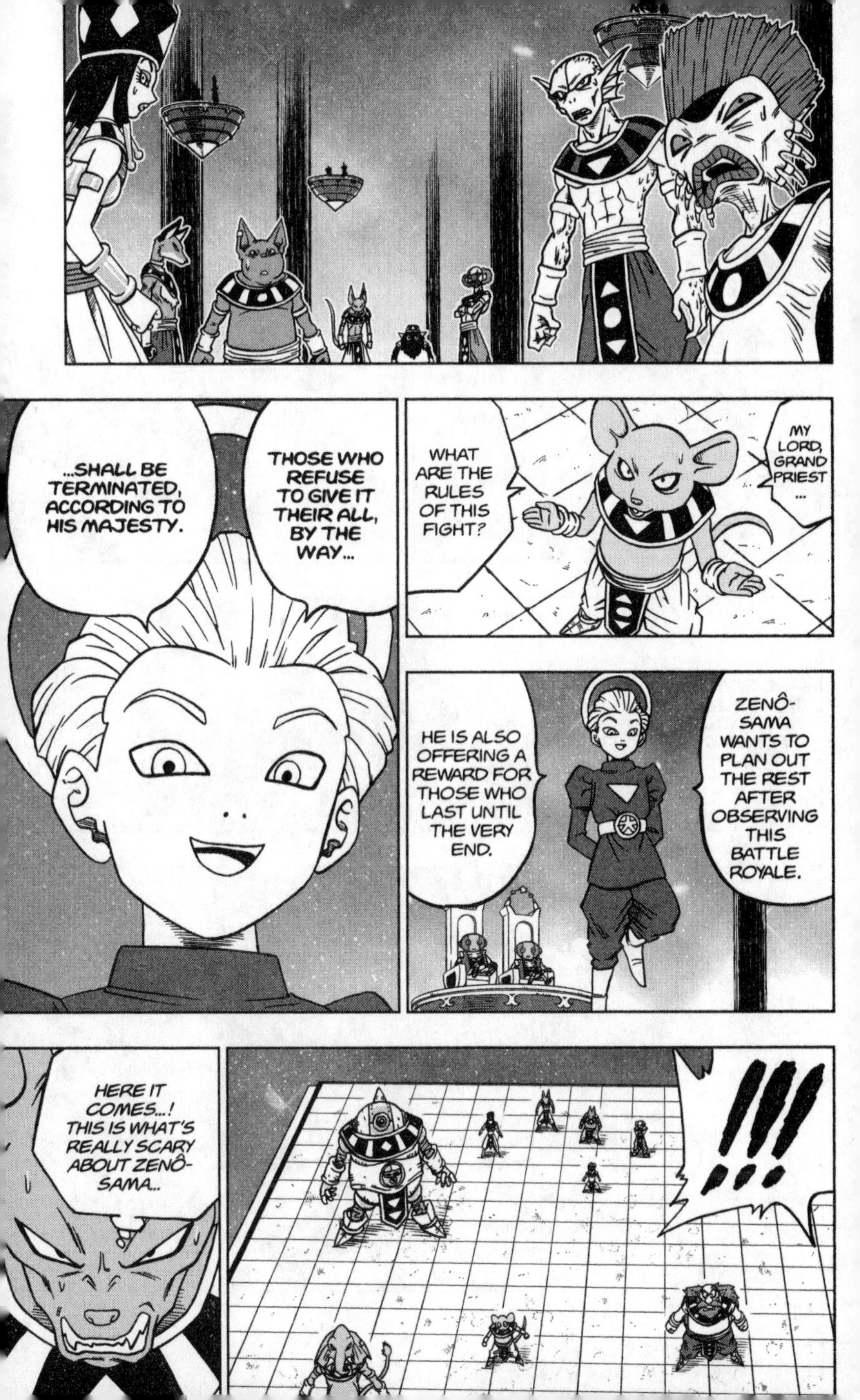
MY LORD, GRAND PRIEST...
WHAT ARE THE RULES OF THIS FIGHT?
ZENÔ-SAMA WANTS TO PLAN OUT THE REST AFTER OBSERVING THIS BATTLE ROYALE.
HE IS ALSO OFFERING A REWARD FOR THOSE WHO LAST UNTIL THE VERY END.
THOSE WHO REFUSE TO GIVE IT THEIR ALL, BY THE WAY...
...SHALL BE TERMINATED, ACCORDING TO HIS MAJESTY.
!!!
HERE IT COMES...! THIS IS WHAT'S REALLY SCARY ABOUT ZENÔ-SAMA...

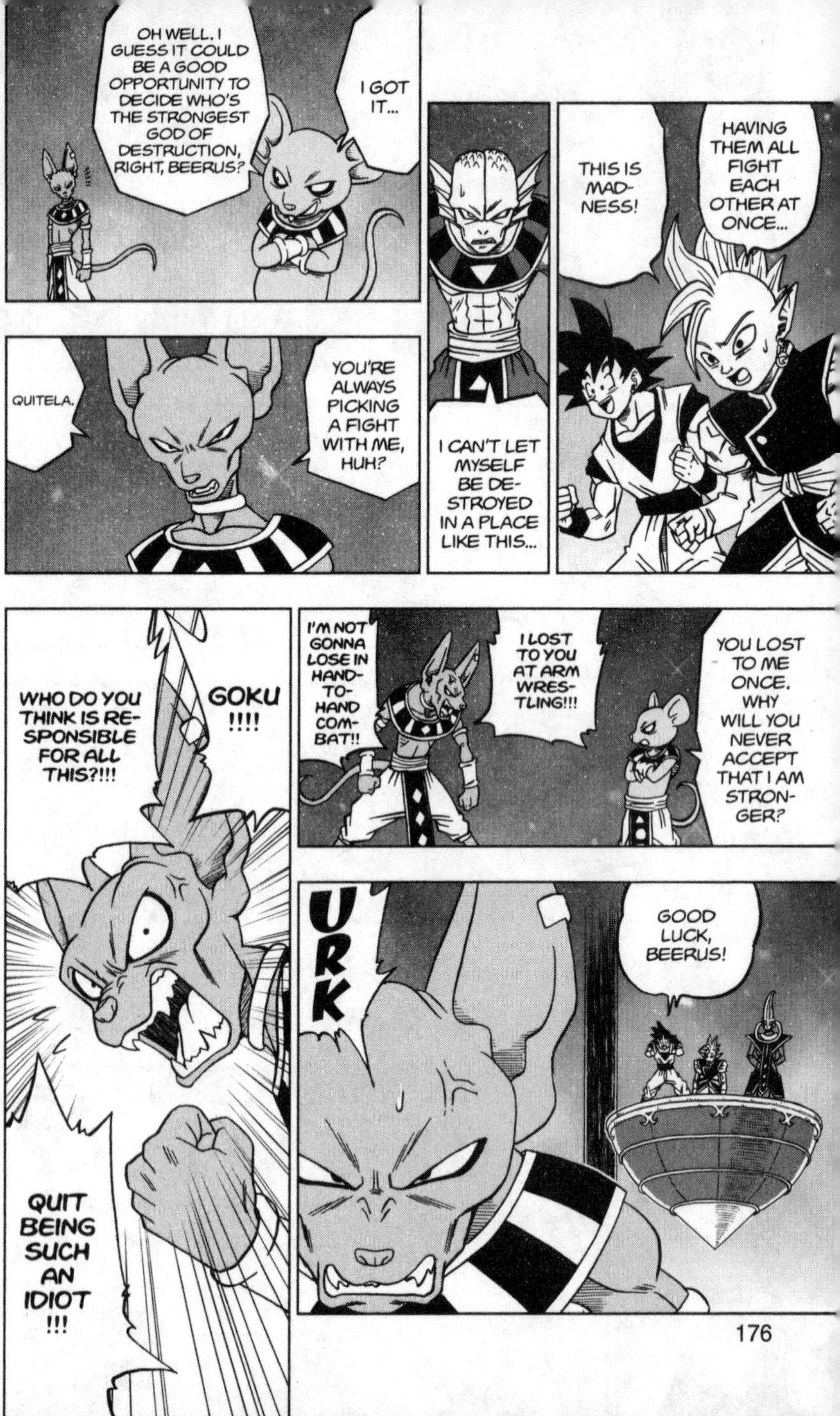
I GOT IT...
OH WELL. I GUESS IT COULD BE A GOOD OPPORTUNITY TO DECIDE WHO'S THE STRONGEST GOD OF DESTRUCTION, RIGHT, BEERUS?
QUITELA.
YOU'RE ALWAYS PICKING A FIGHT WITH ME, HUH?
HAVING THEM ALL FIGHT EACH OTHER AT ONCE...
THIS IS MADNESS!
I CAN'T LET MYSELF BE DESTROYED IN A PLACE LIKE THIS...
YOU LOST TO ME ONCE. WHY WILL YOU NEVER ACCEPT THAT I AM STRONGER?
I LOST TO YOU AT ARM WRESTLING!!!
I'M NOT GONNA LOSE IN HAND-TO-HAND COMBAT!!
GOOD LUCK, BEERUS!
URK
GOKU!!!!
WHO DO YOU THINK IS RESPONSIBLE FOR ALL THIS?!!!
QUIT BEING SUCH AN IDIOT!!!

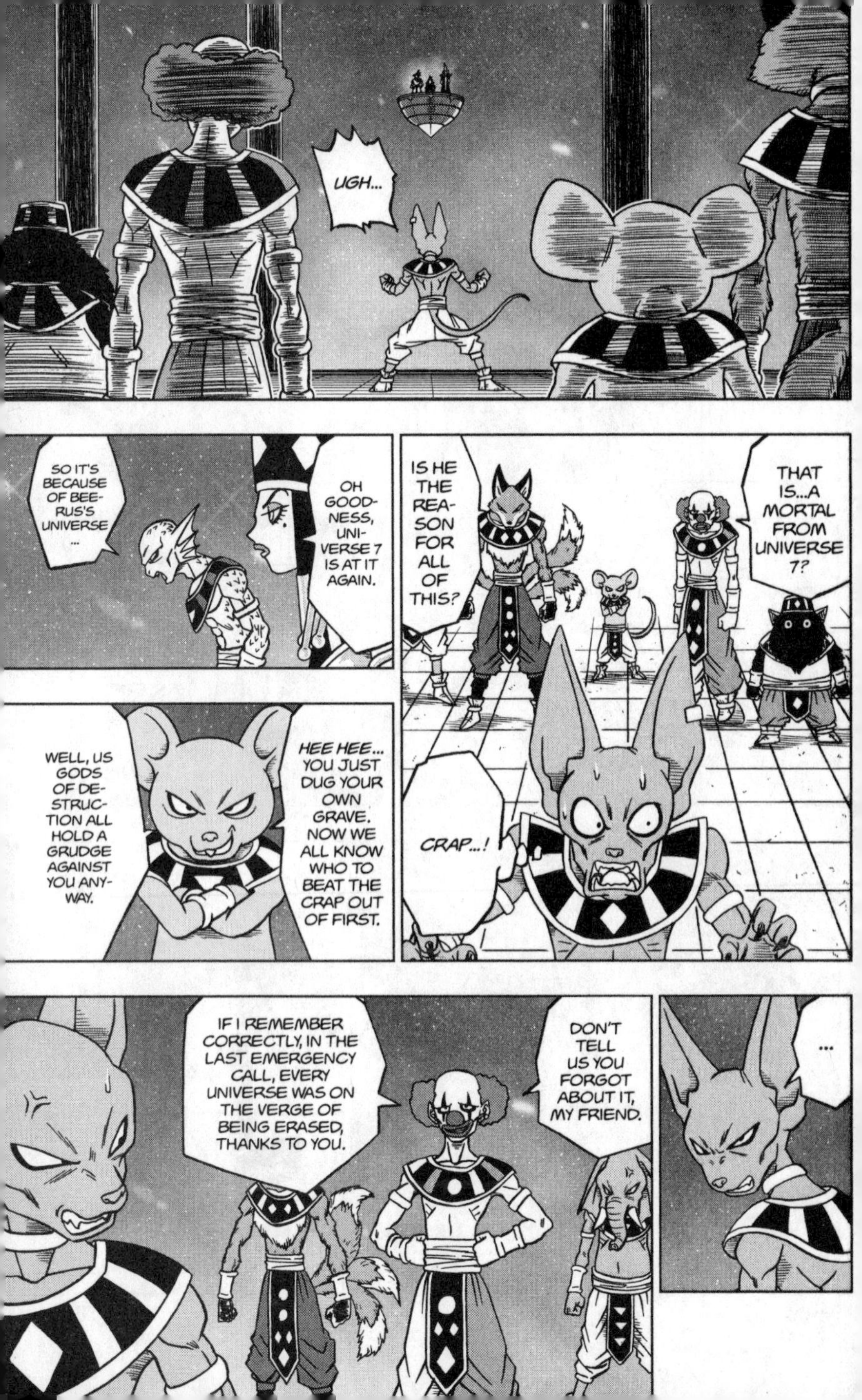
UGH...
THAT IS...A MORTAL FROM UNIVERSE 7?
IS HE THE REASON FOR ALL OF THIS?
CRAP...!
OH GOODNESS, UNIVERSE 7 IS AT IT AGAIN.
SO IT'S BECAUSE OF BEERUS'S UNIVERSE...
HEE HEE... YOU JUST DUG YOUR OWN GRAVE. NOW WE ALL KNOW WHO TO BEAT THE CRAP OUT OF FIRST.
WELL, US GODS OF DESTRUCTION ALL HOLD A GRUDGE AGAINST YOU ANYWAY.
...
DON'T TELL US YOU FORGOT ABOUT IT, MY FRIEND.
IF I REMEMBER CORRECTLY, IN THE LAST EMERGENCY CALL, EVERY UNIVERSE WAS ON THE VERGE OF BEING ERASED, THANKS TO YOU.

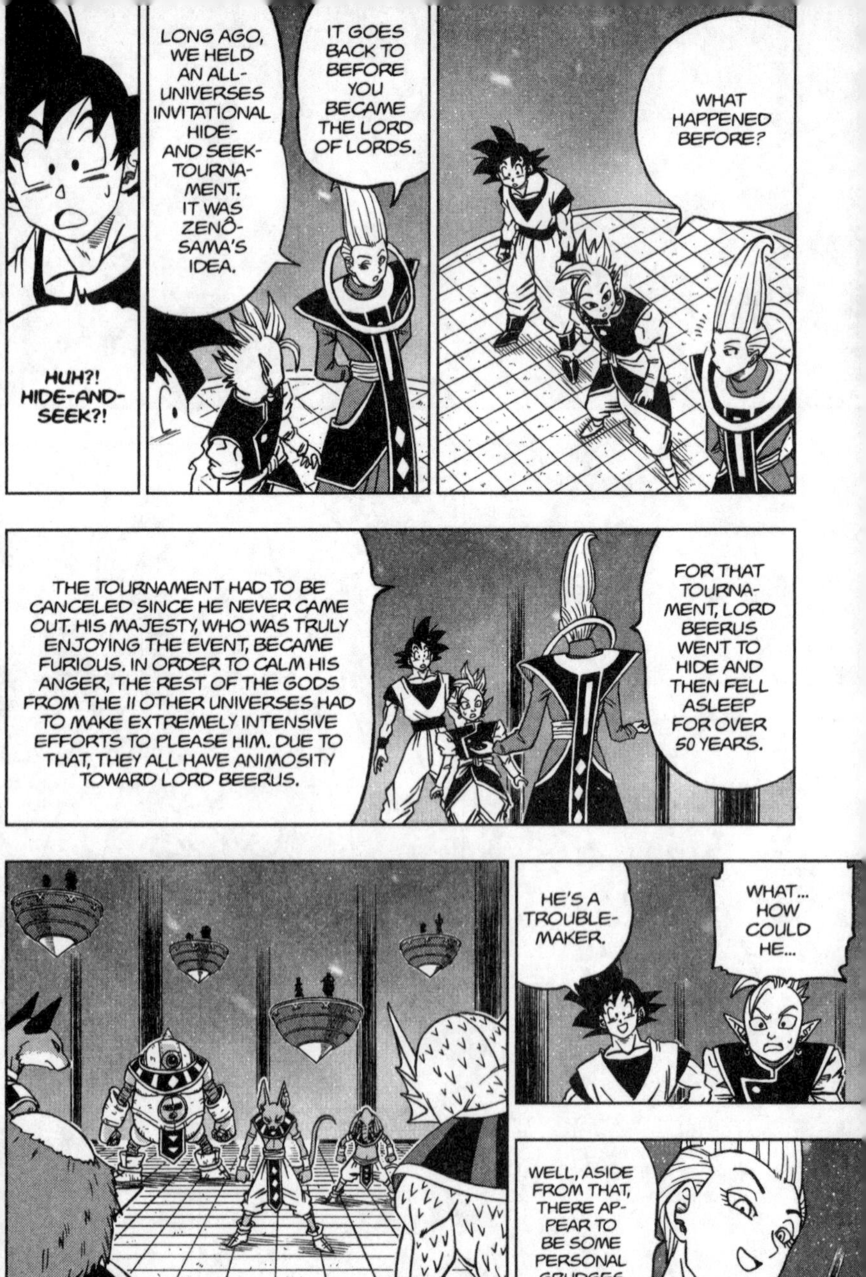
WHAT HAPPENED BEFORE?
IT GOES BACK TO BEFORE YOU BECAME THE LORD OF LORDS.
LONG AGO, WE HELD AN ALL-UNIVERSES INVITATIONAL HIDE-AND SEEK-TOURNAMENT. IT WAS ZENÔ-SAMA'S IDEA.
HUH?! HIDE-AND-SEEK?!
FOR THAT TOURNAMENT, LORD BEERUS WENT TO HIDE AND THEN FELL ASLEEP FOR OVER 50 YEARS.
THE TOURNAMENT HAD TO BE CANCELED SINCE HE NEVER CAME OUT. HIS MAJESTY, WHO WAS TRULY ENJOYING THE EVENT, BECAME FURIOUS. IN ORDER TO CALM HIS ANGER, THE REST OF THE GODS FROM THE 11 OTHER UNIVERSES HAD TO MAKE EXTREMELY INTENSIVE EFFORTS TO PLEASE HIM. DUE TO THAT, THEY ALL HAVE ANIMOSITY TOWARD LORD BEERUS.
WHAT... HOW COULD HE...
HE'S A TROUBLE-MAKER.
WELL, ASIDE FROM THAT, THERE AP-PEAR TO BE SOME PERSONAL GRUDGES TOO.

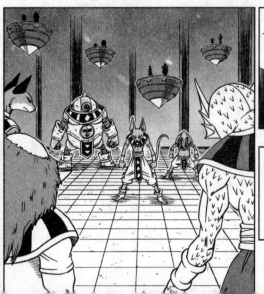

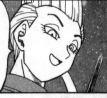

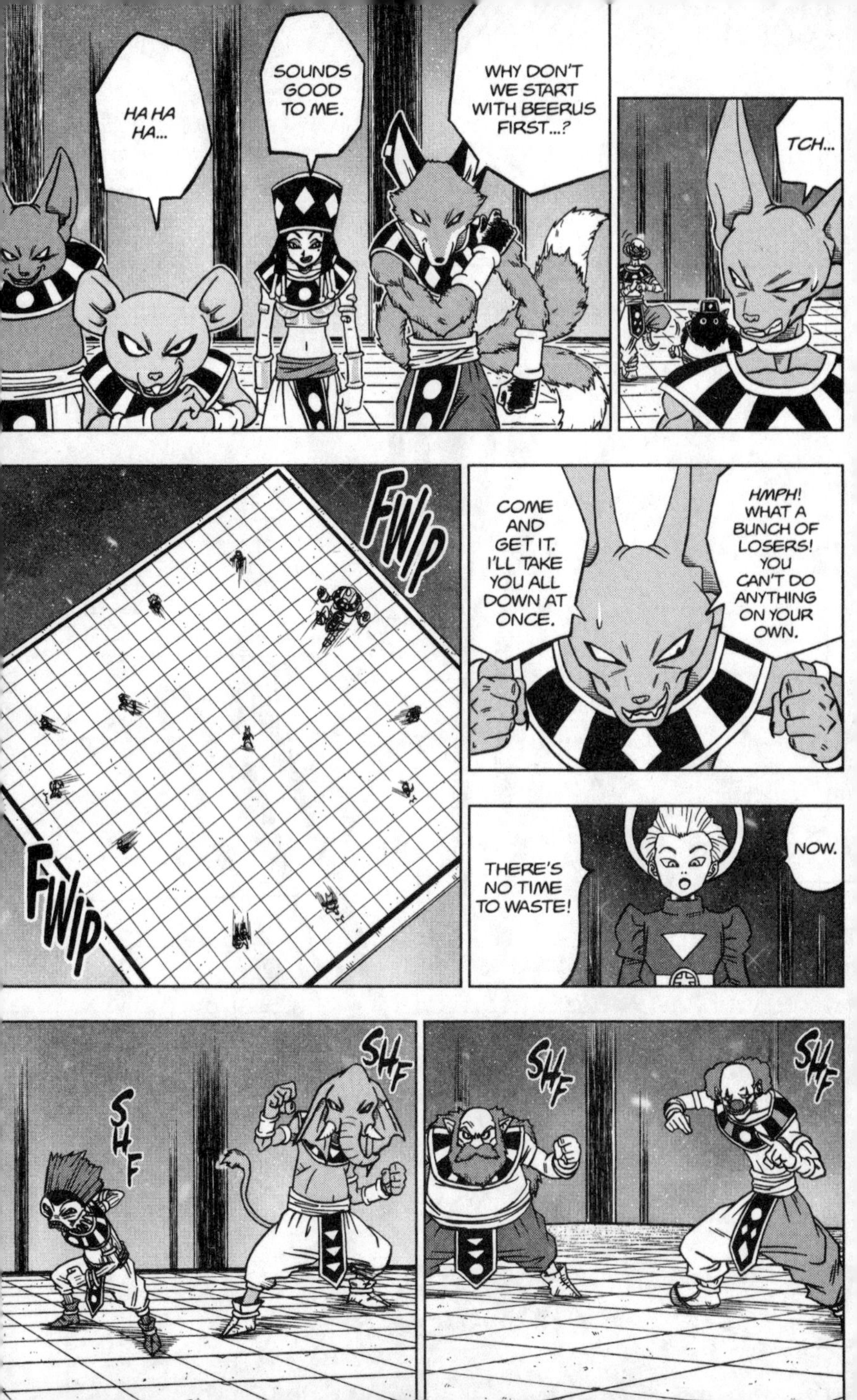
TCH...
WHY DON'T WE START WITH BEERUS FIRST...?
SOUNDS GOOD TO ME.
HA HA HA...
HMPH! WHAT A BUNCH OF LOSERS! YOU CAN'T DO ANYTHING ON YOUR OWN.
COME AND GET IT. I'LL TAKE YOU ALL DOWN AT ONCE.
NOW.
THERE'S NO TIME TO WASTE!
FWIP
FWIP
SHF
SHF
SHF
SHF

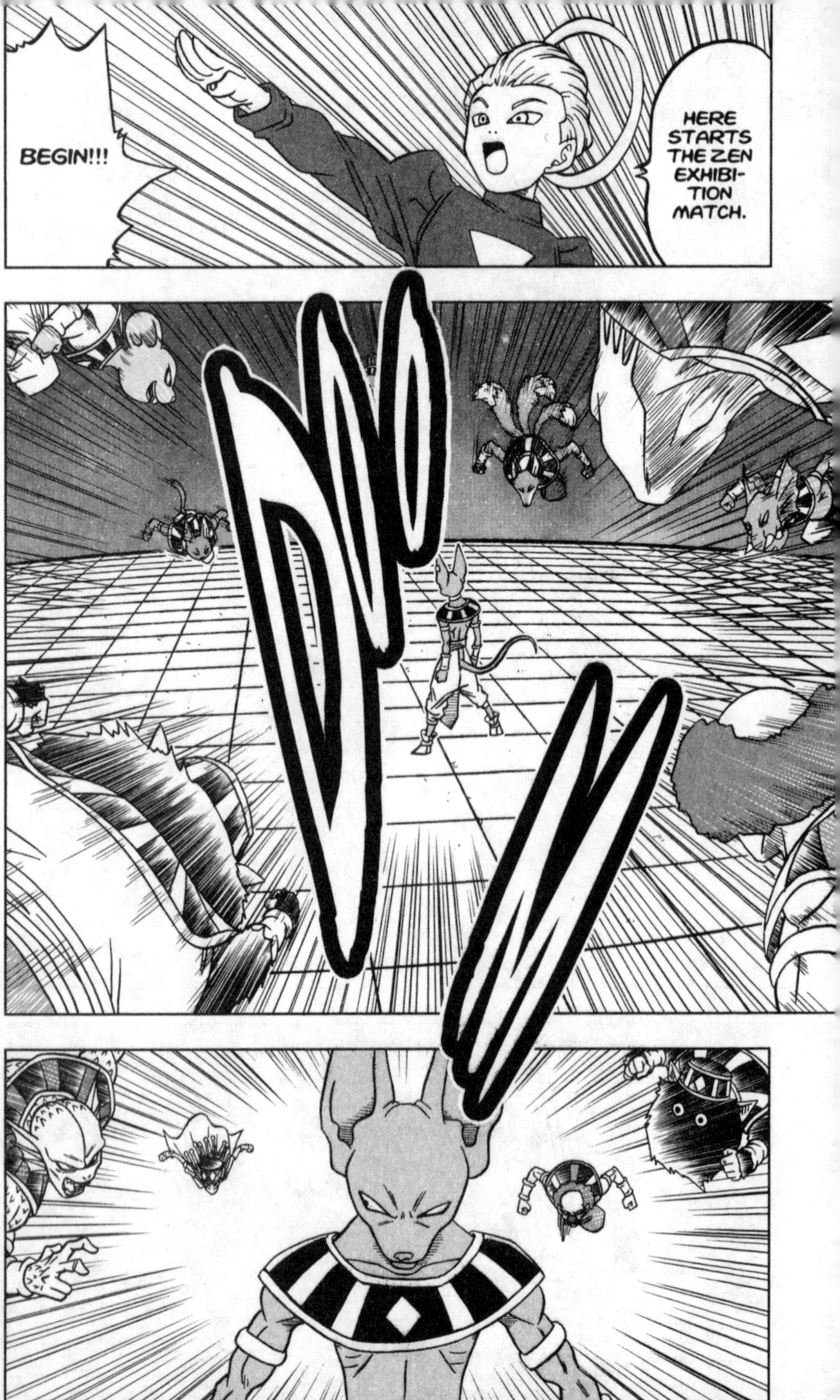
HERE STARTS THE ZEN EXHIBI-TION MATCH.
BEGIN!!!

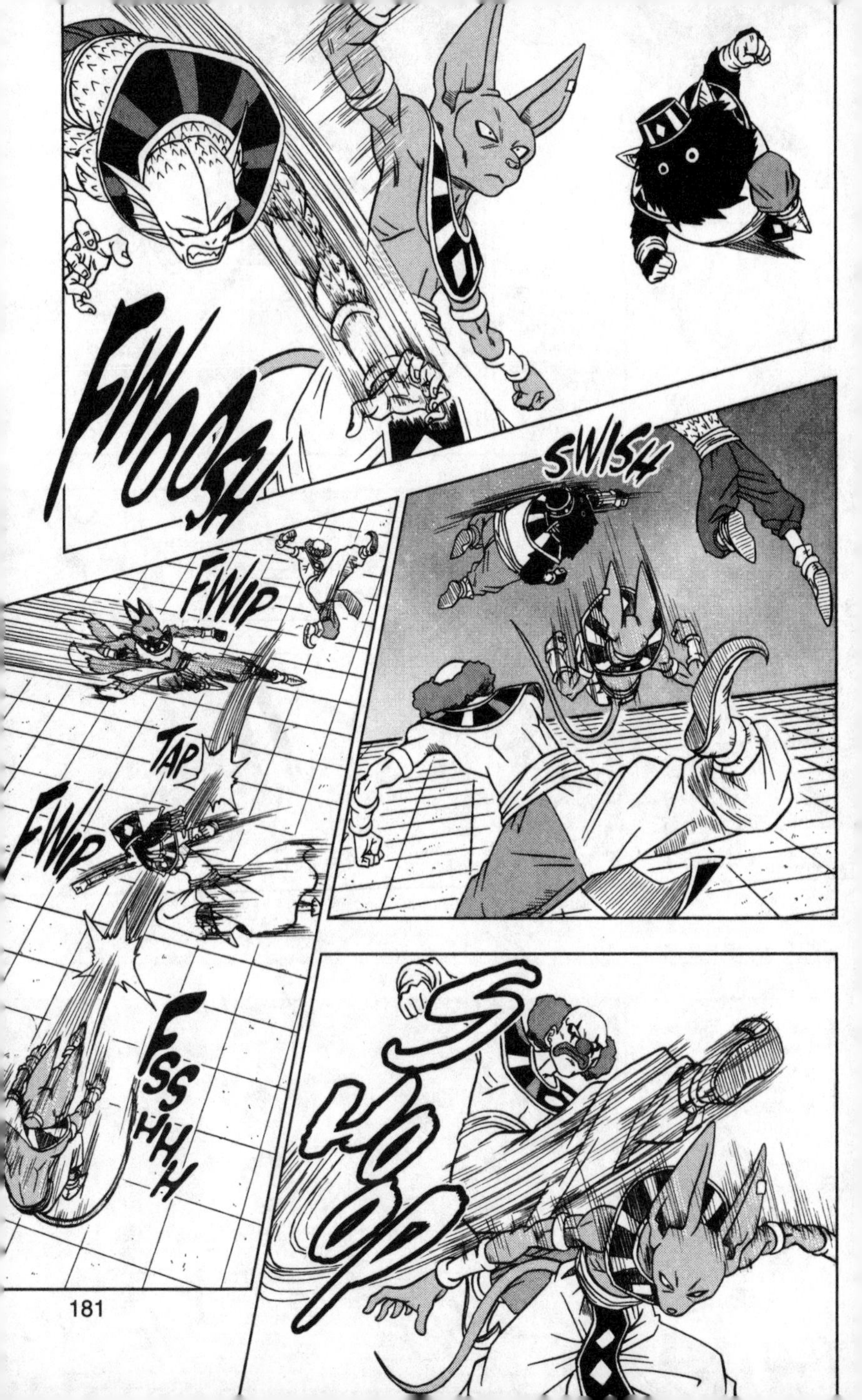
FWOOSH
SWISH
FWIP
TAP
FWIP
FSSHHH
SWOOP

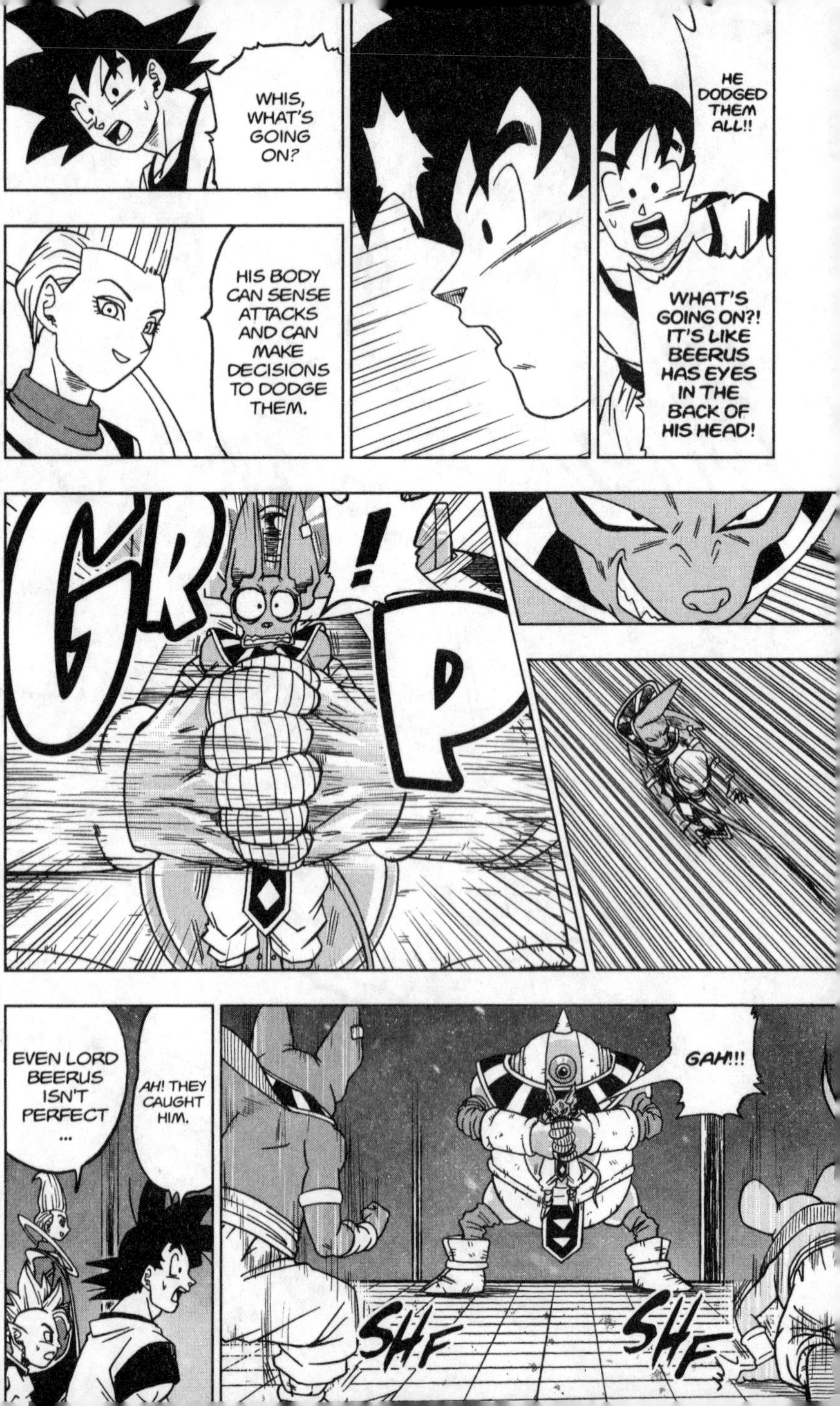
HE DODGED THEM ALL!!
WHAT'S GOING ON?! IT'S LIKE BEERUS HAS EYES IN THE BACK OF HIS HEAD!
WHIS, WHAT'S GOING ON?
HIS BODY CAN SENSE ATTACKS AND CAN MAKE DECISIONS TO DODGE THEM.
GRIP
!
GAH!!!
SHF
SHF
AH! THEY CAUGHT HIM.
EVEN LORD BEERUS ISN'T PERFECT ...

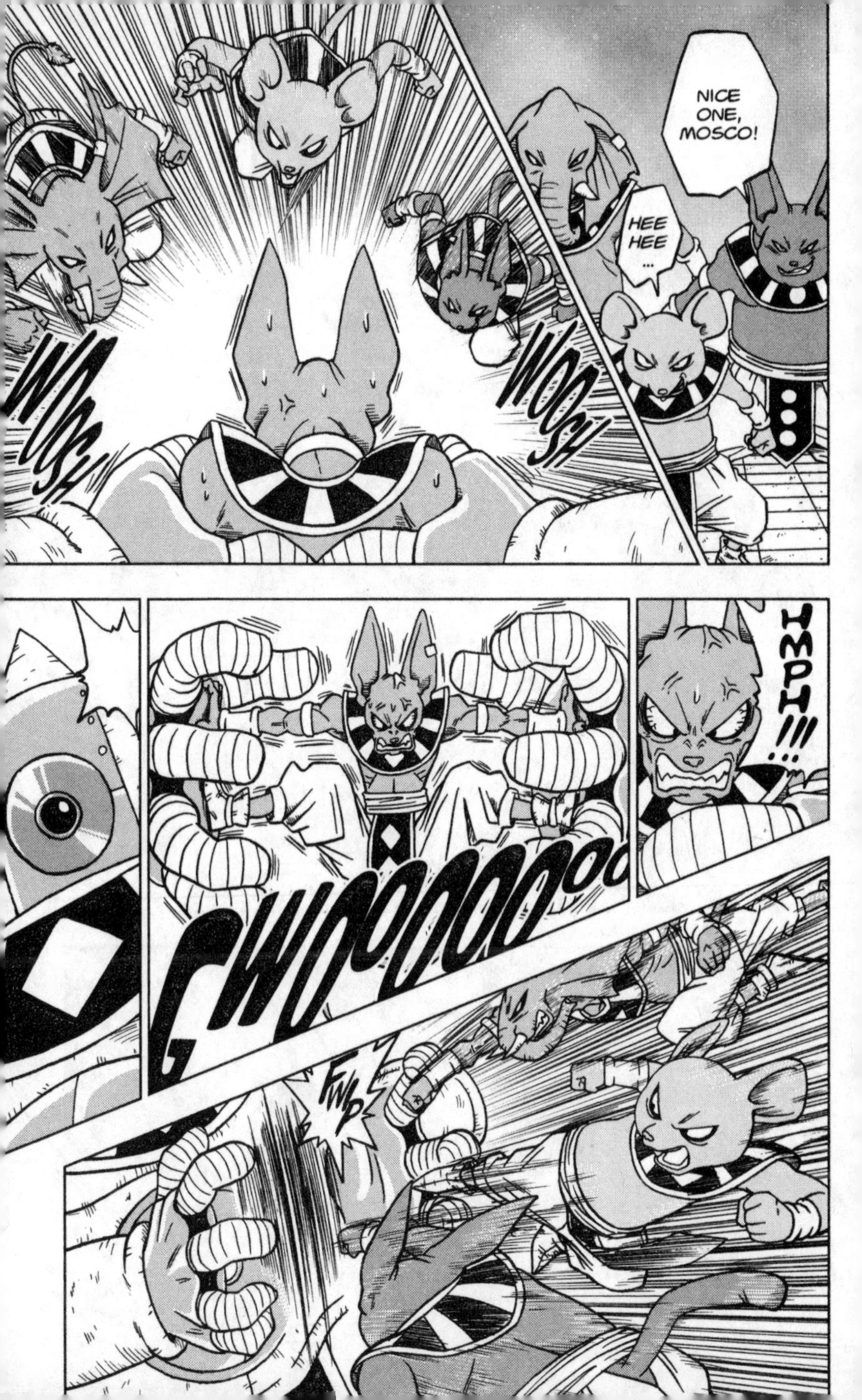
NICE ONE, MOSCO!
HEE HEE ...
WHOOSH
WHOOSH
HMPH!!!...
GWOOOOOOOO
FWIP

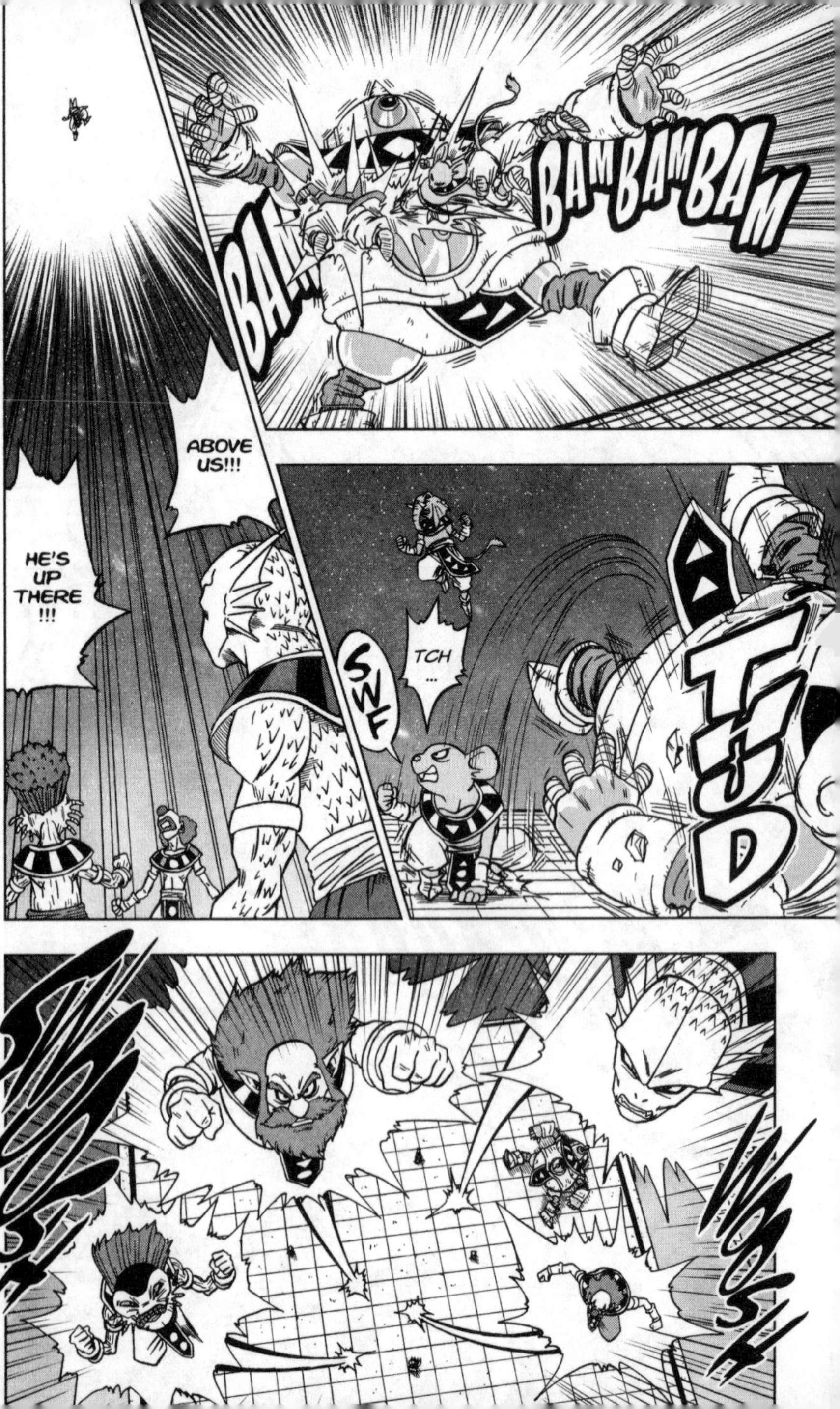
BAM
BAMBAMBAM
TCH ...
SWF
THUD
ABOVE US!!!
HE'S UP THERE !!!
WHOOSH

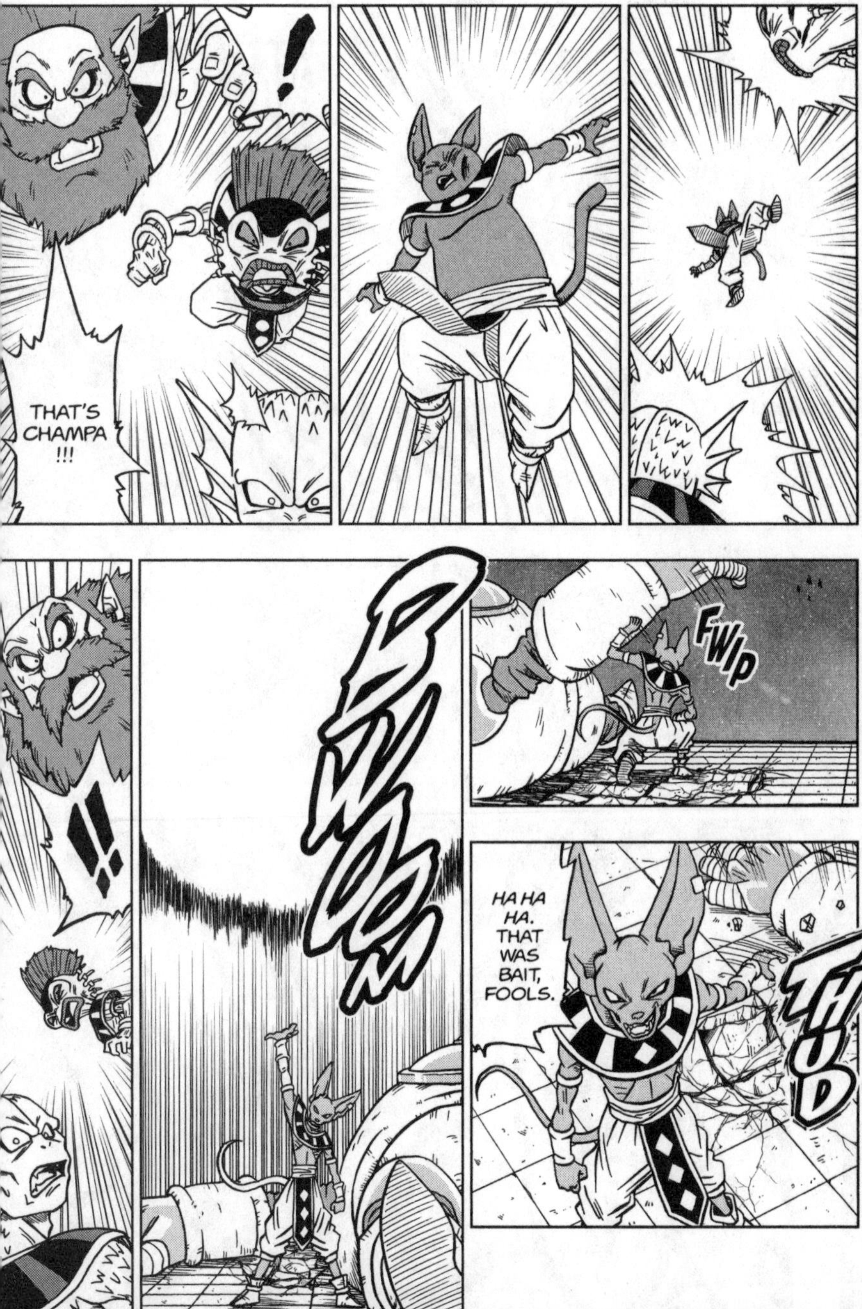
!
THAT'S CHAMPA !!!
FWIP
HA HA HA. THAT WAS BAIT, FOOLS.
THUD
!!

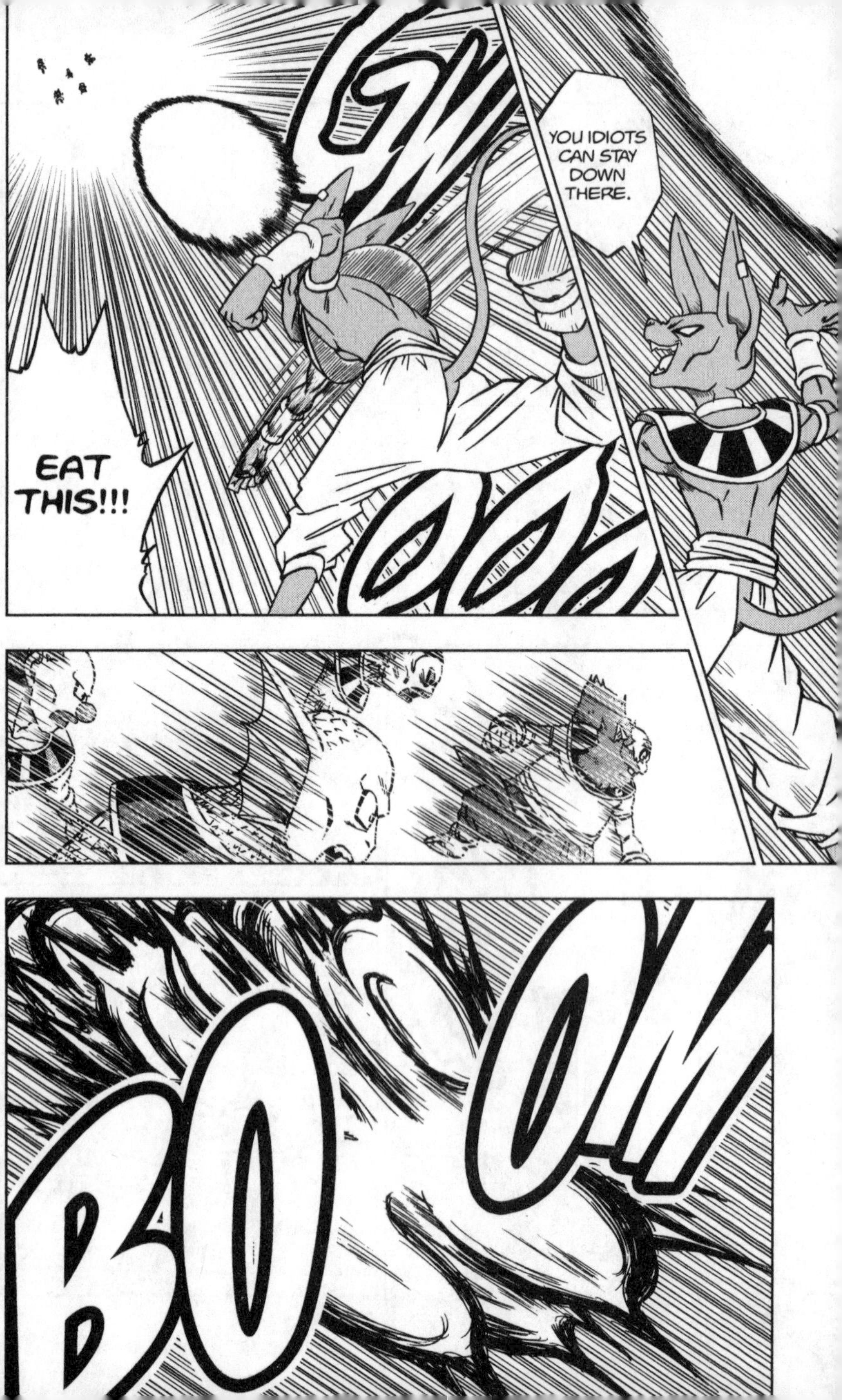
YOU IDIOTS CAN STAY DOWN THERE.
EAT THIS!!!
BOOM

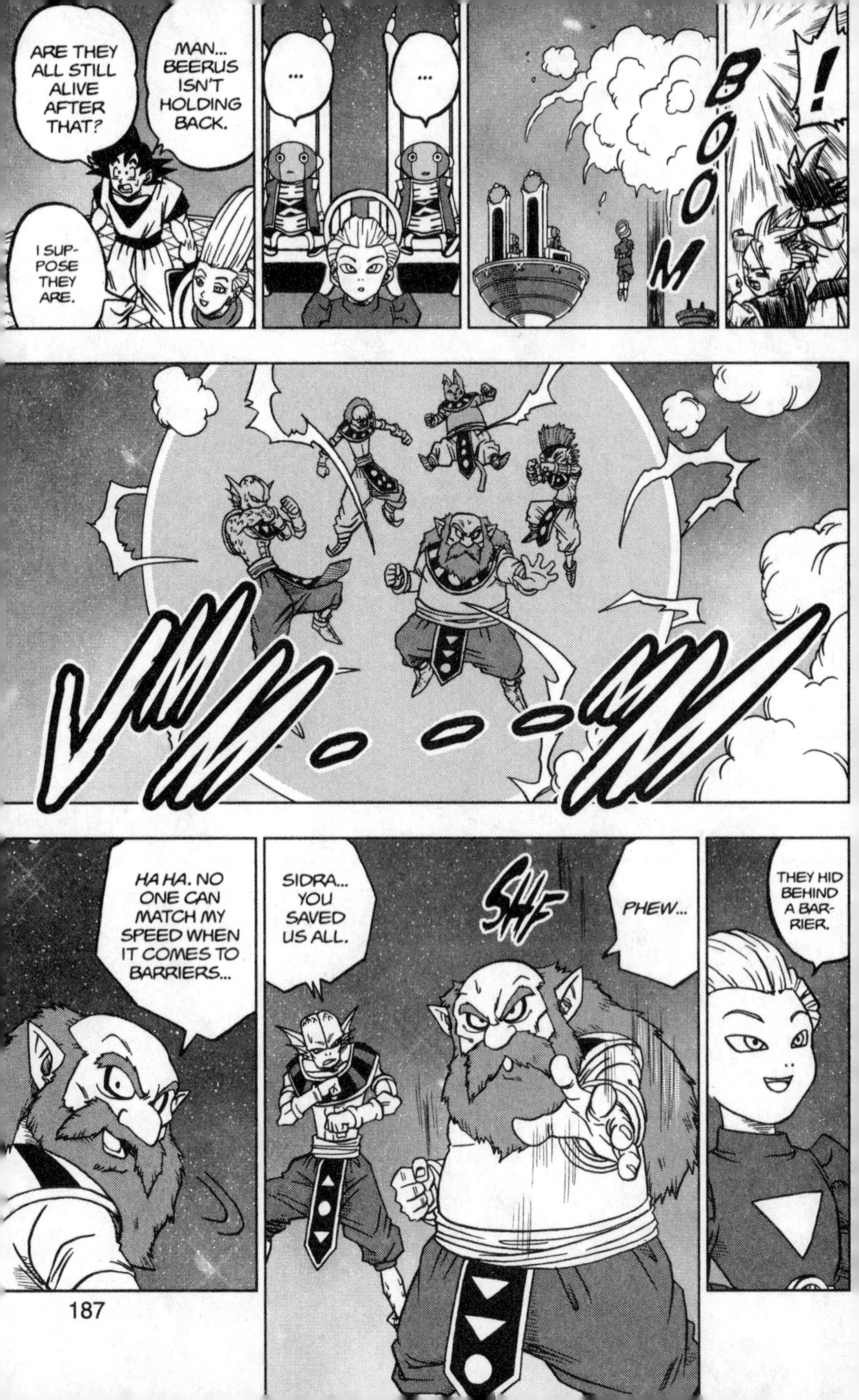
!
BOOOM
...
...
MAN... BEERUS ISN'T HOLDING BACK.
ARE THEY ALL STILL ALIVE AFTER THAT?
I SUP-POSE THEY ARE.
THEY HID BEHIND A BAR-RIER.
PHEW...
SHF
SIDRA... YOU SAVED US ALL.
HA HA. NO ONE CAN MATCH MY SPEED WHEN IT COMES TO BARRIERS...

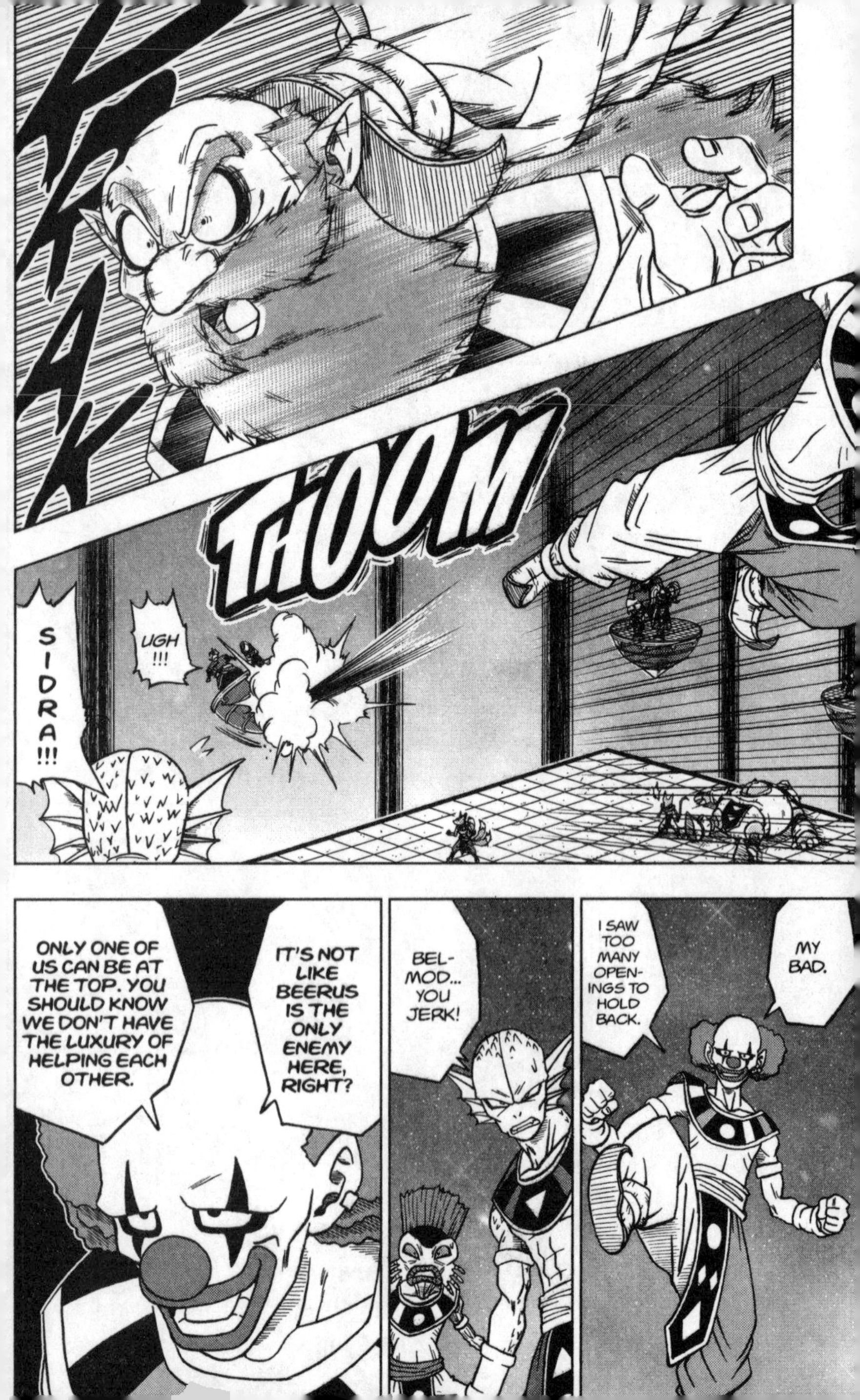
KAK
THOOM
SIDRA!!!
UGH!!!
MY BAD.
I SAW TOO MANY OPENINGS TO HOLD BACK.
BELMOD... YOU JERK!
IT'S NOT LIKE BEERUS IS THE ONLY ENEMY HERE, RIGHT?
ONLY ONE OF US CAN BE AT THE TOP. YOU SHOULD KNOW WE DON'T HAVE THE LUXURY OF HELPING EACH OTHER.

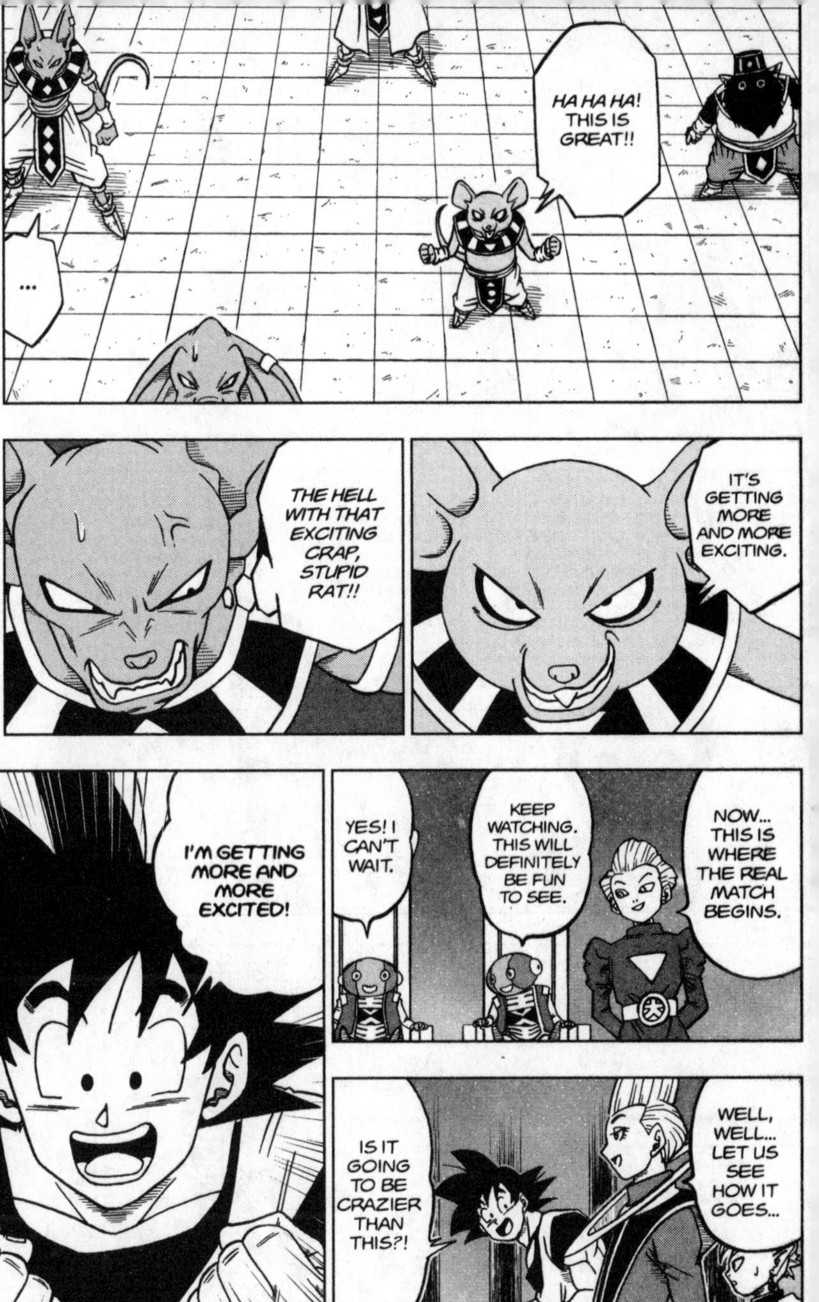
HA HA HA! THIS IS GREAT!!
...
IT'S GETTING MORE AND MORE EXCITING.
THE HELL WITH THAT EXCITING CRAP, STUPID RAT!!
NOW... THIS IS WHERE THE REAL MATCH BEGINS.
KEEP WATCHING. THIS WILL DEFINITELY BE FUN TO SEE.
YES! I CAN'T WAIT.
WELL, WELL... LET US SEE HOW IT GOES...
IS IT GOING TO BE CRAZIER THAN THIS?!
I'M GETTING MORE AND MORE EXCITED!

TO BE CONTINUED!

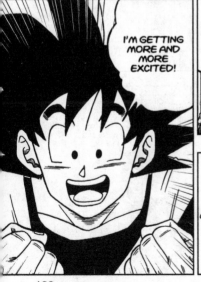

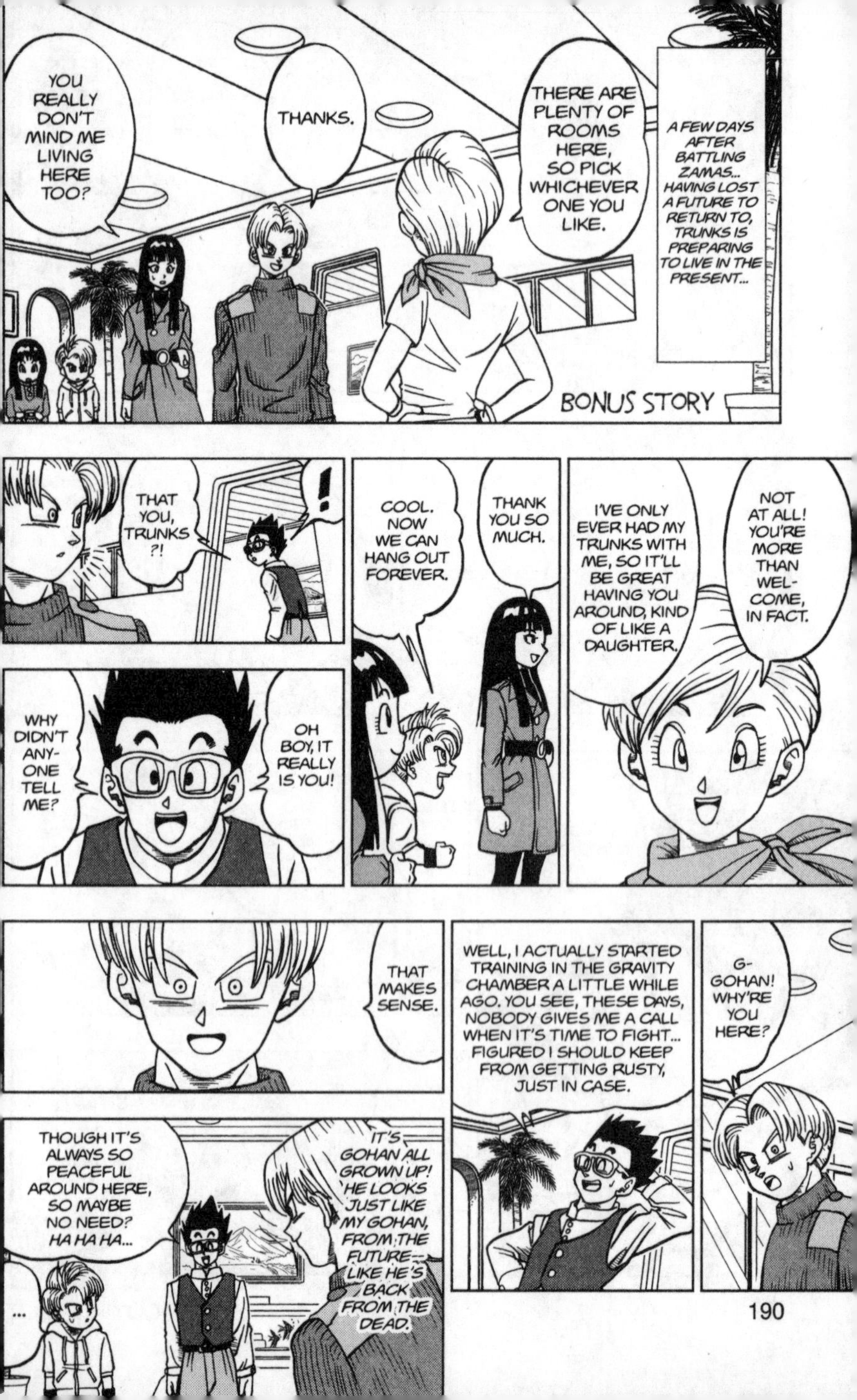

A FEW DAYS AFTER BATTLING ZAMAS... HAVING LOST A FUTURE TO RETURN TO, TRUNKS IS PREPARING TO LIVE IN THE PRESENT...
BONUS STORY
THERE ARE PLENTY OF ROOMS HERE, SO PICK WHICHEVER ONE YOU LIKE.
THANKS.
YOU REALLY DON'T MIND ME LIVING HERE TOO?
NOT AT ALL! YOU'RE MORE THAN WEL-COME, IN FACT.
I'VE ONLY EVER HAD MY TRUNKS WITH ME, SO IT'LL BE GREAT HAVING YOU AROUND, KIND OF LIKE A DAUGHTER.
THANK YOU SO MUCH.
COOL. NOW WE CAN HANG OUT FOREVER.
!
THAT YOU, TRUNKS?!
OH BOY, IT REALLY IS YOU!
WHY DIDN'T ANY-ONE TELL ME?
G-GOHAN! WHY'RE YOU HERE?
WELL, I ACTUALLY STARTED TRAINING IN THE GRAVITY CHAMBER A LITTLE WHILE AGO. YOU SEE, THESE DAYS, NOBODY GIVES ME A CALL WHEN IT'S TIME TO FIGHT... FIGURED I SHOULD KEEP FROM GETTING RUSTY, JUST IN CASE.
THAT MAKES SENSE.
IT'S GOHAN ALL GROWN UP! HE LOOKS JUST LIKE MY GOHAN, FROM THE FUTURE-- LIKE HE'S BACK FROM THE DEAD.
THOUGH IT'S ALWAYS SO PEACEFUL AROUND HERE, SO MAYBE NO NEED? HA HA HA...
...

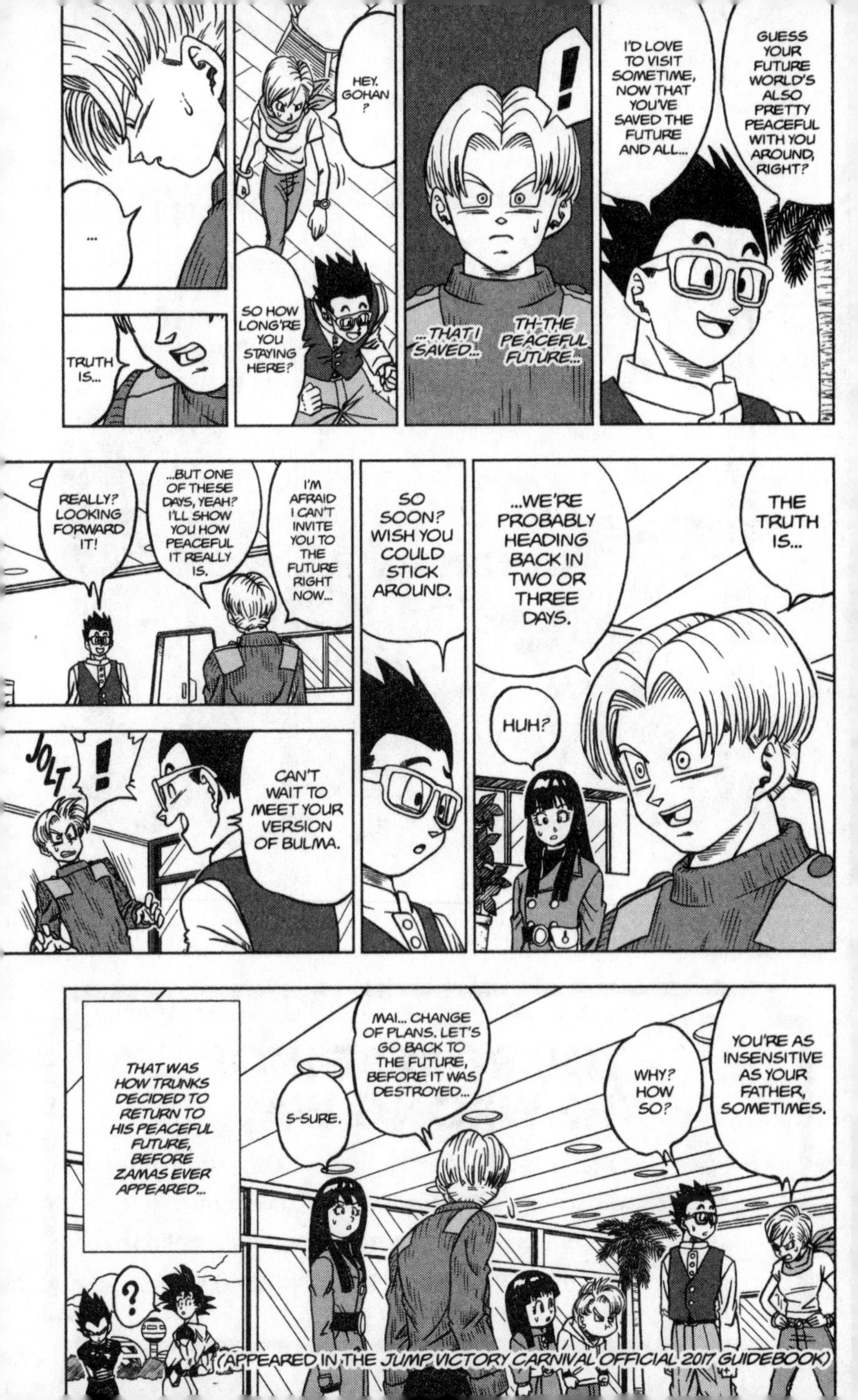
GUESS YOUR FUTURE WORLD'S ALSO PRETTY PEACEFUL WITH YOU AROUND, RIGHT?
I'D LOVE TO VISIT SOMETIME, NOW THAT YOU'VE SAVED THE FUTURE AND ALL...
!
TH-THE PEACEFUL FUTURE...
...THAT I SAVED...
HEY. GOHAN?
SO HOW LONG'RE YOU STAYING HERE?
...
TRUTH IS...
THE TRUTH IS...
...WE'RE PROBABLY HEADING BACK IN TWO OR THREE DAYS.
HUH?
SO SOON? WISH YOU COULD STICK AROUND.
I'M AFRAID I CAN'T INVITE YOU TO THE FUTURE RIGHT NOW...
...BUT ONE OF THESE DAYS, YEAH? I'LL SHOW YOU HOW PEACEFUL IT REALLY IS.
REALLY? LOOKING FORWARD IT!
CAN'T WAIT TO MEET YOUR VERSION OF BULMA.
!
JOLT
YOU'RE AS INSENSITIVE AS YOUR FATHER, SOMETIMES.
WHY? HOW SO?
MAI... CHANGE OF PLANS. LET'S GO BACK TO THE FUTURE, BEFORE IT WAS DESTROYED...
S-SURE.
THAT WAS HOW TRUNKS DECIDED TO RETURN TO HIS PEACEFUL FUTURE, BEFORE ZAMAS EVER APPEARED...
?
(APPEARED IN THE JUMP VICTORY CARNIVAL OFFICIAL 2017 GUIDEBOOK)

YOU'RE READING
THE WRONG WAY!

Dragon Ball Super reads from right to left, starting in the
upper-right corner. Japanese is read from right to left,
meaning that action, sound effects, and word-balloon
order are completely reversed from English order.